The Law of Trusts

BUTTERWORTHS CORE TEXT SERIES

The Law of Trusts

J. E. Penner

Lecturer in Law, London School of Economics
Deputy Chief Examiner in the Law of Trusts, University of
London External LL B Programme

Butterworths
London, Edinburgh, Dublin
1998

United Kingdom	Butterworths, a Division of Reed Elsevier (UK) Ltd, Halsbury House, 35 Chancery Lane, LONDON WC2A 1EL and 4 Hill Street, EDINBURGH EH2 3JZ
Australia	Butterworths, SYDNEY, ADELAIDE, BRISBANE, CANBERRA, MELBOURNE and PERTH
Canada	Butterworths Canada Ltd, TORONTO and VANCOUVER
Ireland	Butterworth (Ireland) Ltd, DUBLIN
Malaysia	Malayan Law Journal Sdn Bhd, KUALA LUMPUR
New Zealand	Butterworths of New Zealand Ltd, WELLINGTON and AUCKLAND
Singapore	Butterworths Asia, SINGAPORE
South Africa	Butterworths Publishers (Pty) Ltd, DURBAN
USA	Michie, CHARLOTTESVILLE, Virginia

© Reed Elsevier (UK) Ltd 1998

A CIP Catalogue record for this book is available from the British Library.

ISBN 0 406 89633 X

Printed and bound in Great Britain by William Clowes Limited, Beccles and London

Visit us at our website: http://www.butterworths.co.uk

Preface

Trusts is a gripping subject; unfortunately it grips most students with anxiety. There is good reason for this: it is difficult. Almost every topic in the law of trusts is complicated by demanding intellectual problems, about the correct solutions to which academics and judges alike disagree. The consequence is that a 'Trusts Made Easy' book is like a 'Physical Chemistry Made Easy' book, a book for fools or the gullible. This is a 'Trusts Made Possible' book. It is a shorter text which explains from first principles what trusts is about, so that by the end of the book you should be 'up to speed' not only on the law, but on the important academic controversies surrounding it, which will be of assistance to readers wishing to do well on a typical LL B exam on the subject. I do not presume that you are already an expert on any area of law. Thus I have tried in the introduction and elsewhere to provide the legal and conceptual building blocks of this subject, even if they are also taught (one hopes they are taught) in other subjects on the standard LL B syllabus. For that reason, if you are only interested in the law of trusts, and not reading for a law degree – say you've just been made a beneficiary under a trust, or your general reading tastes run to the peculiar – this book is also for you.

The law of trusts is judge-made (though it has, of course, been amended here and there by Parliament). That is, it was created by judges over time deciding actual cases, building up the body of rules and principles we today recognise as trusts law. For that reason, if you want to write a really good exam script in the subject, ie get a first, you will simply have to read some cases and not rely entirely on this book, or any other book for that matter. Any textbook is just the author's interpretation of the law, whereas the law itself is found in the cases. To do well you must read them and interpret them by your own lights (taking into account, of course, the views of others mentioned in this book and elsewhere). And if you really want to plumb the depths and soar the heights of trusts law, feel it in your bones and exude it from your pores, reading the cases is a must. (I include a list of 'must read' cases at the end of each chapter.) Making sense out of the body of cases will try every brain cell at your command, so if you fancy yourself a true 'common lawyer', someone who is able to integrate the case decisions in an area of law while at the same time interpreting them to be humane and rational, then this is the subject for you.

Trusts is not a subject you can swot up the evening before an exam. The old saw, 'You can't fatten a hog the night before slaughter', applies here in spades. Read and think; read and pause. Learn to recognise when your brain is full, and stop. Like a box of breakfast cereal your brain will have room for more once the contents have settled. If you start to experience overload, stop, have a cup of tea and do something else for 15 minutes. Then return, and before going on re-read what you were on before. This book proceeds pretty much step-by-step and, at the end of the day, all should be reasonably clear. The only textbook that will ever make perfect sense on first reading is the one you write yourself (and often not even that one). Remember also that the different topics are all part of the same subject, so you will understand each of them better the more you understand all the others. As Wittgenstein said, light dawns gradually over the whole.

I abbreviate the House of Lords to HL, the Privy Council to PC, and the Court of Appeal to CA throughout.

Finally, I must record my thanks, first to Butterworths and Nicola Padfield (the series editor) for being brilliant throughout. Secondly, to Richard Barton, Sean Pettit, Tom Prendergast, and Bill Swadling, whom I love as brothers for reading the manuscript. They bear no responsibility for the final product, but if any egregious errors remain I shall, of course, resent them bitterly – what, after all, is family for?

J. E. Penner
London School of Economics

Contents

Table of statutes

List of cases

CHAPTER ONE

The Historical Origins of the Trust

SUMMARY

The Court of Chancery and the origin of equity

The relationship between equity and the common law

Equity's creation of the trust

The Court of Chancery and the origin of equity

1.1   The law of trusts is the offspring of a certain English legal creature known as 'equity'. The historical development of English law is marked by the existence of a series of different judicial institutions over time; the most significant of these for the modern student are the Courts of Common Law and the Court of Chancery. The Courts of Common Law developed the basic rules and principles which we now recognise as the law of torts (civil wrongs), much of the law of contract, much of the law of restitution, and much of the law of property. The Court of Chancery generated its own rules and principles, which as a body of law are collectively known as 'equity'. Chancery developed the law of trusts, the law of fiduciary obligations, also much of the law of property, the modern laws of breach of confidence and passing off (the law which prevents one trader from 'passing off' his goods as those of another, thus one kind of common law regulation of unfair competition), and, very importantly, a variety of legal remedies, such as the injunction, which the Courts of Common Law were unwilling or unable to provide.

1.2   The term 'equity' does not contrast with 'common law' when the latter is understood to distinguish judge-made law from legislation by Parliament. From that perspective, both equity and the common law are creations of 'common law', bodies of rules and principles developed over time as judges gave reasons for their decisions in actual cases.

1.3 The most important intellectual characteristic of equity is that it was developed by Chancery over the centuries in response to the pleas of individuals complaining of the injustice, in their particular cases, of the common law. Chancery was not, in any proper sense, a modern court of appeal, but rather a court which simply gave different answers from those of the common law to legal problems which arose on the same set of facts.

1.4 The common law was developed and administered in the royal courts, those courts established by the king, in contrast to local manorial courts which were the province of local nobles and which applied local customary law. It was called the 'common' law of England because in theory it applied universally. Equity arose out of the administrative power of the medieval Chancellor, who was at the time the king's most powerful minister. Since the king was regarded as the fount of justice, it was appropriate for the king to hear pleas by his subjects concerning injustices which his own royal courts might have perpetrated, and kings being kings, he delegated the task to his Chancellor. Since the Chancellor was to begin with usually an ecclesiastic, he felt able to concern himself with men's immortal souls, and thus their consciences; thus it was on the basis of 'conscience' that he exercised this royal power to remedy injustice. The Chancellor came to exercise a quasi-judicial function, by which cases called 'suits', as opposed to 'actions' at common law, could be brought before him. The suitor would appeal to the Chancellor on the basis that the rigid application of the common law rules caused injustice in his particular case. In response, the Chancellor, exercising his personal authority, could order a person not to act upon his common law rights if in good conscience he ought not to do so, *in effect* overturning the rules of common law. *In theory*, however, the common law was regarded as unchanged; the Chancellor merely decreed that the parties could not act upon it.

1.5 In time this quasi-legal function of the Chancellor led to the development of a separate court, the Court of Chancery, which became a sort of court of fairness, or 'equity', that tempered what was often regarded as the harsh and rigid application of common law rules. While this was substantially true early on, this contrast between the rigid rules of the common law and the flexible fairness of equity was almost certainly a highly misleading caricature by the end of the 18th century. By then the rules of equity were fast becoming as rigid and technical as any in the common law. Equity, which was once said to vary with the length of the Chancellor's foot to emphasise the personal character of the Chancellor's intervention on the basis of what he understood to be good conscience, had become a second body of law.   18th c

The maxims of equity

1.6   Although Equity developed its own definite rules covering various matters, it also produced a series of 'maxims' or broad principles which manifested equity's general approach to the solution of legal problems. An example of such a maxim is, 'Equity looks to intent, not form'. If, for example, two parties entered into a land transaction, and on their face the documents of the transaction purported that the transaction was not a mortgage, though in substance it was, the court of equity would look beyond the form of the documents, which might be decisive at common law, and treat the transaction as a mortgage. We will encounter various of these maxims as we go along. Like any general legal principles, the maxims of equity have been encrusted with judicial interpretation over the centuries, so it would be a great mistake to treat these maxims nowadays as anything more than devices which assist the interpretation and organisation of particular equitable doctrines.

The relationship between equity and the common law

Equity as a 'gloss' on the common law

1.7   Equity and the common law were not separate but equal systems of rules covering the same matters only differently. Equity has always relied on the existence of the common law, being essentially, in the terms of Maitland (a great equity scholar), a 'gloss on the law'. If you peeled away all the rules of equity, the common law could still stand alone as a comprehensive body of rules covering tort, contract, property, etc. If you peeled away the common law from equity however, you wouldn't have anything like a comprehensive body of rules – equity, was, and remains, a kind of patchwork overlay modifying particular common law rules.

Strife between equity and the common law

1.8   Equity largely worked through the issuance of 'common injunctions,' by which a plaintiff at common law could be enjoined, ie

3

stopped, by a decree of the Court of Chancery, from proceeding with his case, or restrained from enforcing the result. As one might imagine, from the point of view of the common law judges this was tantamount to the Chancellor's denying claimants access to justice. After several attempts by the common law judges to assert the dominance of the common law over the power of the Chancery, and some consequential political strife, it became settled by the end of the 17th century that the decrees of Chancery would prevail. Equity was here to stay. So, for about two centuries, England had a true dual system of courts with two different finely-developed bodies of law.

Remedies at common law and equity

1.9 Different remedies were available from the common law courts and the court of equity. A common law court could order a losing defendant to pay damages, a money sum, to the plaintiff, and in cases concerning land could order a defendant to get off the land so that the plaintiff could take possession. If the defendant refused to pay damages, the Court would empower a sheriff to come round, seize his possessions, and either hold them until he paid or sell them to raise the plaintiff's damages. Similarly, if a defendant refused to get off the land, the sheriff would come round and clear him out. Thus the common law courts had, essentially, only one means of enforcing their decisions: they could separate a person from property. Chancery had a much more sweeping power, which provided scope for a variety of equitable remedies. The Court of Chancery could throw anybody who disobeyed its orders into gaol, for contempt of court. This was not a criminal sentence, where if you served your time you got out. If you refused to carry out an order of Chancery, you rotted in gaol until you decided to comply. (Nowadays, imprisonment for contempt of court is regulated by the Contempt of Court Act 1981, and the court also has powers to act in place of the defendant in certain instances, for example by executing documents, or by appointing others to act in his place; s 39, Ord 45, r 8.) This is the meaning of the phrase that equity acts *in personam*; equity acts on your body. Equity has the power to make you do something, or to stop doing something, because if you refuse, you lose your liberty for as long as it takes. Thus injunctions have their origin in equity. Equity can also rescind contracts, ie tell people to act as if a contract was never formed, and can rectify documents, that is, tell people to carry on as if the document had different terms. As a result, in many cases litigants whose substantive rights lay at common law would seek the *remedial* support of Chancery – so for example, one suffering the smoke of a neighbour's brickworks and unsatisfied with money damages would apply to Chancery for an injunction to shut the brickworks down; or, a contracting party would seek an order from Chancery for the specific performance of the contract in a case where money damages for breach would inadequately compensate.

The Judicature Acts

1.10   The administrative inconvenience of a dual system of courts which dealt in different fashions with the same factual issues is apparent, and by the Judicature Acts 1973-75 Parliament abolished the institutional division between the Courts of Common Law and the Court of Chancery. One High Court was established, the judges of which were henceforth to apply the rules of both common law and equity, where appropriate, in the cases before it; where the rules conflicted, the rules of equity were to prevail. What counts as equity today, therefore, is the body of rules and principles which *derive* from those applied in the Court of Chancery until 1875; judge-made law is a living thing, and so equity has developed since then, in just the same way as has the common law of contract or tort. Despite the abolition of the separate courts, there remain distinct traces of this institutional history which bear directly on the current state of English law.

The fusion of law and equity

1.11   Since 1875 judges apply both common law and equity in the same court at the same time. It remains an open question to what extent the rules and principles of the common law and of equity have been fashioned into one coherent, principled body of law, whether that is, the common law and equity have 'fused'. The fusion question can be framed in this way: Although judges and lawyers now deal with whatever rules of equity and common law apply to the case before them, in what sense should they maintain the distinct historical and intellectual origins of these rules in their heads? Maintaining such a notional distinction will have consequences in so far as the mere fact that a rule arose in the common law or in equity will have consequences for its application. Consider the following old chestnut of the fusion debate: because equity arose in a 'court of conscience' it is said that, as a matter of unalterable principle, all equitable relief is *discretionary*. For example, if a plaintiff seeking the equitable remedy of specific performance of a contract has acted unconscionably in some way himself, then equity will refuse to help him, leaving him to his remedies at common law. The maxim framing this rule is 'He who seeks Equity must come with clean hands'. By contrast, it is said, common law remedies lie 'as of right', the court having no similar discretion. So we now pose the question: should it still matter which court originally devised a particular remedy when judges come to decide how they should apply it nowadays? Surely not. If it remains true that some remedies that arose in equity should only be granted on a discretionary basis (and there may be good grounds for this), this must be justified as a matter of principle which fits into a coherent rationale which explains the remedial rules in that particular area of law. This coherent rationale must, of course, also explain the various restrictions and limitations that exist today upon remedies originally given at common law. Even if an explanation is based upon concerns about justice which were originally given voice by Chancery, that does not entail that the rule must henceforth be identified as an equitable one, any more than we would identify a modern rule of the law of wills as ecclesiastical, because the law of wills was originally the province of the ecclesiastical courts. Nevertheless, this particular version of the 'history is destiny' fallacy lingers. It lingers in part almost certainly because of the theoretical difficulties that have arisen in accommodating the most important single development of equity, the law of trusts, into one coherent law of property. Fusion may seem somewhat straightforward when directed towards remedies, but the idea of ironing out the differences between the common law and equity in property law, is, as we shall see, a different kettle of fish.

Equity's creation of the trust

1.12   The most important development of the preceding institutional history is the law of trusts. Trusts is the only branch of law that LL B students study which arose purely in the Court of Chancery. The law of trusts is worthwhile studying separately from the rest of equity for two reasons. First, the rest of equity is best studied in combination with the common law rules which govern the different substantive areas of law to which these other equitable rules apply. For example, equitable remedies are best examined in the context of studying the various substantive actions, like breach of contract, where they are given; or, if remedies *per se* are the focus of inquiry, it is silly to restrict one's attention to equitable remedies, missing the important points of comparison with common law and statutory remedies. Land law courses necessarily include the substantive development by equity of the land law, and the substantive equitable wrongs of breach of confidence and passing off both happily situate themselves in the study of torts generally or the law relating to intellectual property to which they are also related. Second, matters of pedagogical convenience aside, the law of trusts is worthwhile studying in its own right because the 'trust' – equity's imposition of stringent personal obligations upon a legal owner to hold property for the benefit of another, with the result that he is no longer able to treat the property as his own – may be regarded as the paradigm case of equity's interference with common law rights in pursuit of justice.

The use

1.13   The historical roots of the trust lie in a medieval property device, the 'use'. The history of the land law in the first centuries following the Conquest can be described as the process by which true property or ownership in land arose, as the influence of the social and political structure of feudalism waned. Under feudalism, rights in land basically amounted to rights in a complex hierarchical system of social and political authority and agricultural wealth distribution. This hierarchy was maintained through a system of 'tenures' of land, under which different 'tenants' had rights in the same land. At the top of this ladder was the king, at the bottom the person actually in possession of the land, and in between there might be any number of 'mesne (pronounced 'mean') lords'. It was essentially a system of taxation. Each tenant, starting with the one in possession who through his serfs would produce agricultural goods, passed the wealth of the land upward by doing 'rent-service' of various kinds to the lord immediately above him, and so on up to the king. Thus although a person might have an 'estate', an ownership interest, in some piece of land, this estate was as likely to be a seigneury, *ie* the right to a rent from a tenant immediately below on the feudal ladder, as it was to be an estate giving possession of the land itself. Different kinds of rights and duties defined the different kinds of tenure by which land could be held, such as knight service, the obligation to provide knights or money for arms, or socage, the obligation to provide agricultural products. The use arose as a means of avoiding some of the more disgruntling rules of the tenurial feudal system. Land could not be left by will, but could only be inherited according to the rules of primogeniture, the general effect of which was that the entirety of a man's rights in land passed to his eldest son. This preserved large estates in land, but it meant that a man could not take advantage of his landed wealth to provide for all of his children on his death. Another problem arose if one wanted to benefit certain religious orders. For various reasons it was difficult if not impossible to provide for them by conveying land to them. Finally, certain legal incidents of feudal land-holding could themselves become very oppressive. In particular, if land held in knight-service passed to a minor heir, the lord immediately above on the feudal ladder acquired the 'right of wardship', the right to manage the estate and take all the profits of the land until the heir reached maturity. These elements (amongst others) of land tenure inspired medieval lawyers to avoid them. The avoidance mechanism was the use.

1.14 Although land could not be left by will, there were no similar restrictions on *inter vivos* dispositions, ie dispositions while the tenant was alive. Thus A, a feudal tenant, could convey his property to X, Y, and Z as co-owners. Of course, a mere conveyance would not do A much good if by conveying the land in this way he gave up all rights in it; the property was conveyed *on use*; the conveyance was written to X, Y, and Z *to the use of* someone A wanted to benefit. In general, A could benefit whomever he wanted: his widow for life, all of his children, an order of Franciscan monks, and so on. The common law completely ignored the words 'to the use of'. As far as it was concerned, X, Y and Z were the owners by conveyance, subject to all the feudal duties of their estate, and could do whatever they liked with the land, regardless of the wishes of A. But the Chancellor thought otherwise. It would be unfair to allow X, Y and Z to take the benefit of the land themselves, for they only got it in order to benefit the person(s) A intended, called the 'cestui que use', or the 'cestuis que usent' if there were more than one. (These are terms of old law French – England was conquered by the Normans, after all. The way they are pronounced today would not meet with the approval of the Parisian on the street. 'Cestui(s) que use(nt)' is pronounced 'settee(s) key use'.) The Chancellor enforced the use, ensuring that X, Y, and Z used the land according to the use A dictated. In this way A could effectively create a will of land, by structuring the use so that X, Y, and Z held it for the benefit of those he wished after his death.

1.15 The conveyance was made to co-owners to exploit a particular technical common law rule. The form of co-ownership that was invariably employed was the joint tenancy. Joint tenancy has the significant feature of the right of survivorship, by which upon the death of any joint tenant, his interest disappears – it does not pass to his heir – with the result that there is just one fewer co-owner. Thus if X died, his heir would not inherit a share of the property; neither do Y and Z as the other co-owners; X's interest just disappears. The other common form of co-ownership is 'tenancy in common'. In contrast to the position with joint tenants, the ownership share of a tenant in common passes to his heir. As joint tenants of the legal title to the land, X, Y, and Z would be liable to comply with the feudal duties, but importantly, because of the right of survivorship, the particular worry of a minor heir inheriting the land could be completely avoided. The danger of inheritance would only arise if following a series of deaths only one of the original joint tenants remained, who would then be the sole owner. If *he* then died, his heir would inherit. But that could easily be avoided, for after the death of X, for example, Y and Z could convey the land to themselves and V and W, on the same use. In this way, whenever the number of joint tenants dropped to a low number, a simple reconveyance to another group of joint tenants ensured that the property was never inherited, and so a wardship would never arise.

1.16 The use, therefore, could be employed to avoid all of the rules of feudal tenure mentioned. The benefit of land could be passed to others than those who would inherit under the rules of primogeniture. It could be passed to those who were legally disentitled from holding property, eg religious orders and minors, and finally it could be used to ensure a minor never inherited.

1.17 How should we characterise the use? One way is this: a use is a kind of 'structured gift'. A conveys property to X, Y and Z to the use of someone to whom he wants to give the property but which for various reasons he can't do under the common law rules of property; an obstacle, as we have seen, in feudal times was the rule of primogeniture. The use can also be characterised as a kind of feudal tax-avoidance mechanism. Transferring the benefit of land by way of use enabled feudal tenants to enhance the value of their land, by disengaging it in part from its feudal incidents, particularly those that operated upon inheritance.

9

The origin of the trust

1.18   This book is about the law of trusts, not the law of uses, so what happened? Very briefly: Henry VIII wanted money, and set about getting some by prosecuting with a vengeance his ancient feudal rights as the man at the top of the feudal pyramid. He even had a special court set up, the Court of Wards, to help him do so. Because by this time feudalism was essentially anachronistic, his efforts were branded 'fiscal feudalism'. Vexed at being deprived of the feudal revenues he would otherwise have got but for the employment of uses by his noble tenants, he managed to get Parliament to pass the Statute of Uses in 1535. This statute 'executed the uses': a conveyance from A to X to the use of B was after the Act treated as a conveyance from A to B directly. The title passed from A to X, and then to B as the use was automatically 'executed', cutting out X. It was thenceforth impossible for someone holding the legal title to be bound to benefit another, since there was no longer any use by which he could be bound. How the trust arose in the next century and a half to replicate the use in all but name is an interesting bit of history, but not, alas, to be gone into here. Suffice it to say that by the turn of the 18th century, where a legal title holder X, now called the trustee, held property to the benefit of B, now rendered as 'in trust for B' rather than 'to the use of B', (B was consequently renamed the 'cestui que trust', and now generally called the 'beneficiary'), Chancery would require X to hold the land for the benefit of B, just as if he had formerly held it to B's use.

1.19   Since the incidents of feudalism are now abolished, you might ask why anyone would want to give a 'structured gift' today. Why do people set up trusts? For most private trusts, the basic reason is the same as in medieval times, to provide for loved ones in a way one cannot do, or it would be unwise to do, simply by transferring legal title. One cannot give minors land, so if one wants a minor to have Blackacre ('Blackacre' is the name lawyers always give to a hypothetical piece of land), it must be held on trust for him by someone else. One may be worried that one's son is a spendthrift, and so give money for his living expenses to a trustee to dispense, on condition that the benefit will pass to someone else if he goes bankrupt. One may want someone to have the dividends, ie the income, from shares, and someone else to have the capital. One cannot fragment the legal title to shares to accomplish that. In certain circumstances, the law of taxation also favours giving property by way of trust when one is alive over leaving property to them in one's will, so many trusts are essentially tax avoidance devices.

10

1.20 Note that the structured gift and tax-avoidance functions of the use/trust work in essentially opposite ways. To the extent that the use/trust avoids feudal incidents or taxes, it frees property from restrictions which reduce its value to an owner. On the other hand, the structured gift burdens property, and the structure of benefits under a trust can be very complicated indeed. If the feudal use worked to free land from the institution of feudalism, its modern counterpart, the trust, also ties up property with bonds quite as tight to different social institutions, such as the family, or the workplace, as in the case of a pension fund trust.

Further Reading

Baker (1990), chapters 6,12,13,14,16.

Simpson (1986) chapters I, VIII, IX.

Self-test questions

1. What features distinguish equity from the common law?

2. What does 'fusion' refer to?

3. What was a 'use', what purpose did it serve, how did it work, and how is it related to the trust?

CHAPTER TWO

Property, Obligations and Trusts

SUMMARY

The trust – equitable title and fiduciary obligations

The express trust

The personal and proprietary nature of the trust

The context of insolvency

Testamentary gifts

The trust – equitable title and fiduciary obligations

2.1 In chapter I we operated with the rather vague notion that a trustee 'holds property on trust' for the beneficiaries. It is now time to make this notion explicit and precise. A trust exists whenever equity regards the legal owner of property as having *fiduciary* obligations to hold the property solely for the benefit of, ie on trust for, some other person or persons; those persons equity regards as being the true owners, who may, therefore, be said to have 'equitable title' to the trust property.

2.2 'Fiduciary' obligations are obligations to another person to act with loyalty and good faith in dealings which affect that person, who is called the 'principal'. In the case of a trust, the trustee is fiduciary to the beneficiary. In general, the fiduciary has the power unilaterally to affect his principal's interests by altering his legal position, in particular by entering into contracts or property transactions. Company directors, for example, enter contracts or sell property in the name of their company; a trustee deals with the trust property as its legal owner, but because the property is trust property, in doing so he clearly affects the beneficiary's interests. Fiduciaries may also be able to affect their principals' practical interests. For example, a solicitor is a fiduciary vis-à-vis his client when he gives him legal advice as to how he should act. Obviously, each of these fiduciaries is in the position to cause his principal, whether company, beneficiary, or client, loss. For this reason, equity requires that these persons act with loyalty and good faith.

2.3 We will discuss the different rules which govern the fiduciary relationship in detail in Chapter 11. Here it suffices to say that the trustee's fiduciary obligations of loyalty and good faith require him never to put his own interests in conflict with those of the trust. In particular, he is prohibited from benefiting in any way from his role as trustee to the trust which is not specifically authorised by the terms of the trust, for example to be remunerated or make any profit from the trust. He must also be scrupulous in keeping the trust property separate from his own.

2.4 Equitable title and fiduciary obligations do not always go together; as the solicitor-client example shows, it is often the case that one may have fiduciary obligations to a person, obligations to put that person's interests above one's own in certain respects, without holding any property for them; conversely, in certain cases we shall see that a person may have equitable title to property although the legal owner of it has no fiduciary obligations to him at all. But the two come together in the case of the express trust, which might be regarded as the central case of the trust.

The express trust

2.5 An express trust is a trust which is intentionally set up. Say that I wish to put away some money for the education of my two minor daughters. While this is a nice thing to do, there are obvious problems in just transferring the legal title to property to a five- and a seven-year-old. What I will do, therefore, is to create a trust in their favour. As the original legal owner of the property, I am called the 'settlor', for I 'settle' the property upon my daughters under the trust. (Confusingly, not all express trusts are properly called settlements; settlements are trusts, usually family trusts, in which there are *successive* interests; they will be discussed in the next chapter.) There are essentially two ways in which I can do this. I can simply declare that I now hold such and such property, say 1,000 shares of ABC plc, 'on trust' for my daughters. Or I can transfer the shares to my brother to hold on trust for my daughters. In the former case, called a 'self-declaration' of trust, I become the *trustee*, the holder of the legal title of the shares who must deal with the property according to the terms of the trust; in the latter case my brother does. In both cases I am the settlor, and my daughters are the *cestuis que trust(ent)*, or *beneficiaries*. Most express trusts are created in writing, and the document which contains the terms of the trust is normally called the *trust instrument*. Sometimes this document also works to transfer the legal title of the property from the settlor to the trustee, but often a separate document, sometimes called a *vesting instrument* (because by it the legal title *vests* in the trustee), does this.

2.6 Since, as we have just seen, a settlor can declare himself trustee of property for someone, the settlor and the trustee can be the same person. A settlor can also convey property to a trustee in trust for himself, so the settlor and beneficiary can be the same person. A trustee can also be one of several beneficiaries, as would result from a transfer to B on trust for B and C in equal shares. But what cannot exist is a lone trustee who is also a lone beneficiary. The law does not recognise a division of the individual self so that you would be bound to hold property for your own sole benefit, a defined benefit which gave you rights against yourself and imposed duties on you to yourself.

Beneficial title

2.7 The impossibility of a legal owner being a trustee for himself alone shows that it is incorrect to think that the outright owner of a piece of property, that is, the legal owner of property which is not subject to any trust, has both legal and equitable title; he has the legal title *simpliciter*, and there is no equitable title at all. This is not to say that equity is blind to the legal ownership of property; equity is perfectly aware that a legal owner of property subject to no trust has the benefit of the property himself, having no obligation to hold it for another. 'Beneficial' is the compendious term which describes either the case where a legal owner has the benefit of the property or the case where a beneficiary does: a legal owner of property is the beneficial owner if the property is not subject to any trust; where property is held on trust, the beneficiary under the trust is the beneficial owner. In determining the rights of individuals to property under the law of trusts, the pertinent question is always whether equity recognises a distinct beneficial interest in the property, ie an equitable title, which displaces the legal owner's beneficial interest. The mistake is to think that because a legal owner has the beneficial interest, he has both a legal and an equitable title to the property.

Exercising powers to create an express trust

2.8 You should think of express trusts as the creations of the settlor; an express trust is created when a settlor *effectively exercises his powers of ownership* to do so. Understanding the significance of this will involve a brief digression.

Powers

2.9 A power is the capacity to change or create rights, duties, and other powers. One has the power to enter into contracts; if you and I agree that I will pay you £5 for washing my car, then we give birth to a new legal relationship: we both have rights and duties we didn't have before. I have the right that you wash my car and the duty to pay you £5 for doing so, and you have, correspondingly, the duty to wash it and the right to be paid £5 for doing so. Owners of property have, simply by virtue of their ownership, all sorts of associated powers. If I own Blackacre I can exercise my powers over it to lease it, to give it away, to mortgage it, to licence you to come onto it to have dinner with me, and so on. One of the other things I can do if I own Blackacre is create a trust of it in your favour, either by self-declaration or by transferring Blackacre to a trustee to hold on trust. In the former case, I have imposed a fiduciary duty upon myself to hold Blackacre for your benefit, and have conferred a right upon you to the benefit of Blackacre. In the latter case, the trustee will have undertaken a duty to hold Blackacre for your benefit, and you will have the corresponding right that he does so. Express trusts can be created by the settlor's exercise of his power gratuitously, or because he is obliged to do so under a contract. For example, occupational pension funds are held in trust and arise by virtue of employment contracts.

Operations of law

2.10 New rights, duties, and powers are not only created by individuals exercising their legal powers, but may also arise 'by operation of law'.

Consider the case of a tortious injury, ie an injury which occurs because someone has committed a civil wrong (a 'tort'). If I negligently run you down with my car, you now have the right to sue me for 'damages', ie money compensation. But it would be a dreadful mistake to think that because I was the one who ran you down, I thereby exercised a power of mine to confer upon you a right to sue me for damages. The law only recognises capacities to create new rights, duties, or powers where the law wishes to provide a facility to do things in particular ways: the law recognises a power to enter contracts, or declare trusts, or make a will, because the law is in favour of those things. The law is not in favour of my running people down, so I have no legal powers attached to that capacity. The right to sue someone for damages arises *by operation of law* on the occurrence of your negligently-caused injury because the law regards it as just that you should be able to sue for compensation. The distinction between rights, duties, or powers that an individual creates when he exercises a power, and those which arise by operation of law, is of great significance in the law of trusts: while express trusts are created by a settlor through the exercise of his powers of ownership, other trusts, constructive and resulting trusts, may arise by operation of law on the basis of particular facts. Sometimes it is difficult to tell them apart as we shall see, but telling them apart is crucial, for different rules of the law of trusts apply depending upon whether the trust is an express trust or not.

Revocability

2.11 A settlor may be able to revoke the trust, that is, bring it to an end and get the trust property back, and it is important to understand the legal basis for revoking a trust where it is possible. Trusts are normally created by the settlor transferring property to a trustee while at the same time declaring the terms of the trust, thereby creating the equitable title of the beneficiaries. And just like any other transfer or creation of an interest in property, once the act of transfer or creation is complete, the interest in the property belongs to the recipient, and that is the end of it as far as the transferor is concerned. Thus the settlor cannot think of the trust property as still 'really his'. He cannot get it back, for he is legally out of the picture. In the same way that a donor of an outright gift has nothing to say about what the donee does with the property once the gift is made, neither has the settlor anything to say about the trust, the way it is administered, etc after the trust is created. The equitable interests under the trust belong to the beneficiaries, and they, and only they, may enforce the terms of the trust against the trustee. That is the 'default' position. But in setting out the terms of the trust the settlor may grant himself powers under it. He can give himself a power to bring the trust to an end, that is, to revoke it. He can also give himself lesser powers, such as the power to replace the trustees, or the power to decide the shares of the property that the beneficiaries will take, and so on. But the point to realise is this: if the settlor has a power to revoke the trust or to appoint new trustees, that power must be an express or implied power in the terms of the trust itself; the power derives from the trust terms, not from the settlor's position as the one who originally owned the property. Indeed, under the terms of the trust the settlor may give such powers to anyone he chooses.

The personal and proprietary nature of the trust

The personal fiduciary duties of the trustee

2.12   Since the trustee has legal title to the property in question, the trustee has all the legal rights and powers associated with the property. If land held on trust is occupied by squatters, then it is the trustee who has the right to evict them. It is the trustee who has the power to buy and sell the trust property, so he is the one who makes the trust investments. The trustee must, however, act upon these rights and exercise those powers in accordance with his *personal* fiduciary obligation to apply his ownership of the property in the beneficiaries' best interests.

2.13   This general fiduciary duty to apply his ownership for the beneficiaries' best interests is often sub-categorised into duties of two kinds: 'administrative' and 'dispositive' duties. Roughly, administrative duties govern the trustee's power to make contracts and his powers of ownership to maintain the value of the trust property, which is also called the 'trust corpus' or 'trust fund'. Trustees have the duty to invest the trust property safely and so that it makes a reasonable return. A legal owner of property not subject to a trust has all the same powers, but not the duties. He can invest it, or not, as he chooses, and may engage in dangerously speculative investments. A trustee must invest the trust property and must not do so in a dangerously speculative way. Where appropriate, trustees must also insure the trust property, against fire, for example, if the trust property is a house.

2.14 Dispositive duties are those which require the trustee to dispose of the trust property to the beneficiaries according to the terms of the trust. These are the duties compliance with which delivers to the beneficiaries the particular benefits the settlor intended. In short, they govern the trustee's power as a legal owner to give the property away. For example, the trustee may have a duty to pay one beneficiary the income of shares for ten years, and then transfer title to the shares to another beneficiary. The trustee is not free to benefit whom he would like, like any other legal owner. His duty to exercise his power to give away the property only according to its terms is the essence of any trust.

Legal and equitable title compared

2.15 You will often hear the rights and powers the trustee and beneficiary have in respect of the trust property spoken of in terms of split ownership, expressed as *legal title* and *equitable title* respectively. The idea behind this is that the trustee is the owner at law, and has legal title, while the beneficiary is the owner in equity, and has equitable title. One must, however, take care in the use of the word 'title' here, because it might suggest that the trustee and beneficiary have identical rights, the only difference being that the legal owner's are enforced by the common law, while the beneficial owner's are enforced in equity. Thinking so is a bad mistake, however, for this reason: legal title normally comprises the full panoply of ownership powers, but equitable title rarely does. The legal owner of property, even if he is a trustee, has, in law, all these powers, but only in the limiting case of the *bare* trust does the owner in equity.

Bare trusts

2.16 Under a bare trust, a trustee holds property for a beneficiary on no specific trust terms. Bare trustees are often called *nominees*, to indicate that their role is to do little more that hold the property in their names and do the bidding of the beneficiary. Since there are no specific trust terms, there is no structure imposed on the benefit the beneficiary is to receive; in consequence, in equity it is fully and absolutely his without any restriction, and indeed, the beneficiary has the right to compel the trustee to transfer the legal title to him at any time, collapsing the trust. In this case, then, it is reasonable to say that the trustee is the owner of the property in law, and the beneficiary the owner in equity, because the trustee in such a case must do whatever the beneficiary says with it. Here it makes sense to say the trustee and beneficiary have essentially identical ownership powers, the trustee having legal powers and the beneficiary powers in equity, powers the beneficiary exercises through his directions to the trustee. But this is the limiting case, and it is not by any means the typical case of a trust. In the vast majority of trusts the benefit the beneficiaries receive from the trust property is defined, and therefore limited, by the terms of the trust; beneficiaries under most trusts have essentially none of the powers normally associated with ownership or title. They get the benefit of the property as defined by the terms of the trust, such as it is. That is, of course, the main reason settlors benefit people through trusts in the first place, so that *they* can decide what the beneficiaries will get out of the property, in other words, to give them a specified benefit from the property *without giving them ownership*.

2.17 Hence the mere existence of 'equitable title' indicates nothing whatsoever about the content of rights and duties *between* the legal title holder and the equitable title holder. In particular, the fact that equity recognises such a divided title *does not entail* that the legal title holder should be regarded as owing stringent fiduciary obligations to the equitable title holder in the way that a trustee under an express trust does. While the 'paradigm' case of the trust is the intentionally set-up express trust, trusts can also arise by operation of law. These trusts, of which two kinds are traditionally recognised, ie *resulting* and *constructive* trusts, will be discussed in detail in chapters 4 and 5. For now, it suffices to say that one of the complicating factors of these trusts is that what the operation of law often gives rise to in the case of a resulting or constructive trust is merely an equitable title, ie a beneficiary's equitable proprietary right to some property. The holder of the legal title to this property, while properly named, I suppose, a resulting or constructive 'trustee', is often someone who never undertook to hold the property on trust for anyone, and who may not even know that an equitable title in the property exists; partly because of this, he often has no fiduciary duties whatsoever towards the equitable title holder, as would an express trustee to his beneficiary.

The personal and proprietary nature of the beneficiary's right

2.18 It is now time to consider the beneficiary's right from his perspective. For simplicity we shall assume that there is only one beneficiary. The beneficiary has the personal right that the trustee comply with his duties, and since the trustee is a fiduciary, he must exercise all his powers over the property with the best interests of the beneficiary in mind. Obviously, the net result of the trustee's compliance with his duties is that the beneficiary will receive whatever benefit the terms of the trust dictate. If he is an income beneficiary, for example, he has the right to receive payments when the trust investments generate income. He holds this right against the trustee, who has the correlative duty to pay the beneficiary that income. In this respect, the beneficiary has a right that the trustee pay him an amount of property at a particular time, and therefore he has a right which is very much like the right to be paid a debt, and he can transfer this right by assigning it to a third party. But the beneficiary's right is more than just an assignable personal right against the trustee to be paid his benefit according to the trust terms, for equity regards the beneficiary as being the owner of the trust property itself.

2.19 The beneficiary's right is proprietary in so far as it is a right in the trust property itself, ie, in so far as its fate is tied up with the fate of the trust property. One indication of its proprietary character is that it lasts only so long as the trust property does, that is, will only be effective so long as he is able to find or identify the trust property. If the trust property is stolen through no fault of the trustee and the property cannot be found, or is destroyed through no fault of the trustee, then the trust essentially evaporates, for there is no property to which the beneficiary's rights under a trust can attach. As a consequence of this theft or destruction the trustee's personal duty to dispose of the property in accordance with the terms of the trust likewise disappears, for he is no longer an owner of any trust property. Thus, if the property disappears, then so does the trust, and so does the beneficiary's right. There is a sharp difference between the right of the beneficiary in this respect and the right of the buyer under a contract of sale to be delivered the goods, or the right of a creditor. If the goods which the seller is bound to deliver are lost or stolen before title passes, then the buyer does not lose his contractual right to the seller's delivery of them; he may bring an action for damages for their full value. Similarly, if a debtor is robbed it is no skin off his creditor's nose – the debt did not attach specifically to the property that was stolen, and the debtor cannot use the robbery as an excuse for not paying in full. In the case of the beneficiary, however, he is the one who loses if the trust property is lost or stolen, since equity regards his rights as being dependent upon his continuing 'equitable' title, which attaches to the trust property from the outset of the trust.

2.20 Note, however, that the trustee's personal liability for a breach of trust committed while the trust is up and running continues even if the breach caused the total loss of the trust property. For example, if the trustee commits a breach of trust by investing the trust fund improperly so that all the money is lost, the trustee is personally liable to compensate the beneficiary. This liability is a personal one, for it follows on the failure of the trustee to comply with his personal duty to invest the trust fund properly.

2.21 Because trusts are founded upon a special arrangement in which the legal title to property, and therefore all the legal powers to deal with it, is held by someone who is not permitted to act as if he owns it for his own benefit, they create an obvious danger: if the trustee is an incompetent or a rogue, he is in the position drastically to harm the beneficiary's interest by transferring the trust property to a non-beneficiary. All may not be lost, however; since the beneficiary's right is proprietary he can, where possible, follow the property into the hands of a person to whom the trustee wrongly transferred it, and demand that this new owner hold the property on trust for him – in other words he can assert his equitable title in the property against a subsequent holder of the legal title to the property, just as if that person were the original trustee himself. The only problem is that he cannot claim his rights against *every* subsequent holder of the legal title, and so the proprietary nature of the beneficiary's right is limited.

Claiming equitable title against third parties

2.22 Historically, the law concerning which subsequent holders of the trust property would be required by equity to hold the property on trust for the beneficiary developed piece-meal. Roughly, equity held first that a purchaser for value who had notice of the trust, ie knew he was buying property that the trustee held on trust for another, was obliged to give effect to the beneficiary's rights; then the trust obligation was extended to those who inherited the property from the trustee; then, to a donee (the recipient of a gift) with or without notice of the trust, then to creditors of the trustee who had seized the trust property in order to realise the debts owed them (roughly the equivalent of a trustee's trustee in bankruptcy (**2.32**)). So the development of the beneficiary's right to follow the property was conceived in equity as the transfer of the personal duty of the trustee to others where the circumstances were such that they ought, in good conscience, to hold the property for the beneficiary. Thus this aspect of the proprietary character of the beneficiary's right grew out of equity's willingness to shift personal trust obligations onto subsequent takers of the legal title to the trust property. But this shifting stopped at the door of the *bona fide purchaser of the legal interest in the trust property without notice, whether actual, constructive, or imputed, of the trust*, a person sometimes called 'equity's darling'.

The bona fide purchaser

2.23 If the trustee transfers the legal title to the trust property to someone who has:

- given good 'consideration' for it, ie has given money or money's worth in exchange for it; and who

- has no actual notice, ie knowledge, of the beneficiary's rights; and

- has no 'constructive' notice of them either, ie knowledge of those interests which he would have acquired if he had made all usual and reasonable investigations when purchasing that kind of property; and

- has no 'imputed notice' either, ie any agents working for him in making the purchase have no actual or constructive notice either,

then this purchaser takes the property with good legal title free of any trust obligations, and the beneficiary loses his equitable title in the trust property. The beneficiary's equitable title is extinguished, and he cannot demand the property back from the bona fide purchaser, nor can he demand that the bona fide purchaser act like a trustee and deliver his benefits under the trust as if it still applied to that property.

2.24 There are a few points worth noting. First, the rule applies to the bona fide purchaser of any legal *interest*, not just a *legal title* in the property which someone may acquire. An example is a legal security interest (**2.34**). Where a person who bona fide and without notice advances money to the trustee and takes a legal charge over some trust property, he takes an interest which is not subject to the beneficiary's rights either. The practical upshot in this situation would be that if the trustee failed to pay back the loan, then the lender could 'realise' his security by taking possession of the secured property and selling it to pay off the debt. As a bona fide purchaser, he would prevail over the beneficiary's equitable title to the property.

Bona fide purchasers of equitable interests

2.25   Second, notice that the rule only applies to the case where the purchaser acquires a *legal* interest. If, for example, the trustee in breach of trust grants an *equitable* security interest in the trust property, that is a security interest which equity will enforce but which is not recognised at common law, then A will take subject to the rights of the beneficiary even if he is a bona fide purchaser for value of this interest with no actual, constructive, or imputed notice of the beneficiary's rights. The bona fide purchase rule only applies in a contest between a legal interest holder and an equitable interest holder. In a contest between two equitable interest holders, like the beneficiary and A in this case, the general rule of equity is that the interest which was created first in time prevails. Why is there this difference? It appears to have arisen as a kind of 'jurisdictional' curiosity. The beneficiary and the honest purchaser who has paid good value for his interest stand essentially on an equal footing with respect to their moral claims to the property. The rogue trustee has dealt dishonestly with both, selling the property out from under the beneficiary, and selling a flawed title (because impressed with a trust) to the purchaser. We have the classic case of a rogue and two innocents, and the court is faced with a choice as to whose claim should prevail. However, because the purchaser of an equitable interest was already within the jurisdiction of equity, ie his interest was equitable, equity had to deal with their competitive claims, and adopted the 'first in time' rule. On the other hand, equity did not weigh up the competing claims of the beneficiary and the legal bona fide purchaser. Only if the legal purchaser's conscience was affected could he be subject to the 'conscience'-based jurisdiction of equity; since it was not, equity regarded itself as having no power to intervene against him (see *Pilcher v Rawlins* (1872)). Thus the bona fide purchaser of a legal interest got his legal title free and clear of the trust because of a sort of 'default' rule about the 'conscience'-based jurisdiction of equity.

'Notice' in different contexts

2.26 Finally, about the formulation of the rule: the rule as stated refers to the bona fide purchaser's having 'notice of the trust'. This formulation accurately describes the working of the rule in the context of its historical development, where land was transferred by deed. These transfers were carried out according to a standard conveyancing practice. For example, in the case of the sale of the fee simple of Blackacre, the buyer's solicitor would inspect the past title deeds and the property itself to discover any proprietary interests in Blackacre held by third parties. For example, the neighbouring owner of Whiteacre might have an easement, such as a right of way, over Blackacre. If it were a *legal* interest, this easement would most probably have been created by deed and the solicitor should discover it when inspecting the deeds. Nevertheless, being a legal interest, the rule was that it would bind the purchaser of Blackacre whether his solicitor was able to discover it or not. (Of course, following the purchase, he could sue the seller for damages for not disclosing that Blackacre was subject to this easement.) Blackacre might also be subject to some equitable proprietary interests. For example, the owner of Blackacre might have granted another of his neighbours an equitable right called a 'restrictive covenant' preventing him from using Blackacre in a particular way, for example, developing the land for industrial purposes. Such an *equitable* right would only bind the purchaser if his solicitor actually discovered it or ought to have discovered it by making the proper investigations, and if so, then the purchaser would take Blackacre subject to this equitable right. In essence, then, the extent of notice in this context defined the extent of the rights in the land the purchaser acquired; his legal estate was limited by or subject to all the valid legal interests in the land and all the valid equitable interests in the land of which he had actual, constructive, or imputed notice – if he wanted to buy the land free of those interests, he had to deal with those interest-holders themselves, to buy them out, as it were. On the other hand, those equitable rights not caught by actual, constructive or imputed notice did not bind him at all.

2.27 The rule's operation is quite different in the case of other property. There is no standard 'conveyancing' practice for the sale of other property, like chattels, or shares. Individuals are not expected to investigate the title as they would do if they were buying land, for the simple reason that third parties do not generally have a variety of interests in chattels or shares. Therefore the practical effect of the rule in most circumstances is that the purchaser is only bound if he has actual, constructive, or imputed notice that he is dealing with a trustee of the property who is selling the property in order to effect a *breach* of trust. For example, brokers who buy shares from pension trustees who are selling these shares in the course of following their investment strategy, brokers who will know, of course, that the shares are the property of the pension fund, do not take these shares subject to the trust simply because they know they are dealing with shares held under a trust. Having actual notice of the trust in this case does not require them to hold any shares they buy from the pension fund trustees on trust for the pension fund beneficiaries. They will only take the shares bound by the equitable rights of the pension beneficiaries if they have notice that the trustees are selling the shares as if they held the legal title to the shares for their own benefit, ie in order to perpetrate a breach of trust and defeat the beneficiaries' interests. For that reason, in the case of sales of most trust property, like shares or other investments, with respect to the issue of notice you should think of the rule as follows: a bona fide purchaser for value of the legal title without actual, constructive, or imputed notice that the transaction is made in *breach of trust* will take free of the beneficiary's interests.

Tracing trust property

2.28 Although the beneficiary's proprietary right *in the original trust property* is obliterated by its sale to a bona fide purchaser, all is not necessarily lost, for the beneficiary may acquire a substitute proprietary right by operation of law, the availability of which depends upon what are called 'tracing rules'. If my rogue trustee sells the trust property, say shares, to a bona fide purchaser for £1,000, my equitable title to the shares is extinguished. But since it is clear that the trustee has received the £1,000 in exchange for the shares, the law will trace the value of the shares into the £1,000. The law will keep track of that value if it shifts again, for example into a car which the trustee buys with that money, or into any other property which is exchanged for the proceeds, tracing through one exchange substitution after another. Tracing will only stop when either the property into which I trace that value is lost or destroyed, or the evidence of what substitutions were made runs out, or the property is exchanged for non-property, for example where the trustee blows the trust money on a vacation. The rules of tracing will be discussed in detail in chapter 12. The great thing about tracing value in this way is that it gives the law a basis for giving the beneficiary new rights, in particular proprietary rights (though, as we shall see when we discuss breach of trust in chapter 12 personal rights may depend upon tracing as well). For example, because my value from the shares can be traced into the £1,000, I may be able to claim that I have an equitable title in that money, or if there are subsequent exchanges, I may be able to claim an equitable title in the later exchange products.

Personal remedies for breach of trust against third parties

2.29 Second, all may not be lost even though the beneficiary's proprietary rights run out because the original trust property disappears through loss, theft, or destruction, or can no longer be followed because acquired by a bona fide purchaser, or its value can no longer be traced into substitute property – the beneficiary may have personal rights not only against the original trustee but against others. We shall discuss these rights in chapter 12; in general they arise against any one who dishonestly participates in a breach of trust, and against anyone who receives trust property or its traceable proceeds in the knowledge that it comes to him as the result of a breach of trust.

Equitable 'title' – proprietary or restitutionary?

2.30 Where trust property is transferred in breach of trust, we can conceive of the beneficiary enforcing his *continuing* equitable title in the property against anyone who acquires legal title to it (except for equity's darling). But one can conceive of the beneficiary's equitable 'title' in a different way. Recall the historical development of the beneficiary's ability to enforce the trust against those who took the trust property (**2.23**). One might say that, rather than equity's enlarging bit by bit the enforceability of the beneficiary's title in the trust property, equity instead enlarged the category of subsequent takers upon whom it would impose personal fiduciary obligations in favour of the beneficiary. In other words, rather than enforcing the beneficiary's original equitable interest against 'all the world' save for equity's darling, which would clearly indicate that the beneficiary's equitable interest was continuing and thus proprietary, therefore deserving of the term equitable 'title', equity merely imposed new personal obligations on the subsequent holders of the trust property as a remedial measure – each time equity did this it gave the beneficiary a new personal right against the subsequent legal title holder. On this view, the beneficiary does not have equitable title, but merely a personal interest against the trustee for the time being – however, this interest is well protected, because unless a subsequent taker is equity's darling, equity will impose a new trust obligation upon him to prevent his being unjustly enriched at the beneficiary's expense. Remedial rights which arise by operation of law to prevent a person being unjustly enriched at another's expense are called 'restitutionary', and so we can frame these different conceptions of the beneficiary's right as either proprietary or restitutionary. As it happens, almost everyone believes that the beneficiary's interest is correctly described as proprietary, not restitutionary. But the distinction remains important, and will arise again in different contexts, in particular when we consider the nature of the beneficiary's interest in substitute property into which he has traced the value of the original trust property.

Equitable interests as trust property

2.31 In the foregoing it was assumed for the sake of simplicity that the trustee always holds the *legal* title to the trust property, but as we have seen (**2.18**), a beneficiary's equitable interest is itself a valuable right which can be assigned; such a right can therefore form part of a trust corpus itself. Thus a beneficiary can declare a trust of it, which is called a 'subtrust'. Here the trustee of the legal property holds it on trust for the beneficiary, who in turn holds his right to it under the sub-trust for the sub-beneficiary. Equitable property can take many forms besides a traditional beneficial interest under a trust, in particular with respect to land. Equitable interests in land, such as equitable mortgages, leases, or easements, are well-known proprietary rights in land, and now are protectable under various registration systems. If registered, they will bind everyone who takes the legal title, including a bona fide purchaser. For that reason, certain equitable rights in land are nowadays as secure as legal rights. If rights of this kind are held on trust we again have a case where the trustee holds equitable, not legal title to trust property, and although it would be unusual to regard the trustee's holding of equitable interests in land as 'rights held under a sub-trust', this is technically correct.

The context of insolvency

2.32 One of the main reasons why proprietary rights are valuable is that people and companies can become insolvent. One is insolvent if one has insufficient assets to meet one's liabilities – in other words, one hasn't enough financial resources to meet the demands of all one's creditors. In the case of individuals, the legal device of bankruptcy allows the insolvent individual to get out of this mess and start again afresh. It works roughly as follows: all of the property of the bankrupt, including any rights to be paid any debts owing to him, becomes the property of his trustee in bankruptcy, whose job it is to distribute these assets, the bankrupt's 'estate in bankruptcy', in proportionate shares to the bankrupt's creditors. Thus, if the bankrupt's estate is worth £10,000, and his total debts are £100,000, each creditor will receive 10 pence in the pound for the debt he is owed. Following this distribution, and after a period of time, eg three years the bankrupt is 'discharged' from all his debts, and can begin economic life again, albeit without much in the way of assets. (Certain assets of the bankrupt remain his, and are not used to pay off his creditors: roughly, the property personally required by him in the pursuit of his employment or business and such property as is required to meet his and his family's basic domestic needs.) The analagous process with respect to a company is called liquidation; in essence, the liquidator distributes all of the assets of the company to its creditors on a proportionate basis. Following this distribution the company no longer exists. There is no compendious term which covers both the trustee in bankruptcy and the liquidator of a company, so henceforth when the term 'trustee in bankruptcy' is used it will, for our purposes, comprise them both.

2.33 Proprietary rights become very important in the case of insolvency. If a bankrupt owes you £100, then you are likely to see little money, for as a general creditor you will only be paid a proportionate share of the bankrupt's assets. You might be lucky to see any money at all. To the extent, however, that your rights against the bankrupt are proprietary, then you are in a much stronger position – an asset of the bankrupt which is subject to the proprietary right of someone else is, to the extent of that right, not the bankrupt's own property, and therefore not part of his estate in bankruptcy to be used for distribution to his general creditors – it belongs to the person with the proprietary right. The beneficiary's *equitable* rights to property held on trust stand on the same footing as legal title in this respect in the case of insolvency. The trustee has no beneficial interest in the property he holds on trust, and so neither can his trustee in bankruptcy, who acquires title to all the trustee's legal assets should he become bankrupt, thus the property

29

is not available to the trustee in bankruptcy for distribution to the trustee's own creditors. In short, a beneficiary's equitable rights bind a trustee in bankruptcy. Obviously then, personal rights to be paid sums of money, for example a claim for money damages for breach of contract, are not as valuable in a bankruptcy as proprietary rights, for they give the right-holder no special claim on any particular assets of the bankrupt. For this reason, plaintiffs who have a claim for money against a bankrupt will often try to claim that their past dealings with him created a trust over some of the bankrupt's property, for then they can simply withdraw this property from the bankrupt's estate.

Security interests

2.34 A beneficiary's equitable title is functionally similar to a 'security interest' in the context of insolvency. A security interest is a right that a creditor holds in particular property of his debtor. The classic example is a mortgage over land. In return for providing money, the lender (the 'mortgagee') makes sure that the borrower (the 'mortgagor') grants him a mortgage over the borrower's land. (Contrary to common parlance, it is the lender, then, who gets a mortgage.) A mortgage is a right that the lender has in the land of the borrower, and it has the effect of securing payment of the loan. If the borrower defaults on his contractual repayments of the loan, then (roughly) the lender has the right to take possession of the land and sell it to pay off the loan (plus whatever interest or other costs are specified by the loan contract). All security interests work in essentially the same way. They entitle the creditor who has one, called a 'secured' creditor, to sell the property in question if the borrower defaults on his repayments. Because security interests 'charge' the property with the repayment of a loan in this way, they are often just called 'charges'. The vital point about charges is that they are proprietary rights. They attach to the property itself. If the property passes out of the hands of the borrower into the hands of his trustee in bankruptcy, the lender will still be able to 'realise' his security, ie sell the property to pay off the debt, even though it is no longer held by the borrower. Any of the money proceeds of sale which are not required to pay off the outstanding debt belong, of course, to the trustee in bankruptcy – in other words, the security interest only charges the property to the extent of the sum owed. Security interests are not only created by two parties to a loan agreement. A court can make a 'charging order' against a defendant's property, which gives the plaintiff a charge over the property to secure the payment of an award of damages.

2.35   The justice (or lack thereof) of the beneficiary's right to withdraw his property from the bankrupt's estate is illuminated by a distinction Hayton ((1996a), 14) makes between the beneficiary's interest under the trust when things are humming along in a lawful fashion, and his rights when things go awry. Always remember that a trust, like a contract, is a private arrangement. While it is working, more or less, the beneficiary enforces his rights against the trustee, like a contracting party pressing for performance against the other contracting party. When things go badly wrong because the trust property is transferred away in breach of trust, the beneficiary, in a sense, takes the trust public, and tries to get the property back from third parties. You can make an analogy here with a secured loan. The loan contract is private, but when the borrower goes into bankruptcy, the lender goes public with the contract and claims the actual property itself back from the trustee in bankruptcy, disappointing all those other creditors. You can see why, in these circumstances, Parliament has tried to make things as fair as possible by putting in place public registration systems both for many equitable proprietary rights in land and for security interests, to protect third parties who would otherwise be hurt if caught out by the proprietary effect of these private arrangements. But there is no registration system as such for interests under trusts; they remain private. Thus in order to avoid surprising innocent third parties, the law must be judicious in accepting claims by those who would argue that their past dealings with a bankrupt gave rise by operation of law to a trust over some of his property in their favour, as this will effectively give the claimant a priority over other creditors which may, in the circumstances, be quite unfair.

Testamentary gifts

2.36   A *testamentary* trust is one created as a gift under a will. (Trusts created by living settlors are called *inter vivos* trusts.) Many trusts are created in this way, so a passing familiarity with the rudiments of the law of wills and of intestate succession is very useful. The property of a dead person is called the 'deceased's estate', and it passes to the living in one of two ways: either according to the deceased's will, or if he has no valid will, that is, if he dies 'intestate', then according to the rules of intestate succession. The rules of intestate succession are essentially 'default' rules which distribute the property in the way that most people would have distributed it had they made a will; to their spouse first, then to their children; if there are no spouse or children, then to their parents, siblings, and finally to more distant relations. The person who makes a will is a 'testator', and in his will he nominates one or more 'executors' who will 'prove' the will, ie have the will declared valid by a Court of Probate. The property of the deceased goes to the executors who will pay off the deceased's debts, and then distribute the deceased's estate to those whom he has given it under his will. In the case of intestacy, there is no will to execute; the court will instead appoint one or more 'administrators' who will, like executors, clear up the deceased's affairs by paying his debts, and then distribute the estate according to the rules of intestate succession. Both executors and administrators are called the 'personal representatives' of the deceased.

2.37 For historical reasons, different terms apply to testamentary gifts of different kinds of property. Land is 'devised' by will, and therefore the gift is called a 'devise' and the donees 'devisees'. Generally, personalty is 'bequeathed', but gifts of sums of money are called 'legacies' and their recipients 'legatees'. 'Gifts' will suffice for a compendious term. The gifts under a will do not take effect from the time it is made, but only when comes into operation on the testator's death. Thus if one of the intended recipients dies before ('predeceases') the testator, his gift 'lapses'. With respect to that piece of property, it is as if the testator made no specific gift of it at all. Intended testamentary gifts, including intended trusts which are to take effect on the testator's death, may fail for a number of reasons. The testator may have failed sufficiently to specify either the recipient or the property to be given, for example. Because intended gifts under wills fail, a very important clause in any will is the one in which the testator gives 'the rest and residue' of his estate; this 'residuary' clause gives all the property left over after the specific gifts, of Blackacre to A, of 500 shares in X plc on trust to C for life and then to D absolutely, and so on, are distributed. The recipients under this clause, the 'residuary legatees' (so called whatever kind of property they get) will get more to the extent that any of the specific gifts fail. If there is no residuary gift or for some reason it fails, for example because the named residuary legatees have predeceased the testator, then any property not disposed of by specific gifts in the will will be distributed as if the testator made no will at all, ie under the rules of intestate succession. Thus it is apparent that there is always an incentive for a good fight over the validity of specific gifts in the will – the residuary legatees or, failing them, the intestate successors, will always look carefully at their validity, because they will take the property if a specific gift fails. This applies just as much to specific testamentary gifts which are trusts; indeed, most of the cases concerning the validity of trusts concern testamentary trusts.

2.38 The 'formal' requirements of wills, principally that a will be signed by the testator and attested by two witnesses, are prescribed to ensure that the will truly represents the testator's intentions and, in general, the law will allow no departures from this method. If an entire will is invalid for not being correctly formally made, the deceased's estate is distributed under the rules of intestate succession, no matter how obvious it might be that this was contrary to his actual intentions. Here again is an opportunity for a good fight. Those who would take as intestate successors, if not well provided for in the will, have the incentive to press every reasonable argument that the will is invalid.

2.39 While the main function of a will is to dispose of the testator's property, so that the power to make a will is essentially a legal power of ownership, a testator may (conditionally) impose obligations under a will, otherwise he could never create trusts, which require the creation of the fiduciary duties of trusteeship. The reason why the testator can only *conditionally* impose trust obligations is that no one is ever required to take up the role of trustee; a trustee must undertake these fiduciary obligations voluntarily. On the other hand, it is a principle of equity that a trust will never fail for want of a trustee, and so the court will find someone who will take on the trust; so although the testator's imposition of trust obligations is in theory dependent upon their acceptance by someone, as a practical matter they will be accepted so he can impose as he likes. A testator may also direct his executors or trustees to enter into contractual obligations, for example, to give an interest free loan to his brother in law. What a testator cannot do by his will, of course, is to enter into a contract, ie undertake contractual obligations himself, for when the will takes effect he is, of course, dead.

2.40 The deceased's personal representatives are not trustees for the people who will take the property under the will or on intestate succession (*Stamp Duties Comr v Livingston* (1964)). They are the full legal owners of the deceased's property, though they are under stringent obligations to dispose of his property properly, and for this reason, their role is very trustee-like. Furthermore, prospective beneficiaries under a will or under the rules of intestate succession, although they do not have an interest in the deceased's estate itself as a beneficiary does in the property of a trust, have a right against the personal representatives to administer the estate properly, and this right, like the beneficiary's right to his interest under a trust, can be assigned or bequeathed (Re Leigh's Will Trusts (1969)). Executors are often appointed to be the trustees of the testamentary trusts which a testator specifies in his will.

Further Reading

Matthews (1996); Hayton (1996b); Sealy (1962); Swadling (1997).

Self-test questions

1. What are fiduciary obligations?

2. What is equitable title?

3. What is the significance of 'equity's darling'?

4. What is a security interest, and in what respects is it comparable to a trust?

5. Explain the role of a deceased's personal representatives; in what respects are they like trustees?

CHAPTER THREE

Express Trusts

SUMMARY

Fixed trusts, discretionary trusts, and powers of appointment

Beneficial interests under fixed trusts

The principle in *Saunders v Vautier*

The rule against perpetuities

The enforcement of discretionary trusts and powers of appointment

Beneficial interests under discretionary trusts and powers of appointment

Protective trusts

3.1 Express trusts are very flexible devices for structuring the benefits which property can provide, in particular in ways which are impossible or inconvenient to do simply by making an outright gift. Essentially three ways of doing so can be employed – fixed trusts, discretionary trusts, and powers of appointment.

Fixed trusts, discretionary trusts, and powers of appointment

Fixed trusts

3.2 The beneficial interests under a fixed trust are, as the name implies, fixed, which means that the *share* of the value of the trust property the beneficiary will receive is defined by the terms of the trust. This does not mean that the actual monetary value the beneficiary will receive can be determined from the outset. For example, shares may be held on trust to pay the income to B for his life, and then to transfer legal title to the shares to C. Both B and C know what their interests are, though the particular amounts of income which B may receive from the trust property will vary with the amounts of dividends paid on the shares. Nevertheless, any income will be certain as soon as it comes into existence when a dividend is declared.

Discretionary trusts

3.3 In contrast, the terms of a discretionary trust give the trustee a dispositive discretion. The trustee may have a discretion as to the particular amounts any beneficiary may receive, a discretion as to whether certain individuals receive anything at all, or both. A typical trust of this kind is one in which a testator leaves money in trust for his children 'in such portions as the trustees shall in their absolute discretion see fit'. The main reason for giving the trustee a discretion of this kind is that it allows the trustee to respond to changing circumstances. If one child gets married and has children of his own, it may be sensible to give that child more money. Under a discretionary trust, no individual who is in the class of possible beneficiaries, ie in whose favour the trustee may exercise his discretion, has any interest, ie 'equitable title', in the trust property, until the trustee actually exercises his discretion and declares that such and such a share or amount will go to that individual. The possible beneficiaries have only a hope, or expectancy, of receiving the testator's bounty. However, the fact that the trustee has a discretion does not mean he can do anything he wants – he still has the fiduciary obligation to carry out the terms of the trust, and therefore he *must* exercise his discretion within the trust terms and distribute the trust property. The result of the trustee's having a discretion to select only some of the possible beneficiaries means, of course, that some might not receive an interest at all, in which case they will not really be 'beneficiaries' of the trust. For this reason, the term 'objects' is used. This is a compendious term which covers beneficiaries under a fixed trust, possible beneficiaries under a discretionary trust, and possible recipients under a power of appointment, to which we now turn.

Powers of appointment

3.4 A power of appointment under a trust allows the power-holder to 'appoint', ie give, property to individuals, free of the trust. Consider the following trust term: '£100,000 on trust to pay the income to A for life, and then to my nieces and nephews then living in such shares as he shall in his absolute discretion see fit, with power to A to appoint such of the capital as he shall in his absolute discretion see fit to any of my nieces and nephews'. This starts out as a trust, but A is given a power of appointment to transfer as much of the £100,000 as he wants at any time to the settlor's nieces and nephews before his death. If A exercises the power, he will simply take the property right out of the trust and give it to someone in the class of objects (the nieces and nephews). Because a power of appointment is a power to give away property, it is a power of ownership, although limited by the trust terms. Because powers to appoint property are given to individuals, power-holders are often called 'donees of the power', or 'donees' for short; this terminology is obviously confusing because one naturally thinks of the person *to whom* property is appointed as the donee, not the one who does the appointing. In any case, beware of this term when you read the cases. Powers are generally restricted, essentially in the same ways that discretionary trusts are limited. The settlor can restrict the power so that the power-holder can only appoint to a certain class of objects, the amounts that any object receives can be limited, and so on. A power to appoint to anyone in the world, including the power-holder himself, is called a 'general' power. Such a power essentially amounts to absolute ownership, though a power to appoint to anyone which can only be exercised by will, which obviously cuts out the power-holder himself, is still considered a general power. A 'special' power is a power to appoint to a restricted class of persons, eg the testator's children, even if that class includes the power-holder. A 'hybrid' or 'intermediate' power is a power to appoint to anyone *except for* a restricted class, eg anyone except the settlor or his spouse or children.

3.5 Discretionary trusts and powers of appointment are similar in many respects, but there is a vital distinction (in theory at least) between them: a power-holder, unlike a trustee of a discretionary trust, has *no duty* to exercise the power. Indeed, in general, there is no duty on the power-holder even to consider exercising the power. There are, however, two complicating factors: (1) If a power of appointment is given to a trustee or trustees of the trust, while there is no duty on the trustee any more than on any other power-holder to exercise the power, trustees, because of their fiduciary position, must consider using the power from time to time. In other words, trustees can't simply ignore the power like A in the example above could. So a power is a power whoever gets it, but if a trustee is given the power, he does have duties in respect of it which other power-holders do not. Terms sometimes used to distinguish these situations are 'bare' and 'fiduciary' power – when any old person who is not a trustee has the power, it is called a 'bare power'. When a power is given to the trustee or trustees, it is called a 'fiduciary power'. I suppose these terms do no real harm, so long as one bears in mind that the difference does not lie in the character of the power, as these terms suggest, but in the character of the power-*holder*; a 'fiduciary power' is a power of appointment *held* by a fiduciary or trustee. There is, however, an important practical consequence of giving a power under a trust to 'the trustee' or 'the trustees'; the power is exercisable by whoever are the trustees for the time being, ie not only by whatever particular individuals are the trustees at the outset but by any successor trustees appointed to replace them. A bare power given to a named individual is exercisable only by him. (2) Occasionally, non-trustees are given 'powers in the nature of a trust'. For example, a testator may give his brother a power to appoint property by his (the brother's) will, where in the circumstances it is clear that the testator intends to oblige the brother to make that appointment. Thus the brother is under a fiduciary duty to exercise the power – he *must* exercise it. Just like a trustee of a discretionary trust he must act, though unlike the trustee he is not the legal owner of the trust property. If he fails to act, the court will act for him, in the same way as the court will enforce a discretionary trust should the trustees themselves refuse to act (*Brown v Higgs* (1803)). Powers of appointment are sometimes distinguished from discretionary trusts and 'powers in the nature of a trust', where in both cases there is a duty to act, by being called 'mere' powers, 'mere' indicating the absence of any duty to appoint.

3.6 Because there is no duty upon the power holder to appoint, he might well not, and so there will always be those who will take the property if no appointment is made, who will, in the standard terminology, 'take in default of appointment'. As the provision for A and his nieces and nephews in the example above illustrates, one whole 'trust' can combine the different devices of the fixed trust, discretionary trust, and power of appointment.

Beneficial interests under fixed trusts

Capital and income interests

3.7 Under a trust, the beneficial interests in the trust property can be carved up pretty much any way the settlor wishes. However, there are standard ways of doing so which we shall encounter again and again, in particular dividing the property between 'income' and 'capital' beneficiaries. Consider the following gift: 'To A for life and then to X, Y and Z in equal shares'. A will receive the benefit of the property during his lifetime, but what determines the extent of his benefit? Can he insist that the trustee transfer as much of the property as he wants to him, so that X, Y, and Z will only get what he hasn't used up before he dies? No. A is entitled only to the income of the property, and the income he receives will depend upon the kind of property in the trust. Income on shares consists of the dividends that are paid, on bonds or other-interest bearing investments the interest payments, the rent on land. During A's life X, Y, and Z will get nothing. They are the 'capital' beneficiaries; after A's death they are entitled to the property itself, free of any trust, in equal shares. The value of their interest will fluctuate with the market sale price of the trust property.

Successive interests

3.8   Where there are income and capital beneficiaries there are 'successive' interests. Successive interests are interests in the same property which take effect one after another, usually following the successive deaths of the beneficiaries. In the example above, A will get the benefit for the time being, and only later will the capital beneficiaries X, Y, and Z get any value from the trust property. Traditionally successive interest trusts, called 'settlements', were the province of dynastic families, and were used to define each successive generation's beneficial interest in a family's landed estates with a view to preserving them for subsequent generations. Because land was the subject matter of settlements, successive interests were framed in terms of two freehold estates in land, the life interest and the fee simple. A life interest, unsurprisingly, lasts for the lifetime of an individual, and a fee simple estate is unlimited in time, and therefore a gift of a fee simple amounts to absolute ownership. So a typical gift might be to Fred for life, then to Beatrix for life, then to Albert in fee simple. Fred will enjoy the benefit or income of the property for his life; when he dies Beatrix will get the income for as long as she lives, and when she expires Albert will take the absolute ownership. Due to the significance of the land settlement, the income beneficiary for life of a trust of any kind of property is often called the 'life tenant', the traditional land law term for the present holder of a life estate, and the capital beneficiary the 'remainderman', the corresponding term for one

39

who took the fee simple following a life estate. Successive interests are not, however, restricted to time periods equivalent to the life estate and fee simple. One might make a gift of the income of shares to Richard until he attains the age of 21, and then to Tom for 10 years, and then to Mary absolutely.

Exhaustive and non-exhaustive trusts of income

3.9 Trusts of the income of property can be cut down by giving the trustees a 'power to accumulate', that is, a power to save the income as it arises rather than distributing it to beneficiaries. The accumulations can be directed to go either to the capital beneficiary or to accumulation funds which can later be paid over to the income beneficiaries. Trusts with a power to accumulate are called 'non-exhaustive', for when the power is exercised the distributions to the beneficiaries do not exhaust all of the income. Trusts of income with no power to accumulate are called 'exhaustive'.

Conditional and defeasible interests

3.10 Complicating matters somewhat, there may also be conditional and defeasible interests in property held under a trust. Conditions may be of two kinds, conditions precedent and conditions subsequent. A condition precedent is a condition which must be fulfilled for a gift to take effect, eg 'Blackacre to A in fee simple, on condition that he marries before the year 2000'. A condition subsequent is a condition of defeasance – the gift will come to an end if the condition occurs, eg 'Blackacre to A in fee simple, but if he should become a barrister, then to B in fee simple': if A becomes a barrister, then B will become entitled to Blackacre. Finally, a determinable interest is one which, while similar to a gift defeasible upon condition subsequent, is conceptually different. A gift defeasible upon condition subsequent is regarded as a full gift, of a life interest for example, which might come to an end before running its normal course, ie until the death of the life tenant. A determinable interest is regarded as being reduced from the outset by the determining event, although its actual duration will extend to the maximum period of the basic interest if the determining event does not occur. Thus a life interest determinable upon X's marriage will 'ripen' into a complete life interest if X never marries. The very subtle conceptual distinction between determinable interests and interests defeasible upon condition subsequent, so that the legal effect of a gift 'to Mathilda for life, but if she remarries, to Betty' (a life interest defeasible upon condition subsequent) differs from one 'to Mathilda during her widowhood' (a determinable life interest), has been much criticised for being 'extremely artificial' (Pennycuick VC, *Re Sharp's Settlement Trusts* (1972)).

Vested and absolute interests

3.11 Because interests can be defeasible or contingent, the interest can shift from one person to another. A person's interests are 'vested' if he is entitled to receive the benefits of the property as matters stand at the present. Thus, where there is a gift 'to A for life, remainder to B', A and B both have vested interests, since as things stand right now the property will go to them. It is not to the point that B has only a future interest. His capital interest is still vested, because he is in line to receive it and no one else is. Because this gift is not subject to any condition or defeating contingency (the capital only goes to B (or his heirs) when A dies, but A must die sometime), B's interest is also 'absolute'. An absolute interest is one which cannot be defeated. An example of a person with a vested interest which is not absolute is the unmarried widow Mathilda in the example – the income interest is vested in her and she receives the income, but it is not absolute, for if she remarries she will lose it. Another example is the person who will take property in default of appointment before any appointment is made. Until appointment, he is in line to receive the property, but he is clearly not absolutely entitled for his interest will be defeated by an appointment.

3.12 Although the trust device allows a settlor to distribute his bounty in a variety of ways over a period of time, the law does put limitations on this power. In particular, the law limits his ability to keep the property in the trust and out of the hands of the beneficiaries whom equity regards as the true owners of the property. The two principal means of doing so are the principle in *Saunders v Vautier* and the rule against perpetuities.

The principle in *Saunders v Vautier*

3.13 Although named after the case of *Saunders v Vautier* (1841), the principle is actually of much longer standing, and may be stated as follows:

wherever a beneficiary with a vested interest under a trust is *sui juris*, ie of full age and not a lunatic, he may call for the trust property which represents that interest, and the trustees are obliged to transfer the legal title of it to him; if he is a sole beneficiary, this will result in the complete collapse of the trust. For example, if a settlor creates a trust under which his son A is to receive the income of property until he is thirty, at which time he is to receive the capital, that son can demand the legal title as soon as he reaches 18. This represents a significant limitation upon the settlor's 'freedom of trust', but it can be justified in two ways. First, there might be something of an 'anti-trust' justification, as follows: while it is fine to empower owners to created structured gifts of property where this is essentially the only means of giving the benefits of property, as for example when money is provided for minor children, this power should not be used to allow an owner to control his beneficiaries when they are fully competent to look after themselves. If you give property to someone, you naturally take the risk that they will use that property in ways which are foolish or which otherwise might defeat your hopes. But that is the price of treating people, including donees of property, as autonomous individuals. The law of trusts should not, therefore, allow settlors to treat sane adults as children, and so the principle of *Saunders v Vautier* reflects the law's desire that all individuals, once *sui juris*, should be treated as capable of running their own affairs, including their rights over property. The second justification is related, and concerns the idea of equitable ownership. In the eyes of equity, the beneficiaries are the owners of the trust property, not the settlor. They have the rights against the trustee, and must enforce the trust themselves. When they reach full age the trust, is in essence, in their hands. They can enforce their rights against the trustee or not, may consent to the trustees acting outside the terms of the trust, ie doing what would otherwise be a breach of trust, and as we shall cover in some detail in the next chapter, may vary the terms of the trust as they wish. The settlor has no say in any of this. Thus they are (in theory) in full control of the property via the office of the trustee. But if that is so, why cannot they do with their property what they like, as can any other full owners, and in particular, take the property out of the trust completely if they so desire?

3.14 The operation of the principle varies according to the type of trust. Under fixed trusts, *sui juris* beneficiaries may in principle demand that the trustee transfer the legal title to whatever share of the trust property is theirs, but this is subject to a general limitation that such a transfer must not result in the devaluation of the other beneficiaries' shares. In *Stephenson v Barclays Bank Trust Co Ltd* (1974), Walton J said:

> In general, the [individual *sui juris* beneficiary] is entitled to have transferred to him... an aliquot share of each and every asset of the trust fund which presents no difficulty so far as division is concerned. This will apply to such items as cash, money at the bank or an unsecured loan, Stock Exchange securities and the like. However, as regards land, certainly, in all cases, as regards shares in a private company in very special circumstances...the situation is not so simple, and even a person with a vested interest in possession in an aliquot share of the trust fund may have to wait until the land is sold, and so forth, before being able to call upon the trustees as of right to account to him for his share of the assets.

3.15 More recently, in *Lloyds Bank plc v Duker* (1987), the court refused the request of one beneficiary for the transfer of his proportionate interest in shares of a private company held on trust; the transfer would have given him a controlling block of shares in the company, and as a result his shares would be worth more per share on the open market than the remaining shares in the trust. The judge ordered the sale of all the trust shares on the open market, which, since it would give control of the company, would attract for the whole block of shares a higher price; the beneficiary could then claim his proportionate share of the proceeds of sale. It is important to note that the beneficiary acquired the large proportionate interest in the shares both because certain of the gifts in the original will which disposed of the shares lapsed and through a subsequent bequest. Where a testator or settlor specifically gave one beneficiary a majority interest in a trust of shares, it might be inferred that he intended that beneficiary to take also the market value benefit of a controlling interest, in which case the principle of *Saunders v Vautier* should allow him to withdraw his shares.

3.16 The application of the principle In the case of discretionary trusts is stated in *Re Smith* (1928) by Romer J:

> What is to happen where the trustees have a discretion whether they will apply the whole or only a portion of the fund for the benefit of one person, but are obliged to pay the rest of the fund, so far as not applied for the benefit of the first named person, to or for the benefit of a second named person? There, two people are the sole objects of the discretionary trust and, between them, are entitled to have the whole fund applied to

them or for their benefit. It has been laid down by the Court of Appeal in *In re Nelson* (1918) that, in such a case as that you treat all the people put together just as though they formed one person, for whose benefit the trustees were directed to apply the whole fund.

Therefore, such beneficiaries may together call upon the trustees to transfer the trust property to them as co-owners. If the discretionary trust is one to pay the income only, they can demand the trustee pay the income, as it arises, to them directly as co-owners of it all.

The rule against perpetuities

3.17 As the name implies, the rule against perpetuities prevents settlors from creating perpetual trusts. The rule requires that the beneficial shares of the trust property must get those shares, that is, their rights to the trust property must vest in interest, ie vest absolutely, within a certain period from the time the trust came into effect. The absolute vesting of interests means that the various beneficiaries are all identified and their interests definitely determined to be theirs, and so they may individually or together require the trustees to transfer the trust property to them under the rule in *Saunders v Vautier*.

3.18 The reason for the rule is straightforward: it prevents individuals from directing the use of their property from their grave long after they are dead. The rule ensures that within a certain time after the trust comes into effect, the full equitable ownership of the property gets into the hands of living persons. A detailed examination of the rule is unwarranted here but an outline of its operation is useful, as the effect of the rule will come into play now and again.

3.19 Applying the modern (ie post-17th century) common law rule against perpetuities was a most difficult and complex process, both because of the way the time limit was calculated, and because of the way it took into account the possibility of events occurring which might make a gift fail. The time period of the rule was framed to allow testators to make gifts to their grandchildren that would not vest until the children reached the age of majority, which was 21 when the rule was devised. The rule was devised to make that possible, but also to make sure that this was the limit of what a testator could do to extend the time before his gifts actually vested; in consequence, the allowable time period was framed in a particular way, in reference to 'lives in being' plus a further period of 21 years. The way in which this limit worked is best explained by an example. If I leave property in my will to be divided equally between all my grandchildren who attain the age of 21, under the rule we calculate the time period within which the beneficiaries will become entitled to their shares of the property as follows: If I have any living grandchildren when I die their shares will vest when they each turn 21, and so, being alive at my death, they must turn 21 within 21 years following my death. But I may end up having more grandchildren than them, because my living children may have more kids. My own children who are living at my death are lives in being for the purpose of the rule. (If my wife is pregnant with my child, a child *en ventre sa mere*, as the expression goes, that child counts as a child living at my death, thus a life in being for the purpose of the rule.) The rule now works as follows: obviously, any child born to my children must be conceived before my children die; therefore, the last grandchild of mine which could possibly be born will be conceived no later than the death of my last living child; therefore that last grandchild will turn 21 (ignoring periods of gestation) no later than 21 years after the death of the last life in being. Thus a gift to any or all of my grandchildren who attain their age of majority, 21, must vest, if it vests at all (all of my grandchildren may, as it turns out, die before 21 – that makes the gift fail, but not for perpetuity), within the period determined by the lifetime of the last surviving life in being plus 21 years. Thus the rule can be stated as follows: a gift upon trust is valid if the interests in the trust property of those who are intended to benefit vest, if they vest at all, within 21 years following the death of the last surviving life in being. The following example will show why there were complexities and difficulties applying the rule.

3.20 Say that I have three daughters, all of whom are over 60. They're not going to have any more children, so I'm not going to have any more grandchildren. So if in my will I leave a sum of money to be divided equally amongst my *great* grandchildren who attain the age of 21, that gift will vest within a period determined by lives in being plus 21. The relevant lives in being here are my grandchildren. I will have no more, and the last great grandchild of mine will come into existence (if only in the womb of his mother) no later than the death of my last surviving grandchild. And so none of my great grandchildren will attain the age of 21 (again discounting periods of gestation) later than 21 years following the death

45

of the last surviving life in being. Nevertheless, this gift is void for perpetuity. The courts reasoned that only death prevented anyone from having another child, and so, my daughters being alive, they might yet have another child after my death, although each was over sixty. Such a grandchild would not be alive at my death, so would not be a life in being, and this grandchild could have a child after the death of the last surviving grandchild of mine who was alive at my death, thus after the death of the last surviving life in being. That great grandchild's share would vest more than 21 years after the last life in being. Thus, the gift fails because the rule was applied on the basis of what *could* happen, however unlikely something might be, not on the basis of what was likely to happen or actually happened over time.

3.21 The Perpetuities and Accumulations Act 1964 changed the rules somewhat. In particular it introduced the notion of 'wait and see', by which a gift is valid if it turns out that it vests in the perpetuity period, even though it might not if some possible event or another actually occurs. Secondly, it created a provision by which a settlor can select any period of eighty years or less as the period for his gift, rather than relying on lives in being plus 21 years.

3.22 The rule applies not only to the vesting of fixed interests, but also to interests which arise under discretionary trusts and the exercise of powers of appointment. Special powers of appointment must be exercised, if they are exercised at all, within the perpetuity period, and by parity of reasoning, distributions under discretionary trusts must occur within the perpetuity period as well. By contrast, since general powers are akin to ownership, the rule requires only that the power is acquired during the perpetuity period, since this acquisition in effect vests the interest in the property. It is not clear how hybrid powers are to be treated under the common law rule, though under s 7 of the 1964 Act it appears that any power which does not allow a person to appoint to himself without the consent of anyone else (a general power for the purposes of the Act) will be treated as a special power.

3.23 Finally, as the title of the 1964 Act indicates, statutory rules have been introduced to limit the period in which a settlor can direct that the income of trust property may be accumulated. The details are not important here.

The enforcement of discretionary trusts and powers of appointment

3.24 Up until the decision of the HL in *McPhail v Doulton* (1970) it was a fairly simple matter to distinguish between the way in which the court would enforce the trustees' compliance with a discretionary trust and the way in which it would oversee the exercise of powers of appointment. In the case of both, any distribution in violation of the terms of the trust or power, ie any misfeasance, would be void. The difference lay in the effects of nonfeasance. With respect to discretionary trusts, the trustees are under a duty to exercise their discretion and distribute the property, and if they fail to do so the court must order a distribution. Before *Kemp v Kemp* (1801) the court would, in rare cases, exercise the trustees' discretion to distribute the property unequally to the objects, but following that decision the practice became to apply the maxim 'equality is equity' and distribute the property equally amongst them. In the case of powers, by contrast, the case of nonfeasance presented no problem. There was no duty for the court to enforce.

Certainty of objects

3.25 What changed in *McPhail* was the test of certainty which applied to the objects of discretionary trusts. Normally much of what follows is covered in trust books in the chapter on 'Certainty' (in this book, chapter 7), but being a radical thinker I propose to include it here because it concerns the enforceability of discretionary trusts and powers, and the rights of the objects under them, more than it does certainty *per se*. Certainty of objects is a requirement of both trusts and powers, and means nothing more than that the terms of the trust or power have to indicate with sufficient precision who is in the class of objects.

The 'complete list' test and the 'is or is not test'

3.26 The historical test for certainty of objects for trusts, whether fixed or discretionary, was that for a trust to be valid, one had to be able to draw up a complete list of the objects. In a discretionary trust for the settlor's children, for example, this could be easily accomplished since it was clear that the class of objects comprised the settlor's children and no one else. Whether or not the 'complete list' test was applicable to mere powers of appointment fell to be decided in *Re Gestetner's*

Settlement (1953). The power in question was a power to appoint property to a large and fluctuating group of objects including the settlor's former employees and their surviving spouses. It was held that the power was valid even though a complete list of the possible objects of the power could not be drawn up at any one time. Harman J. stated:

> [T]he document on its face shows that there is no obligation on the trustees to do more than consider – from time to time, I suppose – the merits of such persons of the specified class as are known to them and, if they think fit, to give them something... I cannot see [that] such a duty [makes] it essential for these trustees, before parting with any income or capital, to survey the whole field, and to consider whether A is more deserving of bounty than B ... there is no difficulty ... in ascertaining whether any given postulant is a member of the specified class. Of course, if that could not be ascertained the matter would be quite different, but of John Doe or Richard Roe it can be postulated easily enough whether he is or is not eligible to receive the settlor's bounty.

Thus was born the 'is or is not' test for certainty of objects: since the power holder has no duty to distribute the property, all that matters is misfeasance, ie if he appoints property at all, he must be sure to appoint only to those within the class of objects and not those outside it; all he need know with certainty is whether any particular person is within the class or not; in particular he does not need a complete list of all objects who are eligible to receive.

3.27 In *IRC v Broadway Cottages Trust* (1955), the CA had to decide whether the same test should apply to a *discretionary trust* for a similarly large and fluctuating class including the settlor's employees and their wives and widows. In summary, the arguments against the 'is or is not' test, and in favour of the complete list test, were these: Starting from the principle stated by Lord Eldon in *Morice v Bishop of Durham* (1805), that in order to be valid, a trust must be one which the court can control and execute, various factors made the court's control and execution of such a trust impossible:

- In the absence of a complete list only a subset of the whole class can be identified; such a subset cannot 'claim execution of the trust' or call for the trust property under the principle in *Saunders v Vautier* because the trustees have no duty to distribute to any subset of the whole class; as a result, where the whole class of objects cannot be identified the trustees' duties are 'illusory'.

- Since no complete list can be made, it is impossible to infer that the testator intended a trust for the entire class in equal shares in default of distribution, so the court is unable to deal with a failure of the trustees to distribute by ordering such a division; the court could not order a particular unequal division, for that would be exercising a dispositive (**2.14**) discretion, and that discretion is the trustee's alone.

- The court's ability to execute a trust must be judged in reference to what might happen, not in reference to what is likely to happen. It must be assumed that the trustees for some reason refuse to distribute. This must be assumed also of new trustees replacing old ones who proved recalcitrant. Replacing one set of trustees after another is not execution of the trust by the court.

- The trustee must know or be able to ascertain all the objects whom he might select, otherwise he is merely selecting from *some* members of the class, in which case he is not carrying out the terms of the trust to exercise his discretion amongst all of the objects.

- Similarly, the court cannot mend the invalidity of a trust of this kind by imposing an arbitrary distribution amongst some only of the whole unascertainable class; to create a certain class to replace the uncertain one chosen by the settlor would amount to imposing a different trust.

3.28 The essence of the argument in favour of the 'is or is not' test was that no difficulty in practice in effectively controlling the execution of the trust would arise:

- Having undertaken the trust, the trustees can be assumed to be willing and able to carry it out.

- With respect to malfeasance by the trustees: the 'is or is not' test allows the trustees to ensure that only qualified beneficiaries take benefits, and so the trustees can distribute within the terms of the trust. Conversely, distribution to non-objects can be determined with certainty, and could be restrained by the court on the suit of any qualified member of the class.

- With respect to nonfeasance by the trustees: At the suit of any qualified member, recalcitrant trustees could be replaced, and this process could be repeated. 'The possibility that not only the original trustees but every set of trustees appointed in their place would fail or refuse to do this is so remote that it can for practical purposes be disregarded.' In the unlikely event necessary, the court could declare a trust in default of distribution for a modified class of whose members a complete list could be made.

3.29   The trust failed. Jenkins LJ had this to say:

> We confess to some sympathy for the appellants' argument, which has an attractive air of common sense, but we do not think that it can be allowed to prevail. We think the submissions... to the effect that the trust is not one which the court could control or execute, and that this objection cannot be met by urging the improbability of assistance by the court ever becoming necessary, are well founded. We also agree that... the court would not be executing the trust merely by ordering a change in trusteeship.

At this time, then, one important distinction between discretionary trusts and powers was their respective tests for certainty of objects, which directly reflected the court's consideration that discretionary trusts, being trusts, required possibilities of precise enforcement in the case of nonfeasance which did not apply to powers.

McPhail v Doulton

3.30   Thus the matter stood until *McPhail v Doulton* (1970), which concerned a discretionary trust for a large class comprising employees and ex-employees of a large company and their dependents and relations. Although about a year before the HL in *Re Gulbenkian Settlements* (1968) had confirmed *obiter*, that while the 'is or is not test' was appropriate for powers, the complete list test remained the appropriate test for discretionary trusts, a different panel of their Lordships in *McPhail v Doulton* decided 3:2 that the 'is or is not test' was appropriate for discretionary trusts as well. The majority decision, given by Lord Wilberforce, essentially recognised the 'common sense' arguments put in *Broadway Cottages Trusts*, accepting that in practice trusts for large classes of beneficiaries could be adequately enforced.

3.31   Lord Wilberforce emphasised that the difference between the duties of trustees who held a mere power of appointment and those of trustees who held property on a discretionary basis was a matter of degree:

Any trustee [holding a mere power] would surely make it his duty to know what is the permissible area of selection and then consider responsibly, in individual cases, whether a contemplated beneficiary was within the power and whether, in relation to other possible claimants, a particular grant was appropriate. Correspondingly a trustee with a duty to distribute, particularly among a potentially very large class, would surely never require the preparation of a complete list of names, which anyhow would tell him little that he needs to know. He would examine the field, by class and category; might indeed make diligent and careful inquiries, depending on how much money he had to give away and the means at his disposal, as to the composition and needs of particular categories and of individuals within them; decide on certain priorities or proportions, and then select individuals according to their needs or qualifications. If he acts in this manner, can it really be said that he is not carrying out the trust? ... Such distinction as there is would seem to lie in the extent of the survey which the trustee is required to carry out; if he has to distribute the whole of the trust fund's income, he must necessarily make a wider and more systematic survey than if his duty is expressed in terms of a power to make grants. But just as, in the case of a power, it is possible to underestimate the fiduciary obligation of the trustee to whom it is given, so, in the case of a trust (trust power), the danger lies in overstating what the trustee requires to know or to enquire into before he can properly execute his trust. The difference may be one of degree rather than of principle ...

3.32 As regards the court's enforcement of the trust, Lord Wilberforce thought that no conclusions could be drawn from the fact that in large trusts of this kind, equal division was not a possible means of enforcement:

As a matter of reason, to h[...]
such as the present is cer[...]
last thing the settlor ever[...]
probably would, produce a[...]

Rather, enforcement should b[...]
and the practicalities of the si[...]

Assimilation of the validity test [...]
of trust powers with powers. As[...]
and normally will, be under a fid[...]
what way they should exercise t[...]
compel its exercise. It will interve[...]

3.35 A pu[...]
a 'fraud' on th[...]
to a person who[...]
however, of benef[...]
for example, a powe[...]

'fraud' o[...]

app[...]

and possibly if they are proved to have exercised it capriciously. But in the case of a trust power, if the trustees do not exercise it, the court will; ... the court, if called on to execute the trust power, will do so in the manner best calculated to give effect to the settlor's or testator's intentions. It may do so by appointing new trustees, or by authorising or directing representative persons of the classes of beneficiaries to prepare a scheme of distribution, or even, should the proper basis for distribution appear, by itself directing the trustees so to distribute.

It should be borne in mind that *McPhail* does not appear to alter the traditional enforcement of discretionary trusts where the class of objects is small: if there are no clear indications as to how the trustee ought to exercise his discretion, the court will order an equal division amongst all the objects.

3.33   In the case of both powers and discretionary trusts, the distribution of property must be within the terms of the power or trust. Normally, the objects of the power or trusts will enforce the trust to prevent misfeasance of this kind, by bringing the trustee to court. They have every incentive to do so, of course, for any property distributed outside the proper bounds is property not available for distribution to them. In the case of a power, however, this enforcement is more likely to be undertaken by those entitled upon default of exercise. They hope the power is not exercised at all in the given time period, for any unappointed property is theirs. They are therefore likely to be astute to discover and object to any appointments outside the proper class of objects.

3.34   Besides appointing outside the class of objects, a purported exercise of a power will be invalid if the powerholders never truly applied their minds to what they were doing, as in *Turner v Turner* (1983) where the power holders blindly followed the directions of the settlor without appreciating they had a discretion to exercise.

a power

ported exercise of a power will also be invalid if it constitutes power. A fraud occurs when the appointment is made is properly with the class of objects, with the purpose, tting someone who is not a proper object, where, holder who could only appoint to members of her family appointed to her sister believing and intending that the sister would apply most of the funds for the benefit of a couple with whom she had lived (*Re Dick* (1951)). The leading case is the Privy Council decision in *Vatcher v Paull* (1914) which outlines the basic principles: 'Fraud' does not denote conscious immoral or dishonest wrongdoing, but merely that the power has been exercised with the intention to benefit someone outside the class of objects. Typically, this will be done under a bargain between the appointer and appointee, under which the latter will upon receipt of the property secure the benefit for someone not properly within the class, typically the appointer himself when he is a non-object, though a bargain of this kind is not essential for a fraud to occur. The test appears to be that the power holder has deliberately set out to benefit a non-object by making the appointment to a valid object, and it is irrelevant that the appointee might not, as it turned out, have complied with the appointer's wishes (*Re Dick*). Fraud does not occur simply because the appointer sets conditions on his exercise of the power; only conditions which if fulfilled result in securing the benefit of the appointment for a third party will be bad.

3.36 In the case of nonfeasance, it is clear that the court must enforce the trust by one of the ways mentioned by Lord Wilberforce (**3.32**), according to the nature of the trust. By contrast, since the exercise of mere powers is not obligatory, the general rule is that the courts will only restrain invalid exercises of powers, not require their exercise if the trustees themselves are unwilling. An illustration of these principles is found in *Re Locker's Settlement* (1977). There trustees applied to the court for its approval when they sought to distribute income which had arisen over a three year period some eight years before which they had failed to distribute under a discretionary trust. It was argued that having failed to comply with their duty to exercise their discretion and distribute at the relevant time, that the trustees were now disabled from doing so, and that the court must give effect to the trust by ordering an equal division amongst all the discretionary objects. Goulding J disagreed. Although, following *McPhail* the court had ample power to execute a discretionary trust upon the failure of the trustees to do so, trustees intent upon making good their past failure by subsequently exercising their discretion should be encouraged to do so, as being closer to the settlor's intention than the execution by the court, though in such circumstances the court should 'readily listen' to any misgivings of such a course where the trustees have failed to listen or act upon the beneficiaries requests for distribution; in such a case the ample powers of the court to execute the trust might justifiably be invoked. Furthermore, a distinction may be drawn between powers of appointment and discretionary trusts in this regard. Failure to exercise a power of appointment results in the appropriate gifts over taking effect, so that a power-holder's failure to act normally raises no issue of this kind. Goulding J did not specifically consider the case of a failure of a trustee power-holder to act in a timely fashion. One presumes that the court might have to engage in some remedial measures if it was shown that a gift over came into effect where a trustee power-holder did not even consider exercising his power of appointment as his duty requires. Indeed, in certain cases, the courts will control mere powers to the extent of requiring their exercise. Thus in *Klug v Klug* (1911) the court felt under a duty to direct a transfer of funds (under a power of advancement, **10.37** et seq) 'when one trustee very properly desires to exercise his discretion ... and his co-trustee [who refused to do so because she disapproved of the beneficiary's marriage] will not.' And in the case of pension fund trusts, the beneficiaries who have earned their rights may have legitimate expectations that mere powers held by trustees to augment the benefits to which they are strictly entitled under the trust will be exercised in their favour (*Mettoy Pension Trustees Ltd v Evans* (1991)).

Beneficial interests under discretionary trusts and powers of appointment

3.37   The principle in *Saunders v Vautier* applies to discretionary trusts, but this does not mean that the beneficiaries, if all *sui juris*, are treated as having a vested interest, either individually or together; only if they exercise their *Saunders v Vautier* rights and demand the income or trust property from the trustees do they acquire indefeasible interests *(Vestey v IRC* (1979)). Indeed, rather than 'co-owners' or 'group-owners', until that time each object has his own individual right to retain whatever income is appointed to him, and their individual interests are essentially in competition with each other (Lord Reid, *Gartside v IRC* (1968)). It is worthwhile noticing that one party in many of these cases is the IRC, the Inland Revenue Commissioners. Whether or not an object has a vested interest has been important for purposes of taxation law. (See, eg *Pearson v IRC* (1981); *Re Trafford's Settlement* (1984).)

3.38 In the case of general or hybrid powers, the objects have no rights whatsoever, since the class of objects amounts, essentially, to the whole world, or in the case of hybrid powers, the whole world minus a few. Those entitled in default of appointment will have the only rights to ensure that the power is not improperly exercised. Objects of special powers are in a similar position to objects of a discretionary trust individually, but not collectively. Individually, they may of course retain what is appointed to them, and they can enforce the power by ensuring no invalid appointments are made, and where the powerholder is a trustee (a fiduciary power), can insist upon the trustee properly considering its exercise, though they cannot, of course, insist upon any appointments (*Re Gulbenkian*). But because there is no duty to appoint at all, the objects have no *Saunders v Vautier* rights whatsoever. Their interests are in competition not only with each other, but primarily with those entitled in default of appointment, who are generally regarded not only as the primary objects of the settlor's bounty (*Vatcher v Paull* (1914)), but are regarded as the persons in whom the property is vested, subject, of course, to defeat by the exercise of the power of appointment (*Re Brooks' Settlement Trusts* (1939)).

3.39 The decision in *McPhail* poses some conceptual difficulties. As Hayton (1996b) has said, one of the irreducible core elements of a trust is an obligation owed by the trustee to the beneficiaries. In a *McPhail*-type trust, however, the beneficiaries appear to be little more than postulants, seeking the trustees' largesse but having no enforceable right to it, and perhaps more to the point, little incentive to pursue the remedies which the HL made available to have the court replace the trustees or help devise a scheme of distribution. Since there is no clear likelihood that pursuing such remedies will result in a favourable distribution (ie one that includes oneself), who would bother seeking them? Although Lord Wilberforce was keen to forge rules to reflect the practical, common sense realities of the situation, did he not disregard the rather obvious point that the object of a large discretionary trust may have little more real incentive to enforce the trust than does the object of the mere power? Lord Wilberforce expounds the various approaches the court, 'if called on', might make to enforce the trust in a practical fashion, without considering whether, in reality, these 'practical' remedies are likely ever to be asserted by the objects. For this reason, such trusts may in practice be trusts of 'imperfect obligation' (see **9.20**), depending on the likelihood that the trustees' duties will be enforced. Remember that trusts are private. Should the law create an exception in these cases and require trustees of a *McPhail*-type trust to publicise its existence, in order to increase the chances of enforcement? Should such an obligation extend to powers to appoint to large classes of this kind?

3.40 Besides enforcement, there is also the issue of *Saunders v Vautier* rights and equitable ownership. Whatever such rights discretionary objects have under a *McPhail*-type trust in theory, they are clearly impossible to exercise if the class of beneficiaries cannot combine together because it is unascertainable on the complete list test. Perhaps the most suitable analogy for the *McPhail* situation is the case of the executor of a will and those who will take under it. Recall (**2.30**) that executors are the legal owners of the deceased's estate, but not trustees for the likely recipients, and until such time as the estate is actually distributed, a recipient has only a right to compel the executor to carry out his duties; a recipient has no rights, even equitable rights, in the property itself. The situation under a *McPhail*-type trust seems essentially similar. The objects do not have together, nor individually, any right in the property whatsoever, but merely have a right to the enforcement of the trust. The trustees, for their part, appear to be legal owners subject to the equitable rights of enforcement of the beneficiaries. The practical differences, however, are quite important. To become effective, a will must be admitted to probate, which makes the will public. No publicity is equally required for the *McPhail*-type trust, although one presumes that in many cases trusts of this kind will be testamentary. The more striking feature, however, is that wills must be executed in a fairly short time and the expectant recipients are likely to follow the trustee's actions fairly closely, since the will will tell them what benefits they are intended to receive, and this will make surveillance of the trustees worthwhile. Thus we are faced with the question whether the courts should, as the HL in *McPhail* seemed happy to do, allow settlors to create equitable obligations where the practical likelihood of enforcement appears so much lower than in any other previously recognised trust situation. In *Broadway Cottages* Jenkins LJ refuse to 'spell a valid power out of an invalid trust', ie validate the settlor's gift by allowing the trustees to exercise the trust as if it were a power (see also **7.6-7.7**). Might this not have been a preferable route to take to give effect to the settlor's wishes? Perhaps the test for whether we should recognise a trust is an 'equitable ownership/ *Saunders v Vautier*' test: if there is no person or group who can reasonably be said to have equitable title or at the minimum, practically exercisable *Saunders v Vautier* rights, then it is difficult to hold that the 'trustees' are in reality subject to 'trust' obligations.

Protective trusts

3.41 A beneficiary under a fixed trust, such as a life tenant, has a vested interest in the trust property, which can be assigned, or given as security on a loan, and most significantly, will go into the beneficiary's estate in bankruptcy if he becomes insolvent. A settlor may be happy to give a beneficiary an interest under a trust, but may like to avoid that entitlement going to pay his creditors if he becomes bankrupt. A protective trust is a device which combines a determinable life interest with a discretionary trust to protect trust assets from just this occurrence.

A determinable life interest followed by a discretionary trust

3.42 The protective trust works as follows. There are two trusts: first there is a gift of a determinable life interest in favour of the person the settlor wishes primarily to benefit, for example his son, who is known as the 'principal beneficiary'; on the occurrence of a determining event the trust property is then to be held on a second trust, which is a discretionary trust in favour of a class of objects, which may include the principal beneficiary himself. The determining events always include the situation in which the principal beneficiary's right to income is assigned to anyone else or goes to his trustee in bankruptcy, but typically also includes any case where the beneficiary's interest becomes charged, or more vaguely, 'payable' to anyone else. On the determining event the secondary, discretionary, trust kicks in by operation of law, for the determinable interest automatically terminates when a defeating event occurs – no exercise of any power of revocation is necessary. The situation will now be that the income is distributable at the trustees' discretion to the objects of the secondary trust, 'the secondary objects'. Since an individual object of a discretionary trust has no vested interest in the trust property (**3.37**) neither can his creditors or trustee in bankruptcy, and thus the trust property is kept out of their hands so long as the trustee chooses not to give the bankrupt object any, which he obviously will not.

3.43   It is absolutely essential that the first gift is a determinable life interest and not a life interest defeasible upon a condition subsequent, for any one of three reasons, otherwise the protective trust will not work. The chief reason is that as a matter of historical concepts of property, conditions which prevent the alienation of property, that is the assignment, charging, or transfer by operation of law of property, are absolutely void, whereas determinable interests which determine upon an alienation are not (Burn (1994), 345). Second, and less crucially, a condition subsequent is strictly construed, and if uncertain, eg too vague, the condition is struck down but the gift remains; thus if the condition were struck down in this way the principle beneficiary would take an absolute life interest which would not be protected. Finally, and least importantly, gifts defeasible upon condition subsequent do not end automatically when the condition arises; rather, the happening of the condition gives the secondary donee a right to bring the principle gift to an end; therefore the secondary donee must act. For example, in the case of land, the secondary donee acquires a right to re-enter the land if the defeating condition occurred, but the primary donee's rightful possession of the land lasts until the secondary donee actually re-enters. With respect to the protected life interest in income, at least one of the secondary objects is required to demand that the trustees henceforth apply the property under the secondary trust. Presumably, this would be no more than an inconvenience in most cases; nevertheless, if protective trusts could be framed in terms of conditions subsequent the primary beneficiary's life interest would remain following a forfeiting event, and the trustee would be required to apply the benefits to, for example, a trustee in bankruptcy, until a secondary object acted.

No protective trust for oneself

3.44   Although technically the protective trust works just as well for a settlor who wishes to transfer his own property on protective trusts to avoid the consequences of his own bankruptcy, this is not allowed (*Re Brewer's Settlement* (1986)). The justification is roughly as follows: A may give B a gift structured or limited in whatever ways he wishes, so if he wants B to have an interest, but not B's trustee in bankruptcy should B become insolvent, that's OK. As a donee from A, B cannot expect any particular gift, or any gift at all, and neither can his creditors; if the latter are therefore deprived of A's bounty, they have no just cause to complain. On the other hand, A may not escape his liability to his own creditors by purporting to 'give' his property to himself in the same way. His own property is absolutely his, and must retain the normal 'incident', ie conceptual attribute, of property, of being available to pay his debts.

3.45 On the other hand, a person may put his property on trust for himself, determinable on the event that he assigns or charges or otherwise alienates it – the policy is only against avoiding the effects of bankruptcy. If a settlor includes as one of the events his becoming bankrupt anyway, that provision will be ineffective against his trustee in bankruptcy in accordance with the general policy, but does not make the other events ineffective. So, in Re *Detmold* (1889), the occurrence of one of the other operating events terminated the trust, and so the settlor no longer had an interest which could pass into his estate in bankruptcy when he later became bankrupt. If the settlor becomes bankrupt, so that the life interest passes as one of his assets into the hands of his trustee in bankruptcy, the interest of the trustee in bankruptcy cannot be defeated by the subsequent occurrence of a valid defeating condition (Re *Burroughs-Fowler* (1916)).

The s 33 protective trust

3.46 Protective trusts can be expressly stated in a trust instrument, but may also be created by directing the trustees to hold property for X 'on protective trusts', which automatically invokes the particular protective trust formulated in s 33(1) of the Trustee Act 1925:

> 33.– (1) Where any income, including an annuity or other periodical income payment, is directed to be held on protective trusts for the benefit of any person (in this section called 'the principal beneficiary') for the period of his life or for any less period, then, during that period (in this section called the 'trust period') the said income shall, without prejudice to any prior interest, be held upon the following trusts, namely:–
>
> (i) Upon trust for the principal beneficiary during the trust period or until he, **whether before or after the termination of any prior interest, does or attempts to do or suffers any act or thing, or until any event happens, other than an advance under any statutory or express power, whereby, if the said income were payable during the trust period to the principal beneficiary absolutely during that period, he would be deprived of the right to receive the same or any part thereof,** in any of which

cases, as well as on the termination of the trust period, whichever happens first, this trust of the said income shall fail or determine;

(ii) If the trust aforesaid fails or determines during the subsistence of the trust period, then, during the residue of that period, the said income shall be held upon trust for the application thereof for the maintenance and support, or otherwise for the benefit, of all or any one or more exclusively of the other or others of the following persons (that is to say)–

(a) the principal beneficiary and his wife or husband, if any, and his or her children or more remote issue, if any; or

(b) if there is no wife or husband or issue of the principal beneficiary in existence, the principal beneficiary and the persons who would, if he were actually dead, be entitled to the trust property or the income thereof or the annuity fund, if any, or arrears of the annuity, as the case may be;

as the trustees in their absolute discretion, without being liable to account for the exercise of such discretion, think fit.

3.47 As the s 33 formulation of the events giving rise to forfeiture (in bold above) shows, forfeiture clauses are generally very widely framed so as to apply to any circumstance which might defeat the principal beneficiaries receipt of the benefit of the trust. Notice the initial phrase in bold: 'whether before or after the termination of any prior interest', which indicates that if the trust initially takes effect in circumstances in which the interest will pass to a third party, there will be a forfeiture. This occurred in *Re Walker* (1939): the person who would become a principal beneficiary under a testamentary protective trust was a bankrupt who had applied for his discharge from bankruptcy. The court granted the discharge, but suspended it for one month, and in this period the testator died. Bad timing. Because he was still a bankrupt when the trust came into effect on the testator's death, the interest was forfeit.

3.48 If there is a doubt as to the interpretation of a forfeiture clause, whether the s 33 formulation or an express clause, it is resolved in favour of the principle beneficiary, not primarily because he is the first object of the settlor's bounty – the settlor obviously considered the secondary objects to be worthy of a benefit as well (*Re Sartoris' Estate* (1892))– but for the mundane reason that those who wish to assert their rights based upon a forfeiture have the burden of showing that a forfeiture has occurred (*Re Baring's Settlement Trusts* (1940)).

3.49 The actual words of the clause are all-important, as shown by the pair of cases, *Re Gourju's Will Trusts* (1942) and *Re Hall* (1943). In both cases the principal beneficiaries' income became payable to the Custodian of Enemy Property under the Trading with the Enemy Act 1939 by virtue of their residence in France during the second world war. In effect, if there was no forfeiture, the Custodian would hold the income on behalf of the principal beneficiaries until the war was over or they could return to England to claim it, so it was to the beneficiaries' advantage if there were no forfeiture. In *Gourju*, the will creating the trust incorporated the statutory provision, by which the life interest can terminate upon the happening of any event; Simonds J concluded that the happening of the events made the income payable to the Custodian, so the forfeiture occurred:

> It was urged upon me by council for Madame Gourju that the result of such a decision is a forfeiture by reason of an event which can never have been contemplated by the testator, an event, moreover, of a wholly different character from any event fairly within his contemplation. With that I cannot but agree, but the words of the clause are too strong for me, and I can only express the earnest hope that in the welter of legislation that peace will bring, the hard case will not be forgotten of a beneficiary who, like Madame Gourju, suffers an undeserved forfeiture of her income.

3.50 By contrast, in *Hall* the forfeiture clause was an express provision which did not refer to the happening of events, though it did comprise the principal beneficiary's 'suffer[ing] any act or thing' whereby the property would become payable to someone else. Uthwatt J construed it this way:

> Reading the clause as a whole, it seems to me that it is directed to the forfeiture of the annuity in the event of the annuitant personally doing certain classes of things, such as alienating or charging it, or permitting an act to be done whereby she is deprived of her annuity. It appears not to be directed to a case where the annuity is subject to an alienation which is not the result of the countess's own act. ...She was in France, the normal place for a French national, when her property became subject to the provisions of the Act, and I fail to see how the fact that she was there

and remained there can be said to amount to the doing of an act of the kind which is contemplated by the clause. The question whether she has 'suffered' anything is, perhaps, more open. The word 'suffer' is capable of more meanings than one. I have come to the conclusion that it is proper to attribute to the word in this clause the meaning 'permit'. It is clear that the annuitant has not permitted anything to be done.

3.51   Section 33 of the Act expressly exempts the exercise of a power of advancement from being a cause of forfeiture, and this applies to any trust which incorporates the statutory provision. A power of advancement allows the trustee to advance, or pay, capital to the income beneficiary (**10.37**); the obvious effect of doing so is to reduce his right to income, since as a result there is less capital upon which income can arise, and so, but for the exemption, the advancement could be seen to work a forfeiture. The exemption appears to apply to express protective trusts as well (*Re Rees* (1954)), and may simply be a matter of common sense not requiring any statutory exemption (*Re Hodgson* (1913); *Re Shaw's Settlement* (1951)) – advancements simply secure the benefit of the trust property to the beneficiary by another means, not deprive him of his entitlement to it. Whether the exercise of any other power which affects the principal beneficiary's right to income, such as a power to appoint capital to a third party, causes a forfeiture, is a matter of interpretation of the instrument.

3.52   Under the Trustee Act 1925, s 57 the court may by order 'vary', ie modify, the terms of a trust (**10.44**), and such orders, though they may affect the life tenant's right to income, do not effect a forfeiture:

> If and when the Court sanctions an arrangement or transaction under s 57, it must be taken to have done it as though the power which is brought into operation has been inserted in the trust instrument as an overriding power. (Farwell J, *Re Mair* (1935))

Orders affecting a life tenant's right to income made under the court's divorce jurisdiction to distribute property likewise do not effect a forfeiture (*General Accident Fire and Life Assurance Corpn Ltd v IRC* (1963), CA), and where the court order extinguishes one spouse's protected life interest entirely, this extinguishes the secondary dis-cretionary trust as well – it does not arise as if the extinction of the primary trust counted as a forfeiture (*Re Allsopp's Marriage Settlement Trusts* (1958)). *Re Richardson's Will Trusts* (1963) is an anomalous exception. The case concerned a protective trust which was to operate until the principal beneficiary attained the age of 35, at which time his interest became absolute. On 3 June 1955, the court ordered that a payment of £50 per annum to his ex-wife be charged on his life interest; on 24 October 1955, he turned 35, and on 27 August 1956, he was declared bankrupt. Dankwerts J held that the court order effected a forfeiture. It is difficult not to believe that the result was motivated by the fact that, absent the forfeiture, the trustee in bankruptcy would have acquired the interest in the income subject to the wife's charge, leaving the principal beneficiary nothing. Instead, under the discretionary trust upon forfeiture, the former principal beneficiary was entitled to dis-cretionary payments, which it appears had in fact been made before his bankruptcy.

3.53 It is clear that a forfeiture should occur whenever the principal beneficiary's right to receive the income is transferred or charged either by the beneficiary himself or by operation of law or by another's exercise of his rights, as in Re *Balfour's Settlement* (1938) where by reason of the beneficiary's instigation of a breach of trust the trustees were entitled to impound the income (**12.22**). More difficult is the case of forfeiture upon the condition that the income becomes 'payable to' someone other than the principal beneficiary. In *Re Baring's Settlement Trusts* (1940) it was held that 'payable to' cover a broader range of cases than those where the principal beneficiary's property interest vests in a third party by reason of an assignment or charge. But a forfeiture cannot arise simply because the principal beneficiary has debts of sufficient size that he must devote some of his trust income to paying them off. The income remains payable to him, and he only has the personal duty to pay these debts out of all of his property. In order for a forfeiture to arise under the 'payable to' provision, some third party must be able to demand that the trustee must pay the trust income to him directly, and such circumstances should generally involve the state, as in the cases above concerning the Custodian of Enemy Property and court orders upon divorce. In *Re Baring's Settlement Trusts* an order of sequestration, which allowed third parties to demand payment of the principal beneficiary's income to enforce another order of the court was held to forfeit the life interest. However the cases also appear to indicate that 'payable to' will be construed narrowly, ie to the case where the third party may demand payment of the income as it arises, ie as the trustee receives it or can claim it, eg when dividends are paid on shares or rent on land falls due; a third party's right to demand income which has *already accrued* under the trust, ie funds that were already in the trustee's hands, does not effect a forfeiture (Re Greenwood (1901)). Furthermore, a forfeiture does not occur where a third party did acquire the right to demand payment of the income as it arose, but that right ended before any income actually accrued, on the basis that until any income arose none was actually 'payable' (Re Longman (1955). See also Re Salting (1932).) A trustee's right to require payment from the income for his charges and expenses as attorney to the principal beneficiary causes no forfeiture; it is akin to the appointment of an agent to collect one's rents who has the right to deduct his commission before paying the remainder to the beneficiary (Re Tancred's Settlement (1903)). In Re Westby's Settlement (1950), Lord Evershed MR held that even if such a right to be paid expenses was effective to create a charge over the income, the interest would not be forfeited; a forfeiture clause is directed to protect the beneficiary's net income from the trust after any proper expenses are incurred.

3.54 Following a principal beneficiary's bankruptcy and consequent forfeiture, he may be an object under the secondary discretionary trust, and will be if the s 33 provision is invoked. Following his discharge in bankruptcy, he may be paid income at the trustees' discretion. While still a bankrupt, the trustees may apply income for his benefit, by, for example, providing him with services such as meals or accomodation, but only to the extent that this is for his 'mere support' (Re Ashby (1892)). Any money that is paid directly to him may be claimed by his trustee in bankruptcy, but to the extent that he receives no property in his own right, as when the trustee, at his discretion, pays third parties for services, the trustee in bankruptcy has no claim, for the bankrupt receives no property (Re Coleman (1888); Re Smith (1928)). Unless the trustee has the power to accumulate income, however, he may not retain accrued income in order to pay it to the former principal beneficiary upon his discharge from bankruptcy; the trustee must distribute the income within a reasonable time following its accrual (Re Gourju's Will Trusts (1942)).

Further Reading

Waters (1967); Hayton (1996b)

Must read cases: *Stephenson v Barclay's Bank Trust Co Ltd* (1974); *Re Trafford's Settlement* (1984); *Lloyds Bank plc v Duker* (1987); *IRC v Broadway Cottages Trust* (1955); *Re Gulbenkian Settlement* (1968); *McPhail v Doulton* (1970); *Vatcher v Paull* (1914); *Re Locker's Settlement* (1977); *Re Baring's Settlement Trusts* (1940); *Re Coleman* (1888); *Re Gourju's Will Trusts* (1942); *Re Westby's Settlement* (1950).

Self-test questions

1. What is a fixed trust, a discretionary trust, and a power of appointment, and how do the interests of the objects of each differ?

2. What are income interests, capital interests, successive interests, contingent interests, defeasible interests, and vested interests?

3. Following *McPhail v Doulton* (1970) the distinction between discretionary trusts and powers of appointment held by trustees is only one of degree. Discuss.

4. How does a protective trust achieve its purpose?

5. Eric transferred a block of flats to trustees to hold for him on trust for life or until he 'does or attempts to do or suffers any act or thing, or until any event happens whereby Eric would be deprived of the right to receive the rental income or any part thereof', upon the happening of which they were to hold it on trust for his wife. The rent from the apartment house is collected by agents who deduct a commission. Eric is declared bankrupt, and the next day he assigns his interest under the trust to his brother Philip. Advise Eric's trustee in bankruptcy.

CHAPTER FOUR

Resulting Trusts

SUMMARY

Intentional trusts and trusts which arise by operation of law (TABOLs)

Presumed intention resulting trusts (PIRTs)

Automatic resulting trusts (ARTs)

The nature of resulting trusts and resulting trusteeship

Intentional trusts and trusts which arise by operation of law (TABOLs)

4.1 In the last chapter we considered express trusts, and there I advised that the way to understand express trusts is to think of them as trusts made by the settlor himself when he *effectively exercises his powers of ownership to create a trust*. These trusts might be called 'intentional trusts', because the settlor by effectively exercising his powers to create a trust has produced what he intended. However there are also trusts which arise by operation of law (TABOLs, for short). The law itself imposes trusts in certain circumstances, which is to say that the law itself creates an equitable title for beneficiaries in the property of a legal owner. Resulting trusts, as we shall see, may be either intentional trusts or TABOLs.

Automatic resulting trusts (ARTs)

4.2 Resulting trusts characteristically arise in two situations. In the first, a resulting trust will arise where an express trust fails, or fails in part, for some reason. For example, the settlor may transfer £10,000 to trustees on trust for his niece Barbara. Unbeknownst to the settlor, Barbara has died, so there is no person to take the intended beneficial interest under the express trust. In consequence, the beneficial interest 'results' or 'springs back to the settlor, and the trustees will hold the trust property on bare trust for the settlor. Trusts can also fail in part. If I transfer property to trustees to hold in one-third shares for Tom, Dick, and Harry, and Tom has died, then that one-third share is held on resulting trust for me. Because these trusts arise automatically upon the failure of the intended disposition, these are generally called *automatic resulting trusts*, or ARTs.

Presumed Intention Resulting Trusts (PIRTs)

4.3   Second, there are *presumed intention resulting trusts*, PIRTs. (These trusts are also called, simply, 'presumed resulting trusts', but since presumed *intention* resulting trust is more accurate, that usage will be employed.) There are two categories, purchase money PIRTs and gratuitous transfer PIRTs. If two or more persons put their money together to buy property equity will normally hold that they share the equitable title to the property in proportion to the amount of money each put in, regardless of the way the legal title is held, whether in both of their names, in one of their names, or in the name of a third party. Whoever the legal title holders are, they will hold the property on bare trust for them both in proportionate equitable shares. Similarly, if A pays the whole purchase price of property, but the title is put in B's name, B will hold the property on bare trust for A. These are both cases of purchase money PIRTs. If A, however, simply transfers property he already owns to B *gratuitously*, ie receiving no payment in return – no 'consideration' as lawyers say – B will likewise hold the property on bare trust for A under a gratuitous transfer PIRT. In all these cases, the holder(s) of a legal title will hold the property on bare trust for those who put the value in. The recognition of these trusts is founded upon an evidentiary presumption: in the absence of evidence, equity will presume that someone putting money into the purchase of an asset intends to take a proportionate share, up to the entire value if he pays the full price, or when someone transfers legal title gratuitously to someone equity presumes he intends to create a bare trust in his favour; hence the term 'presumed intention' resulting trust. This presumption, and thus the trust, will be defeated by actual evidence of any contrary intentions of the parties regarding their shares of the beneficial ownership (*Westdeutsche Landesbank v Islington London Borough Council* (1996, HL); see Swadling, (1996)), and of course, an express declaration of trust made by the donor or the joint contributors will displace the operation of a gratuitous transfer or purchase money PIRT, respectively (*Pettitt v Pettitt* (1970) per Lord Upjohn; *Goodman v Gallant* (1986)). Because the law presumes that a gratuitous contribution or transfer *implies* an intention to create a trust, PIRTs are also sometimes called 'implied' trusts.

4.4 The distinction between ARTs and PIRTs was originally drawn by Megarry J in *Re Vandervell (No 2)* (1974) as follows (though it was clearly foreshadowed by Lord Upjohn in *Vandervell v IRC* (1966)). PIRTs are intentional trusts, created by the settlor's exercise of his powers of ownership to create a trust. Because however, the law presumes the settlor's intentions, he need do nothing to prove, by a written document or otherwise, any declaration of trust accompanying the transfer of the legal title to his property, either the trust property itself in the case of a gratuitous transfer PIRT, or his money in the case of his a purchase money PIRT. This evidentiary presumption may, however, be rebutted by evidence that the settlor did not intend to create a trust, eg intended instead to make a gift to the transferee. In contrast, the ART arises by operation of law automatically on the failure of an express trust, indepedently of any intentions of the settlor (though see **4.14**, below). ARTs arise by what is sometimes called the application of 'proprietary arithmetic': if the settlor places property on trust intending to part with the beneficial interest entirely, but for some reason has not, then by subtraction, whatever is left effectively undisposed of results to him.

Presumed intention resulting trusts

Law of Property Act 1925, s 60(3)

4.5 The evidentiary presumption underlying voluntary transfer PIRTs applied equally to transfers of land and personal property ('personalty') like chattels or company shares before 1926. Before 1926, if a gift of land was intended it was necessary to expressly state in the deed of conveyance that the land was conveyed to the use and benefit of the donee in order to displace the presumption. Section 60 (3) of the Law of Property Act 1925 provides, however, that a resulting trust is not to be implied merely because there is no express statement of this kind. Whether this section effectively abolished voluntary conveyance PIRTs of land is undecided by authority – in *Hodgson v Marks* (1971) Russell LJ noted *obiter* in passing that the question was debatable – the orthodox view is that it does (see Chambers (1997), pp 16-19). Regarding personalty, the presumption still technically applies. Since, however, it must surely be the case that most gratuitous transfers are intended to be gifts, the presumption should give way to the slightest contrary evidence, including evidence of the surrounding circumstances and commonsense inferences to be drawn therefrom – the presumption fully applies when it is my round and I buy you a pint, but no judge in his right mind will say that you hold that pint on trust for me.

4.6 The presumption is much more relevant in the case of purchase money PIRTs, and regularly operates where the property in question is land. 'Purchase money' should be read as 'purchase contribution in money or money's worth'. In *Springette v Defoe* (1992) the sitting tenant of a house was entitled to a discount from the market price; when she purchased the property with her cohabitee the value of the discount was treated as a contribution she made to the purchase price in determining her equitable share. In the case of land purchased with the aid of a mortgage, the person(s) raising money on a mortgage, and therefore liable to repay the loan, will be credited with a corresponding contribution. For example, assume A and B purchase a house in their joint names for £50,000, A contributing £10,000 in cash, the remaining £40,000 coming from a mortgage loan under which both A and B are liable. A will therefore have an equitable share of (10 + 20 (half the loan))/ 50 = 60%, and B a 20/50 = 40% share. Note that one's equitable share is determined by the share of one's *liability under the mortgage*, not by *the value of the money one actually repays (Cowcher v Cowcher* (1971)). The result of this is that if the house A and B bought doubles in value in a year to 100,000, and they sell, B will acquire a much better return on the money he has actually paid than A. Assume that following the sale and the repayment of the outstanding mortgage, the profit comes to 40,000: A will receive a 60% share, 24,000, in return for a 10,000 deposit and paying half the mortgage premiums for a year, while B will receive a 40% share, 16,000, for having only paid half the premiums. It may not even be the case that A and B have split the premium payments in half; even if A had paid all the premiums, B would acquire the same 16,000 share, since it is his joint mortgage liability that determines his contribution under the resulting trust. Since this may appear to lead to an unjust result, the courts have on occasion varied the parties' shares via a constructive trust (**5.9** et seq).

70

The presumption of advancement

4.7 The presumption does not operate in all cases of a gratuitous transaction. As Freud might have said, sometimes a gift is just a gift. In these circumstances, it is said that a 'presumption of advancement' operates, although this terminology is misleading; all it means is that the evidentiary presumption of an intention to create a trust does not apply (*Pettitt* per Lord Upjohn). There is no such presumption where A gratuitously transfers property to his wife or his child or to someone to whom he stands *in loco parentis*, ie someone for whom he feels an obligation to provide as would a parent (*Re Paradise Motor Co Ltd* (1968)). In *Pettitt* a majority of their Lordships clearly felt the presumption of advancement was a creature of the nineteenth century which was largely out of date; Lord Upjohn, while willing to apply the presumption said:

> These presumptions or circumstances of evidence are readily rebutted by comparatively slight evidence.

Founding an evidentiary presumption on the theory that, in general, a husband intends to make gifts to his wife but not *vice versa*, and that, in general, fathers, but not mothers, intend gifts to their children, today seems exhorbitantly sexist. While the opinions in *Pettitt* might have suggested the judicial reform or even abolition of the presumptions of advancement, it has not happened (in England) yet. (In Australia the presumption now applies equally to gifts from mother to child: *Nelson v Nelson* (1995).) It may be, as Hayton says (Hayton (1996a), 314):

> ... easier for courts to pay lip-service to the old case law whilst being satisfied on flimsy evidence that the old-fashioned presumption has been rebutted.

4.8 Given that the presumption is merely evidentiary, any evidence of the transferor's or purchase money contributor's actual intentions should displace it, and evidence bearing on the intentions of the transferor or contributor should be construed broadly. *Fowkes v Pascoe* (1875) and *Re Vinogradoff* (1935) make a nice contrast in this regard. In *Fowkes*, a woman of substantial means purchased stock in the name of a son of her former daughter-in-law; the only evidence of the woman's intentions were the surrounding circumstances; since there was no conceivable reason for her transferring the stock to him to hold as her nominee, she must have intended to give it to him; thus the presumption of resulting trust was rebutted. In contrast, *Re Vinogradoff* is an atrocity of a decision. There a woman had transferred £800 of War Loan stock into the joint names of herself and her 4-year-old granddaughter. Following her death, it was claimed that the child held the stock on resulting trust, there being no evidence to establish an intention to make a gift. Given that her granddaughter was four, the probability that the donor intended to make a gift, not constitute her granddaughter her trustee, is about as close to 1 as probabilities get in this life. Furthermore, any express attempt to have done so would have been ineffective anyway, since under the Law of Property Act 1925 an infant (ie a person under the age of majority) could not be a trustee. Undaunted, Farwell J held that the granddaughter held the stock on resulting trust, so the executors of the grandmother's estate were entitled to it. The idea that sensible inferences may be drawn from all the circumstances is the approach taken nowadays.

> In reality the so-called presumption of a resulting trust is no more than a long stop to provide the answer when the relevant facts and circumstances fail to yield a solution. (*Vandervell v IRC* (1966) per Lord Upjohn; see also *Pettitt v Pettitt* (1970))

4.9 For example, in *McGrath v Wallis* (1995), the weak presumption of advancement of a share in a family house between father and son who both contributed to the purchase price was rebutted, or rather, a resulting trust in favour of a father was established, on the basis, first, that at one stage a declaration of trust formally expressing the father's and son's ownership shares in proportion to their contributions was drawn up by the father's solicitors, and though it was never executed no evidence suggested that he had later given his solicitors contrary instructions. Second, as the father was only 63 and in good health, there was no obvious reason to make a gift to his son of an 80% share in the house where he would himself live.

4.10 In the case of a purchase money PIRT, it should be remembered that a gift or a trust are not the only options: A may give B money as a loan, which B then spends to purchase property. Obviously, evidence of such a loan would displace any claim A might make to a purchase money PIRT of the property (*Re Sharpe* (1980)).

Illegality

4.11 Unfortunately, whether a presumption of resulting trust applies or not has been shown to be of crucial significance recently in the case of illegal property transfers. In general, neither the common law nor equity will allow a plaintiff to establish a claim on the basis of evidence which implicates him in an illegal purpose; thus, the equitable maxim, 'he who comes to equity must come with clean hands'. The obvious problem with such a rule is that, as often as not, the defendant to the action, who prays in aid this maxim, has hands just as filthy as the plaintiff, so as between the parties at least, the rule can appear to have unfair consequences. Such a case faced the HL in *Tinsley v Milligan* (1993). Two women who cohabited as a lesbian couple agreed to put the house in the name of one of them in order that the other could misrepresent her assets to the benefits agency, and thus claim benefits to their joint economic advantage. Both were therefore parties to the fraud. They subsequently fell out and Tinsley, the legal title-holder, sought to evict Milligan, who adduced evidence of her contributions to the purchase price to establish a share in the house under a purchase money PIRT. A bare majority of the HL found for Milligan. The only evidence she needed to adduce was of her contribution to the purchase price; on that basis alone her equitable share under a resulting trust was established – she didn't need to say *why* she contributed the money so she didn't need to adduce any evidence of her fraud, and so she escaped the operation of the clean hands principle. The dissenting Lords Goff and Keith would have applied the principle in its more traditional formulation, ie that where evidence of the plaintiff's illegal behaviour which was relevant to the matter came before the court, equity would refuse its assistance. While the majority decision is understandable in light of the fact that Milligan had since admitted her fraud to the Department of Social Services, and that if Milligan had failed her co-fraudster Tinsley would end up with an undeserved windfall, the decision can be criticised for reaching its decision in this technical way. The upshot is that where the evidentiary presumption of resulting trust operates, the fraudster who transfers his property to another, say to defraud his creditors when bankruptcy looms, can retrieve the property when the coast is clear (ie when discharged from bankruptcy or having settled with his creditors who are unaware of the transferred assets) simply by adducing evidence of the transfer. Note that Milligan's later confession was not the ground of the decision, so the case provides no basis for distinguishing between a plaintiff who succeeds in his fraud and one who does not. But where the presumption of resulting trust does not operate, for example, where the fraudster transfers the property to his wife, the fraudster must lead evidence to show that he intended a trust, and so must rely upon evidence of his true intentions for the transfer; since these of course were fraudulent, in his case his unclean hands will deny him a resulting trust. So we have the nice situation that a male fraudster who stashes his property with his son will come a cropper, but a female fraudster doing the same will retrieve her ill-hidden assets.

4.12   The CA recently dealt with the former situation in *Tribe v Tribe* (1995). A man, worried that his liabilities under two leases would be his financial ruin, transferred his shares in the family company to his son in order to safeguard his assets. As it turned out, he sorted out his liabilities under the leases without having to resort to the fraudulent deception. He sought a declaration of trust from the court when his son refused to re-convey the shares. Reviewing past authorities in which the rule was not applied where the intending fraudster had 'repented' and withdrawn from his fraudulent scheme, the court applied this exception, holding that the elder Tribe was entitled to establish a trust on the evidence of his fraudulent intentions, since the scheme had not been acted upon.

4.13   While all rules which deny a plaintiff the assistance of the court where his claim discloses an illegality may appear to unjustifiably favour a defendant, the working of the evidentiary presumptions for and against a resulting trust appear to make the operation of a rule more of a lottery than can possibly be justified: always remember, the presumptions are mere evidentiary presumptions as to intentions – evidence of actual intentions should always be relevant, regardless of which party raises them. The broad application of the rule, as favoured by Lords Goff and Keith, yet tempered by a similarly broad but well-defined set of exceptions based on the plaintiff's prior withdrawal from the scheme, later confession and reparation, and so on, would be preferable (see Rose (1996)).

Automatic resulting trusts

The relevance of intentions to ARTs

4.14   As we have seen, Megarry J distinguished ARTs and PIRTs partly on the basis that the former arose by operation of law independently of the settlor's intention. Recently, Lord Brown-Wilkinson doubted this in *Westdeutsche Landesbank v Islington London Borough Council* (1996):

> Megarry J ... suggests that [such a trust] does not depend on intention but operates automatically. I am not convinced this is right. If the settlor has expressly, or by necessary implication, abandoned any beneficial interest in the trust property, there is in my view no resulting trust; the undisposed-of equitable interest vests in the Crown as *bona vacantia* [ie goods without an owner]...

There are two ways of understanding this. The first is that, despite appearances, in the vast majority of cases where resulting trusts arise on the failure of an express trust to dispose in whole or in part of the beneficial interest in the trust property, the court really does inquire into and assess whether the settlor intended a resulting trust to arise, and finds that he did. This seems fanciful, since courts appear not to make any such inquiry and it seems unlikely that settlors have any actual intentions in this regard at all. If they did, one presumes that they would express them. On the other hand, Lord Browne-Wilkinson may only be saying that despite the normal, 'intention-independent', automatic operation of the resulting trust in these circumstances, there are cases where (1) the facts show that the settlor actually intended to abandon any interest in the trust property if the trust failed, and (2) he did not *express* this intention *as a term* of the trust he created, ie he didn't declare as he did the other terms of the trust that if the trust failed in whole or in part that he abandoned his interest, and (3) because of these 'collateral' intentions the court treats the undisposed of trust property as *bona vacantia*. This does not upset Megarry VC's characterisation, but only modifies it in a very minor way as follows: the ART is not wholly 'intention-independent' in that it may be *displaced* by a settlor's actual intentions to abandon all interest in the trust property which might otherwise result to him to the Crown. This surely occurs in a vanishingly small fraction of trusts, and it is not clear that there have ever been any cases of this kind (**9.50**).

4.15 The complicated way in which an ART can arise is shown by the attempt of a rich industrialist, one Guy Anthony Vandervell, to endow a chair of pharmacology in the Royal College of Surgeons. The facts of the case are somewhat convoluted, but the essential points are clear enough. There were three players: Vandervell himself, who controlled and owned most of the shares of a private engineering company he had founded; the Royal College of Surgeons (RCS); and Vandervell Trustees Ltd. (the trust company), a company which administered two separate trusts, one for Vandervell's children, and one a retirement, profit-sharing and savings fund for Vandervell's employees. The plan to endow the chair in the RCS (as devised by Vandervell's accountant to avoid tax) was to get shares of Vandervell's company into the hands of the RCS, and then Vandervell, using his control over his company, would have the company declare dividends on the shares sufficient to fund the chair; as part of the scheme, the RCS would grant an option to the trust company, so that once the dividends were paid the shares could be retrieved from the RCS. Vandervell duly instructed a bank which held some of the company shares on bare trust for him to transfer the shares to the RCS, and RCS in turn granted an option to purchase the shares for £5,000 to the trust company. The evidence was fragmentary, but at a minimum it was clear that the option was not to be granted to Vandervell himself because he did not want the beneficial ownership of the shares, which would increase his tax liability. Dividends sufficient to fund the chair were declared. In *Vandervell v IRC* (1966) a majority in the HL decided that because the option was essentially an interest in the shares that Vandervell had himself created by the arrangement, he had a beneficial interest in it; therefore, though the option was granted to the trust company, it held the option on resulting trust for Vandervell. Since he held the beneficial interest in the option under a resulting trust, he had a beneficial interest in the shares, for by exercising the option he could regain ownership of them. So although the RCS clearly had a beneficial interest in the shares, so did Vandervell under the option. Under the rules of taxation prevailing at the time, this beneficial interest in the shares entitled the IRC to charge Vandervell large amounts of surtax on the dividends, so as it turned out, the grant of the option proved hugely costly to him.

4.16 Given the relative simplicity of the facts, it is startling how difficult the different judges in the CA and the HL found it adequately to characterise the transaction in which the RCS received the shares and granted the option to the trust company in a way which explains their finding a resulting trust to Vandervell. In *Vandervell (No 2)* (1974), where he closely analysed *Vandervell v IRC*, Meggary J gives the gist of what the judges appeared to think:

> [Quite] apart from mechanism or motive, there is the fact, of paramount importance in relation to any concept of resulting or implied trust, that

it was Mr. Vandervell alone who was providing the property in question. The option was an option over shares of which Mr. Vandervell was the sole beneficial owner. If Mr. Vandervell disposed of those shares in such a way that he brought about the vesting of a major benefit in the college and a minor benefit in the defendant company, then it seems to me that Mr. Vandervell was providing both those benefits, even if his provision of the minor benefit was indirect and not made under compulsion.

Now, when a judge in a trust case says things like 'Quite apart from mechanism or motive', start to worry, for if the law of trusts is about anything, it is about mechanism and motive – in other words it concerns whether or not individuals have effectively exercised various powers of ownership, and the consequences of having done so or having failed to do so. That is what this case concerned and, and so mechanism and motive are all-important. Three legal mechanisms might account for transaction in *Vandervell*:

(1) There were two entirely separate gratuitous transactions – Vandervell gave the RCS some shares, and RCS granted the trust company an option;

(2) Vandervell made a binding contract with the RCS; or

(3) Vandervell made a conditional gift of the shares.

4.17 We can dismiss (1) from the outset. While Vandervell certainly had an independent reason to grant the RCS the shares – it was how he intended to endow the chair – the RCS had no independent reason to give the trust company anything; furthermore as a charity, the RCS could not just give rights to its property away; thus (1) is simply implausible on the facts. (2) is more likely. The contract would be one whereby, in return for granting the RCS the shares and subsequently declaring dividends upon them, the RCS would use the dividends to found a chair of pharmacology in Vandervell's name, and grant the option to the trust company. (3), however, is probably correct: Vandervell made a gift of the shares on condition the option was granted to the trust company. This condition would have to be equitable, not legal. While conditional gifts of land were both perfectly valid at law and common prior to 1926, no similar facility for conditional legal gifts of personalty was ever developed. (See Bell (1989), pp 225-226.) To the extent a gift could be made 'conditional', the 'condition' did not attach to the property, but to the donee. Thus a gift of personalty upon a condition which failed neither revived the donor's title in the property nor gave him any other proprietary right in it (eg a right to re-possess akin to a 'right to re-enter' land). Rather, he had a personal restitutionary claim against the donee, and only against the donee, for the gift's value (*Re Garnett* (1905)). However, conditional gifts of any kind of property are perfectly valid in equity (**3.10**). Thus Vandervell transferred the legal title of the shares to RCS on trust to hold the shares subject to the condition precedent that it grant an option to the trust company to purchase the shares. Upon granting the option, RCS then held the shares either absolutely (subject of course to the option), or on charitable trust to found the chair. Now here's the crucial point. On either (2) or (3) Vandervell gave value to RCS to endow the trust company with a valuable right, the option – in the absence of any evidence of Vandervell's intentions the trust company would hold that option on a purchase money PIRT for him. In other words, Vandervell provided value in the form of shares to the RCS and 'purchased', either by way of binding RCS by contract or by an equitable condition, the grant of the option to the trust company.

4.18   There was, however, evidence of Vandervell's intentions to displace the PIRT. Apparently, the main rationale for requiring the RCS to grant the option was simply to ensure that the shares could be retrieved from the RCS to forestall problems in pursuing a public flotation of Vandervell's company. It was not clear that Vandervell entertained any specific intentions as to who should have the beneficial interest in the option the trustee company was to acquire, except that he did not want to retain or re-acquire any interest for himself in the shares. Save for Lords Reid and Donovan, all the judges found it inconceivable that Vandervell intended the trust company to take the option beneficially – in other words, he must have intended that the trust company was to hold the option on trust for somebody. But what trust? The majority found that the intended trust was simply too vague and undefined to be valid. Now, the court might appear a wee bit mean in their unwillingness to draw inferences from the surrounding circumstances. Both the CA and Lords Upjohn and Donovan considered the possibility that the option was transferred upon trust for such objects as the settlor or the trustee company might declare – this was no help of course, because under such a trust Vandervell would himself be a possible object, and so under the taxing act he would still have retained a beneficial interest. But why stop the process of inference there? If one thing seems clear it was tha Vandervell nor the trust company intended Vandervell to have a interest in the option. A more generous court might, on the facts, have inferred that Vandervell's intention was for the trust company to hold the option on a discretionary trust, the objects being either his children or his employees, subject to a power of Vandervell and the trustees to add further objects, though not Vandervell himself (an intermediate power, **3.4**). This interpretation may, however, be somewhat anachronistic as the validity of an intermediate power was not settled until the 1970s (**7.53** et seq).

4.19   The result was an ART. While a PIRT was not displaced by evidence that Vandervell intended a gift to the trust company – there was no such evidence and most of the judges found such an intention inconceivable – it was displaced by evidence which disclosed that Vandervell had an intention to create an *express* trust. To be sure, it was an imprecise express trust on the court's view – to hold the property for, well, someone, but at any rate not for himself. Nevertheless this intention was sufficient to displace the operation of the PIRT. This express trust failed, since the objects were not sufficiently specified, and therefore the beneficial interest resulted to Vandervell *under an ART*. Most ARTs arise when the settlor transfers property directly to the trustee on trusts which fail to dispose of the beneficial interest, not in the rather complicated way in which Vandervell provided the option for the trust company. Because of that, the judgments in the HL can be confusing, and Megarry J's review of them in his judgment in *Vandervell (No 2)*, while somewhat tedious, is preferable.

4.20   One rule of law which comes out clearly in *Vandervell v IRC* is that simply having a positive intention not to retain any beneficial ownership in property transferred to another, as Vandervell had, will not prevent the transferor from ending up with the beneficial title under an ART, since if the transferor not only has that intention but has also the intention that the transferee is to hold on trust, and the trust fails, then the only possible result is an undefined express trust, which leads to an ART.

4.21   ARTs will come up again in chapter 9, when we discuss trusts which may 'fail' for two particular reasons, where a trust 'purpose' is accomplished or becomes impossible, and on the dissolution of an unincorporated association which defines the class of beneficiaries. Since it is not clear that these cases really are instances of the failure of a trust giving rise to an ART, it is better to discuss the matter there.

The nature of resulting trusts and resulting trusteeship

Trusts 'resulting in pattern'

4.22   PIRTs and ARTs are both resulting trusts in that they are 'resulting in pattern', which is to say that the beneficial interest in the property 'results', ie goes back, to the person whence it came. This very pattern can be used to classify all trusts. In contrast to resulting trusts, there are 'prosulting' trusts (a term I borrow from Birks), that is trusts where the beneficial interest goes forward, to someone other than the person whence the value came. If pattern alone is the only criterion used to identify resulting trusts, then the category of resulting trusts would include many more trusts than just PIRTs and ARTs. Any express bare trust in which the settlor transferred property to a trustee in trust for himself is properly called a 'resulting' trust on this basis. Indeed, any trust in which the settlor receives any benefit whatsoever by whatever means would be a resulting trust. So, for example, if a settlor put property on trust for himself and his wife and children in such shares as the trustee should in his absolute discretion see fit, then if the trustee exercises his discretion in the settlor's favour and gave him a share, he would receive this share under a resulting trust, since he provided the trust property in the first place, and now it has come back, or 'resulted' to him. The usefulness of such a distinction is doubtful; in particular it does not tell us whether the beneficial interest 'resulted' because of the settlor's intention or by operation of law, a criterion which, it will be argued below, distinguishes express trusts and PIRTs from ARTs; second, it does not distinguish between the capacities in which the person to whom value returns receives it, that is as the settlor, or as a beneficiary.

Resulting trusts as intentional trusts and TABOLs

4.23   The paradigm example of an intentional trust is the express trust. However PIRTs fit in this category as well, for remember, PIRTs operate by way of an *evidentiary* presumption as to what the settlor's intentions were, ie as to whether he created a trust or not; the law does not impose a trust on the parties by operation of law. The PIRT is simply an intentional trust which is resulting in pattern, whose recognition by the court is made easier because the settlor benefits from the evidentiary presumption by not having to prove his intention to create a trust, eg by pointing to a oral or written declaration of trust, unless evidence is led by the transferee which tends to show that he actually intended a gift. In other words, while the evidentiary presumption affects the burden of proof, it does not change the nature of the trust as one created by the settlor himself. Assuming that Megarry J was right and Lord Browne-Wilkinson's remarks are to be interpreted as I said they should be (**4.14**), a paradigm example of a TABOL is the ART, for it arises on the failure of an express trust to dispose of the entire beneficial interest in the trust property irrespective of the settlor's intentions, and even, as *Vandervell* shows, where a resulting trust is the last thing the settlor intended or wanted.

The role in which the 'resulting beneficiary' takes

4.24 The distinction between the PIRT and the express trust as intentional trusts and the ART as a TABOL is sharpened by looking at the role or capacity in which someone who has provided value receives a benefit to himself under a trust, ie in cases where a trust is 'resulting' in pattern. Under an express trust or a PIRT, the benefit of the property goes to the person intended to take under the trust, that is, it goes to the person who originally provided the value not because he was the settlor, but because he is a beneficiary under the intentional trust. An individual can be both settlor and beneficiary under a trust (**2.6**). In this sense, the express trust and the PIRT are, though superficially 'resulting' in pattern, are truly 'prosulting' in pattern, because the benefit of the property goes forward from the settlor to the beneficiary. Even though these two roles are filled by the same individual, this individual has rights under the trust because he was the intended beneficiary, not because he was the settlor. By contrast, the benefit an individual gets under an ART arises precisely because he was the settlor. The ART is a new trust imposed by the law in the settlor's favour, under which he is newly a beneficiary, because of the logic of the proprietary arithmetic (**4.4**) – that which he fails to dispose of by his express trust goes back to him.

Resulting trusteeship

4.25 Both the PIRT and the ART are bare trusts, so the legal title holder has essentially only one duty: to do with the property what the resulting beneficiary directs. This is obvious in the case of the ART. In the case of the PIRT, this is so because the evidentiary presumption only goes so far as to presume the location of the beneficial ownership – no other trust terms are presumed. Any further terms of an intentional trust must be proved without the benefit of the presumption. If they are, the trust will not properly be called a PIRT, for the proof of that more complex trust will amount to the proof of an express trust.

A new theory of resulting trusts

4.26 Recently, a new, more expansive role for resulting trusts has been suggested by Birks (1992) and Chambers (1997), based on a re-formulation of the underlying theory of resulting trusts which merges PIRTs and ARTs. According to this thesis, a resulting trust arises whenever a person transfers property or contributes value to a purchase for no consideration and *without the intention to give the beneficial ownership of it* to the recipient; the law gives rise to a trust to prevent the *unjust enrichment* of the recipient, ie if the transferor or contributor did not intend the recipient to take beneficially, the law deems it unjust for him to do so, and makes him hold the property on resulting trust. The Birks/ Chambers thesis broadens the operation of the resulting trust. The difference between the traditional role of the PIRT and the ART and the Birks/Chambers resulting trust is the difference between an intention to create a trust, and an intention not to make a gift This might sound like a distinction without a difference, but it most assuredly is not. The former is a much smaller category; it is one way of passing legal title for no consideration with no intention of making a gift. But there are lots of others. Take this case: I mistakenly pay my gas bill a second time, simply forgetting that I had done so already. Assume for simplicity I pay in cash. The gas company acquires legal title to the money when I pass it to one of its employees, though I do so under a mistake, because I voluntarily hand it over intending title to pass. At common law I am entitled to a restitutionary (**2.30**) personal claim against the gas company for the amount I mistakenly paid. The Birks/Chambers thesis, however, steps in to give me more: although I intended to pay the money to meet a contractual debt to the gas company, the transfer was in fact for no consideration since having paid for my gas once, I received no value in return for my second payment; but clearly I did not intend to make a gift of the money to the gas company; therefore the gas company is a recipient of a gratuitous transfer where I, the transferor, intended no gift, and so according to Birks and Chambers the gas company should hold the money they received on resulting trust for me. Obviously, I will be very happy about acquiring this equitable proprietary right if, following my mistaken payment, the gas company becomes insolvent (2.32 et seq). If Birks and Chambers are right, many common law personal restitutionary claims may be elevated to equitable proprietary rights via this resulting trust, for it makes any recipient who winds up with the transferor's property without paying for it, and cannot prove the transferor intended to make a gift of it to him, a trustee. Swadling (1996) has opposed this view, arguing that the resulting trust is displaced by evidence of *any* intention contrary to the intention to create a trust – the transferee does *not* have to prove that the transferor intended to make him a gift; therefore, in the case of the mistaken payment, since my intention was to transfer the money to the gas company as outright legal owner – how else could I pay the debt I thought I owed? – the presumed intention resulting trust does not arise. The debate, though interesting, shall for the foreseeable future be academic, for in *Westdeutsche Landesbank* the HL unanimously adopted Swadling's view (although Chamber's book-length treatment of the issues was not yet published and so was unavailable to the court).

Further Reading

Birks (1996b); Chambers (1997); Swadling (1996); Rose (1996).

Must read cases: *Vandervell v IRC* (1966); *Re Vandervell (No 2)* (1974); *Pettitt v Pettitt* (1971); *Cowcher v Cowcher* (1971); *Westdeutsche Landesbank v Islington London Borough Council* (1996); *Tinsley v Milligan* (1993); *Tribe v Tribe* (1995).

Self-test questions

1. What are presumed intention resulting trusts (PIRTs) and automatic resulting trusts (ARTs), and what distinguishes them?

2. Maurice and Flo run a business together, and are afraid that they are about to go bankrupt. They each own 25,000 shares of ABC plc,

which they transfer to their son Damian to avoid losing them to their creditors. Maurice then receives a legacy, which he uses to clear their debts. Maurice and Flo now seek the return of their shares, but Damian refuses. Discuss.

3.   What is the difference between an intentional trust and a trust arising by operation of law (TABOL)? Does this distinction illuminate the nature of resulting trusts?

CHAPTER FIVE

Constructive Trusts

SUMMARY

Varieties of constructive trust

Trusts of the family home

The remedial character of the constructive trust

Varieties of constructive trust

5.1 All constructive trusts arise by operation of law, but beyond this common characteristic, there is little that binds the various examples of constructive trusts together as a category. This chapter will very much serve as an introduction to constructive trusts, not a thorough examination, for reasons which will become apparent as we proceed. We will only examine one kind in detail here, the constructive trust of the family home.

5.2 For our purposes we can identify three broad categories of constructive trust: (1) those that arise through the application of the maxim 'Equity looks upon that as done which ought to be done' to give enhanced rights to parties to specifically enforceable contracts; (2) those which preserve the value of a beneficiary's equitable proprietary rights when there has been a breach of trust; and (3) those in which individuals acquire for the first time an interest in another's property because of their past dealings or relationship with the legal owner.

5.3 As to (1), the maxim 'Equity looks upon that as done which ought to be done' reflects the approach of equity when it deals with certain property transactions which typically have two stages. When one buys land, one normally enters into a binding contract of sale, which is later followed by the execution of the documents which transfer title.

85

Whenever the property being sold is unique in the eyes of equity, equity will allow the buyer specifically to enforce the contract of sale; that is, if the vendor refuses to carry out the contract and transfer the title, the buyer is not left to his common law right to sue for damages; equity will order the vendor to transfer the property itself. This is the general position with contracts for the sale of land, because, in the eyes of equity, all land is unique. But moreover, because 'Equity looks upon that as done which ought to be done', equity will treat the vendor *as having transferred* the title to the land to the buyer the moment the contract is agreed. The vendor, then, will hold the land on a constructive trust for the buyer until he transfers the legal title. We shall not examine this sort of constructive trust in any detail, though it will arise now and again, so you must be aware of its existence.

5.4   As to (2), if a trustee should transfer legal title to property in breach of trust to a third party who is not a bona fide purchaser, then the equitable title will remain the beneficiary's (**2.21** et seq). What kind of trustee is the third party? Because he was never intended to hold the property – he holds it because of a breach of trust, after all – he is generally called a 'constructive trustee'. However, it is best to describe him more fully, as a 'constructive trustee of an express trust interest'; that is, the equitable interest in the property remains throughout, and so retains its characteristic as one created by an express trust, but the trustee is not appointed a trustee of the express trust, but rather his 'trusteeship' is constructive, imposed by law, so that the beneficiary can claim his equitable interest against him. To the extent that the trustee's trusteeship is imposed by law, one might class the situation as a constructive trust. However, in the case of a trust to preserve the value of a beneficiary's equitable interest which arises because he traces this value into proceeds acquired by a third party, the trust is truly constructive.

Traceable proceeds

5.5   The beneficiary can, in certain circumstances, trace the value of his beneficial interest into property exchanged for the trust property (**2.28**). Whereas the beneficiary *retains* his equitable title in trust property even though it has been transferred to a third party in breach of trust, he may be able to *acquire* an equitable title in its 'traceable proceeds' that third party receives in exchange for the trust property. If he is able to claim an equitable interest in those proceeds, the third party will hold them on a constructive trust for him – neither the equitable title nor the trusteeship was created by an express trust. The third party did not declare a trust over the proceeds (nor did the transferor of them to him – that person just bought the trust property), nor did he declare himself a trustee. The trust is imposed by law.

5.6 What about traceable proceeds acquired by the express trustee himself, as for example, in breach of trust he sells the trust property to buy himself a new car? Prima facie, one might say that this situation gives rise to a constructive trust over the car: the trustee never declared a trust over the car, so it was imposed by law. What complicates matters here is that a trustee, in the course of properly managing the trust corpus, buys and sells trust property all the time, making investments and so on, and the express trust automatically captures the property exchanged for trust property, bringing into the trust. The trustee doesn't have to declare a trust over the shares he acquires with trust money every time he does so. In view of this, the general attitude of equity is that it will not 'hear' the trustee say that he exchanged trust property for his own benefit. If this is right, then in the case of the trustee, any traceable proceeds are held under the express trust, so long as the beneficiary does not object to the 'investment'. We will return to this matter in chapter 12, when we examine breach of trust in detail.

Personal liability as constructive trusteeship

5.7 Where a breach of trust occurs the trustee is personally liable to the beneficiary to make up the loss; that is, the beneficiary has a personal money claim against the trustee for whatever losses were caused by the breach of trust. This remedy is particularly important where the trust property was transferred away in breach of trust and it can neither be followed nor traced. Others besides the trustee, however, may be personally liable for breach of trust. Where the trustee is assisted in his breach of trust by an accessory, whether by the accessory's receiving or handling the trust property or otherwise, the beneficiary will have a personal claim against the accessory to make good the loss caused by the breach. Unfortunately, the traditional terminology for describing the accessory's liability is to say he becomes a 'constructive trustee', because he acquires the same personal liability as the original trustee. But the accessory need never have acquired title to any trust property. It is his assistance in the breach that makes him liable, so it is now better to refer simply to his accessory liability, rather than confusingly to call him a 'constructive trustee'. Again, we shall return to these matters in chapter 12.

5.8 (3) is a problematic category, for the power of equity to create property rights, ie equitable title, for one individual in the property of another, in order to do justice because of his past dealings or relationship with the legal owner, has not been informed by entirely coherent principles. As an introduction a couple of examples will suffice. Those familiar with land law will be aware of what are called 'constructive trusts of the family home'. If P and Q, who is usually P's spouse, come to an informal agreement or arrangement that Q is to share in the ownership of the property in which they live, the legal title to which is in P's name alone, and Q then relies on the arrangement to his detriment, Q will acquire an equitable share in the property under a constructive trust. The second example arises in a completely different context; it has been held that an employee standing in fiduciary relationship to his employer who accepts a bribe to breach his fiduciary duties will hold the bribe money on constructive trust for his employer. Although they do not have any informal agreement to this effect as in the case of P and Q and the family home, the fiduciary relationship, it has been argued, is sufficient to give the employer an equitable title in his ill-gotten gains. Breach of fiduciary obligations and constructive trusts which may arise as a result will be examined in chapter 11. The only constructive trust we shall examine in detail in this chapter is the constructive trust of the family home.

Trusts of the family home

5.9 Broadly speaking, what concerns us here are the circumstances under which it is just for law to vary the property rights between individuals in what is usually the most significant asset either one of them owns (or both of them co-own), because of their relationship to each other or their past dealings together. While traditionally the typical relationship was that between husband and wife where the husband was the sole legal owner of the matrimonial home, in principle and practice the relationship or dealings can be between any two or more individuals: between unmarried cohabitees, whether straight or gay, parents and (adult) children, or any others (*Cooke v Head* (1972)). Indeed, the significance of this law is now much reduced for married couples than for others, for disputes over beneficial ownership typically arise on the breakdown of a relationship, and the courts are empowered to vary the property rights of spouses upon divorce (Matrimonial Causes Act 1973, s 24; Matrimonial Property and Proceedings Act 1970, s 37). No similar jurisdiction exists for other cohabitees. Nevertheless, determining the beneficial interests in the family home under these rules remains important in cases where one of the couple, married or not, becomes bankrupt, for only that person's share will be available to his trustee in bankruptcy for distribution to creditors.

5.10 Different common law jurisdictions have taken different theoretical approaches to the power of equity to vary property rights. For example, in New Zealand, the courts have emphasised the reasonable expectations of the party claiming an equitable share in the property; thus a wife who in all the circumstances can reasonably claim to have expected a share in the family home given the parties' conduct, and who has relied upon those expectations, will be successful (*Gillies v Keogh* (1989)). In Canada the courts have emphasised the unjust enrichment that the defendant would obtain if the plaintiff were to receive no share in the property; thus, for example, a husband who has benefited throughout the marriage by his wife's raising their children and domestic work will hold the legal title upon constructive trust for himself and his wife in appropriate shares (*Pettkus v Becker* (1980); *Sorochan v Sorochan* (1986)). In England, the foundational HL decisions in *Pettitt v Pettitt* (1970) and *Gissing v Gissing* (1970) laid down the 'common intention' approach.

5.11 *Pettitt* can in one sense be regarded as the negative side of the coin, and *Gissing* the positive. In *Pettitt* their Lordships were unanimously concerned to refute the proposition that the courts had a general jurisdiction to rearrange the property rights of cohabitees on the breakdown of their relationship in whatever way seemed 'fair and just in all the circumstances'. They revealed, however, a variety of opinions as to the circumstances in which the court could find that one party had acquired a beneficial interest in the property of another. *Gissing*, in particular the speech by Lord Diplock, provided that basis: where the parties had a common intention that the beneficial interest in the property was to be shared, the best evidence of which being an actual agreement, and that common intention was acted upon by the plaintiff to his detriment, then the defendant would hold the property on constructive trust for them both in the intended shares.

The requirement that the plaintiff act to his detriment

5.12 Why, if a common intention to share the property is proved or inferred from all the evidence, does this not operate as a declaration of trust, albeit an informal one, which validly creates the trust? Why must the plaintiff also show that he acted to his detriment on the parties' arrangement? The problem is the existence of a statutory requirement, s 53(1)(b), which provides that an oral declaration of trust of land is unenforceable. (Formality requirements will be discussed in detail in chapter 6.) Equity will therefore not enforce a purely voluntary informal trust of land. But, as Hayton ((1996), 366) puts it:

> Equity acts *in personam* to prevent [the defendant] pleading the lack of formalities, so [the plaintiff] gets what was agreed. [The plaintiff's] interest should date from the time she commences to act to her detriment in the contemplated manner so that it is then inequitable for [the defendant] to deny her an interest.

5.13 So, while a common intention is necessary, it is not sufficient to establish a constructive trust. The plaintiff must also show he acted to his detriment in reliance on the agreement or understanding (*Midland Bank plc v Dobson* (1986)). The extent and quality of reliance should match what was expected under the parties' common understanding, but in many cases this is unclear. In *Grant v Edwards* (1986) Browne-Wilkinson VC said:

> In many cases of the present sort, it is impossible to say whether or not the claimant would have done the acts relied on as a detriment even if she thought she had no interest in the house. Setting up a house together, having a baby, making payments to general housekeeping expenses... may all be referable to the mutual love and affection of the parties and not specifically referable to the claimant's belief that she has an interest in the house. As at present advised, once it has been shown that there was a common intention that the claimant should have an interest in the house, any act done by her to her detriment relating to the joint lives of the parties is, in my judgment, sufficient detriment to qualify ... Accordingly, in the absence of evidence to the contrary, the right inference is that the claimant acted in reliance [on the common intention] and the burden lies on the legal owner to show that she did not do so.

5.14 Following a wealth of case law interpreting *Pettitt* and *Gissing*, the HL again spoke in 1990. In *Lloyds Bank plc v Rosset* (1990) Lord Bridge, giving the only judgment of a unanimous House, provided what is now the authoritative enunciation of the basic principles:

> The first and fundamental question which must always be resolved is whether, independently of any inference to be drawn from the conduct of the parties in the course of sharing the house as their home and managing their joint affairs, there has been at any time prior to acquisition, or exceptionally at some later date, been any agreement, arrangement, or understanding reached between them that the property is to be shared beneficially. The finding of an agreement or arrangement to share in this sense can only, I think, be based on evidence of express discussions between the partners, however imperfectly remembered and however imprecise their terms may have been. Once a finding to this effect has been made it will only be necessary for the partner asserting a claim to a beneficial interest against the partner entitled to the legal estate to show that he or she has acted to his or her detriment or significantly altered his or her position in reliance on the agreement in order to give rise to a constructive trust or proprietary estoppel.

> In sharp contrast with this situation is the very different one where there is no evidence to support a finding of an agreement or an arrangement to share, however reasonable it might have been for the parties to reach such an agreement if they had applied their minds to the question, and where the court must rely entirely on the conduct of the parties both as the basis from which to infer a common intention to share the property beneficially and as the conduct relied on to give rise to the constructive trust. In this situation direct contributions to the purchase price by the partner who is not the legal owner, whether initially or by payment of mortgage instalments, will readily justify the inference necessary to the creation of a constructive trust. But, as I read the authorities, it is at least extremely doubtful whether anything less will do.

Evidence of a common intention is to be read objectively, as a reasonable person would do, from the statements or conduct of the parties. In particular, a dishonest actual intention of the legal owner will not defeat an agreement or understanding objectively viewed, as for instance, where the legal owner makes an excuse for putting the title in his name alone, as in *Eves v Eves* (1975) where the excuse was that the female partner was too young to own property, or in *Grant v Edwards* (1986) where the legal owner said placing the female partner's name on the title would prejudice her in her divorce proceedings.

5.15   The common intention may be one in which the parties decide on their respective beneficial shares from the outset, or may be one in which the parties decide that each should get a 'fair' share according to the contributions each had made directly or indirectly to the acquisition of the property, in which case the court will obviously have leeway in determining the extent of the beneficial interests (*Gissing v Gissing; Midland Bank plc v Cooke* (1995)). In *Huntingford v Hobbs* (1992) the female partner paid about 61% of the purchase price of the property, and with the male partner jointly undertook to repay the mortgage which funded the remainder. On the facts, however, it appeared that there was a common intention that the male partner would pay all the mortgage instalments, and so in determining their respective shares, the CA credited him with the full value of the mortgage loan contribution to the purchase; by the same token, however, on the sale of the property the value of outstanding mortgage debt was debited entirely from his share of the proceeds.

5.16   *Rosset* makes clear that the limits within which a common intention can be inferred merely from conduct are narrow. From the first, the activities of a husband (doing odd jobs about the house to keep it in repair and minor renovations and improvements) and of a wife (cooking, cleaning, and raising the kids) doing what husbands and wives 'normally' do were regarded as wholly insufficient evidence of a common intention to share the property beneficially (*Pettitt; Gissing; Burns v Burns* (1984)). The requirement of direct contributions to the purchase price 'initially or by payment of mortgage instalments' seems to confuse constructive trusts with purchase money PIRTs. Contributions to the initial purchase price will give rise to a PIRT unless made by the husband to a purchase in the sole name of his wife; however payments of mortgage instalments do not give rise to a resulting trust (*Cowcher v Cowcher* (1971)), unless the court is tacitly applying 'backward tracing' to such payments. 'Backward tracing' is tracing value through a debt into the property that is purchased with it. Thus, if my rogue trustee uses £5,000 of trust money to pay off a bank loan, then I trace into the product he purchased with the loan money; if he purchased a car with the loan money, I trace the value of the trust money into that, and claim equitable title to the car. It would be perfectly sensible to apply a backward tracing purchase money PIRT analysis to the payment of mortgage instalments, but the courts have never said that was what they were doing. The orthodox view, therefore, must be that the mortgage instalments are contributions referable to the acquisition of the property under a common intention constructive trust, a constructive trust inferred, however, from nothing more than the very paying of the instalments. Query whether this does not amount to a backward tracing purchase money PIRT under different terminology.

5.17 The recent decision in *Midland Bank plc v Cooke* (1995) represents something of a departure from these principles. A house was purchased in Mr Cooke's name alone, with his savings, a mortgage taken out by him, and a wedding present from his parents. Mr and Mrs Cooke testified under oath that they had made no agreement concerning the beneficial interest in the house. The CA decided that the wedding present was a gift to both Mr and Mrs Cooke, and therefore, since the money was half hers, Mrs Cooke acquired an interest in the house under a purchase money PIRT. If resulting trust principles were to define their respective shares, Mrs Cooke would have an interest of approximately 7% due to her share of the wedding gift. The CA decided her share was 50%. It declined to adopt the view that where a party's interest was defined purely by their contribution to the purchase price, no common intention being proved, all other conduct is irrelevant to determining that party's beneficial interest. Where one party has successfully asserted a beneficial interest in the property, the court should undertake a survey of the entire course of conduct between the parties to determine their respective beneficial shares; furthermore, Waite LJ said:

> ... positive evidence that the parties neither discussed nor intended any agreement as to the proportions of their beneficial interests does not preclude the court, on general equitable principles, from inferring one.

This statement must be doubted in view of the HL's reasonably clear statements in *Gissing* and *Rosset* that a common intention constructive trust can only arise on the basis of a real common intention.

The constructive trustee is a bare trustee

5.18 The legal owner holding the family home under a constructive trust is just a bare trustee vis-à-vis the equitable owner of a share. There are no other 'terms' of the trust with which he has fiduciary obligations to comply. The plaintiff and defendant are merely co-owners in equity to the extent of their respective shares.

Third parties and insolvency

5.19 The plaintiff's equitable proprietary interest under the constructive trust will be capable of binding third parties who deal with the legal title-holding defendant (eg *Williams & Glyn's Bank v Boland* (1980, HL); *Kingsnorth Finance Ltd v Tizard* (1986)), though it will not do so in all cases (eg *City of London Building Society v Flegg* (1988)); the details will not be considered here. The standard practice of purchasers or mortgagees of land is to make such inquiries as to avoid being caught by the plaintiff's interest. Of greater concern, perhaps, is the position of third parties where the legal title holder, usually the husband, goes bankrupt. For example, a wife who acquires an equitable share of the property under a constructive trust will take the value of that share free of the claims of her husband's creditors. Given how common it is these days for title to the family home to be shared, it is perhaps somewhat precious to manifest much concern for the unsecured creditors in these circumstances, since it is not very plausible that *they*, as opposed perhaps to a mortgagee, advanced money to the husband relying on a belief that he owned the whole of, rather than co-owned, his family home. The sale of the property now 'co-owned' by the husband's trustee in bankruptcy, who wants to realise the husband's share in money, and the wife, who generally wishes to remain in occupation, will not be postponed for more than a year in most circumstances (*Re Citro* (1991)), so the trustee can get the money out of the house quite smartly.

Proprietary estoppel

5.20 Notice that in the passage from Lord Bridge's decision in *Rosset* that he mentions the constructive trust and 'proprietary estoppel' in the same breath. While proprietary estoppel in its various forms is a much older doctrine than the common intention constructive trust, they are similar. Where a defendant represents by his words or conduct that the plaintiff will acquire some entitlement to his land, and the plaintiff acts to his detriment in reliance upon the representation, the defendant may be 'estopped', ie stopped, from standing on his strict legal rights to the land in order to withdraw the entitlement. The two main differences between the common intention constructive trust and proprietary estoppel are first, that the former relies upon some common understanding or agreement, while the latter is based upon the defendant's representations, and second, that the only result of the operation of common intention is a constructive trust, whereas in the case of a proprietary estoppel the plaintiff will acquire the 'minimum equity to do justice' (*Crabb v Arun District Council* (1976); *Pascoe v Turner* (1979)); the court may award not only an equitable interest in the property, but more appropriate lesser interests, such as a licence to occupy or a charge on the property for money expended. In this respect, proprietary estoppel is a more flexible doctrine. Hayton (1996a), 373 et seq) argues that the distinction between common intention constructive trusts and proprietary estoppels is illusory, and that the courts should draw upon their experience of applying both doctrines to reach the equitable result, an approach suggested by Browne-Wilkinson VC in *Grant*. A full examination of proprietary estoppels and comparison with constructive trusts is beyond our purposes, but even the brief comparison above is suggestive – how different in most cases will an informal 'common' understanding be from an informal representation by the defendant legal owner which is reasonably acted upon by the plaintiff?

The remedial character of the constructive trust

5.21   All trusts arising by operation of law may appear to have a 'remedial' nature: if a right is created by the law, then surely it must be an application of the principles of justice in response to a fact situation demanding it. Thus the constructive trust arises because it would be unconscionable for the legal title holder to deny his cohabitee the equitable interest they agreed the latter should have, so the law provides one. But *all* legal rules are intended to express the principles of justice, and indeed, learning the law is in part finding out what justice means. So one cannot call a rule remedial simply because it is explained by reference to principles of justice. In the context of this discussion, a remedial equitable interest is one which is awarded by a court (although parties may anticipate what a court will award and act accordingly, as when a negligent driver (or rather, his insurance company) pays compensation to the person he injured so avoiding an expensive legal action). Are there remedial constructive trusts of this kind?

5.22   The contrary view is that constructive trusts are simply the consequences of particular equitable rules of title, rules governing the transfer or loss or acquisition of equitable property rights in various transactions; this is generally called an 'institutional' view of such trusts. Save for the vendor's constructive trust and the 'constructive' trust under which a recipient who is not a bona fide purchaser holds trust property, constructive trusts look less like they arise from rules of title and more remedial than do, for example, ARTs (chapter 4), which also arise by operation of law. The rule giving rise to an ART is pretty clearly a rule of title, which essentially provides that an owner retains or gets back any property he fails to dispose of effectively. In contrast, a common intention constructive trust is more like an equitable mushroom that arises from the legal mycelium whenever the conditions are right, not so much as the result of a modification of the rules governing title transactions, but as a remedy which is afforded on the basis of the parties' ongoing behaviour, in particular the course of action which amounts to detrimental reliance. The distinction is not watertight, of course, because any rule by which a title is transferred or a new title arises can be considered a rule of title, no matter how nebulous the rule actually is. Nevertheless, it is fair to say that the rule giving rise to an ART looks more like an 'automatic' rule of title, whereas the rules, such as they are, governing common intention constructive trusts, look a lot more like considerations taken into account by the court when deciding to 'award', as it were, an equitable interest (See *Muschinski v Dodds* (1985) per Deane J).

5.23 In English law the constructive trust must be regarded as institutional in the sense that, where one arises, it is like any other equitable property right – it comes into existence when the facts which trigger the operation of the law occur, and so it binds third parties from that time just as much as any other equitable property right does (*Re Sharpe* (1980)). The idea, which appears to be accepted at least theoretically in other jurisdictions (in particular the US (American Law Institute, *Restatement of Restitution*, para 60) and Canada (*Rawluk v Rawluk* (1990)), that the trust arises only when the court declares it, but has effect retroactively to the time when the facts which justify the award occurred, has not found favour in England, for the very good reason that there is something fishy and apparently unjust about declaring a property interest with retroactive effect, for proprietary rights bind third parties. It is fishy because if I acquire a property from X in which the law regards Y as having no interest, it is not clear how I simply by owning the property I could become subject to Y's rights which arise by virtue of a later court order against X – it seems illegitimately to mix up personal and proprietary rights, since once X has sold me the property, it is no longer connected to him personally any more than it is to anyone besides its current owner, ie me. It tends toward injustice, for if Y has no right against X when I buy the property (since the court has not by then made the remedial order), there is no way that I can protect myself from Y's right. I cannot even be a bona fide purchaser without notice, since there is nothing in existence of which I can take notice. Even if the courts may minimise the effect of the award on third parties by setting particular conditions on the trust, for example that it be subject to particular third party rights, this requires the court to be vigilant in protecting the rights, possibly unknown, of parties not before court, and in any case seems *ad hoc*.

5.24 On reading the cases you might think that in reality the law of trusts gives judges such discretion that their 'finding' a constructive trust on the facts virtually amounts to 'awarding' the plaintiff a retrospectively effective equitable interest. Nevertheless the HL in *Pettitt* certainly denied that the courts should have such a discretion. The more interesting question is whether the courts should have a discretion to award a plaintiff an equitable interest which takes effect only from the date of the court order, along the lines favoured by Hayton ((1996a), 375 et seq). Such an equitable title would automatically be subject to the rights of innocent third parties in the property acquired before the award. Such a prospective constructive trust, ie one operating from the date of the court award, will not assist the plaintiff if the defendant is bankrupt, but will protect the plaintiff if the defendant goes bankrupt before the plaintiff gets his share out of the property, and will entitle the plaintiff to the actual property, which will be worthwhile if the property itself, rather than just its value, has significance for the plaintiff. Such a prospective constructive trust has never been awarded under English law, though in *Muschinski v Dodds* (1985) the High Court of Australia made just such an order.

Further Reading

Gardner (1993); Birks (ed) (1994, Vol II, Part IV).

Must read cases: *Pettitt v Pettitt* (1969); *Gissing v Gissing* (1970); *Grant v Edwards* (1986); *Lloyds Bank plc v Rosset* (1990); *Midland Bank plc v Cooke* (1995).

Self-test questions

1. What are some examples of constructive trusts? Do they have any common features?

2. Phillippa and Paul purchase Whiteacre together for £50,000. Phillippa contributes £10,000, Paul £1,000, and the remainder is raised by way of a mortage on Whiteacre, for the repayment of which Paul is solely liable. Paul loses his job and Phillippa pays all the mortgage instalments. Paul starts a business which fails, and has been declared bankrupt. The house is now worth £100,000. Discuss.

3 What is the difference between the 'remedial' and 'institutional' views of constructive trusts?

CHAPTER SIX

Formalities and Secret Trusts

SUMMARY

The purpose of formalities

Declarations of trusts in land: s 53(1)(b) of the Law of Property Act 1925

The doctrine of *Rochefoucauld v Boustead*

Dispositions of subsisting equitable interests: s 53(1)(c)

Formal requirements on testamentary gifts: s 9 of the Wills Act 1837

Informal testamentary trusts: secret and half secret trusts

The purpose of formalities

6.1 The law sometimes imposes a requirement on the *form* of legal transactions before it will regard those transactions as effective, typically a requirement that the transaction be made or recorded in writing. The law may impose formalities for different purposes, but three are of particular relevance to transactions in equitable property.

As a cautionary measure

6.2 Property rights, including equitable interests under a trust, are very valuable rights. They should not be effectively dealt with in a casual or informal way, just in case the transferor did not seriously consider the consequences of his act. The formality of writing, in particular the requirement that the transferor signs his name, is suited to this purpose, because these days even the most benighted rube understands that when he signs his name to a document which is not a personal letter he is generally doing something of legal consequence.

For evidential purposes – I

6.3 Writing requirements provide documentary evidence which make frauds more difficult on the presumption that it is easier to get away with lying to the court about what someone said than it is to successfully forge documents and lie to the court about their origin.

For evidential purposes – II

6.4 Documentary evidence also prevents the administrative problems that might arise when the memory of oral transactions has faded. Also, when transactions are complicated, the writing down helps the parties to be clear about what they intend. Finally, in the case of trusts, the writings are useful simply as a paper record for the trustee which ensures that he does not commit an inadvertent breach of trust by, say, paying income to a former beneficiary who has since assigned his equitable right to the income to someone else.

6.5 It is a maxim of equity that 'equity looks to intent not form'; equity has never itself insisted on formal requirements for any transactions. Parliament however, by statute, has imposed formal requirements on the creation and transfer of equitable interests, and equity must take due regard of them. Here we will be concerned, first, with the formalities for creating a trust, that is bringing into existence equitable rights, and then formalities for the transfer, or assignment, or disposition of already existing equitable interests, that is, the existing rights of beneficiaries under a trust.

Declarations of trusts in land: s 53(1)(b) of the Law of Property Act 1925

6.6 Section 53(1)(b) of the Law of Property Act 1925 provides:

> A declaration of trust respecting any land or any interest therein must be manifested and proved by some writing signed by some person who is able to declare such trust or by his will;

Section 53(1)(b) applies only to land. There is no similar provision with respect to personalty: therefore there is no formal requirement for the declaration of a trust of personalty. Thus you can orally declare that you hold your copy of this book on trust for your mother, and if you mean it, then you do.

6.7   Section 53(2) of the Act provides:

> This section does not affect the creation or operation of resulting, implied or constructive trusts.

To the extent that resulting, implied, and constructive trusts arise by operation of law, this provision is strictly speaking unnecessary, or inserted *ex abundante cautela* (out of an abundance of caution), for there can be no formality requirements for trusts which arise by operation of law. The clause does save PIRTs, however, since these are intentional trusts, not TABOLs (**4.23**). Although somewhat unusual, where a party undertakes to create a trust of land as his side of a contract, a contractual constructive trust (**5.3**) will arise, and so a failure to declare the trust in writing will not result in the trust being unenforceable. Since contracts for any disposition of land must be in writing (Law of Property (Miscellaneous Provisions) Act 1989, s 2), in the case of trusts declared in fulfilment of a contractual obligation there will invariably be a writing anyway.

6.8   The person 'able to declare such trust' under s 53(1)(b) will normally be the settlor, of course. This is plain where the trust is self-declared, ie the legal owner of land declares that he shall himself hold the land on trust. A somewhat complicated example is the case of *Rochefoucauld v Boustead* (1897), a case which turned on the failure to declare a trust in writing. The plaintiff, the Comtesse de la Rochefoucauld, had mortgaged her estates in Ceylon, and the mortgagee demanded payment of the mortgage debt. Having insufficient funds following her divorce, Boustead orally agreed to buy the estates from the mortgagee at a price sufficient to cover the mortgage debt and expenses, and hold the estates on trust for her, subject to her paying off the purchase price and further expenses. Since Boustead purchased the beneficial title from the mortgagee which he impressed with the trust in the plaintiff's favour, so he should have signed the necessary writing. Where A transfers land to B to hold on trust for C, A has the beneficial title before the transfer of the land to B, so is the one able to declare the trust. If he transfers the title but fails to declare the trust in writing, A should remain the appropriate signatory if anyone is, simply because it is A's intentional trust which we are concerned about. It seems doubtful, though, whether A's writing should be effective to enforce the trust against B, since the whole point of the section is to make oral declarations of trust unenforceable, and the declaration which matters must be the one A makes prior to or at the time legal title is transferred to B, ie when he still has the beneficial interest. Youdan (1984) argues that B, the legal owner, may sign the writing as the one who would be beneficial owner if there were no trust. Where B is willing to do so, his production of the writing is, however, better regarded as his own self-declaration of trust giving effect to A's wishes. In *Gardner v Rowe* (1828) an express trust was found valid though later evidenced by a writing of the trustee, but the case turned on the doctrine of *Rochefoucauld v Boustead*, not on the writing point, so it does not decide the issue.

The doctrine of *Rochefoucauld v Boustead*

6.9 Section 53(1)(b) uses the words 'manifested and proved by some writing', which have been interpreted to indicate *not* that a purported declaration of trust is void without such a writing, but that it is *not enforceable* in law; the express trust exists and binds the parties, but the beneficiary cannot invoke the assistance of the court to make the trustee carry it out. In *Rochefoucauld v Boustead* (1897), however, the CA did enforce the oral express trust, because it would be a fraud for a person taking the land as a trustee to plead the statute and keep the land for himself. 'Equity will not allow a statute enacted to prevent fraud to be used as an instrument of fraud', and so the court will allow parol (ie oral) evidence to prove the express trust, despite s 53(1)(b).

6.10 In *Bannister v Bannister* (1948) an elderly woman conveyed two cottages to her brother-in-law at a below market price on the understanding that she should be able to live rent-free in one of them for the rest of her days. When he tried to evict her, the CA declared that he held one of the cottages on trust to give effect to the agreement. It did not matter that the brother-in-law had no fraudulent intent when the property was transferred; the fraud consisted of relying upon the absence of writing when the sister-in-law tried to enforce her beneficial interest. Scott LJ described the trust as a constructive trust, without however giving any reasons for this classification. The constructive trust analysis may appear to be preferable to the express trust analysis simply because it gives an identical result without appearing to disregard the statute, since constructive trusts are specifically exempted from formality requirements by s 53(2).

6.11 *Rochefoucauld* and *Bannister* were both two party cases. How should the doctrine apply in the three party case, ie where A transfers land to B upon trust for C. If one adopts the constructive trust approach, the law may impose the result most justified in the circumstances – in some cases the constructive trust should be a bare trust for A, which merely prevents B's unjust enrichment, in others it should reflect the terms of the unenforceable express trust, so carrying out A's intention. In general in the three party case a trust in favour of A is preferable because it gives due weight to the statute, for the express trust is not enforced, yet at the same time B's fraud is prevented. Moreover, the cautionary purpose is served: if A still wishes to carry out his intentions, he can declare the trust again; if he does not, then the trust saves him from the effect of his oral declaration. Moreover, C can hardly complain that a *fraud* has been perpetrated against him simply because he has not received a gratuitous benefit from A. A constructive trust in favour of C should only be found where C relied to his detriment either because of a representation by A or because B has acted to carry out the trust, or perhaps, where A is no longer able to declare a trust in C's favour afresh, for example because he is dead, a case we shall consider when we look at secret trusts (**6.36** et seq). These considerations apply with even greater force to the case where A makes a self-declaration of trust in favour of C, for A cannot defraud himself, and appear to justify the result in *Rochefoucauld*, a self-declaration case. Boustead gratuitously promised the plaintiff to buy the estates for her benefit; thus he was the settlor of the trust, and the cautionary purpose should normally counsel the court to find no trust at all and allow him to renege, for it would be no fraud if Rochefoucauld did not receive this gratuitous benefit. The court's analysis of the facts is not well reported, but Boustead had, apparently, been giving effect to the express trust, upon which the plaintiff might have relied, and so in all the circumstances the decision was probably correct.

Disposition of subsisting equitable interests: Law of Property Act 1925, s 53(1)(c)

6.12 Section 53(1)(c) of the Law of Property Act 1925 provides:

> A disposition of an equitable interest or trust subsisting at the time of the disposition must be in writing signed by the person disposing of the same, or by his agent thereunto lawfully authorised in writing or by his will.

The section refers to a 'disposition' of an existing equitable interest. We shall be concerned almost entirely with what counts as a disposition for purposes of the section. 'Equitable interest or trust' refers to equitable interests in both land and personalty (*Grey v IRC* (1959)). Notice also that by this section, unlike s 53(1)(b), a disposition must be in writing – if not in writing, it is absolutely void, not merely unenforceable.

6.13 The section might be interpreted either broadly or narrowly. The predecessor section in the Statute of Frauds 1677 upon which it was based required writing for 'grants and assignments' of equitable interests; if that were taken as the intended meaning of 'disposition', then the section would have a fairly narrow compass. It would not apply to surrenders or releases of one's equitable interest, for there the beneficiary merely gives up his interest; he doesn't grant it to another. Similarly, if a beneficiary's declaration of trust over his interest in favour of someone else wouldn't be caught, since he does not assign or grant his equitable interest but retains it in order to give effect to the sub-trust. In *Grey v IRC* (1959) the HL unanimously held that that 'disposition' was to be given its natural meaning, which would appear to cover *every* transaction (not being an operation of law) by which any individual is able to alter a beneficiary's equitable entitlement under the trust. It would apply not only to every act of the beneficiary by which he somehow deals with his interest, but would also include the exercise by anyone of any power, such as a power to appoint, which might affect the beneficiary's equitable interest. Not only does the cautionary purpose apply in all these cases, but the purpose called 'evidential II' (**6.4**) does also: trusts can be extremely complicated, and a paper record of various transactions concerning the equitable interests is vitally important, so important that it would be justified if the law insisted upon writing as the price of their validity (see Green (1984)). The cases, however, do not reveal such a straightforward approach. We shall consider the different transactions in turn.

Assignment to a third party

6.14 Assignments are clearly caught by s 53(1)(c): if A, for example, holds an equitable income interest in shares under a trust, and wishes to assign it to X, he must do so in writing; a purported oral assignment is absolutely void.

Declaration of trust

6.15 It is generally accepted that where a beneficiary declares a trust of his equitable interest, creating a sub-trust, s 53(1)(c) does not apply. If the equitable interest is in land, any trust must be evidenced in writing by s 53(1)(b), but if the equitable interest is in personalty, such as a trust of company shares, an oral declaration of sub-trust appears to be valid. The rationale for the exception is that, while the declaration of the sub-trust does have the effect of extinguishing the beneficiary's *beneficial* interest in the trust, either in whole ('I declare that I hold my income interest on trust for Tim, Tom, and Tammy, in such proportions as I see fit') or in part ('I declare that I hold my income interest on trust for Trevor for life and then for myself absolutely'), and so in that sense is a disposition, it is not a disposition in the sense that the beneficiary retains his entire equitable title to give effect to the sub-trust. Thus, in the same way that a legal owner of property does not dispose of his legal title when declaring a trust over it, the equitable owner does not dispose of his equitable interest when he declares a sub-trust.

6.16 An exception to this exception is, however, also widely accepted in the academic literature, to wit: if the beneficiary declares a bare sub-trust, ie 'I declare that I hold my life interest upon trust for Ted absolutely', then the declaration is void unless in writing. The idea is that the beneficiary is now a mere conduit between the trustee and the sub-beneficiary. The sub-beneficiary should approach the trustee directly for his benefits, since it is pointless for the trustee to pay the beneficiary/sub-trustee and for him to immediately turn around and pay the sub-beneficiary. If this is right, then the declaration of a bare sub-trust amounts to an assignment of his equitable title and should count as a disposition under s 53(1)(c). Certain nineteenth-century cases, *Onslow v Wallis* (1849), *Re Lashmar* (1891), and *Grainge v Wilberforce* (1889), seem to suggest that the beneficiary/sub-trustee drops out of the picture in this way, although their authority for this proposition is disputed (Green (1984)). A different argument along these lines is sometimes made: if the sub-trustee has some 'active duties' to perform under the trust, such as the sub-trustee's discretion in the Tim, Tom, and Tammy example above, rather than being a mere conduit, then he does not drop out of the picture, and therefore the sub-trust is not in essence an assignment, and so an active duty sub-trust is valid without writing. In other words, this trust cannot simply collapse, the sub-trustee dropping out of the picture. Both the bare trust/non-bare trust and active duties/no active duties distinctions seem slender reeds upon which to rest a difference in the requirement of writing. The idea seems to be, that, because the beneficiary drops out of the picture when he creates a bare, or no active duties, sub-trust, he has effectively assigned his interest. But even if those nineteenth century authorities apply, it would seem that the beneficiary/sub-trustee drops out not by virtue of his own declaration of the sub-trust, but either by operation of law, which collapses the sub-trust giving the sub-beneficiary rights against the trustee automatically, or because the sub-beneficiary leaps over his head to the trustee, taking his beneficial rights to the source, as it were, under the principle of *Saunders v Vautier*. Surely the beneficiary/sub-trustee could not himself insist on quitting the scene; the trustee could always choose to pay him and let him deal with his own sub-trust. If this is right then he does not drop out of the picture by his own hand. In any case, distinguishing between these sub-trusts to alter writing requirements seems unmotivated in light of the various purposes for which formalities are imposed. Feel free, therefore, to argue that either all sub-trusts should require writing (as does Green (1984)), or that none should, though be careful to mention these distinctions in an exam answer, since they will have attached themselves limpet-like to the brain of the typical trusts law examiner.

Directions to the trustee to hold the equitable interest for another

6.17 If A directs his trustee to hold his equitable interest for a third party, it is generally accepted that this requires writing. This is in effect an assignment achieved, not by dealing with the third party directly, but by instructing the trustee henceforth to treat the third party as the beneficiary. *Grey v IRC* is usually cited as authority for this proposition, although as we shall see it actually concerned a different transaction. Nevertheless, the rationale for the application of s 53(1)(c) is straightforward. The beneficiary here, by his own act, extinguishes his own beneficial interest in favour of another, and so there is little to distinguish this from an assignment.

Directions to the trustee to hold the equitable interest on new trusts for another, and variations

6.18   Now we will discuss the 'big three' cases of this topic, *Grey v IRC, Vandervell v IRC* (1966), and *Re Vandervell (No 2)* (1974). The courts made something of a hash of all of them, so it is difficult to say exactly what each decided, hence the 'and variations' above.

6.19   *Grey* involved an attempt to avoid paying *ad valorem* stamp duty on the setting up of a trust. *Ad valorem* stamp duty is a tax charged on documents which transfer the *beneficial* interest in property. For example, when you transfer title to a house, *ad valorem* stamp duty is payable, '*ad valorem*' indicating that the amount of the duty is a percentage of the market value of the property. At the time *Grey* was decided, stamp duty was payable on the transfer of shares. So, for example, if you transferred shares to Theresa on trust for Ben, the beneficial interest passed from you to Ben, and so *ad valorem* stamp duty was chargeable on the share transfer document. If by some means you could get the shares into a trust for Ben without having to use a document that transferred the beneficial title, then you could avoid paying *ad valorem* stamp duty. Furthermore, any transfer document which did not transfer a *beneficial* interest only attracted a fixed stamp duty of 50p. So a transfer of shares from one trustee to another, eg when a trustee retired, only cost 50p stamp duty, since the beneficial interest remained with the beneficiary throughout. Say you wanted to transfer shares to Theresa on trust for Ben, but avoid *ad valorem* stamp duty. Here's how you could do it: declare that you hold the shares on trust for Ben. Shares are personalty, so you can declare such a trust orally: no document, so no stamp duty. Now retire from the trust in favour of a new trustee, Theresa, and transfer the legal title in the shares to her. The share transfer will be stampable at 50p, not *ad valorem*, because it does not transfer the beneficial interest, which already lies with Ben. The only catch in this scheme is that if you write a document recording your declaration of trust too soon after your oral declaration, the Revenue will regard the writing as a document which transfers the beneficial interest to Ben, and you will pay *ad valorem* stamp duty on it (*Cohen and Moore v IRC* (1933)). By this means, then, you could transfer the shares to Theresa on trust for Ben paying only 50p in stamp duty. The settlor in *Grey* was not so lucky.

6.20   In *Grey*, the settlor owned 18,000 company shares, which he desired to transfer in equal amounts into six trusts for his grandchildren which he had already set up. He transferred the shares to the two trustees of the grandchildren's trusts, but to hold the shares on bare trust for himself, and so, since the beneficial interest remained with him, the transfer document only attracted 50p stamp duty. He then orally directed the trustees to hold the shares in six separate and equal blocks upon the pre-existing grandchildren's trusts. Five weeks later the trustees executed a document declaring that they held the shares on the children's trusts. The Revenue argued that this document was stampable *ad valorem* because it transferred the beneficial interest in the shares from the settlor to the grandchildren. The trustees argued that the settlor's oral direction did so, and that such a direction did not require writing under s 53(1)(c) to be valid. The HL unanimously decided that such a direction was a disposition within s 53(1)(c) and so needed to be in writing; therefore the oral direction was void. Somewhat strangely, the later writing in which the trustees stated that they held the shares on the grandchildren's trusts was regarded as validly transferring the settlor's interest; the case therefore also appears to stand for the proposition that a later writing may retroactively validate an invalid oral disposition. Although the settlor was not expressed as a party to the deed declaring the trusts, he did sign it, and so the participation of the beneficiary is necessary for this to work.

6.21 What precisely does the case decide? The settlor's direction was clearly not a direction to the trustees to hold his equitable interest for his grandchildren in equal shares. That would simply have made them equitable co-owners of the shares under the same bare trust. Neither was it a self-declaration of trust, in which he declared that he would henceforth hold the shares on trust for the grandchildren on trusts identical to the ones he had already set up for them with the trustees. Rather, he directed his trustees in their nominee capacity to divide the shares into equal lots and thereafter hold the lots as trustees of the grandchildren's trusts, each trust to receive one lot. The important point is that the trustees were not to continue to hold the shares as nominee trustees for new beneficiaries, but to hold the shares in their quite separate capacity as trustees of the grandchildren's trusts. Because the trustees of the grandchildren's settlement were the same two persons who were the settlor's nominee trustees, the legal title did not have to be transferred, but this should not obscure the point. A trustee is a separate trustee to each of the trusts he administers, and must keep the property of the different settlements separate. For example, in this case, the trustees would be required either to divide the share certificates equally into six lots, or use the share serial numbers, to allocate particular lots to each of the different grandchildren's settlements (see Green (1984)). At a minimum, therefore, the case decides that an oral direction to bare trustees to hold the trust property on different trusts which they also administer is void unless in writing, though a later writing may be effective as a 'belt and braces' device to cure a prior invalid oral direction. However Green (1984) is clearly right to argue that the case must also be authority for the proposition that a direction to bare trustees to transfer the property to other trustees on different trusts is similarly void unless in writing, since the situations are identical except for the fact that in the former the trustees of both trusts happen to be the same persons, and this is no reason to distinguish between the two. However, in *Vandervell v IRC* the HL unanimously decided that an oral direction to a trustee to transfer the legal title to shares to different trustees on new trusts was valid. The HL didn't, apparently, realise they were deciding this, but they did.

6.22   Review the facts of *Vandervell v IRC* (**4.15**). The Revenue's first argument was that the first part of the transaction, the transfer of the shares held on bare trust for Vandervell by the Bank to the RCS on Vandervell's oral direction failed because this amounted to a disposition of his equitable interest under the bare trust, and therefore he needed to be in writing under s 53(1)(c). The point their Lordships thought they were deciding was this: Is A's oral direction to his trustee to transfer the legal title to shares held on bare trust to a third party absolutely, ie so the third party acquires the beneficial legal title to them, valid, or must it be in writing under s 53(1)(c)? They all decided that s 53(1)(c) did not apply and so the oral direction was valid. The reasoning of their various Lordships was brief and does not repay intense scrutiny (see Green (1984)). For his part, Lord Upjohn said this:

> [I]f the intention of the beneficial owner in directing the trustee to transfer the legal estate to X is that X should be the beneficial owner I can see no reason for any further document or further words in the document assigning the legal estate also expressly transferring the beneficial interest; the greater includes the less. X may be wise to secure some evidence that the beneficial owner intended him to take the beneficial interest in case his beneficial title is challenged at a later date but it certainly cannot, in my opinion, be a statutory requirement that to effect its passing there must be writing under section 53(1)(c).

To the extent that Lord Upjohn is satisfied because the transfer of a legal title involves a document anyway, and so a 'further' document seems superfluous, he has forgotten that the rule of law he has just propounded will apply equally to chattels, which can be transferred out of the trust by delivery – the result is that a trustee may give away trust property on the basis of an oral direction with no writing whatsoever. Second, the point is not whether a legal transfer normally includes the beneficial interest – of course it does; the question is whether it does in this case, where the beneficiary has not expressed in writing his intention to give up the beneficial interest. Finally, Lord Upjohn's concern that X, the recipient, might want some sort of writing is interesting, since it indicates he is fully aware of the kind of trouble that oral dispositions can cause, not only the X's of the world, but beneficiaries, who might be defrauded on the basis of supposed oral directions, and trustees, who may later have to prove oral directions to show that their actions were not in breach of trust.

6.23   You will recall, however, that their Lordships unanimously decided that the grant of the option from RCS to the trust company was Vandervell's own doing, somehow part of the arrangement he set in motion, most likely a conditional gift in equity giving rise to the option held on trust by the trust company (**4.16** et seq). That was why on the failure of the express trust of the option there was an ART in his favour. But if this is true, which it must be because that is the decision of the case, then the transfer by the bank of the shares was a transfer subject to some kind of equitable obligation, that is, subject to some trust. In consequence, their Lordship's decision that the oral direction by Vandervell was valid is authority for the proposition that an oral direction to a trustee to transfer property held on bare trust to another person *on trust* for a third party, is valid. This of course directly contradicts the broader basis of decision that Green (1984) argues is the right inter- pretation of *Grey*. Most commentators, however, take their Lordships at their word and it is textbook gospel to say that *Vandervell v IRC* decides only that an oral direction to a bare trustee to transfer the trust property to a third party absolutely for his own benefit is a valid disposition. This decision is commercially convenient, it is said, because it allows nominee trustees of shares, like brokers, to sell them on the oral directions of their beneficiaries. This justification is specious: the buying and selling of shares amounts to the trustee's exercise of his power of investment (**10.2**), and in general trustees never have to get the written direction of the beneficiaries to manage the trust property in this way, that is, s 53(1)(c) does not apply, because these 'dispositions' of the trust property are not the disposition of anyone's equitable interest, but merely dealings with the trust corpus in which those equitable interests lie. The only difference in the case of a bare trust is that the beneficiary has the right to tell the trustee how to exercise any of his powers, including the power of investment. The exercise of this power, then, has nothing to do with the trustee's defeating or extinguishing a beneficiary's interest by *giving* the trust property away, or extinguishing part or all of the beneficiary's entitlement under the trust (whatever its specific property) on the basis of oral instructions. As with the bare sub-trust/non-bare sub-trust distinction above, feel free to argue these points, but in an exam recite the accepted catechism to begin with.

6.24 The Vandervell saga continued in *Vandervell (No 2)*. Once the Revenue made its claim for the surtax, Vandervell and the trust company decided to exercise the option. The trustees used £5,000 from the children's trust and purchased the shares. The trustees wrote to the Revenue informing it that the shares were now held under the children's trust. As he had done for the RCS, Vandervell then exercised his control over his company and had various dividends declared on the shares over the next few years, amounting to more than a million pounds; in doing so he intended to provide for his children, and subsequently wrote a will leaving them nothing more. After his death, the executors of his will claimed that none of the preceding transactions had worked to displace Vandervell's beneficial interest in the option; therefore in the shares purchased through its exercise the dividends declared on those shares were his property in equity as well; hence the executors claimed that the trust company held the shares on trust for Vandervell's estate. (While Vandervell would be obliged to repay the £5,000 to the children's settlement plus interest, the use of the children's trust money did not mean they became the beneficial owners.)

6.25 The CA decided that a valid trust had been declared in favour of the children, and so the dividends properly belonged in the children's trust. The CA gave a number of reasons, most of which are insupportable. The only plausible one, and pertinent to our discussion, is in this passage from Lord Denning MR's decision:

> A resulting trust for the settlor is born and dies without writing at all. It comes into existence whenever there is a gap in the beneficial ownership.

It ceases to exist whenever that gap is filled by someone becoming beneficially entitled. As soon as the gap is filled by the creation or declaration of a valid trust, the resulting trust comes to an end. In this case, before the option was exercised, there was a gap in the beneficial ownership. So there was a resulting trust for Mr Vandervell. But, as soon as the option was exercised and the shares registered in the trustee's name, there was created a valid trust of the shares in favour of the children's settlement. Not being a trust of land, it could be created without any writing. A trust of personalty can be created without writing.

Hayton ((1996), 71) and Green (1984) both assume that what makes Lord Denning's decision even possibly correct is a finding on the facts (however erroneous) that the trust company had the power to declare trusts of the option or shares purchased with it; by exercising the option and holding the shares on trust for the children the trust company declared a trust that 'filled the gap' in the beneficial interest, which declaration the CA found did not attract the requirements of s 53(1)(c). On this view the case has a tinily narrow ambit, to wit: where a trustee holds property upon bare trust for a settlor, but that trustee has the power under the trust to declare new trusts of the property, his exercise of that power need not be in writing. But this interpretation cannot stand with the facts of *Vandervell v IRC*, nor with Lord Denning's own words: Vandervell held under an *ART*, an automatic resulting trust – a trust which simply cannot contain any special powers of this kind for the trustees or anyone else. An ART is the barest of bare trusts. So even if on the facts the express trust Vandervell had intended the trustee company to hold the option under gave the trustee company the power to declare new trusts, that trust failed for uncertainty, and nothing of it lingered in the ART that arose upon its failure. Rather, the CA decision, per Lord Denning MR at least, appears to be that because Vandervell was fully aware of and assented to the trustee company's exercise of the option to hold the shares on the children's trust, his assent amounted to an oral declaration of trust. So the case is authority for the proposition that where a settlor transfers personal property on trust, yet fails to make an effective oral declaration of trust, so that an ART in his favour arises, his subsequent oral declaration of trust is valid, his beneficial interest under the ART not requiring to be disposed of in writing under s 53(1)(c). This decision is not in conflict with *Grey*, since there the settlor intentionally transferred property on bare trust for himself. In *Vandervell (No 2)*, by contrast, Vandervell had tried to do what was perfectly legitimate, ie transfer personalty to a trustee on orally declared trusts, only the oral declaration failed for uncertainty. If the settlor remedies the situation by declaring trusts which are certain, why should that declaration require writing when the first didn't? This, indeed, would appear to be the one case where an exception to s 53(1)(c) is justified, since one might say that the second, valid, declaration is part and parcel of one transaction in which the holder of legal title to personal property (or the equivalent, assuming that Vandervell had the right to transfer the legal title to shares by orally directing the bare trustee Bank to do so, ie that *Vandervell v IRC* is rightly decided) transfers it on trust – and that, of course, is the one case of an oral declaration of trust which is perfectly valid, there being no equivalent to s 53(1)(b) which applies to personalty.

Releases, surrenders, and disclaimers

6.26   A release and a surrender are the same thing. A beneficiary surrenders his interest when he clearly indicates that he no longer wishes to benefit under the trust. If the beneficiary has a vested interest, for example a life interest in shares, what follows is an ART in favour of the settlor, if the trust is *inter vivos*, or in favour of the residuary legatees, if the trust is testamentary. If the beneficiary has only a contingent interest, eg he is the object of a discretionary trust or power of appointment, then his surrender just removes his name from the list of possible objects; there is no ART because he has no vested interest in any property upon which it could operate. Section 53(1)(c) should apply to surrenders or releases, since they clearly amount to the beneficiary's disposing of his entire equitable interest in favour of others, even if he does not know or care who will benefit under the trust by his surrender. There is, however, no good authority on the point, almost certainly because any careful trustee will insist that a beneficiary surrendering his interest will do so in writing. *IRC v Buchanan* is perhaps of some small assistance. There the CA interpreted 'disposition' as used in the Finance Act 1943 to include the exercise by a beneficiary of a special power under a trust to surrender her life interest in favour of her children.

6.27   A person *disclaims* an interest under a trust when he refuses any beneficial interest from the outset. The only authority for the application of s 53(1)(c) to disclaimers is *Re Paradise Motor Co* (1968). The CA held that 'a disclaimer operates by way of avoidance, and not by way of disposition'. A person disclaiming 'avoids', that is, never obtains any equitable interest, and therefore never acquires anything to dispose of: s 53(1)(c) has no application. This characterisation of disclaimers seemed entirely *ad hoc*, to avoid one more complication in a case in which the beneficial ownership to shares had to be determined on vague and ill-remembered oral testimony, and the authority referred to (*Re Stratton's Deed of Disclaimer* (1957), CA) actually takes the *opposite* line: that a beneficiary takes the benefit of an equitable interest from the moment the gift becomes effective in his favour, and therefore his disclaimer *does* amount to a disposition extinguishing a right he presently enjoys. Little weight, then, should be given to the decision. Certainly the purposes behind the section apply just as much to disclaimers as to other dispositions.

Agreements to assign or vary equitable interests for consideration

6.28 As we have seen (**5.3**), in the case of specifically enforceable contracts for the transfer or creation of rights in property, equity will impose a contractual constructive trust on the grantor of the interest. This doctrine operates just the same in the case of assignments of equitable interests where the interest is 'unique' in the sense that a failure to receive it under the contract cannot be adequately compensated by money damages. *Always* remember (some judges do not, eg Lord Wilberforce in *Chinn v Collins* (1981)) that this constructive trust depends on the availability of specific enforcement of the contract, and this in turn depends on whether the property is unique in this way. For example, private company shares are, since they cannot be freely purchased on the open market, but public company shares are not.

6.29 In the case of an agreement to assign equitable interests under a trust, the contractual constructive trust that arises is a constructive sub-trust. The beneficiary holds his equitable interest on constructive sub-trust for the purchaser. This is not a *bare* sub-trust until the purchaser pays up. Until he does, the beneficiary can refuse to assign the underlying equitable title. When the purchaser does pay up, the beneficiary holds his equitable interest on bare sub-trust for him. If you believe in the view that a bare sub-trustee drops out of the picture (**6.16**), then this sub-trust collapses, and the assignment is effective without any writing. If you demur from this view, the purchaser can insist upon the beneficiary transferring the equitable interest to him in writing. In either case, once the purchaser pays for the interest, he is the full beneficial owner of it and may enforce this interest with the full weight of equity behind him.

6.30   In *Oughtred v IRC* (1960) the contractual constructive trust was employed in an attempt to avoid stamp duty. Mrs Oughtred and her son Peter both held interests in a trust of private company shares. They agreed to vary their equitable interests, as a result of which Mrs Oughtred would acquire the entire beneficial interest in the shares under a bare trust; in return she would transfer a separate block of shares to Peter. Following the agreement, Mrs Oughtred and Peter executed a deed which declared that Mrs Oughtred now had the entire beneficial interest in the shares. The trustees then formally transferred the legal title to the shares to her absolutely. The question before the court was whether the formal share transfer attracted *ad valorem* stamp duty, or only a 50p duty because by virtue of the constructive trust, she already beneficially owned the shares in equity. The HL majority held that the formal share transfer attracted *ad valorem* stamp duty, but largely on what might be called the 'principles of stamp duty law'. Lord Jenkins held that while the purchaser under a specifically enforceable agreement has a proprietary interest of some sort, that doesn't prevent the subsequent transfer of the property which completes the transaction from being stampable *ad valorem*. After all, *ad valorem* stamp duty was payable (and remains payable) on documents transferring title to land even though the purchaser acquires the beneficial interest when the contract is agreed under the paradigm example of a contractual constructive trust. Lord Radcliffe dissented, accepting that upon the agreement being made Mrs Oughtred became the absolute owner in equity, and so felt that the share transfer did not transfer any beneficial interest.

6.31   The view that the constructive trust arising on the specifically enforceable agreement is sufficient to create an enforceable equitable interest has been endorsed since, outside the stamp duty context, by Megarry J in *Re Holt's Settlement* (1969), where there was an agreement to vary the interests under a trust, and by a majority of the CA in *DHN Food Distributors Ltd v Tower Hamlets London Borough Council* (1976) where the interest in question was in land. Most recently, the CA in *Neville v Wilson* (1996) held that the equitable interest in a private company shares could pass by virtue of a contractual constructive trust arising on a specifically enforceable, though oral, agreement.

Testamentary trusts: Wills Act 1837, s 9

6.32 Section 9 of the Wills Act 1837 provides that for a will to be valid it must be signed by the testator and attested by two witnesses. The section applies to any testamentary gift, including testamentary trusts. Unless properly signed and attested, an intended testamentary gift fails. Formalities are of obvious importance here, as a will takes effect when the testator is dead, so we will not hear any oral evidence from him as to his intentions. (It is worthwhile reviewing **2.36-2.40** at this point.)

Non-testamentary gifts giving an interest on death

6.33 Not every gift by which the donee takes an interest on the donor's death is testamentary. For example, I can declare that I hold Blackacre on trust for myself for life, and then for you. My personal representatives will hold Blackacre for you from my death. This *inter vivos* trust immediately vests in you a future interest in Blackacre. For a gift to be testamentary it must be *revokable* and *ambulatory*. A valid testamentary gift, ie one in a will, can be revoked or amended by the testator any time before his death, though he must do so in writing in compliance with s 9. A document which amends a will in part is called a 'codicil' and becomes part of the testator's whole will. 'Ambulatory' means that a will, while valid when properly made, just walks along without immediate effect, only operating when the testator dies. Thus gifts which would have been valid had they been made *inter vivos* when the testator made his will may fail at the time of his death, because in the interval things may happen to his legatees, to him, or to his property. A gift 'lapses' if the intended legatee predeceases the testator; the property goes back into the deceased's estate, and from there either to the residuary legatees or intestate successors. When a testator makes a will, he may leave specific gifts, eg of his car to X or his house to Y, or pecuniary legacies, eg £10,000 to Z. The testator might be rich when he makes his will, but bankrupt when he dies. Before any property is distributed under a will, all of the testator's creditors must be paid, and some of his property might have to be sold to do this. Thus the particular items of property and the total wealth distributable under the will can never be ascertained until his estate is administered. A specific gift *adeems*, ie fails, if the testator's estate does not include the specific property; if for example, he sold his car then any specific gift of the car in his will fails. A gift *abates* when a legatee's gift is proportionately reduced because there is insufficient property to satisfy all the testator's gifts. Thus a pecuniary legacy may abate anywhere down to zero if the testator is not as rich at his death as he thought he would be when he made his will.

6.34   Even if the *inter vivos* trust of Blackacre above is made revocable, it is not truly ambulatory since until revoked it cannot lapse by reason of your pre-deceasing me – if you die first then your successors will take the fee simple in Blackacre when I die. Nor will the gift adeem or abate if it turns out that I am deeply in debt when I die – the beneficial interest in Blackacre has been disposed of *inter vivos*, and cannot form part of my estate.

6.35   Besides *inter vivos* trusts giving an interest which vest on the death of a settlor, property can 'go' to others on one's death by operation of the right of survivorship on jointly held property (**1.15**). Thus if I transfer Blackacre to you and me as joint owners, or set up a joint bank account in our names, then if I die before you, you become the sole owner as my joint interest just disappears on my death. I can also take out a life insurance policy naming you as the beneficiary; the policy will pay out to you on my death. In *Re Danish Bacon Co Ltd Staff Pension Fund* (1971) Megarry J held that the right of an employee to nominate someone who will receive death in service benefits under a pension fund was not testamentary and therefore not subject to s 9 requirements. Megarry J also held that such nominations do not require writing under s 53(1)(c), since the nominator is not disposing of any subsisting equitable interest – the benefit only arises on his death. (See also *Baird v Baird* (1990).)

Informal testamentary trusts: secret and half secret trusts

6.36   Secret and half secret trusts are testamentary trusts which fail to comply with the Wills Act because they are not disclosed or disclosed fully in a valid will. Typically, a fully secret trust (FST) arises when T appears to take an absolute gift under A's will, but T has informally agreed with A to hold the property on trust for B. Secret trusts, however, can arise when there is no will at all: If T is A's intestate successor, he may also informally agree with A to hold the property he gets on trust for B (*Sellack v Harris* (1708)). After A's death, T, whether a legatee under A's will or A's intestate successor, is in the position to deny the informal trust and keep the property for himself fraudulently.

6.37 A half secret trust (HST) is one in which the existence of the trust is apparent on the face of the will, but the terms of the trust are not disclosed, eg 'I leave Blackacre to X on trusts which I have communicated to him'. Unlike the fully secret trust case, X is not in the position to deny the trust, and so cannot fraudulently take the property himself, for he is clearly a trustee for someone, and of course equity will not allow him to take the property beneficially.

6.38 Why should anyone wish to make informal testamentary trusts of this kind? One possibility in the case of fully secret trusts (FSTs) is simply that the legatee or intestate successor has persuaded the testator to do so, in order to perpetrate a fraud. The legatee might say, 'Don't give your property in a will – that will only lead to a great deal of squabbling in court – leave it all to me and I will do what you wish without fear of legal challenge.' Generally, however, secret trusts are intentionally created by the testator to ensure the secrecy of testamentary gifts. Since wills must be proved in a Court of Probate the contents of a will become public. (You can purchase of copy of anyone's will at Somerset House in London; they have done a brisk business in Princess Diana's will.) Testators wishing to provide for their secret lovers or other objects which would embarrass them or rather, harm their posthumous reputations, may instead of leaving them property by will leave property absolutely to a friend who agrees to hold the property on trust secretly for these beneficiaries. If the testator regards the obligation the legatee undertakes as only a moral obligation, and the legatee is trustworthy, then legal enforcement is not required. The imposition of such moral obligations does not interfere with the effect or policy of the Wills Act, for in law the legatee becomes the absolute owner under the will, and moral obligations to the deceased do not upset that. The question is whether and in what circumstances informal promises to a testator should be given legal effect? Should the enforcement be restricted to the case where the testator is truly a victim of an intentional fraud, or should a testator's scheme to create a secret testamentary gift, colluded in by his secret trustee, also be enforced despite the Wills Act? Originally, it appeared that equity would enforce the promise as a trust obligation over the property only in the case of actual fraud. Equity would not allow a fraudulent legatee to plead that the trust was invalid under the Act on the basis 'equity will not allow a statute enacted to prevent fraud to be used as an instrument of fraud'. This is the 'fraud theory' of the enforcement of secret trusts, but the leading nineteenth century case, *McCormick v Grogan* (1869), HL, is ambiguous as to what counts as fraud.

6.39   In *McCormick*, the testator left all his property to his friend Grogan. On his deathbed, he told Grogan that he had left all his property in his will to him, to which Grogan replied, 'Is that right?'. The testator also told him where to find the will and a letter with it. There was no further communication between the testator and Grogan. The letter to Grogan detailed a large number of gifts in pursuit of which he desired Grogan to apply the money, although he left much to Grogan's discretion. Grogan did not make all of the detailed gifts, and one non-recipient, McCormick, sought to have Grogan declared a secret trustee. The HL refused to do so, but their Lordships' conception of the fraud in response to which equity will make the legatee a trustee is ambiguous. Their reasons suggest either that the necessary fraud is (1) a fraudulent scheme on the defendant's part *to induce* the property owner either to make a will in the defendant's favour (or not revoke a will in his favour), or refrain from making a will because the defendant will take on his intestacy, in which the defendant misrepresents his true intentions, falsely promising to carry out the owner's wishes, thereby acquiring the owner's property on his death for his own benefit; or (2) merely the defendant's 'fraudulent' refusal, when he receives the property on the owner's death, to comply with an agreement with the original owner upon which the owner relied in disposing of the property as he did. (1) is obviously much narrower, and amounts to saying that a testator who attempts to make informal testamentary gifts will fail to do so by operation of the Wills Act, unless he was fraudulently induced to avoid making a valid testamentary gift by a legatee or intestate successor who benefits from the fraud. (2) essentially allows the testator to opt out of the strictures of the Wills Act; so long as he effectively communicates his testamentary intentions to a legatee or intestate successor, who agrees to carry them out, this joint endeavour to defy the Wills Act will succeed because equity will enforce the agreement against the legatee.

6.40   Whatever the actual state of the authorities in 1869 which led to their Lordships' ambiguous characterisation, (2) is the way the law has developed. As stated by Lord Sterndale MR in *Re Gardner* (1920):

> The obligation upon the [secret trustee] seems to me to arise from this, that he takes the property in accordance with and upon an understanding

to abide by the wishes of the testatrix, and if he were to dispose of it in any other way he would be committing a breach of trust, or as it has been called in some of the cases a fraud. I do not think it matters what you call it. The breach of trust or the fraud would arise when he attempted to deal with the money contrary to the terms on which he took it.

The recent case of *Re Snowden* (1979) provides a good example of the current ambit of the court's willingness to enforce FSTs. There an indecisive testatrix, after making various particular gifts in her will, left the residue of her estate to her brother, he knowing her wishes for the money. Her brother died six days after she did, and the question was whether on very insufficient evidence a trust of the residue was undertaken by him. Megarry VC found that the testatrix had only imposed a moral, not a legal, obligation upon her brother, so there was no secret trust. However, he pointed out that only some cases of secret trust involved the possibility of fraud, and there was none here – the secret trustee could not personally benefit by any fraud, for he had died – the question was whether there was a secret trust which would take the property out of his estate on death. While the burden of proof that a secret trust exists lies on the person who asserts its existence, in cases where there is no fraud the normal civil standard of proof, ie what is more likely on the balance of probabilities, applies. The state of the law now is well put by Hayton ((1996), pp 92-93):

> Testators, today, who do not want their testamentary wishes to become public by admission to probate as part of their will can take advantage of the doctrine of secret trusts to make provision for mistresses, illegitimate children, relatives whom they do not wish to appear to be helping or organisations which they do not wish to appear to be helping. Indecisive, aged testators can also leave everything by will absolutely to their solicitors, from time to time calling upon or phoning their solicitors with their latest wishes.

Equity's enforcement of secret trusts has, therefore, allowed testators to make informal, even oral, testamentary dispositions in flat defiance of the Wills Act; to opt out of it, as it were. The only 'fraud' necessary is the legatee's refusal to carry out his agreement with the testator, the agreement being to carry out an informal testamentary disposition so that the testator can bypass the provisions of the Wills Act. In its confused appreciation of fraudulent behaviour in this context equity allows a testator to make an informal will just because he uses a human instrument, ie his legatee, to do so. By reposing his informal, even oral, will in this human vessel he can succeed where another testator committing his wishes to an unattested paper cannot, because the unattested paper 'cannot commit fraud', even though the human legatee and the unattested paper are fulfilling exactly the same function.

Fraud and HSTs

6.41   The trustee of an HST can lie about the trust upon which he holds the property, telling the world it was for his own mistress rather than the testator's, for instance, but he cannot deny there is any trust and take the property for himself like the fully secret trustee can, as he is a trustee on the face of the will. As a result, because the court would only get round the Wills Act in the case of fraud, it was not settled until the 1929 HL decision in *Blackwell v Blackwell* whether HSTs should be enforced. The gift in *Blackwell* was as follows: 'I give and bequeath to my friends ... the sum of twelve thousand pounds free of all duties upon trust to invest the same as they in their uncontrolled discretion shall think fit and to apply the income and interest arising therefrom yearly and every year for the purposes indicated by me to them ...' The appellants argued that where the trustee was named in the will, there could be no fraud under any version of the fraud theory in *McCormick v Grogan*; the question was merely one of for whom is the trust held; if there is no further validly expressed intention which specifies the trust terms, then the trust fails and the trustee holds under an ART for the residuary legatees. The HL disagreed, allowing parol evidence to prove the terms of the trust. The HL removed this impediment by adopting a new variation on 'fraud'. According to Lord Buckmaster, the defendant's fraud is not falsely to induce the testator to make a gift in the defendant's favour, nor to refuse to comply with his promise to the testator, but to cheat the testator's intended donees of their intended benefits – the fraud is a fraud on the secret beneficiaries.

6.42   This reasoning is circular. As Sheridan (1951) points out, to consider the fraud as a fraud 'on the beneficiaries' begs the question. There is no fraud on an intended beneficiary if a gift intended for him 'fails' for formal invalidity, for if it is an invalid trust, he is not a beneficiary. The question is whether a half-secret trust is a valid or invalid *means* of making someone a beneficiary despite the Wills Act. If it is not, then there is no fraud. By thinking of the intended beneficiaries *as* properly entitled beneficiaries from the outset, is to assume what needs to be shown, ie that failing to enforce a half-secret trust abets a fraud.

The 'dehors the will' theory of HSTs

6.43 Viscount Sumner provided a further reason for the result, articulating what is now conventionally called the '*dehors* (ie outside) the will' theory of secret trusts:

> The limits, beyond which the rules as to unspecified trusts must not be carried, have often been discussed. A testator cannot reserve to himself a power of making future unwitnessed dispositions by merely naming a trustee and leaving the purposes of the trust to be supplied afterwards, nor can a legatee give testamentary validity to an unexecuted codicil by accepting an indefinite trust, never communicated to him in the testator's lifetime. ... To hold otherwise would indeed be to 'give the go-by' to the requirement of the Wills Act, because he did not choose to comply with them. It is communication of the purpose to the legatee, coupled with the acquiescence or promise on his part, that removes the matter from the provisions of the Wills Act and brings it within the law of trusts, as applied in this instance to trustees, who happen to be legatees.

Under the '*dehors* the will' theory, secret trusts are regarded as *inter vivos* declarations of trust by the testator; the only atypical feature is that the trusts are not constituted, ie the property is not transferred into the hands of the trustee, until the testator's death, through his will. Therefore secret trusts operate outside the will, and therefore the Wills Act has no application.

6.44 The *dehors* the will theory is fundamentally unsound. In the first place, the theory should be called the '*dehors* the Wills Act' theory to reflect what it means. The argument is that secret trusts are *inter vivos* trusts, therefore not testamentary, therefore not within the ambit of the Wills Act. Of course secret trusts are outside the *will*: wholly in the case of FSTs, partly in the case of HSTs. But that entails nothing whatsoever about the application of the Wills Act – every informal testamentary disposition is outside the will; if it were a formally valid testamentary disposition it would *be* a will, or part of one. So the theory depends upon establishing that secret trusts are not testamentary dispositions at all, so the formality requirements of the Wills Act simply do not apply.

6.45   But, alas, secret trusts *are* testamentary dispositions. They are perfectly revocable by the testator – he can either revoke the trust *per se* by communicating with his secret trustee and cancelling or modifying the arrangement, or more simply, he can execute another will deleting or modifying the gift to his legatee (or by just writing a will if the fully secret trust operates on intestacy), thus ensuring that the '*inter vivos*' trust he declared is never constituted. Secondly, and more fundamentally, such a trust simply cannot be an effective *inter vivos* trust because in order to be effective the testator would be declaring a trust of 'future' property, and such a declaration is invalid, ie creates no trust. Future property just refers to property which doesn't exist yet. Now you might think that if I own Blackacre, and I tell you that I'm giving it to you in my will to hold on trust for Albert, then what's wrong with that? Blackacre exists doesn't it? The point however is that I'm not declaring a trust over Blackacre now – I could do that, but that would *take Blackacre out of my estate on death*. But I haven't done that. I am declaring a trust over property which may or may not be in my estate on death. Even if I do my utmost to ensure that Blackacre will be in my estate, it may turn out that I have to sell it before I die, or I may die in such debt that Blackacre will have to be sold by my executors. This, of course, is even more obvious in the case of a pecuniary legacy, eg a secret trust of £5,000. There is a further problem in the case of an *inter vivos* trust of a pecuniary legacy: unless you actually identify the actual money, ie the very notes and coins, the trust fails for uncertainty of subject matter. A person cannot just say, 'I now hold £5,000 on trust for you', even if he's worth millions; before the trust is valid he must segregate or otherwise identify the money which is the property of the trust (**7.35** et seq). Clearly, there's no way of doing that now with money only identified some indefinite time in the future by executors following their administration of the estate. Therefore a legatee's hope of receiving any property of any kind under a will is considered by the law to be a mere *spes*, Latin for a mere expectancy, which one can never count upon getting. As a testator, I am in no better position in this respect before I die than a legatee. So the fact of the matter is that secret trusts are imposed over property which will only be ascertained upon the administration of the testator's estate, and are subject to ademption and abatement like any other such gifts (for an interesting example, see *Re Maddock* (1902)). They are, therefore, ambulatory, and therefore, testamentary. Of course the Wills Act applies to them. The *dehors* the will theory is just an attempt to cloak the embarrassing jam equity has got itself into with its willingness to flout the Wills Act.

6.46 It is submitted that the true reason for the decision in *Blackwell* is the obvious *pragmatic* one, here stated by Viscount Sumner:

> In[both fully and half secret trusts] the testator's wishes are incompletely expressed in his will. Why should equity, over a mere matter of words, give effect to them in one case and frustrate them in the other?

In other words, though there might be a valid *juridical* basis for enforcing FSTs but not HSTs, ie that there's no possibility of fraud in any meaningful sense in the latter, the different rules would be in *pragmatic* conflict, ie, the law would look like an ass. Once equity has sold the Wills Act up the river by allowing testators to give it 'the go-by' with FSTs, it seems rather irrational to stop there and deny equity's enforcement to HSTs, and might well lead to apparent injustice, since from the testator's perspective the decision to use the words 'on trust' in his will can hardly seem to him to be of much consequence; furthermore, it would seem strange if a person who complied with the Wills Act as much as he could while keeping his gifts secret, by declaring in his will that the gift was held on trust, should be in a worse position than one who keeps everything secret. The result is, then, that both FSTs and HSTs, if properly created, are formally invalid testamentary trusts which equity will enforce.

6.47 Although the '*dehors* the will' theory is insupportable, certain decisions appear to depend upon it. In *Re Young* (1950), the testator's chauffeur was to receive a gift under an HST, but he had also attested the will; under s 15 of the Wills Act 1837, gifts to attesting witnesses fail (attesting witnesses must be able to give unbiased evidence about the validity of the will's execution, and a legatee's interest might bias him in favour of validity). Dankwerts J held that the chauffeur did not take 'under the will', so was able to receive the gift under the HST. Section 15 does not normally apply to trustees in a will, for they receive no *beneficial* interest, but presumably, if the *dehors* the will theory applies, s 15 should defeat both an HST and an FST if the trustee attests the will. This may appear a bit odd in the case of the HST, for the trustee is identified as a trustee on the face of the will. But the *dehors* story says that he is not a trustee *under the will*, so s 15 should apply to him as much as to a trustee of an FST. Of course, one might argue that s 15 should not apply to any trustee, secret or not, since none take a beneficial interest, but such a view cannot stand alongside *Re Young*, for that would be to have it both ways.

6.48   If secret trusts are *inter vivos* trusts, then s 53 should apply; in particular, s 53(1)(b) should apply to secret trusts of land. North J accepted *obiter* in *Re Baillie* (1886) that formal requirements would apply to an HST of land; An oral FST of land was found to be valid in *Ottaway v Norman* (1971), although it must be stressed that the formalities point was not raised.

6.49   An alternative version of the '*dehors*' theory was advanced by Romer J in *Re Gardner (No 2)* (1923), which is that the secret *trustee* is the one that declares an *inter vivos* trust over the property he shall receive under the will; that of course, is even more obviously ineffective as a declaration of trust over a mere *spes*. Such a declaration is at most a declaration of a future intention, and a mere intention will not be enforced by equity. Romer J decided that the interest that was to go to a beneficiary under a secret trust did not lapse when she pre-deceased the testator, because she was a beneficiary not under a testamentary trust, but under the *inter vivos* trust declared by the secret trustee. This logically follows from the finding that the legatee declares himself a secret trustee, but for the reason stated, such a trust is invalid, so the decision should not be followed.

Communication and acceptance

6.50   In order to prove an FST or an HST, the evidence must show (1) the intention of the testator to create a trust; (2) timely communication of that intention to the intended trustee; and (3) timely acceptance by the intended trustee of the trust obligation. The communication may be by the testator's agent (*Moss v Cooper* (1861)), and so long as the secret trustee undertakes the obligation to carry out the trust, he may 'sail under sealed orders', that is, the testator can provide him with an envelope containing the terms of the trust not to be opened until his death (*Re Keen* (1936); *Re Boyes* (1884); *McCormick*). However, the testator must have decided the terms of the trust when the communication is made; 'The devisee or legatee cannot by accepting an indefinite trust enable the testator to make an unattested codicil' (*Re Boyes*). There must be an actual acceptance of or acquiescence in the trust obligation (*McCormick*); the imposition of a merely moral obligation is insufficient (*McCormick; Re Snowden*).

6.51   The orthodoxy governing what counts as timely communication and acceptance of the trust differs for FSTs and HSTs: an FST must be communicated to and accepted by the secret trustee before or after the execution of the will, but before the testator's death (*Moss v Cooper*); the rationale here is that because a will is revocable, he may execute his will and then communicate the trust to the intended secret trustee; if the latter refuses the trust obligation, the testator can make another will revoking the gift and leaving the property to someone else (*Re Gardner*, per Warrington LJ). In contrast, HSTs must be communicated before or at the same time as the making of the will.

6.52 This stricter HST rule for timely communication and acceptance arises for no good juridical reason, since the testator can still revoke the gift in the will if his intended trustee does not agree to undertake the trust just as easily as the testator of an FST can. Commentators almost universally abhor the difference in the communication rules, and, for example, in Ireland (*Re Browne* [1944] IR 90) and the US (Restatement of Trusts, para 55(c), (h)), the rule that communication and acceptance may occur any time before the testator's death applies to HSTs as well as FSTs.

6.53 The leading case is the CA decision in *Re Keen* (1937) £10,000 was given to two trustees:

> ... to be held upon and disposed of by them among such person, persons, or charities as <u>may</u> be notified by me to them or either of them during my lifetime.

The court found that before the execution of the will, one trustee was adequately notified as to the terms of the trust by being given a sealed envelope containing the name of the intended beneficiary; though told not to open it until the testator's death, he understood it to contain the terms of the trust: 'a ship which sails under sealed orders is sailing under orders though the exact terms are not ascertained by the captain till later'. The trust failed, however, for two reasons. The first, which is sometimes referred to as the 'broad' ratio, was that Lord Wright MR found that 'may' (underlined above) referred to future communication of the trusts, ie communication after the execution of the will. Such a clause was bad: because it contemplated future dispositions, the testator was reserving to himself the power to make future unwitnessed dispositions and so giving the 'go-by' to the Wills Act, and it therefore violated the principles laid down by Viscount Sumner in *Blackwell*. Even if the clause could be read to encompass prior communications, so long as it contemplated future ones it must be invalid.

6.54 The 'narrow' ratio was simply that the evidence of the trust, ie a trust communicated prior to the execution of the will, was inconsistent with the clause in the will as Lord Wright MR interpreted it, not necessarily defensibly, ie as encompassing only future declarations of trust. One may argue that the broad ratio was unnecessary for the decision, and therefore strictly speaking, *obiter*, so that the actual rule governing post-execution communications of HSTs remains open. Nevertheless, the rule invalidating post-execution communications is generally regarded as settled, if wrong. In *Re Bateman* (1970) the rule was applied as if no doubt could be entertained about it.

6.55 The rule is typically explained as the result of a confusion of the doctrine of HSTs with the rule governing the incorporation by reference of documents into wills. Where a will refers to a document existing when the will is executed, that document becomes part of the properly attested will even though it is not itself properly attested; in other words, it is incorporated into the will. Because the existence of the half secret *trustee* is identified in the will, the courts have confused this with a reference to a *trust declaration* which has been made when the will is executed. For this reason, the courts have seen it somehow appropriate to limit the enforcement of HSTs to those communicated and accepted prior to or contemporaneously with the will's execution. If it weren't for this confusion, the argument goes, then surely the FST rule would apply, because as stated above, the FST can give the go-by to the Wills Act by allowing post-execution communications, so why not HSTs?

6.56 Perhaps, however, it is not that the judges have confused the enforcement of HST with the incorporation of documents, but have realised the *pragmatic* conflict that would arise between the enforcement of HSTs and the doctrine of incorporation by reference if post-execution communications were allowed. The crucial point is that both HSTs and incorporable documents are clearly referred to in the will. Whatever theory of HSTs you prefer, the proving of the HST looks like an exercise in filling in a gap in the will, much as the incorporation of an outside document does. Indeed, the practical similarities between HSTs and documents incorporated by reference are so apparent that Matthews (1979) argues that the *juridical* basis of HSTs is an expanded doctrine of incorporation by reference, ie to incorporate properly evidenced oral testamentary trusts. In view of this, a more expansive rule for admitting HSTs, ie allowing the proof of HSTs created after the execution of the will, would have the embarrassing consequence, embarrassing, that is, for any jurisdiction which is supposed to operate under the formalities of a Wills Act, of giving a wider ambit to unattested *oral* testamentary dispositions referred to in a will than to unattested *written* ones. As a result, the communication rules for HSTs may best be understood simply as an unprincipled but pragmatic half-way house between the doctrines of FSTs and incorporation by reference, and that it is futile to search for any more theoretically satisfying basis. The corollary is, of course, that the courts find it somewhat less embarrassing to have different communications rules for different secret trusts purely on the basis of the insertion of the word 'on trust' in the document.

Failure of a secret trust to be established

6.57   If the testator intends to create an FST, but fails to communicate it to the trustee and so is not accepted by him before the testator dies, then the gift under the will is not impressed with any trust, and the trustee takes absolutely (*Wallgrave v Tebbs* (1855); *Proby v Landor* (1860)). In general, if only one of two trustees is informed of and accepts the trust before the testator's death, then only he will be bound by the trust; the other receives his property absolutely, having undertaken no trust obligation. However, there appears to be a special rule for the case of trustees who receive the property as joint tenants (as opposed to as tenants in common (see **1.15**)) where only one joint tenant has accepted the trust before the testator makes his will; in that case both are bound. In *Re Stead* (1899) Farwell J doubted that any good reason supported this rule, but accepted it as authoritative. Perrins (1972) argues that the uninformed legatee should only be bound by the representation of his co-legatee when that representation induced the testator either to make a gift to the two of them in his will or not revoke a gift to the two of them in his will, on the principle that no one should profit from the fraud of another, and that nothing should turn on whether the legatees take as joint tenants or tenants in common.

6.58   If a legatee is told that he is to hold on trust, but the terms of the trust are never communicated to the trustee within the testator's lifetime, he is still a secret trustee, though on a trust which fails: he will hold the property on ART for residuary beneficiaries or intestate successors (*Re Boyes* (1884)). The trustee will similarly hold on ART if the trust is fully communicated, but the trust fails, like any testamentary trust might fail, for uncertainty (see chapter 6) or illegality: thus, in *Moss v Cooper*, the *residuary legatees* successfully pleaded that the legatees held the property they received on a secret trust to apply his property to charitable purpose in violation of the Mortmain and Charitable Uses Act 1736; the trust was proven, failed for illegality, and the secret trustees therefore held the property on ART for the residuary legatees.

6.59　No cases have decided what should happen if a fully secret trustee were to renounce the gift or predecease the testator. In *Re Maddock* (1902) Cozens-Hardy LJ opined *obiter* that if the legatee renounced the gift or died during the lifetime of the testator, the secret beneficiaries would get nothing. In *Blackwell*, by contrast, Lord Buckmaster said *obiter* that he 'entertained no doubt' that if an FST were proved on the evidence, the court would not allow it to be defeated by the trustee's renunciation. He did not consider the case of a fully secret trustee who predeceased the testator. This should probably be dealt with as a problem of timing and reliance: does the testator have a realistic opportunity to alter his will? If yes, then the trust should fail if the trustee renounces, or predeceases the testator. If the testator is unable to make a new will, the trust should be proved against the secret trustee or his personal representative if dead. No such problems arise in the case of HSTs, for the court will not allow a trust to fail for want of a trustee, (assuming the terms of the trust can be proved despite the half secret trustee's death).

6.60　In the case of HSTs, the result of any failure of the testator to specify the trusts will be that the trustee will hold the trust property for the residuary legatees, or if none, for the intestate successors. In *Re Colin Cooper* (1939) the testator made a will in which £5,000 was given to two trustees under an HST, having communicated the trust before the execution of the will. Two days before he died, he revoked the will except for the HST, but he also increased the sum to be held on the HST to £10,000; the increase was not communicated to the trustees, and the CA held (1), that the first £5,000 was to be held on the half-secret trusts, for that was the extent of the subject matter communicated; the remainder went on ART into the estate, and (2) the fact that the gift of £5,000 was technically not the one in the first will, ie the will to which the communication of the trust applied, did not matter, as they were in substance the same gift. The general principle of (1), that the trust only binds to the extent communicated, applies to fully secret trusts as well. However, there the question arises, who would get the increase? One might say that, as the increase was not impressed by any communicated trust, then the trustees should take it as an absolute gift. On the other hand, by parity of reasoning with *Re Boyes*, one might argue that once obliged, even the fully secret trustee can only take *as* a trustee, so any increase which fails to get into the trust cannot go to him beneficially, but must be held on ART.

6.61 In the case of HSTs, complications can arise between the directions given in the will and the directions communicated to the trustee – the rule is that the instructions in the will prevail in any conflict. In *Re Huxtable* (1902), £4,000 was given in the will for charitable purposes agreed by the testator and the trustee. Evidence was admissible to prove the charity was for the relief of sick and poor members of the Church of England, but not admissible to prove that only the income on £4,000 was to be spent this way, and that the trustee was to dispose of the principal as he wished on his death, for on the face of the will the whole £4,000 was given to charity, and evidence of the trustee's power to dispose of the principal would contradict the will. *Re Gardner* provides something of a contrast. The testatrix left all her property to her husband for his benefit during his life, 'knowing that he will carry out my wishes'. Thus at first glance this gift of a life estate might appear to be the subject matter of an HST (though the words do not clearly manifest an intention to create a trust; see **7.11**), with an intestacy with respect to the remainder, since that was not disposed of by the will. However, in view of the evidence, the CA decided that the testatrix's intention was to give her husband the benefit of the life estate, while he held the remainder which came to him as her intestate successor under a fully secret trust to give it to certain beneficiaries under his will.

6.62 The question also arises whether evidence of the half secret trust can show that the half secret trustee is himself to benefit from the trust. In general a person named as a trustee may only take a beneficial interest if that is clearly indicated, and on the face of the will in an HST, that obviously is not the case, so in that sense evidence proving that the trustee is to take under an HST may be regarded as contradicting the will. In *Re Rees* (1949) the testator left his entire estate to his solicitor and a friend as trustees 'they well knowing my wishes concerning the same'. The friend died shortly after the testator, and the evidence of the solicitor was that the trustees were to make certain payments and keep the surplus. The CA held that the substantial surplus went on intestacy. Lord Evershed, MR said that evidence they were to take a beneficial interest would conflict with the terms of the will, since they were named as trustees. In *Re Tyler* (1967), Pennycuick J stated *obiter* that he did not find this reasoning 'easy' and that in principle, evidence is admissible to prove all the terms of a trust, including a trust in favour of a trustee. Evershed MR's decision undoubtedly turned in part on the consideration that:

> In the general public interest it seems to me desirable that, if a testator wishes his property to go to his solicitor and the solicitor prepares the will, that intention on the part of the testator should appear plainly in the will and should not be arrived at by the more oblique method of what is sometimes called a secret trust.

6.63 As is apparent from the tone of the foregoing, the present author thinks that equity should not enforce secret trusts and half secret trusts, but should require them to fail as testamentary gifts not complying with the Wills Act, except in rare cases where a feckless testator really has been fraudulently induced to make a gift to the legatee, for example by being told that the law will not allow him to give his intended beneficiary any property under a will. No assistance should be given to any scheme by the testator to avoid the Act. *Inter vivos* trusts, joint tenancy, and insurance policies can all be used to make secret post-mortem gifts by those who cannot come clean about their preferred objects of bounty even after their death. Equity should not provide a further means which so exhorbitantly flouts the policy of the Act.

Further Reading

Youdan (1984); Green (1984); Sheridan(1951); Hodge (1980); Matthews (1979); Perrins(1985); Watkin (1981).

Must read cases: *Rochefoucauld v Boustead* (1897); *Grey v IRC* (1959), *Vandervell v IRC* (1966), and *Re Vandervell (No 2)* (1974); *McCormick v Grogan* (1869); *Blackwell v Blackwell* (1929); *Re Keen* (1936).

Self-test questions

1. Explain the operation of s 53(1)(b) of the Law of Property Act 1925 and the doctrine of *Rochefoucauld v Boustead*.

2. What do *Grey v IRC*, *Vandervell v IRC*, and *Re Vandervell (No 2)* decide?

3. Trustbank plc holds 50,000 shares of Zinc Ltd as nominee trustee for Sam. Sam transfers 150,000 shares of Gold Ltd to Trustbank stating that he wishes to provide for his children.

(i) Sam orally directs Trustbank to hold 50,000 shares of Zinc on trust for his three children, Albert, Jane, and Charlotte, in such shares as Trustbank shall in its absolute discretion appoint. Several months later, for revenue purposes, Trustbank makes a written declaration that it holds the shares on trust for the children.

(ii) Sam orally directs Trustbank to transfer 50,000 Gold shares to Albert absolutely, which it does.

(iii) Sam orally directs Trustbank to hold 50,000 of the Gold shares on trust for Jane. Sam tells Jane that he has done so, and Jane demands that Trustbank transfer the shares to her, which it does.

(iv) Trustbank declares that it holds the remaining 50,000 shares of Gold on trust for Charlotte.

Sam dies, leaving his entire estate to his lover, Fred. Fred disputes the validity of the preceeding transactions. Discuss.

4. In 1993 Samuel made his will, leaving £50,000 to Tina and Trish, and Blackacre to John 'on trust for such persons as I shall instruct him'. In 1994 Samuel mailed Tina a letter which enclosed a sealed envelope; the letter instructed Tina that the sealed envelope was not to be opened until after Samuel's death. Also in 1994, Samuel had lunch with John and told him that he should hold Blackacre on trust for Margaret, Samuel's mistress; John agreed to do so. Samuel died a couple of weeks ago. Tina opened the sealed envelope to discover that it states that she and Trish are to hold the £50,000 on trust for Samuel's illegitimate daughter, Francesca.

Advise Margaret and Francesca.

5.   Is there a theoretical basis for secret trusts which justifies their enforcement?

CHAPTER SEVEN

Certainty

SUMMARY

Certainty of intention: the family gift context

Certainty of intention: the commercial context

Certainty of subject matter and objects: common issues

Certainty of Subject Matter – particular issues: the 'whatever is left' trust; the identification of specific property out of a larger amount

Certainty of Objects – particular issues: outright gifts, fixed trusts, and *Burrough v Philcox* trusts; powers and *McPhail* trusts; conditions precedent defining a class

Administrative unworkability and capriciousness

Effects of uncertainty

7.1 A declaration of trust must be 'certain', which means that a settlor must declare the terms of the trust with sufficient 'certainty' or precision for the trustees to know what they must do, or the intended trust fails.

The three certainties

7.2 The traditional elements of this sufficiency of declaration are known as the 'three certainties', following *Knight v Knight* (1840): certainty of intention, certainty of subject matter, and certainty of objects. The first concerns the question whether what the putative settlor did or said amounts to a declaration of a trust over his property. The second requires that the property which is to form the trust corpus is identifiable. The third requires that the intended beneficiaries, the 'objects' of the trust, are identifiable.

One should distinguish the certainty of intention from the other Certainty of intention is like the 'intention to create legal relations' ontract law; it concerns the question whether the putative settlor really meant to create a trust at all. When we deal with the second and third certainties, we are past that point. We know what the person intended, whether a trust, a power of appointment, or an outright gift: these secondary certainties concern the efficacy of the settlor's expression, or the workability of his intentions: does he provide an instruction that can be carried out? Or is it too vague, or too difficult, or even impossible to implement? A severe difficulty in identifying the subject matter or objects may indicate that no trust was intended: uncertainty of subject matter (*Mussoorie Bank Ltd v Raynor* (1882)) or objects (see, eg *Lambe v Eames* (1871)) has a 'reflex action' which indicates an uncertainty of intention to create a trust.

Certainty of intention: the family gift context

7.4 'Equity looks to intent, not form' fully applies to declarations of trust. No particular formula is necessary, not even the use of the word 'trust'. Neither is it necessary for the settlor to know that, technically, that is what he is doing. In *Paul v Constance* (1977) Mr Paul and Mrs Constance lived together as man and wife though not legally married. He opened a bank account in his own name with money received as compensation for an injury at work. Because of their dealings with the account – they both drew upon it to play bingo and deposited their winnings in it – and because on several occasions Mr Paul declared to Mrs Constance, 'the money is as much yours as mine', the Court held him to have declared a trust of the property in equal shares for himself and Mrs Constance. Thus very informal declarations of trust of personalty are possible (as we have seen, writing is required in the case of land (**6.6**)).

7.5 Many trusts are testamentary gifts, so finding a trust will often depend on construing wills to infer the testator's 'intention'. Uncertainty can arise because there are ways in which a testator may deal with his property which might superficially resemble trusts, but are not. Wills sometimes contain gifts subject to charges: for example, 'I give the leasehold interest on my factory to James, my son, absolutely, but subject to his paying £10,000 per annum to my widow, Jane'. The gift has been made subject to a charge, but James is not a trustee for his mother. Wills may also contain conditional gifts, eg 'Blackacre to James on condition he pays £10,000 per annum to my widow for life, and upon his failure to do so, to Claire for life'. If James doesn't comply with the condition, then the property will go to Claire. But again, James is not a trustee.

Trust or power of appointment?

7.6 It may also be unclear whether a settlor intends to impose a trust on the recipient or intends merely to give him a power of appointment. Consider: '£100,000 to my trustees for distribution to such of my relations as my trustees shall in their absolute discretion think fit': does 'for distribution' mean 'to be distributed', an imperative direction imposing an obligation upon them to distribute, or is it rather to be interpreted as 'available for distribution', thus creating no obligation but giving the trustees a power which they may exercise if they so choose?

7.7 Several rules of construction may determine whether a trust or a power of appointment is intended:

(1) If there is an explicit gift over in default of appointment, eg 'my shares in X company to my trustees, with power to appoint to my children in such portions as my trustees shall in their absolute discretion decide, and in default of appointment, to the London School of Economics', there is a power of appointment, for if the settlor provides for the case where the trustees did not appoint, clearly they are under no duty to do so.

(2) The second rule is a specification of the first. In order to find a power on the basis of a gift over, the gift over must specifically arise on default of appointment. For example, a residuary gift (**2.37**) is not a gift over for this purpose. Residuary clauses deal with failures of all kinds; nothing, therefore, can be inferred about any specific gift just because the will contains a residuary clause.

(3) Finally, if there is no gift over in default of appointment, one must determine the true intentions of the testator by construing the will or settlement as a whole. For example if the testator uses words which clearly indicate his intention to create a trust with respect to some of his gifts, but does not in the gift under consideration, the court is apt to conclude that there is no trust – the testator knew

what words to use to create a trust, and did not (see *Re Weekes'
Settlement* (1897)). The settlor's use of the word 'power' is not
determinative, but words such as 'shall' or 'to be', as in 'shall
distribute' or 'to be divided amongst' seem quite clearly to be
imperative, strongly indicating the imposition of a duty, and thus a
trust. Finally, where a trust is intended but fails for a reason that would
not invalidate a similarly framed power, the court will not save the
gift by treating it as a power (*IRC v Broadway Cottages Trust* (1955);
Re Shaw (1957)).

7.8 Settlors may create a power of appointment 'coupled' with an implied
trust in default of appointment. It is perfectly possible to give someone a
power to appoint certain property, in default of which appointment the
property goes either to the objects of the power itself, rather than to
another class of objects. In cases where there is a gift over in default to
the same people who are the objects of the power of appointment, then
the power is, in essence, nothing more than a power to vary the shares
that the objects would otherwise receive under the gift over.

7.9 In *Re Weekes' Settlement* (1897) a testatrix left property to her
husband with a 'power to dispose of all such property by will amongst
our children in accordance with the power granted to him as regards
the other property which I have under my marriage settlements'. There
was no gift over, so that did not decide the issue. The husband died
intestate. The children argued that the testatrix's words indicated *a
general intention* that the husband should leave the property in question
to all the children in equal shares if he didn't appoint particular shares
to them, in other words, that he was given a power coupled with an
implied trust in default of appointment. Their argument failed. The court
did not find it possible to construe from the document that the property
should be held on trust for all the children jointly if he did not appoint.

7.10 In *Burrough v Philcox* (1840) the pertinent instruction in the will
was as follows:

> ... but in case my son and daughter should both of them die without
> leaving lawful issue, then for the said estates to be disposed of as shall be
> hereinafter mentioned, that is to say, the longest liver of my two children
> shall have the power, by a will, properly attested, in writing, to dispose
> of all my real and personal estates amongst my nephews and nieces or

their children, either all to one of them, or to as many of them as my surviving child shall think proper.

Here the court found a general intention that the class of nieces and nephews and their children should benefit. Lord Cottenham LC said:

[W]hen there appears a general intention in favour of a class, and a particular intention in favour of individuals of a class to be selected by another person, and the particular intention fails, from that selection not being made, the Court will carry into effect the general intention in favour of the class ... and in such case, the Court will not permit the objects of the power to suffer by the negligence of the [powerholder] donee, but fastens upon the property a trust for their benefit.

Precatory words

7.11 'Precatory words' are words of prayer or request in wills, for example, this testator's direction from *Mussoorie Bank Ltd v Raynor* (1882): 'I give to my dearly beloved wife ... the whole of my property ... feeling confident that she will act justly to our children in dividing the same when no longer required by her'. Clearly the testator had in mind that his wife would, following her use of the property, pass it on to his children, but did he intend her to hold the property on trust – for her own use for life, say, and then for their children after her death? A run of cases leading up to the middle of the nineteenth century provided authority for a 'doctrine of precatory trusts', by which such expressions were held sufficient to create trust obligations (see *Palmer v Simmonds* (1854)). In *Lambe v Eames* (1871) however, the CA refused to find that a testator's gift of his estate to his widow 'to be at her disposal in any way she may think best, for the benefit of herself and her family' was a trust. James LJ said:

[I]n hearing case after case cited, I could not help feeling that the officious kindness of the Court of Chancery in interposing trusts where in many cases the father of the family never meant to create trusts, must have been a very cruel kindness indeed.

In *Mussoorie Bank* the same attitude was adopted by the HL, and the 'doctrine' of precatory trusts was effectively abolished. Nevertheless in the proper context words which on their face look merely precatory may establish a trust. In *Comisky v Bowring-Hanbury* (1905) the words 'in full confidence that ... at her death [my wife] will devise it to such one or more of my nieces' were taken to establish a trust for the persuasive reason that immediately following this direction was a statement to the effect that in the event that the wife failed to devise the property to one or more of the nieces herself, it should be divided equally amongst them. It therefore seemed clear that the testator intended his nieces to take following her death, so the wife really held the property on trust for herself for life, and then for the nieces, with a power to vary the niece's particular shares by her will.

7.12 Occasionally it is difficult to tell whether someone intended to declare a trust or merely stated an intention to make a future gift. In *Jones v Lock* (1865) a man on return from a business trip responded to his infant child's nurse's statement that he had 'not brought baby anything' by pressing a cheque made out to him for £900 into the wee child's hand and said, 'Look you here, I give this to baby'. He later contacted his solicitor, expressing the intention to invest the £900 and more for the benefit of the child, as well as to alter his will in the child's favour. Before doing so he died. Though sympathetic, the court was unwilling to find the father's actions a declaration of trust. He intended to deal with the property in the cheque for the benefit of the son, no doubt, but not as a trustee, but as the full owner until such time as he had made his intended arrangements with his solicitor. The court regarded his 'declaration' as merely a declaration that he was now able to provide for his son and intended to do so.

Certainty of intention: the commercial context

7.13 There are different legal bases upon in which property, in particular personalty such as goods for sale or raw materials, can be dealt with in the commercial context to serve different ends, including the trust. Which basis is used will, in general, be determined by the intentions of the parties. Here we will briefly consider bailments and agency, retentions of legal title, and equitable charges, in the case of goods and raw materials, and then consider the 'Quistclose' trust of money.

Bailment and agency

7.14 If A rents machinery to B, B acquires possession of the property, though not legal title. This transfer of possession is called a bailment; A is the bailor, and B the bailee. Although B has duties to A in respect of the property (to return it in good shape, for instance), this is not a trust, since the legal title is never B's. If B is also A's agent with power to sell the property, again, B is not a trustee; he merely has the power to transfer A's legal title to a buyer. As agent B is a fiduciary to A, who must act in A's best interests when dealing with A's property, but he is still not a trustee of it. Normally, when an agent sells property of his principal under his authority to do so, the money proceeds are his own. He is simply in debt to the principal in that amount (minus, usually, his commission). If the money proceeds are stolen, it is his loss; he owes the principal all the same. Sometimes the contract requires the agent to hold the proceeds of sale on trust for the principal, and here there is a trust, even if the agent may, before remitting the proceeds, deduct his commission (see, eg *Royal Brunei Airlines Sdn Bhd v Tan* (1995)).

Retention of legal title

7.15 A number of legal arrangements may underlie A's supplying raw materials to B, a manufacturer. A may just sell the raw materials to B, for cash or on credit. Where A provides the materials to B on credit, A may worry about B's becoming insolvent, and so in the contract of sale A may employ what is called a reservation of title or 'Romalpa' clause (*Aluminium Industrie Vaassen B V v Romalpa Aluminium Ltd* (1976); *Clough Mill Ltd v Martin* (1984)), under which the legal title to the materials remains with A until (1) they are sold by B after they are incorporated into his manufactured products, whereupon the title to them passes to the buyer of the products, or (2) B has paid off all outstanding debts to A, whereupon the title passes to B himself. If B becomes insolvent, A can reclaim all of the materials B has on hand. There is no trust here; the legal title to the goods simply remains with A until either (1) or (2) occur.

Equitable charges

7.16 Alternatively, the legal title to the raw materials may pass to B under the contract, but A may try to establish that he has an equitable charge (**2.34**) on them, which will make him a secured creditor. If B is a company, however, which for obvious reasons is often the case, the equitable charge must be registered or it is void against B's general creditors or his liquidator (Companies Act 1985, s 395). Thus even if A is able to establish, through the interpretation of the contract, that he has an equitable charge over company B's property, this is unlikely to help in company B's insolvency for it is unlikely that A will have registered the charge if its creation was simply a consequence of the proper interpretation of their contract.

A trust of the materials?

7.17 A, however, may have one more string to his bow. If A can claim that he transferred the legal title to the materials to B 'on trust' for himself, so that he, A, becomes the equitable beneficial owner, then A may reclaim the property upon B's insolvency. The leading case is *Re Bond Worth Ltd* (1980). In *Re Bond Worth* the supplier purported to transfer legal title to fibre to a company for its manufacturing purposes, while retaining equitable title for itself, as well as acquiring equitable title to the manufacturer's products incorporating the fibre and to the proceeds of sale of those products. The court held that such an arrangement created an equitable charge on the fibre, the products, and the proceeds. It now appears to be orthodoxy that while legal retention of title clauses with respect to transferred chattels are effective, those that purport to 'retain' equitable title will be treated as charges, but the reasoning is questionable (see Hayton (1996a), 121; Worthington (1996), 15-24). There is a sound policy reason for this position though: the registration requirement for charges against companies means these interests will be publicly ascertainable by prospective creditors.

The Quistclose trust of money

7.18 The position is significantly different in the case of money advanced by A to B to enable B specifically to pay off certain debts (*Quistclose; Carreras Rothman Ltd v Freeman Mathews Treasure Ltd* (1985)) or to pursue certain projects (*Re EVTR* (1987)). Quistclose (Q) was an investment company that advanced £209,000 to Rolls Razor (RR) in order to allow the latter to pay a dividend which it had already declared. It was accepted by all concerned that if RR had used the money to pay the dividend, then RR would simply have owed Q £209,000 (plus interest); had RR paid the dividend and then gone into liquidation, Q would have been an ordinary creditor. RR was in trouble and did indeed go into liquidation, but before paying the dividend. The HL held that RR held the money on trust to pay the dividend, and that upon their failure to do so, the money was held upon trust for Q.

7.19 The decision was surprising given the commercial context. Normally if A lends money to B, the money immediately becomes B's legal property and A becomes an ordinary creditor; it doesn't matter that A pays the money to B under certain conditions, ie to spend it only on certain business projects. If B spends the money otherwise, he just commits a breach of contract, but not a breach of trust. What intentions of the parties determine that a trust of this kind, rather than a simple debtor-creditor relationship, will arise? The best explanation is given by Millett (1985): if you can interpret the arrangement as one in which *B is, in essence, spending A's money to achieve a purpose which A cannot by spending his own money directly,* a Quistclose trust will arise. In *Quistclose* itself, Q was hoping to stave off RR's bankruptcy by ensuring that RR was able to pay its declared dividend. If, however, A had tried to do that itself, it would have revealed to the world RR's desperate circumstances. So it could only do so by putting the money in RR's hands. While this seems a reasonable explanation of *Quistclose* and subsequent 'staving off bankruptcy' cases, you might well wonder whether the court should give its aid to such schemes by recognising a trust where normally it would only recognise a debtor-creditor relationship, which by their very nature misrepresent to the world, and in particular to prospective creditors, the true financial state of a company. On the other hand, you may think these attempts at company rescue praiseworthy, and that those who try them should not suffer unduly if they fail, as they might if rescue funds are treated like any other kind of loan.

7.20 In *Re EVTR* the *Quistclose* trust principle was extended. There the appellant, who had won a quarter of a million pounds on premium bonds, advanced £60,000 to his old employer to enable it to purchase new equipment. The company contracted with the equipment supplier, paying over the £60,000. The supplier provided temporary equipment until the new equipment could be delivered. The company became insolvent before the new equipment arrived, and the supplier refunded £48,000 to the company. The CA held that, though the funds which had been advanced were paid out, the trust continued to the extent that when the ultimate purpose failed, the refund was held for the original provider. Dillon LJ said:

> True it is that the £60,000 was paid out by the company with a view to the acquisition of new equipment, but that was only at half-time, and I do not see why the final whistle should be blown at half-time.

The problem here, of course, is that the company's payment out of the money appears to be the only appropriate point at which its relationship with the provider of the funds becomes that of debtor and creditor. If that is not full-time, what is? When the equipment has been used for a while? What if it turns out that after a year the equipment turns out not to be much use, and is sold? Are the proceeds of that sale to be held on trust for the original provider? Had the purchase gone ahead so no refund arose, the court would have dated the transition from the trust relationship to one of debtor and creditor when the money was paid, and so should it here. It is submitted that the CA must have imposed some kind of constructive trust giving the provider an equitable title in the traceable proceeds of his loan money. There was, however, no basis in authority for such a trust, and it seems to give the provider an unjustifiable priority over the company's other creditors.

7.21   In the recent *Re Challoner Club Ltd* (1997) Lloyd J held that a rescue fund failed for uncertainty. The fund was provided by the members of the club (a limited company) in order to save it from insolvency, and it was held separately from the club company's other assets. The club company failed and the liquidators demanded the fund as a company asset, and won. Because the rescue fund could be used freely by the company in any way to stave off insolvency, the circumstances in which the money could properly be used could not be exhaustively spelled out, and the trust therefore failed for uncertainty. Now, if an express trust fails for uncertainty of terms, that means it fails because the trustee's obligations to get the property to the objects are too imprecisely expressed, in other words, there is uncertainty as to subject matter or objects or both. The normal consequence of that is an ART; here the funds would go back to the contributing members, not to the liquidators. But the decision may well be correct, because, as stated above (**7.3**), uncertainty of subject matter or objects can have a 'reflex' action on certainty of intention. Though the members and directors may have used the term 'trust', and felt they were creating a trust, the uncertain terms suggest that there was no actual intention to create a trust rather than a simple loan, which they vainly hoped might be unaffected by the club's insolvency. Remember, the normal intention in this context is one to make a loan; a Quistclose trust should only arise where a clear trust intention is shown to displace it.

7.22   Trusts may also protect prepayments by customers. In *Re Kayford* (1975) a mail order company unilaterally decided to place all of the money

144

it received as prepayments for goods in a special account, only drawing upon the account when it filled an order. It was held that, upon the company's liquidation, the money in the account was held in trust for the customers even though they were unaware of the arrangement. While there is nothing particularly difficult about inferring or finding such a unilateral declaration of trust by the company, under insolvency law such a declaration appears to be an illegitimate preference of the company favouring some creditors over others. Should the court recognise a company's intentions if they have this result? A more extreme example of this kind is found in *Neste Oy v Lloyd's Bank plc* (1983). An agent for shipowners received money from them to pay various liabilities they incurred, for example to ports where their ships were berthed. The moneys were paid into the agent's general account, not held separately. One final payment by a shipowner was received by the agent after it had ceased trading. The court held that this last payment was held on *constructive* trust – in other words the court *imposed* a trust despite the actual intentions of both of the parties, on the basis that any honest recipient of the payment in these circumstances would have understood that the sum ought to be repaid immediately. It seems wrong, however, simply to find a kind of Kayford-type prepayment trust rather than the ordinary debtor-creditor relationship when neither party makes the slightest gesture to declare a trust, simply because someone is unlucky given the timing of someone's insolvency. There are *always* creditors who advance that unlucky last prepayment or make that unlucky last shipment of goods on credit to a company just before it becomes insolvent.

Certainty of subject matter and objects: common issues

7.23   Modifying Emery's (1982) classification we can divide up the common sources of uncertainty of subject matter and objects into three categories:

- conceptual uncertainty;

- evidential uncertainty; and

- 'whereabouts' uncertainty.

Conceptual uncertainty concerns the problem of vagueness in the language used by the testator. For example, if a testator gives 'a lot' of his estate to 'my shorter employees' in equal shares, we appear to be faced with a problem. How much is 'a lot', and who, of all his employees, count as the 'shorter ones'. Evidential uncertainty may arise because, while the language used to identify the property or persons is precise enough, it seems unlikely or impossible to find the evidence which will allow the trustees to carry out a settlor's, in particular a testator's, instructions. Consider 'the fishing rod which I used to catch a prize salmon on September 7, 1968, I give to the woman I had dinner with that night in celebration'. This bequest is conceptually certain both in subject matter and object – he caught the fish with only one rod, and only one woman dined with him. But determining which of the fishing rods the testator owned at his death is the prize-winning one, and who the lucky woman is, may be impossible simply because there is no reliable evidence. Finally, the whereabouts problem; consider this bequest: 'The photograph of me with Winston Churchill I give to my nephew Paul'. On its face, there appears no problem at all. There is no conceptual or evidential uncertainty making it difficult to determine which photo is the right one and who Paul is. But what if it turns out that the testator kept the photo hidden somewhere in his 60-room mansion, Grandacre, and secondly, that Paul emigrated somewhere (no one remembers precisely where) in 1973? It may be just impossible to locate either the photograph or Paul.

Whereabouts uncertainty

7.24 We can start with the whereabouts problem, because it is essentially no problem at all (see *Brown v Gould* (1972), per Megarry VC). No trust ever fails because the whereabouts of the property or the object is presently unknown. The trustees would not be required to pull down Grandacre in order to eliminate every possible hiding place for the photo. The gift is valid, and Paul may be put in possession if and when the photograph ever turns up. In a roughly similar fashion, trustees are required to hold a gift to a person whose whereabouts are presently unknown, and give it to him if and when he ever turns up. In *Re Gulbenkian* (1970) Lord Upjohn opined that, in the case of a beneficiary of a class gift whose whereabouts were uncertain, the trustees could apply to the court for a direction to pay his share into court. In short, the problem is correctly thought of as one confronting the trustees when faced with their duty to distribute the trust property, not as a problem concerning the very existence of the trust.

Evidential uncertainty

7.25   Evidential uncertainty of either subject matter or objects defeats an outright gift, a trust for a specified individual, or a fixed trust. The reasoning is straightforward: if the settlor expresses his gift in such a way that evidence must be adduced to identify the property or the person and that evidence is not available, then the gift or trust simply cannot be executed according to its terms. This does not mean that any requirement of evidence defeats an intended gift. There are rules which govern how evidence can be adduced to give effect to a testator's wishes expressed in his will, the general point of which is to ensure that such evidence only gives effect to the testator's declared wishes but does not serve to change or make ambiguous what the testator put in his will, and similar rules should govern the admission of evidence in the case of trusts generally. Evidential uncertainty of objects causes particular problems in the case of discretionary trusts and powers, which will be discussed below (**7.43**).

Conceptual uncertainty

7.26   Conceptual uncertainty arises from the settlor's use of imprecise or vague language to express his intentions. Vagueness is an ineliminable aspect of language. Vagueness can be understood as the problem of the uncertain boundaries which arise when we try to apply our words to things in the world. For example, the word 'tall' appears to have very uncertain boundaries; 'tall' is not a synonym for '5'10" or over'; it is not that precise. People may disagree whether Jim is tall, and an individual may be in a quandary himself as to whether Jim is tall or not. Jim may be 'on the borderline' for 'tall'. Vague terms will certainly apply in some cases – Paul, who is 7'8" is certainly tall – heavens, he's *very* tall – and certainly not apply in others – to Stephen who is 4'11" – but there will be a range of cases for which the application of the term is indeterminate, or *uncertain*. We can make a rough and ready distinction between two kinds of vagueness. 'Degree' vagueness covers words like 'tall'; 'tall' clearly refers to a scale, height, along which we can place individuals. The second kind of vagueness is 'category' vagueness. An example is 'furniture'. 'Furniture' is a term which applies to certain household objects. A sofa is certainly furniture, and a dinner plate is certainly not. But what about a carpet? Or a refrigerator?

7.27 In everyday communication vagueness is not a problem because, in context, we can draw boundaries which are sufficiently workable to understand what we are up to. When greater precision is wanted, we can stipulate a meaning for a term which provides a more precise boundary for its application. For example, we can stipulate that for our purposes, 'tall' means '5'10" or over', or if we run a department store, we can stipulate that furniture includes carpets if carpets are sold in the 'furniture' department. While these stipulations are arbitrary, that does not mean they are unreasonable. '5'10" or over' is a reasonable stipulation for tall, although reasonable people might choose different measures, but '4'11" is not, since that boundary does not reflect anything like the normal borderline area where 'tall' is thought to be vague.

7.28 In some cases courts are willing to determine a boundary for a vague term, in other cases not. In *Palmer v Simmonds* (1854) the words 'the bulk of my said residuary estate' were held to indicate too uncertain a proportion of the residuary estate to establish a trust. The judge did assume that ' the bulk' meant more than half but that that was still too imprecise to establish the subject matter of the trust. In *Re Golay's Will Trusts* (1965) the gift of a 'reasonable income', to go along with a life interest in a flat, did not fail for uncertainty. Ungoed-Thomas J said,

> The court is constantly involved in making such objective assessments of what is reasonable and it is not to be deterred from doing so because subjective influences can never be wholly excluded.

In other words, the court was willing to stipulate a meaning for 'reasonable income'. Vague words are not useless, even at the borderline. Their vagueness at the borderline just requires us to do some work, that is, stipulate criteria for a term's application to give a working definition which is precise enough for the task at hand. Did the court have better reason to do this in *Re Golay's* than in *Palmer*?

7.29 The same problem arises for certainty of objects. The career of the expression 'my old friends'/my 'friends' is particularly interesting. Although 'old friends' and 'my friends' were held to be conceptually certain in *Re Gibbard* (1966) and *Re Barlow's Will Trusts* (1979), in the former the court was applying a test for certainty which was later rejected by higher courts (*Re Gulbenkian* (1968)), and the latter concerned a gift subject to a condition precedent, where, apparently, a lower standard for certainty is required (**7.49**). In *Re Barlow's Will Trusts*, Browne-Wilkinson J denied that the meaning of 'friends' was 'too vague to be given legal effect', and he stipulated criteria for its application:

> Without seeking to lay down any exhaustive definition ... it may be helpful if I indicate certain minimum requirements: (a) the relationship must have been a long-standing one; (b) the relationship must have been a social relationship as opposed to a business or professional relationship; (c) although there may have been long periods when circumstances prevented the testatrix and the applicant from meeting, when circumstances did permit they must have met frequently.

In contrast, Lord Upjohn used 'old friend' as a paradigm example of conceptual uncertainty in *Re Gulbenkian* (1968), as did Megarry VC in *Brown v Gould* (1972):

> If there is a trust for 'my old friends,' all concerned are faced with uncertainty as to the concept or idea enshrined in these words. It may not be difficult to resolve that 'old' means not 'aged' but 'of long standing'; but then there is the question how long is 'long.' Friendship, too, is a concept with almost infinite shades of meaning.

Resolution of uncertainty by outside opinion

7.30   Should a settlor be able to express his directions as precisely as he can, but provide that if there is dispute over their meaning or application, recourse may be had to a living individual who shall settle the matter? In *Re Coxen* (1948), the settlor made a gift of a residence to his widow, which was however to end 'if in the opinion of my trustees she shall have ceased permanently to reside therein'. Jenkins J held:

> If the testator had insufficiently defined the state of affairs on which the trustees were to form their opinion, he would not I think have saved the condition from invalidity on the ground of uncertainty merely by making their opinion the criterion... in my view the testator by making the trustees' opinion the criterion has removed the difficulties [in deciding whether the determining event has occurred, which] may necessarily be a matter of inference involving nice questions of fact and degree.

Re Coxen thus stands for the proposition that an opinion clause cannot cure conceptual uncertainty, but may allow an individual to determine matters of fact as to whether the concept applies in any particular case.

Thus Hayton ((1996a), 157) says that opinion clauses may cure evidential, but not conceptual, uncertainty. In *Re Leek* (1967) the objects of a trust were 'such other persons as the company may consider to have a moral claim upon' the settlor; Harman LJ said:

> It was argued that ... the trust was too vague ... If the trust were for such persons as *have* moral claims, I would agree with this view, but this is not the trust. The trustees are made the arbiters and the objects are such persons as they may *consider* to have a moral claim; and I do not see why they should not be able on this footing to make up their minds and arrive at a decision. (italics original)

7.31 In *Re Tuck's Settlement Trusts* (1978) the CA considered a condition on the inheritance of a baronetcy, that the wife of any heir must be of 'Jewish blood' and 'worship according to the Jewish faith'; in the case of doubt the decision of the Chief Rabbi in London was to be conclusive. Lord Denning MR said:

> I see no reason why a testator or settlor should not provide that any dispute or doubt should be resolved by his executors or trustees, or even by a third person ... if there is any conceptual uncertainty in the provision of this settlement, it is cured by the Chief Rabbi clause.

Lord Denning's view does not, however, represent the law, for though all of the judges upheld the settlement, Lord Russell and Eveleigh LJ did so on a different basis. Lord Russell did not consider the Chief Rabbi clause since he did not find the condition to be uncertain. Eveleigh LJ said that the settlor:

> ... is in effect saying that his definition of Jewish faith is the same as the Chief Rabbi's definition. Different people may have different views or be doubtful as to what is 'Jewish faith', but the Chief Rabbi knows and can say what meaning he attaches to the words ... I therefore do not regard the settlor as leaving it to the Chief Rabbi to discover what the settlor meant or to provide a meaning for the expression used by the settlor when the meaning is in doubt ... The fact is that the Chief Rabbi knows what he means by 'Jewish faith' and the testator has said that he means the same thing.

Thus in Eveleigh LJ's view the Chief Rabbi's opinion is regarded not as determining the meaning of the settlor's words by providing workable criteria for them; the Chief Rabbi's opinion is merely evidence of the settlor's opinion. In practice does this not amount to letting the Chief Rabbi determine the meaning of the settlor's words? In *In Re Tepper's Will Trust* (1987) gifts were subject to the condition that the recipients 'shall remain within the Jewish faith and shall not marry outside the Jewish faith'. Scott J, following Eveleigh LJ, held that *Re Tuck's* established the admissibility of evidence to elucidate the meaning of terms like 'the Jewish faith'.

7.32 In general, courts try not to invalidate trusts if a reasonable construction can be placed on the words which will make them valid (*IRC v McMullen* (1981) per Lord Hailsham), but individual judges vary in their willingness to find a 'benignant' construction. As a result, settlors are faced with uncertainty about the extent to which a court will allow the determination of a vague term. In a recent examination of vagueness in legal language, Endicott (1997) cites the example of the 'anti-rave' provision in the Criminal Justice and Public Order Act 1994, s 63 by which the police are empowered to shut down sound equipment at a 'gathering' where the music 'by reason of its loudness and duration and the time at which it is played, is likely to cause serious distress to the inhabitants of the locality'. To further assist the judge 'music' is defined to include 'sounds wholly or predominantly characterised by the emission of a succession of repetitive beats' (presumably to capture the essence of the music that ecstasy-users prefer, but alas, unsuccessfully to distinguish it from the sound of a pneumatic drill). While it may be excessive to grant settlors the freedom to create legally binding obligations with the use of language as vague as that employed by Parliament, it may not be churlish to suggest that judges, given as they are to making sense of such statutory provisions, should make some reasonable effort to ensure the validity of trust provisions couched in vague language. Where an opinion clause empowers the trustees or a third party to establish criteria for applying the settlor's words, that does not mean they can choose any criteria at all. As Browne-Wilkinson J's decision in *Re Barlow's* shows, the provision of criteria, while necessarily arbitrary, can be more or less reasonable, and the courts could act if the criteria chosen were irrational or perverse; they need not, therefore, be worried that reference to opinion clauses ousts the jurisdiction of the court to determine whether a provision is conceptually certain. Of course the courts must remain the ultimate arbiters of which clauses are just so vague that any determination of criteria for them would, in effect, be writing the will or the settlement for the settlor. But this cannot be said of opinion clauses of the Chief Rabbi kind which save the courts from having to determine criteria themselves for terms which should be given a determinate meaning, and they should welcome the help.

The 'whatever is left' trust

7.33 In *Sprange v Barnard* (1789) a testatrix left £300 in securities to her husband 'for his sole use; and at his death, the remaining part of what is left, that he does not want for his own wants and use', was to be divided equally amongst three others. The court held that the husband was entitled absolutely, for a trust of what property remained after the husband's use 'would be impossible to be executed'; similar negative attitudes to this kind of 'whatever is left' trust are found in *Lambe v Eames* (1871) and *Mussoorie Bank Ltd v Raynor* (1882).

7.34 More recently, however, In *Ottaway v Norman* (1972), the Australian (*Birmingham v Renfrew* (1936)) 'floating' or 'suspended' trust analysis was applied. The son and daughter in law of the deceased claimed that he had left his house, its contents, and his money to his housekeeper to her for her use so long as she lived, but on trust to leave the property to them on her death. Brightman J opined that there was a valid trust of the house and contents (the latter being subject to normal wastage and wear and tear), which he was content to assume was 'in suspense' during the housekeeper's lifetime, attaching to the property only upon her death. It is not clear from this 'floating trust' analysis whether the 'floating trustee' has any obligations to preserve the property during his life. May he spend as much as he wants? Could the housekeeper in *Ottaway* have sold the house and spent the proceeds living on the Costa del Sol? In *Birmingham* the court said that gifts 'calculated to defeat' the trust could not be made, but such an obligation seems so nebulous as to be unenforceable. In *Ottaway v Norman* the trust did not extend to the money the housekeeper received under the will. Such a trust would be 'meaningless and unworkable' unless the money was given with the obligation that it be kept separate from her own money, and there was none.

The identification of specific property out of a larger amount

7.35 In *Boyce v Boyce* (1849) a testator left three houses to his widow, instructing her to give whichever one his daughter Maria chose to her, and to give the other two houses to his daughter Charlotte. Maria died before choosing any house, and the gift to Charlotte failed for uncertainty. The court held that the gift was of the *other* houses that remained following Maria's choice. Since she made none, the ascertainment of such *other* houses became impossible, and so the gift failed.

7.36   While *Boyce* turns on quite unusual facts, it is one instance of a more general problem which has recently arisen as an important issue in the commercial context, that of identifying which specific things, out of a larger class of things, are to be held as the subject matter of a trust. While in *Boyce* the failure turned on Maria's failure to select a property, in the commercial cases the failure generally turns on the failure of a seller of goods to choose particular goods to satisfy the buyer's contract; once identified, but only then, may those goods serve as the subject matter of a trust if one was intended by the parties. In *Re London Wine Co (Shippers) Ltd* (1986) a company which dealt in wines went into receivership. Its customers had purchased wine but left it in the company's possession for storage, and naturally assumed that they could retrieve 'their' wine and that it was not part of the insolvent company's assets. Unfortunately, the customers did not become legal owners of any wine. Although the company represented to them that it held particular cases of wine in storage for them, and even charged them storage fees, in reality the company did not allocate any particular cases of wine to any particular customers, and in general did not ensure that it had on hand sufficient quantities to meet all the customer's purchases should they all have demanded actual delivery of their purchases all at once. Wines were only allocated to any individual customer when he actually took delivery. Under sale of goods law, legal title to goods does not pass under a contract of sale until such time as the seller actually appropriates specific property to the contract. In a thorough review of the case law, Oliver J decided that, for essentially the same reason, the company did not hold any of the wine on trust for the customers: it could not be said with any certainty which wines were the subject matter of a trust for any particular customer.

7.37   *Re London Wine* was recently approved by the PC in *Re Goldcorp Exchange Ltd* (1994), a case involving similar claims against a dealer in precious metals. While sympathising with the customers, Lord Mustill affirmed that a right in property, whether legal or equitable, cannot exist in the air, hovering over an undifferentiated mass of property; it can only exist in relation to property which is specifically ascertained, ie identified. For fans of fusion, the decision is also right as a matter of policy, for insisting upon one set of 'certainty of subject matter' rules which applies both to the transfer of legal title and to the creation of equitable title. If the common law and equity are ever to produce a rational law of property, they cannot diverge on matters as fundamental as this. In particular, equity should not develop its own 'flexible' notion of certainty of subject matter just in order to provide the sympathetic result in a particular case.

7.38   Unfortunately, before the decision in *Re Goldcorp* was given, the CA delivered its decision in *Hunter v Moss* (1994), which throws this area of law into some turmoil. Mr Moss was the owner of 950 shares of a private company. In order to place his finance director, Mr Hunter, on the same footing as his managing director in respect of their interests in the company, he purported to declare (as the court found) a trust of 50 of those shares. He later sold the 950 shares when the company was taken over by a larger concern, keeping all the proceeds for himself. Hunter claimed a proportionate share of the proceeds of that sale, ie the proportion which would be his in equity if the declaration of trust were valid. There was a problem, however, in that Moss had never done anything to segregate or identify any particular lot of 50 shares out of the whole 950 he was to hold on trust for Hunter. Although the case concerned 'intangible property', ie shares, not goods, there seems no good reason to distinguish the clear rule in *London Wine*, approved in *Goldcorp*, that a trust cannot exist unless and until the property to which it relates is specifically ascertained (although the CA appears to have distinguished *London Wine* on a goods/intangibles distinction without further reasoned argument). In order to have specifically ascertained the property in this case Moss would have needed either to isolate share certificates to the specified amount, or at least indicate the registration numbers of the shares to be held on trust. Nevertheless, Dillon LJ held that the trust was effectively declared. His decision was based on an analogy, to wit: since a testator may validly bequeath 50 of his 950 shares of X Ltd without previously segregating them, Mr Moss should equally be able to create an *inter vivos* trust of 50 of his 950 shares of X Ltd without previously segregating them. But under a will there is no immediate trust of any of the property for any of the intended legatees until the estate is properly dealt with by the executors, paying off the testator's debts and so on (**6.33** et seq). The legatee's proprietary interests in specific items of property, whether shares or shoehorns, only arises when such property is actually identified for distribution. As Hayton (1994) points out, the *inter vivos* situation analogous to the testamentary bequest is the case where A properly transfers legal title of his 950 shares to B to hold on trust to distribute 50 of them to C, not Moss's declaration in this case. The decision leads to obvious problems. Assume such a trust. What happens when Moss deals with the 950 shares? Say he sells 100 shares (properly transferring title) to Fred. Whose shares are these? Hunter's or Moss's? If they are Hunter's, Moss has just committed a breach of trust; if they are not Hunter's, he has not. One does want to know whether a breach of trust has occurred. Martin ((1997), 96) suggests that this worry is insubstantial, since the rules of tracing (**2.28, 12.42** et seq) may be notionally employed: thus, we proceed *as if* Moss did segregate 50 shares out of the 950, but then immediately mixed them again with the other 900, so we have a mixture of 950 shares, just like the case where a trustee in breach of trust mixes £50 of trust money in his bank account, raising the balance to £950. Under the rules of tracing, Hunter will be able to trace his value into particular shares in the 950, which particular shares he traces into depending upon the circumstances. But this is a strange way to deal with a certainty problem, that is by assuming that in the very act of declaring a trust a person also makes himself a trustee in breach. The better view is Moss has not properly created a trust at all, and while he might have been contractually *obliged* to do so (under a term of Hunter's employment contract with him), it is conceptually confused to deal with his *failure to make himself* a trustee by treating him *as a trustee in breach*.

7.39   One of the strange aspects of this case was that it was argued as if Hunter was a volunteer, ie that Hunter did not argue that Moss was obliged by a term of Hunter's employment contract to transfer 50 of the shares to him or hold 50 shares on trust for him. One can only speculate why; perhaps Hunter felt that he would have a difficult time proving that he had provided any new consideration for Moss's promise of the shares. But as Hayton (1994) points out, and as we shall see in chapter 8, equity does not normally perfect imperfect transactions by creating equitable rights for people who haven't paid for them. If Hunter is to be treated as a volunteer here, then he does not suffer any loss if the trust fails, and there are no obvious special factors to compel the court to bend over backwards and find an otherwise uncertain, and therefore invalid, trust valid. The situation would be different had Hunter actually provided consideration, but the right response in that case is probably not to adopt Martin's tracing approach: Hayton suggests that the court should impose an equitable charge on Moss's shares in favour of Hunter to the value of the 50 shares. An alternative approach would be the imposition of a constructive trust on Moss over the whole 950 shares, to hold them in shares of 1/19 for Hunter and 18/19 for himself, thus creating an equitable co-ownership of the shares. This approach accords with the recent amendment to the Sale of Goods Act 1979 (Sale of Goods (Amendment) Act 1995) which holds that purchasers of unidentified goods from an identified bulk will obtain legal title to the bulk as co-owners in shares proportionate to their purchases. It seems overly fanciful to adopt a notional segregation and re-mixing and the immediate invocation of the rules of tracing when these other, more straightforward, techniques are available.

Trusts of residue

7.40   One last point on certainty of subject matter, which I stress because students regularly get this wrong in exams: a testamentary gift or trust of the residue under a will is NOT UNCERTAIN. In the course of executing the will, the executors will determine to the very penny the residue of the estate. 'That is certain which can readily be made certain', the saying goes, or 'id certum est quod potest reddi certum', if you prefer Latin.

Certainty of objects: outright gifts, fixed trusts, *Burrough v Philcox* trusts

7.41   In these cases, the object or each member of a class of objects must be known with certainty, or the gift or trust will fail. Thus a gift of '£1,000 to Jim' will fail if there is uncertainty as to who Jim is. The same goes for a trust of the income of 1,000 shares of ABC plc for Jim. Similarly, in the case of a gift to or fixed trust for a class, the trust fails unless the entire class can be ascertained with certainty. For example, '£100,000 on trust to pay the income to my children in equal shares' will fail unless each of the settlor's children can be ascertained. Thus the test of certainty in these cases is the 'complete list test' (recall **3.26**). The same test applies to a '*Burroughs v Philcox*'-type discretionary trust (**7.10**), because each individual in the class will take an equal share should, for some reason, the trustee fail to appoint the trust property, just as the objects of a fixed trust for a class do.

7.42 A settlor may create a trust for a class whose members may be unborn, as in a trust for his grandchildren. Until they are born, of course, these objects are not ascertained, but that does not invalidate the trust for uncertainty of objects. These objects will be identified with certainty over the course of the trust as long as it is not perpetuitous (**3.17** et seq).

Powers and *McPhail* trusts

7.43 Previously (**3.24** et seq) it was discussed why the 'is or is not' test for certainty of objects was held to apply both to powers and to *McPhail*-type trusts. The *McPhail* case was remitted to the High Court for determination whether the trust was valid under the 'is or is not' test. Thence it went up to the CA as *Re Baden (No 2)* (1972). The trust was for, amongst others, employees and their 'dependents' and 'relatives'. 'Dependents' was not regarded as uncertain at all; it had been used in many other deeds and by Parliament to describe individuals financially dependent upon others for their support. 'Relatives', however, led to a difference of opinion. 'Relative' means a descendent from a common ancestor, and so everyone has an indefinite, though undoubtedly large, number of distant relatives about whom they have never heard; if such persons were to be included in the class, then it would be a very large class indeed, and if one thinks in grand historical terms, we may all descend from those original australopithecenes that managed to scrabble out a living in the Olduvai gorge some millions of years ago. There is nothing *conceptually* uncertain about 'descendant from a common ancestor'. The problem turns entirely on proving the connection, ie upon evidential uncertainty.

7.44 Sachs LJ made a clear distinction between conceptual and evidential certainty; the 'is or is not' test applies to the former, and 'the court is never defeated by evidential uncertainty'. It is a question of fact whether 'any individual postulant has on inquiry been proved to be within [the class]; if he is not so proved then he is not in it.' Thus it was perfectly alright that 'relative' means a descendant from a common ancestor. Someone offering sufficient proof of that 'is' within the class; someone unable to do so 'is not'. Sachs LJ did not say who has the onus of proof, though presumably if any postulant must be proved to be within it to take, then the trustees would have to be satisfied so that their decision would stand in the face of a challenge by another beneficiary. Thus although Sachs LJ would not allow evidential uncertainty to defeat the trust, he does rely upon the existence of evidence to define the boundaries of the class.

7.45 Megaw LJ introduced a factor of substantial numbers into the 'is or is not' test: if it could be said with certainty that a substantial number of beneficiaries fell within the class, the class was certain. If this means that only those may take who are within the 'substantial numbers' within the class on the evidence available to trustees at the outset, eg a list of company employees and their spouses and children, then this appears to cut down the class contrary to the settlor's intentions and re-introduce a version of the 'complete list' test. More likely, the 'substantial numbers' merely establishes the validity of the trust. In that case, however, it gives no guidance to the trustee when considering the extent of any survey he must make of the class before distributing, ie the extent of the consideration he must give to distributing to those not within the 'substantial numbers', yet who may fall within the class intended by the settlor.

7.46 Stamp LJ refused to allow evidential certainty to intrude upon or patch up the problems caused by a conceptually certain term: if 'relatives' means descendants of a common ancestor, one either glosses the word or the trust is void for uncertainty; the 'is or is not test' is a test of a class defined by the concepts the settlor used; it cannot be watered down to a test which depends upon a burden of proof, for that makes the test one of evidential certainty, not conceptual certainty, and raises the problem that only one or a few possible objects bring forward the suitable proof:

> [I]t is not enough that trustees should do nothing but distribute the fund among those objects of the trust who happen to be at hand or present themselves.

Rather, the trustees must survey the class of objects and so the test must indicate the scope of this duty, not merely to the validity of making a payment to a particular individual who presents himself:

> [I]t would in my judgment follow that, treating the word relatives as meaning descendants of a common ancestor, a trust for distribution such

as is here in question would not be valid. Any 'survey of the range of the objects or possible beneficiaries' would certainly be incomplete, and I am able to discern no principle on which such a survey could be conducted or where it should start or finish.

However Stamp LJ found authority for interpreting 'relatives' to mean next of kin, and on that basis found the trust valid.

7.47   One notes an important distinction between Stamp LJ's and Sachs LJ's opinions regarding the character of the trustees' duties. Sachs LJ seems concerned only that the trustees are able, with certainty, to distribute the money only to valid recipients, and therefore he focuses the 'is or is not' test on the status of 'any given postulant'. Stamp LJ emphasises the trustees' duty to survey the class, and from this perspective he is surely right that no sensible survey could be made of the employees and all those who have descended from a common ancestor, for that would be like surveying the UK. Almost certainly the trustees will think of 'relatives', when 'surveying the field', as the employees' near relatives. This difference reflects different senses in which a large, discretionary trust is a trust. For Stamp LJ, the whole class of objects really do have the right to be considered, and therefore the trustees must have a sensible picture of them as a whole; there appears a fairly traditional right-duty relationship between the class of beneficiaries and the trustees. For Sachs LJ, the objects are much less like a class, appearing rather as applicants or postulants to a fund for which they might qualify for a distribution, and the trustees are like power holders who may benefit particular individuals; their only duty is to make sure they get on with the job and distribute the funds, and so they need a solid test of whether or not any individual distribution is legitimate.

7.48   Together Sachs and Megaw LJJ found that 'relative' meaning 'descendent of a common ancestor' was not an invalidating term on the 'is or is not' test, though it remains so on the 'complete list' test. Thus a trust for one's 'relatives' in equal shares fails unless 'relatives' is read as next of kin.

Conditions precedent defining a class

7.49   One may make gifts subject to conditions precedent in equity (**3.10**). For example, one might give Blackacre to one's daughter conditional upon her obtaining a 2:1 degree. Notice that the condition does nothing to identify the donee. Here we are concerned with conditions precedent that do. In *Re Barlow's Will Trusts* the testatrix directed her executor to allow any of her friends to buy paintings from her collection at below market value. Thus the condition precedent, friendship, defined *a class* of potential donees, and so the standard of certainty required here makes a useful point of comparison with that for certainty of objects of a trust. Browne-Wilkinson J held that the executor was not required to determine a class of donees defined by the term 'friends', but rather that the direction should be construed as a series of individual gifts to such persons who could satisfy the criteria for 'friendship', on which criteria he gave guidance as we have seen above. As a result, the decision in *Re Barlow's Will Trusts* appears to establish that, in the case of gifts with a condition precedent that defines a class, first, an 'is or is not' rather than a 'complete list' test is appropriate and, second, that the court will be liberal in determining criteria for vague terms.

Administrative unworkability and capriciousness

7.50 At times, we all don't know when to stop. Just before concluding his judgment in *McPhail*, Lord Wilberforce said this:

> There may be a ... case where the meaning of the words used is clear but the definition of beneficiaries is so hopelessly wide as not to form 'anything like a class' so that the trust is administratively unworkable or in Lord Eldon LC's words one that cannot be executed ... I hesitate to give examples for they may prejudice future cases, but perhaps 'all the residents of Greater London' will serve. I do not think that a discretionary trust for 'relatives' even of a living person falls within this category.

Here we will try to give some kind of sensible meaning to this added condition on the validity of trusts, but it may be a hopeless enterprise.

7.51 In the first place, there is some ambiguity in respect of 'so hopelessly wide'; does this refer specifically to the size of the class, so that any discretionary trust for eight million or so would necessarily fail? Would that make sense given the court's willingness to validate the *McPhail* trust, where on broad reading of relative – descendant of a common ancestor – the class was surely huge, certainly in the millions.

Why should mere size render the trust administratively unworkable anyway? Large numbers will not entail that the trustees will be stampeded with postulants; indeed, it is more likely that the beneficiaries of a small family trust, having the incentive to harangue the trustees, give trustees more trouble than any trust of the *McPhail* kind would. If the problem is the survey the trustees must undertake, the difficulty of doing that surely has more to do with whether the class or various sub-classes within it are defined in such a way as the trustees can determine the settlor's intentions regarding how they are to distribute within it, than with absolute numbers. But second, 'hopelessly wide' may not refer to the size of the class, but to the class definition; that is what the grammar of Lord Wilberforce's statement suggests. But what is it for a definition to be 'hopelessly wide'. Hopelessly vague?

7.52 The only reported case in which a trust has failed for administrative unworkability is *R v District Auditor, ex p West Yorkshire Metropolitan County Council* (1985). The council was about to be abolished, and it proposed to transfer its remaining funds, £400,000, on trust for 'any or all or some of the inhabitants of the County of West Yorkshire' in order to benefit them in various ways, amongst which included informing all interested and influential persons of the consequences of its abolition. Lloyd LJ decided:

> A trust with as many as two and a half million potential beneficiaries is, in my judgement, quite simply unworkable. The class is far too large ... It seems to me that the present trust comes within the ... case to which Lord Wilberforce refers. I hope I am not guilty of being prejudiced by the example which he gave. But it could hardly be more apt, or fit the facts of the present case more precisely.

Significantly, Lloyd LJ dismissed the idea that anything but the size of the class was at work to invalidate the power, in particular 'capriciousness', ie that the class was 'an accidental conglomeration of persons who had no discernible link with the settlor':

> [T]hat objection could not apply here. The council had every reason for wishing to benefit the inhabitants of West Yorkshire.

Yet significantly, he stated:

> What we have here, in a nutshell, is a non-charitable purpose trust.

161

Such trusts are normally invalid (chapter 9), because a trust for a purpose has no beneficiaries, and thus no one to enforce it. Therefore administrative unworkability may mean that the class of beneficiaries is 'hopelessly wide' because the trust is not really for a class of individuals at all; it is really a trust to carry out a purpose which is masquerading as a valid trust by the inclusion of a bogus class of beneficiaries.

7.53 Further guidance must be gleaned from three cases dealing not with discretionary trusts, but with 'intermediate' powers, ie powers to appoint to anyone in the world except for a specified class: *Blausten v IRC* (1972), *Re Manisty's Settlement* (1974), and *Re Hay's Settlement Trusts* (1981). In *Blausten* Buckley J held that such a power was only valid in this case because any appointment by the trustees required the settlor's consent; this set metes and bounds on the exercise of the power. Otherwise it would have been invalid.

7.54 In *Manisty* Templeman J took quite the opposite view. As he saw it, the 'is or is not' test required only that it could be said with certainty whether any individual was an object of the power, and though the class of objects of an intermediate power were unlimited, there was no difficulty determining that. On this point Buckley J in *Blausten,* like Stamp LJ in *Baden (No 2),* focused on the duty to survey, while Templeman J, like Sachs LJ, emphasised the validity of any particular appointment. On the question whether a trustee is given any guidance in his exercise of the power in such a case, Templeman J was not perturbed, for the expectations of the settlor are often not difficult to discern; though 'all the beneficiaries are equal some are more equal than others'; while the terms of the power itself may not guide the trustees, that does not mean that they may not sensibly exercise it, which is presumably why the settlor gave them absolute discretion to do so. And it appears that the trustees' duty to survey the entire class of objects is not onerous:

> If a settlor creates a power exercisable in favour of his issue, his relations, and the employees of his company, the trustees may in practice for many years hold regular meetings, study the terms of the power and the other provisions of the settlement, examine the accounts and either decide not to exercise the power or to exercise it only in favour, for example, of the children of the settlor. During that period the existence of the power may not be disclosed to any relation or employee and the trustees may not seek or receive any information concerning the circumstances of any relation or employee. In my judgment it cannot be said that the trustees

in those circumstances have committed a breach of trust and that they ought to have advertised the power or looked beyond the persons who are most likely to be the objects of the bounty of the settlor.

7.55 Significantly, Templeman J directly related the concept of administrative unworkability to the idea of capriciousness by reference to Lord Wilberforce's example:

> The court may also be persuaded to intervene if the trustees act 'capriciously', that is to say, act for reasons which I apprehend could be said to be irrational, perverse, or irrelevant to any sensible expectation of the settlor; for example, if they chose a beneficiary by height or complexion or by the irrelevant fact that he was a resident of Greater London ... The objection to the capricious exercise of a power may well extend to the creation of a capricious power. A power to benefit 'residents of Greater London' is capricious because the terms of the power negative any sensible intention on the part of the settlor. If the settlor intended and expected the trustees would have regard to persons with some claim on his bounty or some interest in an institution favoured by the settlor, or if the settlor had any other sensible intention or expectation, he would not have required the trustees to consider only an accidental conglomeration of persons who have no discernible link with the settlor or any institution. A capricious power negatives a sensible consideration by the trustees of the exercise of the power.

Here we have another candidate for the meaning of administrative unworkability: the settlor's direction is so capricious that no trustee could discern a sensible way to carry it out. However it is doubtful that there is any real standard for capriciousness that will defeat a trust. In *Bird v Luckie* (1850) Wigram VC said:

> No man is bound to make a will in such a manner as to deserve approbation from the prudent, the wise, or the good. A testator is permitted to be capricious and improvident ...

And the English case generally cited as authority for the court's power to strike down capricious directions is a purpose trust case. In *Brown v Burdett* (1882) the testator's instruction to trustees to block up the rooms of a house for 20 years was struck down.

7.56 In *Hays* Megarry VC opined that the width of a power *per se* could not invalidate it if it were given to a non-trustee. The difficulty arises when the power is given to a trustee, whose fiduciary position requires him to deal with the power responsibly. He said:

> [T]he duties of a trustee which are specific to a mere power seem to be threefold. Apart from the obvious duty of obeying the trust instrument, and in particular of making no appointment that is not authorised by it, the trustee must, first, consider periodically whether or not he should exercise the power; second, consider the range of objects of the power; and third, consider the appropriateness of individual appointments.

Megarry VC specifically rejected Buckley J's view that an intermediate power (if not saved by the settlor's consent provision as in *Blausten*) would be invalid as creating a class so wide as not to form a true class:

> I do not see how mere numbers can inhibit the trustees from considering whether or not to exercise the power.

He held the intermediate power valid. With regard to administrative unworkability, he simply pointed out that Lord Wilberforce's words concerning administrative unworkability were directed to discretionary trusts, not powers. With regard to capriciousness, he doubted Templeman J's analysis of a power to benefit 'residents of Greater London':

> In saying that, I do not think the judge had in mind a case in which the settlor was, for instance, a former chairman of the Greater London Council ...

Unfortunately Megarry VC went on to say this:

> Of course, if there is a real vice in a power, and there are real problems of execution or administration, the court may have to hold the power invalid.

A real vice in a power? Real problems of execution or administration? It is hardly helpful of Megarry VC to conclude a discussion of what makes a power bad or administratively unworkable by throwing out a couple of novel criteria for invalidity which he leaves unexplained.

7.57 Megarry VC did, however, say this regarding discretionary trusts, although the statement is clearly obiter:

I consider that the duties of trustees under a discretionary trust are more stringent than those of trustees under a power of appointment, ... and as at present advised I think that I would, if necessary, hold that an intermediate trust [ie a trust by which the trustees could appoint to anyone save a specified class] is void as being administratively unworkable.

But why? The mere presence of a duty to distribute neither clarifies nor muddies the trustee's task – it just means the trustee must distribute the property. If the task cannot be carried out, it would seem as impossible to carry it out for both powers and trusts, and conversely, if it can be carried out for one, it can be carried out for the other. It seems an inadequate reason to hold an 'intermediate' trust void.

7.58 McKay (1974) considers five possible interpretations of 'administrative workability': (1) the beneficiaries of a valid class have no common attributes; (2) the class is too large; (3) the trustees will be unable to perform their administrative duties; (4) the court will be unable to execute the settlor's directions; and (5) the trust is capricious. In view of the past cases in which trusts or powers which have been held by the court to be valid, McKay argues that not only is there no discernible flaw in the trust for 'residents of Greater London' which should render it invalid, but also that:

None of the possible bases upon which [administrative unworkability] could or has been said to rest satisfactorily provides a substantive base for it ... this is principally due to the disruptive influence acceptance of any of those grounds would have on both the decided cases and the presumed spirit and intention of *McPhail v Doulton* itself.

7.59 Here's a final suggestion drawn from Lord Reid's opinion in *Re Gulbenkian*, where he said:

I could understand it being held that if the classes of potential beneficiaries were so numerous that it would cost quite disproportionate enquiries and expense to find them all and discover their needs or deserts, then the provision would fail.

Consider the following discretionary trust: '£1,000 on trust to be distributed amongst those persons who have given their place for the settlor on a bus in such amounts as my trustees shall in their absolute discretion see fit'. The problem here seems to be that in order to determine which persons are eligible, the trustees will have, at a minimum, to advertise, and will probably have to conduct some investigations of those coming forward to determine the validity of any payments; thus in order to carry out any survey of the objects the trustees will have to deal with evidential difficulties, and £1,000 will not be enough to enable them to do so if the recipients are going to receive any worthwhile amounts. Thus, in line with Lord Wilberforce's view that the equal division of the trust fund amongst all the beneficiaries of the *McPhail* trust would benefit no one, the costs of administering this trust would probably result in no payments being made; thus to carry out the trust would result in its defeat in practice. On that basis, one might well say that the trust is administratively unworkable. And if one does want seriously to argue that the duties of a trustee to survey the field are more onerous than those of the trustee of a mere power, we may, if we interpret administrative unworkability in this way, explain why administrative unworkability only applies to invalidate trusts and not powers: regarding this example, we might allow a power to stand, for if anyone who gave up their seat on the bus to the settlor showed up and proved that he had done so, he could be paid by the trustees. The extent of the power-holder's survey would be simply to take the claims of postulants seriously, rather than having to make some effort to hunt them down. Conversely, the trustee of a discretionary trust *must* carry out some sort of search simply because the trustee *must* distribute the fund and therefore *must* find someone who can be paid, and ex *hypothesi*, that search would exhaust the trust fund.

Effects of uncertainty

7.60   At the risk of stating the obvious: if there is uncertainty as to whether a trust obligation has been imposed when property is given, then the recipient takes the gift absolutely, free of any trust obligations. If there is uncertainty of subject matter, then there can be no disposition of property to found the trust, and thus the intended trust fails. If there is uncertainty of objects, ie there is no one the court is willing to hold to be beneficiaries or objects of a power, the trustees will hold the property on ART, or as part of the residue if the failed trust is testamentary.

Further Reading

Emery (1982); Hopkins (1971); Grubb (1982); Hayton (1994); McKay (1974).

Self-test questions

1. What is uncertainty of intention, and how does it relate to uncertainty of subject matter or objects?

2. What is conceptual uncertainty and what may be done to resolve it?

3. What is administrative unworkability?

4. Are the following testamentary gifts valid, and if so, what duties do the executor/trustees have in giving effect to them?

(A) £100,000 to Fred on trust to provide for his wants in his remaining days and to leave what is left to Tom by will.

(B) £200,000 on trust for distribution as the trustees shall in their absolute discretion see fit, to persons or dependants of persons who have had coal miners in the family for at least three generations.

(C) £50,000 to my trustees to advance the same on interest-free loan, such loan to be repaid not later than 21 years after the operation of this will, to my friend Barbara so that she can start up her own accountancy practice.

(D) The residue of my estate to my trustees for distribution to such persons and in such proportions as they in their absolute discretion see fit, save that no distribution whatsoever shall be made to my wife or children.

CHAPTER EIGHT

The Constitution of Trusts

SUMMARY

Equity will not assist a volunteer

Perfecting an imperfect gift: I: the *Re Rose* principle; II: the rule in *Strong v Bird*; III: *Donationes mortis causa*; IV: proprietary estoppel

Covenants to settle

The equitable enforcement of covenants to settle

The enforcement of covenants to settle at common law

The trust of the benefit of a promise to settle

Fortuitous vesting

Concluding considerations on covenants

8.1   A trust is fully set up, or constituted, only when the property is in the hands of a person who is properly bound to be a trustee. The issues which arise concerning the constitution of trusts are closely tied up with equity's general principles for dealing with gifts, and so we shall begin by considering gifts in general. A gift is any transaction which benefits an individual who has not paid, ie given any consideration, for it; such an individual is called a 'volunteer'.

8.2   In *Milroy v Lord* (1862) Turner LJ laid down three 'modes' of making a gift:

*   an outright transfer of the legal title to the property (or the outright assignment of an already existing equitable interest);

*   a transfer of the legal title of the property to a trustee to hold on trust; or

169

- a self-declaration of trust.

8.3 In the case of a self-declaration, the constitution of the trust is automatic; the title to the trust property is in the hands of the trustee as soon as the declaration is made because he made the declaration. Where the settlor transfers property to B on trust for C, he must both effectively declare the trust, and effectively transfer the title to the property to B – it is this second step which constitutes the trust.

'Equity will not assist a volunteer'

8.4 The maxim 'equity will not assist a volunteer' describes an important guiding principle of the court of equity. The principle has two main strands:

- equity will not enforce gratuitous promises; and

- equity will not perfect an imperfect gift.

Equity will not enforce gratuitous promises

8.5 If A promises B that he will give him Blackacre, or if A promises B that he will put Blackacre in trust for him, and A refuses to deliver on his promise, equity will not enforce the promise at B's request. As Hackney (1987), 118) puts it, 'You cannot sue for presents in equity'.

Equity will not perfect an imperfect gift

8.6 In *Milroy v Lord*, Turner LJ said:

> [I]n order to render the settlement [ie the gift] binding, one or other of these modes [**8.2**, above] must, as I understand the law of this Court, be resorted to, for there is no equity in this Court to perfect an imperfect gift. The cases I think go further to this extent, that if the settlement is intended to be effectuated by one of the modes to which I have referred, the Court will not give effect to it by applying another of those modes. If it is intended to take effect by transfer, the Court will not hold the intended transfer to operate as a declaration of trust, for then every imperfect instrument would be made effectual by being converted into a perfect trust.

Thus the three 'modes' of conferring a benefit are three *mutually exclusive* 'modes'; equity will not treat the intentions of a donor to make an outright gift, where the property for one reason or another fails to pass from the donor to the donee, as a self-declaration of trust. *Jones v Lock* (1865) and *Richards v Delbridge* (1874) are illustrative. In *Jones v Locke*, the 'cheque for baby' case **(7.12)**, everything turned on the true intentions of the father. Although he intended to make provision for the infant in various ways, he did not intend to declare a trust of the cheque. As a result, the court found that there was no self-declaration of trust, and the court would not give aid to one claiming the benefit of an imperfect gift. Similarly, in *Richards v Delbridge*, the court would not devise a trust in order to perfect the ineffective legal assignment by Delbridge of the lease to his mill and the stock in trade of his business to his grandson.

8.7   Equity will also not perfect an ineffective transfer of the legal title to property to an intended trustee to constitute a trust by treating the intending settlor as having made a valid self-declaration of trust. If the property fails to get into the hands of the intended trustee, there is no trust.

8.8   But be careful to note what 'equity will not assist a volunteer' does not mean: it does not mean that volunteers who are *already* beneficiaries under an *existing* trust have no rights in a court of equity. As beneficiaries of a constituted trust they are fully entitled to the benefit of the trust, have equitable proprietary rights in the trust property, have the right to sue the trustees to enforce the trust, and so on. It doesn't matter whether they are volunteers or not at this stage. Indeed, most trusts are for volunteers, since most trusts are created by settlors to benefit family members who have certainly never paid the settlor for their benefits under the trust. Equity is not in the business of dismantling *effectively* transferred gifts, or dismantling *effectively* constituted trusts. In short, equity will not assist volunteers *to become* donees or beneficiaries under a trust, but once a person is a donee or a beneficiary, it matters not one whit whether he paid for the privilege or got it for free (*Ellison v Ellison* (1802); *Paul v Paul* (1882)).

Non-volunteers

8.9   By contrast, by *extreme contrast*, the intended non-volunteer beneficiary of a trust, ie one who has given consideration, may rely on the eager assistance of equity to constitute the trust. Obviously, an intended 'donee' who has given consideration for an 'outright gift' is in a different position as well, which is reflected in a complete change of terminology. A 'donee' who has given consideration is not a donee: he's a buyer under a contract of sale. He will therefore have common law legal rights for damages if the seller refuses to perform, and in the case of land and unique chattels, equity will not only order specific performance if the seller refuses to transfer the property, equity will regard the title to the property as having passed the moment the contract is formed (**5.3**). In the case of a promise to create a trust for which the intended beneficiary has provided consideration, equity will again specifically enforce the promise and find a constructive trust in his favour.

Future property

8.10   Promises to transfer property on trust, or 'promises to settle', often involve 'future property', which we have already encountered (**6.45**); future property is property which someone *might* receive, such as a legacy under a will, or royalties from the sale of a book. It is thus no more than a *spes* or mere 'expectancy'. The case of future property provides an example of equity's willingness to perfect an imperfect legal transaction where consideration is given. Because future property does not exist, it obviously cannot be transferred. Thus if I execute a deed whereby I purport to assign to you all the royalties from a book not yet published, that deed assigns nothing, for no royalties exist; thus at common law, an assignment of future property is totally ineffective. If the assignment is gratuitous then equity of course will not take any steps to make the intended assignment effective either. If, however, you give consideration for the assignment, then equity will perfect this imperfect transaction: equity will treat the assignment of future property as a contractual obligation *to* assign the future property if and when it is received (*Re Ellenborough* (1903)).

The general principle behind all of this is that equity is happy to come to the aid of someone who has given consideration for the benefit of property, but is unwilling to do so on behalf of a volunteer. Nevertheless, there are a number of exceptions to this basic rule.

Perfecting an imperfect gift: I – The *Re Rose* principle → for shares

8.11 In *Re Rose* (1952), the CA interpreted *Milroy v Lord* to the effect that, while equity cannot perfect a gift where a donee has not done everything in law which he must do to transfer his title, it will treat as effective an intended transfer where the donee has done everything he is obliged to do to make the gift valid. In *Re Rose* the donor had properly executed a share transfer form and delivered it, with the appropriate share certificate, to the donee. Though the legal title to the shares did not pass until the donee registered the transfer with the company, the court held that, in equity, such a gift is valid from the time that the donor does everything he is obliged to do to transfer the shares. After he has done that, and until such time as the shares are registered in the donee's name, the donor holds the shares as a trustee for the donee. If a dividend were declared in this period, the donor would accordingly hold the dividend payment upon trust for the donee as well.

8.12 *Re Fry* (1946) may appear to be out of line with this view. In that case a donor of British company shares who was resident in America was required by law to obtain the consent of the British Treasury before he could effectively transfer his legal interest. While the donor had done everything he could, in that he had completed the transfer form in favour of his son and had submitted the necessary forms to the Treasury, he died before the Treasury had given permission for the transfer. Romer J held that the donee had obtained no interest in the shares, and applying *Milroy v Lord*, refused to treat the transaction as having passed the beneficial interest in equity. Romer J thought that it was up to the donor to obtain, not just apply for Treasury permission, and that furthermore, since the Treasury might have sought further information before granting permission, the donor might well have had an opportunity to scuttle his own gift; therefore the donor had not done everything necessary to divest himself of his interest in the shares nor relinquished his power over them.

8.13 *Mascall v Mascall* (1984) is a case applying the *Re Rose* principle to registered land. There the court held that the intending donor had made a complete gift in equity by executing the registered land transfer document and handing it, with the land certificate to the donee. Again, as in *Re Rose*, until registration of title the donor holds the land in trust for the donee.

173

II – The rule in *Strong v Bird*

8.14 At common law the appointment of a debtor to be one's executor had the effect of cancelling the executor's debts to the estate. This result was determined by the application of the following technical reasoning: the executor, on becoming the owner of the testator's property and the successor to all of the testator's rights in action, was placed in the position of having to sue himself to recover the debt; since one cannot have a right of action against oneself, the debt was effectively cancelled. Originally equity prevailed over this rule and made the executor account for the money to the deceased's estate, but in *Strong v Bird* (1874) the court of equity held that the common law rule should prevail, *if, and only if, the testator had manifested an intention to forgive the debt in his lifetime and this intent continued up to his death*. This is something like the perfecting of a gift, since the debt is regarded as discharged without a formal release of the debt being made.

8.15 The rule was extended in *Re Stewart* (1908) to apply not only to imperfectly released debts, but also to imperfect gifts, again if, and only if, the testator had manifested an intent to give the gift in his lifetime and this intent continued up to his death. Whatever the merits of this extension of the rule, it should be understood that with this extension equity is now positively assisting a volunteer. In *Strong v Bird* itself, the court simply allowed the common law rule to stand in particular cases, ie where the continuing intention of the testator was to release the debt. But there has never been any common law rule whereby an ineffective attempt to make a gift during the testator's life is made effective upon the putative donee's being appointed his executor. Equity is acting off its own bat to assist a volunteer in this case.

8.16 Here are the oft-quoted words of Neville J in *Re Stewart*:

> The reasoning is first that the vesting of the property in the executor at the testator's death completes the imperfect gift made in the lifetime and secondly that the intention of the testator to give the beneficial interest to the executor is sufficient to countervail the equity of the beneficiaries under the will, the testator having vested the legal estate in the executor.

The first leg of this reasoning emphasises the 'fortuitous' vesting of the property: equity will perfect the imperfect gift just because it gets into the hands of the person it was intended for. The second leg appears to state that the rationale for perfecting the gift is that the gift was intended for the donor's executor, as if a donor's appointment of someone to be his executor has special significance in this regard. While one may presume that a testator has faith in the trustworthiness and competence of his executor, it is dubious to believe that many, or indeed any, testators pick their executors in the knowledge that in doing so they will perfect any invalid gifts or releases of personal debts made to them during their lifetime. The rule seems to work purely on the basis of the 'fortuitous' vesting of the property in the hands of the executors.

8.17   This view supports the extension of the rule in *Re James* (1935) to imperfect gifts made to someone who on the *intestacy* of the donor is appointed one of the administrators of the deceased's estate (**2.36**). This extension was doubted in *Re Gonin* (1979) by Walton J, who would restrict the application of the rule to executors, for they are chosen by the testator, while administrators are chosen by the court, usually from amongst a number of people who might serve. Extending the rule to administrators turned the rule into 'something in the nature of a lottery'. The rule in *Strong v Bird* itself creates an unprincipled lottery however, because one cannot truly suppose that the appointment of a testator indicates anything about the testator's intentions to perfect imperfect gifts – as a rule by which imperfect gifts are perfected by fortuitous vesting, it applies just as much to the administrator as to the executor. The original reaction of equity to the common law rule regarding the release of executor's debts is the right one; he should account to the estate for the debts he owes it. Once *Strong v Bird* overturned this sensible attitude of equity, then there can be nothing but a lottery in which some individuals will have imperfect gifts perfected, and others not, purely on the basis of who ends up, by hook or by crook, as the personal representative of the deceased. The rule has nothing to recommend it and the HL, which has never affirmed it, should overrule it the first chance it gets.

8.18   Applying the rule depends upon showing the deceased had a 'continuing intention' to release the debt or make the gift. It is important to understand what 'continuing intention' means. In *Re Pink* (1912) Kennedy LJ said:

[A] continuing intention on the part of the testator means ... a continuing intention that the gift should have been given at the time it was given.

Thus the deceased's intention must be that he had made an immediate gift which he thought was effective, and maintained that view up until his death. Thus properly understood, the deceased's intention is better framed as his *continuing belief* that he had released the debt or made an outright gift. The doctrine specifically does not cover an intention to make an *inter vivos* gift in the future, a promise to make a gift, or the intention to give the property at one's death. Hayton ((1996a), 240) questions whether the restriction to failed immediate gifts is consistent, since once equity has gone so far as to assist volunteers simply because of fortuitous vesting, why should it not allow the perfection of promises or intentions to give *inter vivos* or testamentary gifts. Kodilinye (1982) points out that the present rule at least reflects the situation as the deceased understood it to be – ie his view was that he had given away the property or released the debt, while the suggested extension would enforce promises that the deceased knew full well that he hadn't complied with. The point is well taken, but on Hayton's extension of the doctrine it would still have to be proven that the deceased has a continuing intention to carry out the promise; thus in both cases the doctrine would equally give effect to the deceased's wishes, and from that perspective it is difficult to distinguish between the merits of the two situations.

8.19 The rule in *Strong v Bird* requires that the property of a gift to be perfected is specific and identifiable as subject matter which might have been previously transferred in accordance with the deceased's beliefs/ intentions. Thus ineffective gifts of or promises to give future property or sums of money, cannot be perfected by the rule.

8.20 Following *Re Ralli's Will Trusts* (1963), in which Buckley J made reference to the rule in *Strong v Bird* in finding that a trust was constituted when the property fortuitously came into the hands of the trustee, it appears that the rule applies to perfect not only imperfect gifts but unconstituted trusts where the intended trustee becomes the deceased's personal representative. Again, the deceased must have maintained the continuing belief or 'intention' that he had constituted the trust, though in fact the transfer to the trustee was ineffective.

III – Donationes mortis causa

8.21   *Donationes mortis causa* (singular *donatio mortis causa*), also called deathbed gifts, are gifts which are made *inter vivos*, but which take effect on death. They escape the formalities provisions of regular testamentary dispositions, and so therefore their scope is very restricted.

8.22   *Cain v Moon* (1869) laid down the essential requirements for a valid *donatio mortis causa* (DMC):

*   The gift must be in contemplation, though not necessarily expectation, of death. All the reported cases deal with a donor suffering from illness, but, for example, going into battle or attempting to climb the Matterhorn should do.

*   The donee must in some respect receive the property in question before the death of the donor; what this amounts to turns on the nature of the property; for a chattel, the donee must take possession or acquire the means to do so, eg the key to a box in which it is held. Receiving some clear token of the property will suffice, as in *Woodard v Woodard* (1991)where receiving the keys to a car, though not the logbook, was sufficient. For a bank account balance, some 'indicia of title' must be transferred, such as the deposit book; in case of shares the delivery of share certificates has been held to work (*Dufficy v Mollica* (1968), and the CA recognised a DMC of land for the first time in *Sen v Headley* (1991) where the indicia of title transferred was the title deeds.

*   Finally, the circumstances must show that the property is to revert to the donor if it turns out that he recovers or does not die as contemplated; in other words, the *gift must be made conditional on the donor's impending death*. It is a common error in exams to assume that all imperfect gifts following which the donor soon dies can be perfected as DMCs – only gifts *conditional* on the donor's death may be. A DMC was held valid where the donor died from pneumonia rather from the incurable disease in contemplation of which the gift was made (*Wilkes v Allington* (1931); this case is generally understood to stand for the proposition that, so long as the gift is made in contemplation of death, it matters not whether the testator dies in the particular way he expected.

IV – Proprietary estoppel

8.23 In certain cases of proprietary estoppel (**5.20**) the court, to give effect to the plaintiff's 'minimum equity', will do what amounts to perfecting an imperfect gift. In *Pascoe v Turner* (1979) a man who declared to the woman with whom he was living as her husband that the house was 'hers and everything in it'. She spent most of her savings on the house. Following their separation he tried to turn her out. The court held that the minimum equity in the case was for the man to transfer the fee simple to the woman.

Covenants to settle

8.24 Covenants are promises formally expressed by being written in a deed; formerly deeds needed to be sealed, typically by a blob of wax or a red wafer affixed to the document; now (Law of Property (Miscellaneous Provisions) Act 1989, s 1) deeds must be signed and witnessed, and seals are no longer required. If the covenantor, the party who makes the promise in a deed, fails to perform what he promised, the covenantee, the party to whom the promise was made, may bring an action at common law for damages. Covenants are very much the product of formal legal thinking: the deed itself was all important. If the seal fell off the deed, then the covenantee could not sue upon it. If after having the covenant enforced against him, the covenantor left the deed undefaced in the covenantee's possession, the covenantee could sue on it and be awarded damages again. Thus, covenants are expressions of voluntarily-undertaken obligations which, because they are expressed in a particular form, can be enforced at common law.

8.25 Covenants must be distinguished from contracts. The modern law of contract developed entirely separately from the law of covenants. The modern law of contract does not require any formal expression of an agreement for it to be legally binding (except in so far as formality requirements have been imposed by statute, eg Law of Property (Miscellaneous Provisions) Act 1989, s 2 requires contracts for the sale of land to be in writing). In the course of its development of contract law the courts developed the doctrine of consideration. Why and how it particularly arose is complicated, but in its modern formulation it essentially requires that in order for a voluntarily-undertaken obligation, roughly, a 'promise', to be legally binding, the person to whom it is made, the promisee, must have given consideration for it. The doctrine of consideration has nothing to do with the law of covenants. A covenant is formal means by which the common law allows persons to make legally binding promises, *regardless* of consideration.

8.26 While equity will not assist a volunteer, equity will in many cases assist those who have given consideration, by for example, ordering the specific performance of a contract in certain circumstances. But combine the maxim 'equity looks to intent not form' with 'equity will not assist a volunteer' and it is clear that in equity a gratuitous promise is a gratuitous promise whether in a deed or not, and so equity will not enforce a promise just because it is in a deed even if the common law will. If I make a legally binding contract to buy your Rembrandt, I will have given good consideration, and so not only may I sue you for damages if you fail to deliver the Rembrandt, I may get an order for specific performance from equity (now governed by Sale of Goods Act 1979, s 52) because it is unique and money damages would be inadequate. If, however, you promise to give me the Rembrandt in a covenant, though I can still sue you at common law for money damages if you fail to deliver, I cannot get specific performance from equity, for equity will not assist a volunteer.

Covenants to settle and marriage settlements

8.27 A 'covenant to settle' is simply a covenant to create a trust, eg 'I, X, hereby covenant with Y that I shall transfer Blackacre to Y on trust for Z'. While X may covenant with Y to transfer property to him on trust for Z in any circumstance, covenants to settle were typical provisions in marriage settlements. A marriage settlement is a trust created by a man and a woman in contemplation of marriage. Normally the property is vested in separate trustees, but in certain cases the husband would be the trustee. Marriage settlements were popular amongst the propertied classes in the nineteenth century, and essentially allowed the wife of the marriage to have control over the property she brought into the marriage, for at common law, a married woman's property became her husband's; it could thus be squandered by a wastrel husband, and if the wife died before her husband without 'issue', ie without having had children, the property brought into the marriage would pass to him and thence to his heirs. Thus the families of wives settled property upon them in trust, first, to allow the woman control

179

over the property she brought into the marriage, for the settlement would give the wife certain powers over it, and secondly, the trust would direct that the property of the wife would be held on trust for her next of kin, ie her own relations, if she should die without issue.

8.28 Typically marriage settlements included covenants with the trustees of the settlement by both the husband and wife to settle 'after-acquired' property on the trusts of the settlement. 'After-acquired property' is simply property acquired after the date of the marriage, and such covenants typically restricted the obligation to property above a certain value. Coming from rich families, both the husband and wife were likely to inherit significant wealth only after the marriage began, and the inclusion of such inherited wealth in the marriage settlement would naturally be 'part of the bargain' which established their position in the dynastic line of both families. Thus both the husband and wife would make a covenant with the trustees to transfer to them, on the trusts of the marriage settlement, any property they would receive over, say, £100 in value. These covenants were not made for any consideration recognised at common law. Indeed, the common law did not recognise contracts between husbands and wives. Equity, by contrast, regarded marriage as 'the most valuable consideration imaginable' (*A-G v Jacobs-Smith* (1895)), and so though equity would not enforce these promises to settle because they were formalised as covenants, it would enforce them because 'marriage consideration' had been provided. Furthermore, equity regarded the issue of the marriage and their issue, ie the children and grandchildren, to be 'within the marriage consideration', and thus able to enforce the covenants. The doctrine of marriage consideration applies *only* to marriage settlements, that is settlements made *in contemplation* of marriage. A husband and wife *who are already married* who set up a trust for themselves and their children do not create a marriage settlement, and the children are not within any marriage consideration.

The enforcement of covenants to settle by equity

Covenants in marriage settlements

8.29 Because equity recognises marriage consideration, it is willing to enforce covenants to settle in marriage settlements, that is, it will order the covenantor to transfer the property to the trustees of the settlement, thus constituting the trust over the property specified in the covenant.

Pullan v Koe (1913) is a typical case. The settlement included the usual covenant by the wife to settle after-acquired property of £100 or more. The wife received £285; she spent part of it and put the rest into bonds in her husband's name. On the husband's death, the trustees of the settlement sued his executors for the transfer of the bonds to them so they could hold them on the marriage settlement trusts. The court held that it was the duty of the trustees to enforce the covenant, and equity would order specific performance of the covenant, as there existed beneficiaries of the marriage settlement who were within the marriage consideration. The court held further that the £285 was impressed with the trust the moment the wife received it, equity looking upon that as done which ought to be done. Thus not only would equity insist on specific performance of the covenant, but that the trust was constituted by way of constructive trust the minute the covenant *could* be performed.

8.30 *Re Plumptre's Marriage Settlement* (1910) is a counterpart case: here, the next of kin, who were to take the property if there were no issue of the marriage, but *not* within the marriage consideration, sued to enforce a covenant to settle after-acquired property. Their suit failed. The court would not order specific performance, as they were volunteers. Eve J relied upon the unanimous CA decision in *Re D'Angibau* (1880), in which Cotton LJ emphasised the distinction between a fully constituted trust, under which volunteers beneficiaries have just as much right as beneficiaries who have given consideration, and a gratuitous promise to create a trust, which will not be enforced against the promisor at the suit of volunteers.

8.31 What happens if a wife receives after-acquired property (bound by a covenant to settle) at a time when there are children of the marriage, but she never transfers the property to the trustees, and later the children die? Can the next of kin argue that the trust was immediately constituted by way of constructive trust as in *Pullan* when the wife received the property, since at that time the covenant was specifically enforceable, there being children of the marriage within the marriage consideration? Once a trust is constituted, it is constituted for all the beneficiaries, volunteers or not (**8.7**); even if it is constituted as a result of a beneficiary who has given consideration suing to enforce the covenant, once the trust is constituted by the covenantor transferring the property to the trustees, it is constituted for non-volunteer and volunteer beneficiaries alike (*Davenport v Bishopp* (1843)). So if the wife had transferred the property to the trustees, the trust would have been constituted for all the beneficiaries, and if the children died the next of kin would have a perfect right to their benefits under the terms of the settlement. Therefore, does not the application of the 'equity looks upon that as done ...' to constitute the trust immediately via a constructive trust also constitute the trust for the next of kin? Alas, no. Apparently, the trust constituted by the constructive trust becomes unconstituted again, believe it or not, when those within the marriage consideration disappear, because the constructive trust evaporates. According to Eve J in *Re Plumptre's Marriage Settlement*:

> [T]he argument founded on the rule that equity looks on that as done which ought to be done is, in my opinion, met and disposed of by [the view that], this rule, although usually expressed in general terms, is by no means universally true. Where the obligation to do what ought to be done is not an absolute duty, but only an obligation arising from contract, that which ought to be done is only treated as done in favour of some person entitled to enforce the contract as against the person liable to perform it.

So volunteers like the next of kin cannot rely upon any constructive constitution of the trust.

8.32   Although we have specifically looked at promises to settle where the consideration is marriage consideration and the promise is expressed in a covenant, the principle that equity will assist someone who has given consideration for the creation of a trust is of general application. Contracts to create trusts occur all the time in the commercial world, as for example, a contract whereby an agent is obliged to hold proceeds of sale on trust for his principle (**7.14**). Consideration has been given for that promise to 'settle', and equity will not hesitate to enforce it. The proceeds will be regarded as held by the agent on constructive trust when he receives them.

The enforcement of covenants to settle at common law

8.33   So far we have considered the equitable enforcement of promises to settle, and we see that where consideration has been given, equity will order the promisor to transfer property to the trustee thereby constituting the trust, and that in the meantime the promisor will hold the property in question upon constructive trust. On the other hand, where the intended beneficiary is a volunteer, equity will not order the constitution of the trust. This is all quite straightforward. So far the fact that these promises to settle have been expressed in covenants has not really mattered; if these promises had been made orally, the results would have been exactly the same. Equity is not concerned with form, and its willingness to enforce promises to settle turns, as we have seen, on whether consideration (including marriage consideration) for the promise has been given, not on the form in which the promise has been expressed. Now, however, the nature of covenants does become important, for these are promises which are enforceable at common law irrespective of whether any consideration had been given.

8.34 Consider the standard covenant to settle. S, the settlor/covenantor, promises to transfer the property to T, the trustee/covenantee, on trust for B, the beneficiary, who is not himself a party of the covenant, and who is a volunteer. The question now is whether T should be able to enforce the covenant *at common law*, and what this would mean. At first glance, there appears no reason why he should not. At common law T is a covenantee, and therefore the promisee of a legally enforceable promise. Can he not therefore bring a common law action for damages for breach of covenant against the covenantor, thereby getting money to the value of the property that ought to have been transferred on trust into his hands, and thereby constitute the trust himself? The answer appears to be 'no', although the cases which establish this have been extensively criticised.

8.35 The principle case is *Re Pryce* (1916), where Eve J held that covenantees/trustees ought not to enforce a covenant to settle in favour of next of kin who were volunteer beneficiaries. Eve J reasoned as follows:

> '[V]olunteers have no right whatever to obtain specific performance of a mere covenant which has remained as a covenant and has never been performed': see per James LJ in *In re D'Angibau*. Nor could damages be awarded either in this Court, or, as I apprehend, at law, where, since the Judicature Acts, the same defences would be available to the defendant as would be raised in an action brought in this Court for specific performance or damages. In these circumstances, seeing that the next of kin could neither maintain an action to enforce the covenant nor for damages for breach of it, and that the settlement is not a declaration of trust constituting the relationship of trustee and cestui que trust between

the defendant and the next of kin, in which case effect could be given to the trusts even in favour of volunteers, but is a mere voluntary contract to create a trust, ought the Court now for sole benefit of these volunteers to direct the trustees to take proceedings to enforce the defendant's covenant? I think it ought not; to do so would be to give the next of kin by indirect means what they cannot obtain by any direct procedure, and would in effect be enforcing the settlement as against the defendant's legal right to [the property in question].

The statement from Re D'Angibau (1880) that volunteer beneficiaries may not obtain the *equitable* remedy of specific performance of a covenant, while true, is not obviously relevant; it does not dispose of the question whether a trustee/covenantee may sue on the covenant *at common law*. To the extent that the next statement indicates that damages would not only be unavailable in equity but also at law for breach of covenant following the Judicature Acts, it is just wrong (see Elliot (1960)). If the statement is only that the volunteer beneficiaries would be unable to get damages in equity (because volunteers) or damages at common law (because not parties to the covenant), then again, this is true, but as with the preceding statement, not obviously relevant. The real heart of the decision lies in the statement that by allowing the trustee/covenantees to sue at common law, the next of kin would achieve by indirect means what they could not achieve directly, and this would in effect, allow the enforcement of the covenant to settle by volunteers, in violation of the general principle. The case is most easily criticised by pointing out that Eve J here seems to have allowed equitable principles to exceed their proper jurisdiction. The general principle, recall, is that 'equity will not assist a volunteer', not 'equity will stand in the way of a volunteer'. By ordering that the trustee/covenantees may not sue, Eve J appears to trench upon the trustee/covenantee's common law rights. What has equity to say about whether a covenantee at common law sues upon his covenant? The covenantee is not seeking the assistance of equity at all; he is not asking for specific performance, but for the common law remedy he is entitled to by his common law right to enforce the covenant. From this perspective, Eve J has no jurisdiction to direct the covenantee one way or another, and so the case is wrongly decided.

8.36 Several authorities go the other way: two, *Fletcher v Fletcher* (1844), *Re Cavendish Browne's Settlement Trusts* (1916), will be discussed below. Most recently the decision in *Cannon v Hartley* (1948) seems to conflict, if not in letter, then in spirit, with *Re Pryce*. In *Cannon* a man, on separating from his wife, covenanted with both his wife and daughter to settle after-acquired property upon them, but did not. The daughter, who had given no consideration but was a party to the covenant, sought to enforce the covenant at common law. Romer J considered that *Re Pryce*, properly understood, was authority only for the proposition that equity would prevent the enforcement of a covenant to settle when the plaintiff was both (1) a volunteer and (2) not a party to the covenant. Romer J awarded the daughter substantial damages for her father's failure to settle the property, stating:

> In the present case the plaintiff, although a volunteer, ... is a direct covenantee under the very covenant upon which she is suing. She does not require the assistance of the court to enforce the covenant for she has a legal right herself to enforce it. She is not asking for equitable relief but for damages at common law for breach of covenant.

The narrowing of *Re Pryce* on the basis that it only applies to non-parties to covenants seems dubious, for equity is not concerned with the formality of who is a party to the covenant – it is not concerned with covenants at all but the promises they express, whether to parties or non-parties; with respect to the promise itself it is the issue of consideration that matters, and the daughter here was a volunteer. The essence of Romer J's decision, that equity's assistance is not being invoked, for she is suing at common law, and further, that equity will not interfere in her doing so, seems to take the exact opposite approach to that of Eve J in *Re Pryce*.

8.37   *Re Pryce* was followed in *Re Kay's Settlement* (1938) (albeit reluctantly by Simonds J), and the latter was followed in *Re Cook's Settlement Trusts* (1964), so the principle that trustee/covenantees may not sue the covenantor at common law for damages must be regarded as authoritative. Assuming however, that these three first instance decisions may be met, if ever considered by the higher courts, by judges more in sympathy with Romer J's views than Eve J's, we must explore the consequences of allowing a trustee/covenantee to sue upon the covenant at common law.

8.38   If the trustee is allowed to sue upon the covenant, what remedy will he obtain? It seems quite clear that he will not be able specifically to enforce the covenant in favour of the beneficiary, that is, obtain an order that the covenantor transfer the property on trust to him, for an order of specific performance is an equitable remedy, and the trustee is a volunteer. (*Beswick v Beswick* establishes that a party to a valid contract, ie. one who has given consideration, may obtain an order for specific performance which benefits a volunteer third party, but in the case we are considering both the trustee/covenantee and the beneficiary are volunteers, so this equitable remedy is unavailable.)

8.39 If the trustee/covenantee brings an action at common law damages for breach of covenant, he may recover on either of two bases. First:

> ... for breach of a covenant to pay a certain sum, the measure of damages (if that is the appropriate expression) is the certain sum. (Elliot (1960))

On an action for an agreed sum, the remedy is the payment of that sum (see Treitel (1987), 779). Alternatively, according to the normal rule of common law damages for breach of contract, the damages will be measured by the covenantee's loss. Here again, the covenantee's loss is the value of the promised property. It is sometimes argued that the trustee/covenantee has suffered no real loss himself, for it is the intended beneficiary who has really suffered a loss by the covenantor's breach of covenant; therefore the covenantee's damages will be nominal unless he can recover damages for the volunteer beneficiary as a third party, and the common law will generally not allow him to do so (*Woodar Investment Ltd v Wimpey Construction (UK) Ltd* (1980), HL). This is misconceived. Though in the deed the covenantee is to hold the property 'on trust for' the beneficiary, the common law, you will recall (**1.14**) has always ignored the words 'on trust for'. It is no answer to a claim in damages for breach of contract at common law that the plaintiff is a trustee who was contracting for others, and the same is true here.

8.40 If this is right, then the trustee/covenantee who is allowed to sue at law will recover the value of the trust property the covenantor promised to transfer. It is here where things start to fall apart, for we must now ask, does the recovery of these substantial damages constitute the trust the settlor/covenantor intended? Another way of putting this is: for whom does the trustee/covenantee hold the damages? The mere receipt of that property doesn't make the trustee/covenantee a trustee of it unless equity is willing to recognise the trust obligation. Or rather, the intended beneficiary will only be able to enforce a trust over that property against the trustee/covenantee if equity recognises that he holds the damages on trust for him. If this operation of securing the covenanted property is done entirely at common law, then it is still up to equity to decide whether the property is to be held on trust. In order to understand the issues at stake here, we must first make a digression.

The trust of the benefit of a promise to settle

8.41 Most commentators accept that the Re *Pryce* unenforceability problem is avoided where the covenant to settle is a special one which creates an 'immediate binding trust of the promise', perhaps like this: 'I hereby covenant to transfer £1,000 to Fred to hold on trust for Alice, and the benefit of this covenant shall forthwith be held by Fred on trust for Alice.' The idea is that in the case of the normal covenant to settle, the covenantee is not a trustee of anything until he receives the trust property, at which time the trust is constituted and he becomes a trustee. Until that time, he holds his common law rights to enforce the covenant for himself absolutely. This special kind of covenant, however, makes him a trustee at the outset, and the subject matter of the trust is his common law rights under the covenant. This might seem a strange sort of trust property, but it is not at all. The right under the covenant is a personal right, but then so is every contractual right a trustee may acquire on behalf of the trust in administering it, as, for example, the right against a bank to the balance of the trust bank account. All can serve as rights held on trust. That is not the problem with the 'trust of the benefit of the promise idea'. The problem is that, according to this idea, in the normal case of a covenant to settle like those in Re *Pryce* and Re *Kay* the covenantee is *not* the trustee of his rights under the covenant for the intended beneficiary. This is entirely implausible. In the normal case, the trustee/covenantee is already a trustee of property under a settlement into which the covenanted property will go if the covenant is performed. Thus when the settlor covenants with the trustee to transfer property to him to hold on trust for the beneficiaries of the settlement, the trustee is immediately constituted trustee of the legal right to sue under the covenant. This is so simply because he undertakes in the covenant to hold the property he will receive under it *as a trustee* for the beneficiaries. As Hackney (1987), 117) puts it:

> At no stage does the transaction operate at common law alone, giving [the covenantee] any rights under the covenant, since the covenant is

made to him as a trustee, any more than would a simple transfer of property to Y on trust for Z give Y beneficial property rights at common law.

The alternative analysis, that the covenantee covenants for himself, would mean (1) that it is up to the covenantee whether or not to enforce the covenant; since he covenants for his own benefit, it is up to him whether he pursues his rights to become a trustee; (2) that it is up to the *settlor/ covenantor* to enforce the trust against the covenantee when he receives the trust property, not the intended beneficiary. If, when the covenantee receives the covenanted property, he refuses to hold it on trust for the beneficiary, then he is merely acting in breach of covenant, not breach of trust, for there is no trust until he constitutes it according to his obligation. The intended beneficiary is not a beneficiary yet, and is not a covenantee (ie a party to the covenant), so he has no rights to enforce it. Therefore to assume that the mere receipt of the intended trust property by the covenantee constitutes the intended trust is to confuse equitable ownership with a common law obligation. It would be up to the settlor (or following his death, his personal representative) to enforce the covenant and require the covenantee to hold the property on trust, and he has no obligation to the intended beneficiaries to do so. There is a further problem if he tries to enforce it – since the trustee is not to hold the property for his own benefit, the settlor gives him no consideration for holding the property on trust (any remuneration he might receive under the constituted trust comes from the beneficiaries, not from the settlor). Thus equity will not enforce the obligation against the trustee by an order of specific performance, requiring him to hold the property on trust. The settlor is left to his common law remedies; this will either be damages for breach of covenant, which will essentially amount to the value of the trust property, or restitution of the value of the property transferred. The upshot is that if the covenantee does not covenant as a trustee, *neither the settlor/covenantor nor the intended beneficiaries* can enforce the covenant to constitute the trust. These considerations strongly suggest that such covenants, in which the covenantee does not covenant as a trustee, are exceedingly rare. The courts, to their credit, have never given any explicit approval of this analysis, and certainly the decisions in *Re Pryce* and *Re Kay* do not in any way seem to depend upon it; indeed, if they thought that, it would be odd that they were willing to hear arguments, because the cases were applications by *trustees* seeking directions of the court as to how they should act *as trustees*. Nevertheless, it is orthodox to say that if in these cases the trustees had held the benefit of the covenant on trust from the outset, their enforcement of the covenants would have been allowed. Support for this proposition is supposedly gleaned from two cases where it is said that covenants were enforced because, exceptionally, there was an immediate binding trust of the covenant, *Davenport v Bishop* (1843) and *Fletcher v Fletcher* (1844).

8.42 *Davenport* involved a suit by a husband against the heir of his deceased wife for the transfer of property from the heir into the husband's marriage settlement. The heir obtained the property by succession when the wife died, but it was property which the wife, when alive, was bound to transfer to the trustees of the settlement under a typical after-acquired property covenant. The husband was not a volunteer, but since there was no issue of the marriage, a relation who was a volunteer would benefit if the property was transferred into the settlement. The heir argued that while the property should go into the trust so as to give the husband his benefit, the volunteer beneficiary under the settlement should be denied any benefit from the property, having given no consideration. In other words, the heir argued that even where someone who had given consideration wished to enforce the covenant and constitute the trust, he could only constitute it for himself, as it were, not for any volunteer beneficiaries. Not surprisingly, Knight Bruce VC found such an idea insupportable, affirming the basic principle that a trust, once constituted, is constituted for all the beneficiaries, volunteers or not. In passing, he said:

> The surviving trustee of the settlement, or his representative, may be thought to be a trustee of the covenant for the benefit both of Mr. Davenport and of the heirs of Miss Lucas [volunteers].

Put in context it is clear that Knight-Bruce VC is simply making the same point in a different way, that the trustee, when suing on the covenant on behalf of a non-volunteer, in effect also sues for the volunteers, for by constituting the trust he does so for all the beneficiaries. It is not a statement that the trustee may sue for volunteers in special circumstances where he is a 'trustee of the covenant'. Indeed the decision turns on Knight Bruce VC's accepting that if there was only a volunteer beneficiary, the trustee could not constitute the trust. The result, then, is that the case re-iterates the *Re Pryce* line of cases – that trustees/covenantees are always trustees of the promise in a covenant, but that does entail that equity will allow them to enforce a gratuitous covenant to settle.

8.43   In *Fletcher v Fletcher* (1844), a father had covenanted to transfer property upon trust to named persons as trustees for his sons, but did not do so. Wigram VC held that the covenant was enforceable by either the named trustees or the intended beneficiaries. The essence of his judgment on the enforceability point is in these lines:

> According to the authorities I cannot, I admit, do anything to perfect the liability of the author of the trust, if it is not already perfect. This covenant, however, is already perfect. The covenantor is liable at law, and the Court is not called upon to do any act to perfect it.

What Wigram VC has decided here is simply that a covenantee may sue a covenantor *at common law* for the trust property. In other words, the decision is simply a decision contrary to the ruling in *Re Pryce*. He only then goes on to consider an objection by counsel, that there could not be a trust of the benefit of a covenant. Wigram VC did not think 'there is any difficulty in that'. Therefore, while the case is authority, contrary to *Re Pryce*, that a trustee/covenantee may sue at common law on the covenant, it does not make the right of the trustee/covenantee to do so depend upon finding 'a trust of the benefit of the covenant' as if that were something special. *Re Fletcher* is not the only authority which contradicts *Re Pryce*. In *Re Cavendish Browne's Settlement Trusts* (1916) Younger J held that trustees were entitled to substantial damages for the breach of a covenant to settle. The case is badly-reported. *Fletcher* is one of the cases listed as having been cited to the court, but there is no indication that the case turned on the particular finding of a trust of the benefit of the covenant.

8.44   In *Re Cook's Settlement Trusts* (1964) Buckley J considered an argument that the covenant created an immediate binding trust of the promise, but decided against on the ground that there cannot be a trust of a promise to transfer future property. This is simply ill-founded. (See, eg *Lloyd's v Harper* (1880)). As a result it is difficult to know what the case stands for, but since there was no analysis of *Fletcher*, one should not draw the conclusion that the case lends weight to the thesis that *Re Pryce* prevents the enforcement of a covenant because the covenantee is not a trustee of the benefit of it.

8.45   We can now return to the question of what *Re Pryce* actually stands for, and the related question for whom would the covenantee hold the damages he was awarded If he were able, *pace Re Pryce*, to sue on the covenant at law. If the preceding consideration of the 'trust of the benefit of the covenant' idea is correct, then virtually all covenantees of covenants to settle are trustees of their rights under the covenant. If that is so, then the decision in *Re Pryce* does not mean that the court is interfering in the enforcement of a covenantee's common law right to make himself a trustee; he is a trustee already. The court is directing a trustee not to use his common law rights to 'get in', or realise a common law claim to, property, just because the common law right is founded on a voluntary promise. By the same token, *Re Pryce* means that the court will not allow a beneficiary to enforce a common law right held by the trust, if this right is only the benefit of a voluntary promise enforceable at common law. In short, equity will not allow a trustee or a beneficiary to enforce a voluntary promise to bring property into the trust. If this is right, it is simply not clear how equity would respond to the case of a trustee who does enforce his rights at common law to win substantial damages. On one hand, equity might require the trustee to hold the damages on trust for the intended beneficiary, for the covenantee is a trustee after all, and equity's refusal to assist a volunteer ought to be restricted to preventing the enforcement of a voluntary promise to settle when equity's assistance is required, or, perhaps, when its directions are sought – it may be significant that in both *Re Pryce* and *Re Kay* the trustees were seeking the advice of the court as to whether they should enforce the covenant at common law. This view might be strengthened by the attitude of the court to 'fortuitous vesting' (**8.15**), which we turn to shortly. If the court is willing to treat the settlor/covenantee's trust as constituted so long as the property gets into the trustee's hands, then the court may treat the trustee/covenantee's own actions which result in this as equally constituting the trust. Certainly if *Re Pryce* were overruled, and trustees were not prevented by equity from suing on covenants, the result would be that they would hold the damages on trust for the intended beneficiaries.

8.46 If, however, *Re Pryce* remains an authority, and a trustee/covenantee sues and wins damages (ie without having sought the directions of the court first as to whether he might do so – Hayton (1996), 234) argues that equity will step in and make the trustee/covenantee hold the damages on *resulting trust* for the settlor, ie the covenantor who he has just successfully sued at common law. Why? Since equity will not assist a volunteer equity will not allow the beneficiary to enforce a trust of the damages against the covenantee. This would be in line with the preceding analysis of Re Pryce but takes it one step further: not only will equity not enforce a constituted trust of the benefit of a promise in the volunteer's favour, but it will not enforce a trust over the proceeds of the enforcement of that promise by a volunteer (at common law) either. But, says Hayton, neither can the trustee/covenantee keep the damages for himself, because he undertook the covenant as a trustee. Equity will therefore make him hold the damages upon resulting trust for the covenantor, putting them both back in the position they were at the beginning. This, so the argument goes, justifies Re Pryce. The court of equity stops the whole pointless process from the outset. Clever, don't you think?

Fortuitous vesting of the trust property

8.47   In Re Brooks's Settlement Trusts(1939), Lloyds Bank were trustees of a marriage settlement, under which the wife had a power of appointment. One of her sons created for himself and his wife and children a voluntary settlement, of which Lloyds Bank were also the trustees, to which settlement he assigned all his interest in any property he might receive as a result of his mother's appointing property to him from her marriage settlement. His mother did, by deed, appoint property to her son. Before this appointment, Lloyds Bank held legal title to this property as trustees for the mother; if they carried out the appointment by complying with her exercise of their power of appointment they would transfer the property to the son. But Lloyds Bank had a second role, as trustees of the son's own settlement, and according to this settlement this self-same property was to go into it. So Lloyds Bank held the property either as trustees of the mother's settlement, under which they ought to pay the money out to the son, or they held it as trustees of the son's own settlement, as property which properly belonged in it. The question, then, was whether the son's assignment of any property he might receive by way of his mother's power of appointment, combined with the fact that the trustees had the legal title to the property, amounted to the constitution of the son's settlement. Farwell J decided it didn't:

> The son had no more than a mere expectancy under the marriage settlement until the appointment was made. That being so, the son, when

he assigned his interest under the [marriage] settlement to the trustees of [his own] voluntary settlement, ... was assigning, or purporting to assign, something to which he might become entitled *in futuro* – not a contingent interest, but a mere expectancy. It is clear on the authorities that he cannot be compelled to allow the trustees to retain the appointed sum, and that he can call on the trustees to pay it over to him.

Farwell J said that in the case of an assignment for value, ie where there was consideration, the trustees could hold the property on trust, enforce the covenant as it were, on the principles of *Re Ellenborough* above, ie on the basis that equity would treat the assignment of future property as a promise for consideration to assign the property if and when received. But here, as there was no consideration allowing equity to treat the invalid legal assignment of a mere expectancy as a valid promise to assign, and further that there was clearly no declaration by the son as a trustee himself, Farwell J held that the son retained beneficial ownership of the property appointed, and ordered Lloyds Bank to pay the money to him.

8.48   Farwell J viewed this result as unfortunate, and said that the law:

... makes it impossible to enforce the [son's] voluntary settlement, even to the extent of permitting the trustees of that settlement to retain, as subject thereto, the money in their hands.

This appears to indicate that Farwell J might have reached the opposite result had the so-called property in question not been a mere expectancy at the time of the son's assignment. In other words, had the property contemplated in the covenant not been future property, the covenant might have been held to bind the son, and the trustees could have devoted the property to the voluntary settlement. But even if that were the case, the son still would not have abided by the covenant and assigned the property into the voluntary settlement. The trustees would still have legal title only because of their multiple roles, not because the son had assigned the property, in other words merely by virtue of the fortuitous vesting of the property. But, as Hayton ((1996), 235) argues, given the decision that Farwell J made it was not consistent of him to think there would have been a different result had the son's assignment been for existing property, for the case turns not on the law regarding the effectiveness of legal assignments, but on equity's refusal to assist a volunteer. If there had been consideration for the son's assignment, then equity would have assisted; equity would not have let the fact that this was an assignment for future property stand in its way – equity will treat an assignment of future property as an enforceable promise to assign where consideration is given (**8.10**). On this interpretation, then, an expansive view of the maxim 'Equity will not assist a volunteer' was taken, giving rise, according to Hayton, to the principle that 'only the settlor (or his agent) can constitute a trust'; a trust should not be regarded as constituted by mere chance, as opposed to by the settlor's own act.

8.49 The counterpart case supporting the validity of fortuitous vesting is *Re Ralli's Will Trusts* (1964). Here a wife covenanted in her marriage settlement to assign property she acquired during the course of her marriage. The after-acquired property in question was a reversionary interest under her father's will, which fell in after her mother died, but which she never assigned. She died, and as it turned out, the sole remaining trustee of the marriage settlement was also the executor of her will, so he became the legal owner of the reversion she ought to have assigned to the marriage settlement when she had first received it. Buckley J decided the case on the terms of the original marriage settlement, holding that under a clause of the settlement the wife declared that she held any existing property on trust for the marriage settlement, and further that the reversionary interest was existing property at the time of the creation of the settlement; therefore, the wife had declared herself a trustee of the reversion on the trusts of the marriage settlement from the outset; consequently her executor held the property on the same trust when he received the legal title to her estate. But Buckley J went on to state, *obiter,* that even if this were not the case, the property became subject to the settlement trusts by the fortuitous circumstance that the trustee of the settlement was the same person as the executor of the will:

> That the [trustee] holds the fund because he was appointed trustee of the will is irrelevant. He is at law the owner of the fund and the means by which he became so have no effect on the quality of his legal ownership. The question is: for whom, if anyone, does he hold the fund in equity? In other words, who can successfully assert in equity against him disentitling him to stand on his legal right?

Buckley J held that the wife, if she were alive, could not make such an assertion against the executor/trustee (and her legatees under her will could not be in a better position) because in order to assert her right to the fund, she would have to show that the trustee could not conscientiously withhold it from her; but all the trustee had to do was point to the covenant to show that in conscience he *should* withhold it from her. It was the beneficiaries under the covenant who in equity had the superior claim upon his conscience. Buckley J accepted that the constitution of the trust in this case would be fortuitous, and that if the executor of the wife's will had been someone different, so would have been the result. But this naturally turned on the fact that the operation of the maxim 'equity will not assist a volunteer' is in a sense inherently fortuitous, for it only goes so far as to prevent a court assisting a volunteer in transferring property to constitute a trust; it doesn't compel a equity to positively divest volunteers of the benefits once their trustee obtains legal ownership. Such a view is, of course, in direct conflict with the principle that Hayton asserts, that 'only a settlor or his authorised agent can constitute a trust'.

8.50   There is a lurking problem in Buckley J's framing of the principle upon which fortuitous vesting operates, which is this: he says essentially that a trustee as bare legal owner must decide who, in equity, has the best claim upon him. Here the question was: in what capacity did the trustee/executor hold the fund – as trustee of the marriage settlement or as executor of the will? Now it may perhaps be fair to demand that a trustee/executor in the context of a close family arrangement like this one might ask himself such a question and be bound to take cognisance of the answer; if therefore, in this case, the trustee/executor paid out the money to the legatees under the will he could be properly held to be in breach of trust. But is it at all sensible to make this question-posing approach into a general principle determining whether a trustee is in breach of trust? Take the case of Lloyds Bank in *Re Brook's*, which is undoubtedly the trustee for thousands of separate trusts. *Qua* legal owner, Lloyds Bank owns all that trust property as a single legal owner, and in Buckley J's view, Lloyds merely looks round to the various equitable claims that can be made upon it under those thousands of trusts in order to decide where its duty lies. But in the case of a large trustee like a bank that is a counsel of nonsense. Clearly it must (for accounting purposes at least) segregate the trust property it legally holds into separate accounts relating to the different trusts it administers. Should a bank really be in breach of trust if property is appointed under one trust, and it pays it out without knowing that such property is also subject to a covenant in another trust, which it is administering quite separately?

Is a bank or any other professional trustee required to keep a list (if such a list could even be kept) of actual and possible cross references between all the trusts it administers? Can Buckley J really be suggesting that trustees ought to be required to survey all their trusts as a unit, treating themselves as legal owners of a big pile of property, and checking to make sure that none of the provisions overlap? Surely not. Trustees have the duty to treat themselves as separate trustees for separate settlements, and to keep the property in separate funds, and consequently they should not be liable for failing to find cross-connections that give rise to fortuitous vesting, at least unless and until a beneficiary whose equitable rights are constituted by the fortuitous vesting notifies the trustees. This problematic aspect of imposing a fiduciary obligation to cross-check what might be very unrelated trusts surely indicates that Buckley J's *obiter dictum*, if it is correct at all, must be restricted in its operation to cases where the trustees are actually aware of the interlocking connexion between the trusts which work to vest trust property fortuitously. A final point: Buckley J based his decision in part on the rule in *Strong v Bird*. Even if the extension of this rule to the perfecting of trusts which the testator intended in his lifetime by the vesting of the trust property in the executor or administrator is correct, its application to the facts in *Re Ralli* is questionable. Buckley J did not refer to any evidence of a continuing intention to constitute the trust, and the requirement of continuing intention is the only thing which keeps that rule within any manageable bounds at all. The application may, perhaps, be explained, by considering the covenant itself to be evidence of a continuing intention where no other evidence is available.

Concluding considerations

8.51 The complications in this area of law arise from a failure of fusion (1.11) of equity and the common law to take place with respect to gratuitous obligations. It should not matter that the recognition of binding but gratuitous promises was first recognised by the common law. If the law (meaning the English legal system, not the common law) provides a means by which gratuitous promises can be made legally binding, then that means should be available for promises of all kinds unless good reason is given otherwise, and no reason is discernible in the cases which would rule out binding, gratuitous promises to settle. 'Equity will not assist a volunteer' is a slogan, not a reason, in this respect.

8.52 Precisely the same point applies to the availability of orders for specific performance. It should not matter that equity devised the remedy of specific performance. It should be employed by the court whenever it is just to do so, and its use or restriction should not depend upon its historical provenance, but upon principled reasons as to why its use is appropriate in one circumstance but not another. While it may well be the case that such principled reasons may be gleaned largely from past decisions of the court of equity, it makes no sense to say that only judges acting as equity judges have a coherent grip on the remedy and that therefore it is not a remedy of the legal system as a whole. It should be available on demand to judges to employ wherever it appears appropriate to do so. If the law treats a gratuitous promise to transfer that Rembrandt as legally binding because expressed in a covenant, then the enforcement of that right should turn on the same principles as apply to a right arising under a contract for consideration, unless there are good reasons why not. Specific performance is given under a contract because the Rembrandt is unique and so money damages would be an inadequate remedy. Therefore specific performance ought to be given to enforce the same obligation expressed in a covenant, though gratuitous, since money damages are just as much an inadequate remedy here and for precisely the same reason.

Further Reading

Kodilinye (1982); Elliot (1960); Hackney (1987) 110 et seq; Hornby (1962); McNair (1988).

Must read cases: *Milroy v Lord* (1862); *Re Rose* (1952); *Re Stewart* (1908); *Re Pryce* (1916); *Re Kay's Settlement* (1938); *Cannon v Hartley* (1948); *Re Brook's Settlement Trusts* (1939); *Re Ralli's Will Trusts* (1964).

Self-test questions

1. In 1985 Fred and Barbara created a settlement on their divorce for their then minor children, Claire and Eric. The trustee of the settlement was Tony, Barbara's brother. The settlement was originally constituted by the transfer of £100,000 to Tony, and in the trust instrument were

included covenants by both Fred and Barbara to settle one-half of any property either might thereafter acquire by legacy or inheritance.

In 1987, Fred made a separate covenant with Tony to transfer one half of any royalties on his new book, to be held on the trusts of the settlement. The book earned £50,000, but Fred never transferred any money into the settlement.

In 1988, Barbara received a legacy of £250,000 in shares of G Ltd. She has always paid the dividends to Claire, and said on numerous occasions that she intended to give the shares to Claire. On 10 July 1995, she made an appointment in early August with her solicitor for the purpose of executing the share transfer to Claire.

On 13 July 1995, Fred and Barbara both died from food poisoning after attending Eric's university graduation. Fred left all his property to his brother Stuart, who is also the executor of his will. Barbara died intestate, and Tony and Claire have been appointed administrators of her estate.

Advise Eric.

2. In what circumstances will equity perfect an imperfect gift? Are any reforms in the law indicated?

3. To what extent is this a correct statement of the law: 'Only a settlor can constitute a trust'?

CHAPTER NINE

The Beneficiary Principle and Property-holding by Unincorporated Associations

SUMMARY

The invalidity of pure purpose trusts

Powers for purposes

Anomalous valid purpose trusts

Valid trusts for persons limited by a purpose: *Sanderson* trusts

Gifts to unincorporated associations

The dissolution of unincorporated associations

Less than unincorporated associations: the case of political parties

The rule against perpetuities

9.1   The 'beneficiary principle' can be stated thus: for a trust to be valid, it must be for the benefit of ascertainable individuals, ie specific beneficiaries. The corollary of this rule is, roughly, that equity will not recognise a trust to carry out a purpose, since the benefits of carrying out a purpose cannot be localised to specific individuals. Hence, the principle is also framed as the 'no purpose trusts' rule.

9.2   The second main subject of discussion here is property-holding by unincorporated associations. An unincorporated association is a collective body of individuals, like a student law society, which does not have its own legal personality like a company does, hence the name *unincorporated* association. According to the prevailing theory of unincorporated associations, what binds the individuals together is a contract. Each member is party to a contract agreed amongst them all that creates the legally binding rules of the association. So, for example, the contract amongst the members of a student law society may set rules about joining or leaving the society, about membership fees, about electing a president or treasurer, and so on.

9.3   In *Conservative and Unionist Central Office v Burrell* (1982) Lawton LJ stated four criteria for the existence of an unincorporated association: such an association will exist where there are:

> [1] two or more persons bound together for one or more common purposes, not being business purposes,[2] by mutual undertakings, each having mutual duties and obligations, [3] in an organisation which has rules which identify in whom control of it and its funds rests and on what terms and [4] which can be joined or left at will.

The existence of mutual undertakings giving rise to mutual duties and obligations is normally read to indicate that the members are bound by a contract *inter se* (ie amongst themselves). The last requirement, ie that the association can be joined or left at will is ill-put. Read strictly, it must be doubted, because there may be rules limiting both who can join the association and upon what basis, and similar rules about leaving. The idea underlying this criterion is that any individual enters the contract *inter se* voluntarily.

9.4   Unincorporated associations are of interest here because if an individual wishes to devote his money to the carrying out of a purpose, in particular after his death, then one way of doing so is to give money to an unincorporated association whose own purposes are those of the settlor. If the settlor wishes to promote fox-hunting with a testamentary bequest, he might consider making a gift to a local hunt association, to spend on its purposes. What we will be concerned with here is the way in which these unincorporated associations hold property, given that they have no legal personality, and secondly, whether a settlor's intention that the association devote the gift to a specific purpose has any legal effect.

The invalidity of pure purpose trusts

9.5   The two most quoted statements expressing the 'no purpose trusts rule' come from the case of *Morice v Bishop of Durham* (1804, before Sir

William Grant MR, 1805 on appeal to Lord Eldon LC). Both emphasise that for trust to exist (putting charitable trusts to one side), there must be someone who will have standing to bring the trustees to court to enforce the trust obligations against the legal owner. Thus the court must find definite objects, ie beneficiaries, who can bring the trustees to court. Sir William Grant MR said:

> There can be no trust, over the exercise of which this Court will not assume a control; for an uncontrollable power of disposition would be ownership, and not trust ... There must be somebody, in whose favour the court can decree performance.

Implicit in this statement is the view that only those who are intended to benefit qua beneficiaries have standing to enforce it. This rule is in essence parallel to the 'privity' rule of contract law; only those who are right-holders under the trust may enforce it, not every Tom, Dick, or Mary who might like to see it carried out.

9.6 From this point of view, the beneficiary principle can be regarded as a corollary of the certainty of objects requirement: if a trust is expressed in terms of a purpose, then it will be impossible to determine any definite objects of the trust, and therefore there are no persons at whose insistence and for whose benefit the Court can order the trustee to carry out the trust. Lord Eldon clearly equates the court's control over the trust with the existence of ascertainable objects and indeed, subject matter:

> As it is a maxim, that the execution of a trust must be under the control of the court, it must be of such a nature, that it can be under that control; so that the administration of it can be reviewed by the court... unless the subject and the objects can be ascertained, upon principles, familiar in other cases, it must be decided, that the court can neither reform mal-administration, nor direct a due administration.

9.7 The best statement of the principle, however, is Roxburgh J's in *Re Astor's Settlement Trusts* (1952). In 1945, Viscount Astor made a settlement of most of the shares of 'The Observer Limited'. The income from the trust fund that was set up was to be applied to a number of purposes, including the maintenance of good understanding between nations, the preservation of the independence and integrity of newspapers, editors, and writers, the protection of newspapers from control by combines, and the improvement of newspapers. It was admitted that the purposes were not charitable (see chapter 13). Roxburgh J framed the beneficiary principle in this way:

> The typical case of a trust is one in which the legal owner of property is constrained by a court of equity so to deal with it as to give effect to the equitable right of another. These equitable rights have been hammered out in the process of litigation in which a claimant on equitable grounds has successfully asserted rights against a legal owner or other person in control of property. Prima facie, therefore, a trustee would not be expected to be subject to an equitable obligation unless there was somebody who could enforce a correlative equitable right, and the nature and extent of that obligation would be worked out in proceedings for enforcement.

According to Roxburgh J, either the legal owner of the property is under an equitable obligation or he is not. If he is, then someone else must have corresponding equitable rights against him which can be enforced. If he is not, then he can deal with the property as he wishes because he is the beneficial owner. Roxburgh J sees no ground between these two alternatives, and it is submitted that he is perfectly right. The very existence of a trust turns on their being a trust obligation to someone who, in consequence, has equitable ownership of the trust property. If we take the requirement of equitable ownership seriously, speaking about the need for someone with standing to enforce the trust is a distinctly second-order way of framing the beneficiary principle. The essence of the principle is that for a trust to exist, there must be someone other than the trustee who has the real beneficial ownership of the trust property. If there is no such person, then not only is there no person *to enforce* obligations against the trustee, but more fundamentally, there are *no trust obligations to* enforce, for the legal owner owns it for his own benefit absolutely.

9.8 Since, however, in cases of this kind the settlor has clearly intended to create a trust by transferring the property to a trustee, the trustee cannot keep the property for himself. An ART arises, because the settlor has failed effectively to dispose of the beneficial interest in the property. In this case he fails to do so because he tries to do the impossible – create a trust without a beneficiary, which for equity is no trust at all.

9.9 There is a well-established exception to this rule in the case of trusts for charitable purposes. The duty to enforce charitable trusts fell on the King as *parens patriae,* and on to the Attorney-General as his legal representative. 'But,' said Roxburgh J:

> ... if the purposes are not charitable, great difficulties arise both in theory and in practice. In theory, because having regard to the historical origins of equity it is difficult to visualise the growth of equitable obligations which nobody can enforce, and in practice, because it is not possible to contemplate with equanimity the creation of large funds devoted to non-charitable purposes which no court and no department of state can control ... If the purposes are valid trusts, the settlors have retained no beneficial interest and could not initiate them. It was suggested that the trustees might proceed ex parte to enforce the trusts against themselves. I doubt that, but at any rate nobody could enforce the trusts against them.

9.10   So the trust failed. Roxburgh J further decided that the trusts were also void for uncertainty, citing in particular the phrases 'different sections of people in any nation or community', 'constructive policies', and 'integrity of the press'. In response to the suggestion that the trustees could themselves apply to the court *ex parte* for a scheme of distribution of the trust income, he said:

> It is not, I think, a mere coincidence that no case has been found outside the realm of charity in which the court has yet decided a scheme of ways and means for attaining enumerated trust purposes. If it were to assume this (as I think) novel jurisdiction over public but not charitable trusts it would, I believe, necessarily require the assistance of a custodian of the public interest analogous to the Attorney-General in charity cases ...

Should the court take a different point of view following *McPhail v Doulton*, where Lord Wilberforce decided that the court has jurisdiction, at the trustees' request, to devise a scheme for the distribution of trust money in the case of a large trust for an indeterminate class of persons. Should the court now do the same in the case of a purpose trust?

9.11   In *Re Denley's Trust Deed* (1968) Goff J appeared to narrow the 'no purpose trusts' rule considerably, while at the same time arguing that he was not diminishing the effect of the beneficiary principle, properly understood. The case concerned an *inter vivos* trust of a piece of land:

> ... to be maintained and used as and for the purpose of a recreation or sports ground primarily for the benefit of the employees of the company

203

and secondarily for the benefit of such other person or persons (if any) as the trustees may allow to use the same... .

The gift was properly limited to a perpetuity period. Goff J held that the gift was valid:

> I think that there may be a purpose or object trust, the carrying out of which would benefit an individual or individuals, where the benefit is so indirect or intangible or which is otherwise so framed as not to give those persons any locus standi to apply to the court to enforce the trust, in which case the beneficiary principle would, as it seems to me, apply to invalidate the trust, quite apart from any question of uncertainty or perpetuity ... The present is not, in my judgment, of that character, and it will be seen that ... the trust deed expressly states that, subject to any rules and regulations made by the trustees, the employees of the company shall be entitled to the use and enjoyment of the land ... [I]n my judgment the beneficiary principle of *Re Astor* ... *is* confined to purpose or object trusts which are abstract or impersonal. The objection is not that the trust is for a purpose or object per se, but that there is no beneficiary or cestui que trust ... Where, then, the trust, though expressed as a purpose, is directly or indirectly for the benefit of an individual or individuals, it seems to me that it is in general outside the mischief of the beneficiary principle.

Goff J held that the class of beneficiaries was ascertainable at any given time, and thus satisfied the certainty of objects requirement on the 'complete list' test. Following *McPhail* one presumes that the class of beneficiaries need only satisfy the 'is or is not' test to be certain.

9.12   What precisely is the effect of a trust for individuals framed in terms of a purpose? While the benefited individuals have standing to enforce the trust, what does this amount to? May they enforce the trust only in order to make the trustees carry out the purpose, or may they combine to defeat the purpose under the rule in *Saunders v Vautier*, insisting that the trustee, for example, lease the land and divide the profits between them? Have they an ownership interest, or just an interest in receiving whatever benefit would come to them through the serving of the purpose? Goff J does not discuss this. His only remarks concerning any disputes while the trust is up and running concern disputes between different groups of benefited individuals, which give no guidance as to how a dispute between the trustees and these individuals is to be resolved, for example had the employees wanted the commercial profits of the land, not its use as a playing field.

9.13 Goff J's decision has received some *obiter* consideration. In *Re Grant's Will Trusts* (1979), where Vinelott J said that the case was:

> ... altogether outside the categories of gifts to unincorporated associations and purpose trusts. I can see no distinction in principle between a trust to permit a class defined by reference to employment to use and enjoy land in accordance with rules to be made at the discretion of trustees on the one hand, and, on the other hand, a trust to distribute income at the discretion of trustees among a class, defined by reference to, for example, relationship to the settlor. In both cases the benefit to be taken by any member of the class is at the discretion of the trustees, but any member of the class can apply to the court to compel the trustees to administer the trust in accordance with its terms.

It is not clear whether there really is 'no distinction' between the two classes of cases. In the latter case, the discretionary trust is one in which the *class* of beneficiaries is defined by the individuals' relationship to the settlor, but their *individual* shares are entirely at the trustee's discretion. In this case the trustees' discretion is wholly dispositive, a matter of who within the class shall benefit at all, and in what amounts. In the *Re Denley* case, the mere power of the trustees to make rules governing the enjoyment of the land does not amount to a discretion over who and in what proportion the beneficiaries may benefit from the property. This is a mere administrative discretion, to ensure that all the employees may enjoy the sports ground as much as possible; the trustees would be in breach if they framed rules governing the use of the land which intentionally excluded a particular group of employees. This view cannot stand as an interpretation of *Re Denley* which respects the actual facts and Goff J's decision. Rather, it reads down the case to the point of overturning it in substance.

9.14 *Re Denley* was also considered in *Re Lipinski's Will Trusts* (1976), which we will consider further below. Oliver J adopted the passage quoted from Goff J' decision as being 'in accord with authority and with common sense', but did not discuss precisely how *Re Denley* should be applied to the *Re Lipinski* facts, where a gift expressed to be for the purpose of constructing new buildings was given to an unincorporated association. In particular, finding the gift valid he said the following:

> [I]t seems to me that whether one treats the gift as a 'purpose' trust or as an absolute gift with a superadded direction or ... as a gift where the

205

trustees and the beneficiaries are the same persons, all roads lead to the same conclusion.

The vital point here is that on the latter two treatments of the gift, the testator's expressed purpose may be entirely ignored, either on the basis that as a 'superadded direction' it merely expresses a motive for the gift, or on the basis that, the trustees and the beneficiaries being the same persons, the property is absolutely owned, and thus on *Saunders v Vautier* principles the beneficiary/trustees may do with the property what they like. This seems at odds with the impression Goff J clearly gives that the trustees are to carry out the purpose.

9.15   Thus both Vinelott J's and Oliver J's interpretations appear to be killing *Re Denley* with kindness. While they are happy to agree that the *Re Denley* trust was valid, in doing so they effectively gut the decision, at least in so far as it expanded the scope of valid purpose trusts. Finally, recall *West Yorkshire Metropolitan County Council* (**7.52**). One of the reasons Lloyd LJ gave for finding that trust for all the residents of West Yorkshire bad was that it amounted to an invalid purpose trust which could not be treated as a case like *Re Denley* because the class being so large, there were no ascertainable beneficiaries.

9.16   In parallel with the treatment of *Denley, Quistclose* (**7.18** et seq), which at first glance appeared to validate another new kind of purpose trust, one to devote funds to a particular business purpose, seems also to have been made safe and warm within the beneficiary principle by subsequent interpretation. While the exact limits to what a settlor can accomplish with such a commercial trust remain unsettled, such trusts can be explained without treating them as purpose trusts. Recall that A transfers the legal title to money to B to apply the money in a particular way, which in *Quistclose* was to pay a dividend to shareholders; if the money is so applied, the trust evaporates and B becomes a mere debtor to A, who merely owes A the equivalent sum of money as an ordinary debt; but if, because of supervening events, it becomes impossible to apply the money as intended, B holds the money on trust for A. This could be explained as a purpose trust, as follows: A transfers the money to B upon trust to carry out a particular purpose; if the purpose is carried out, the trust evaporates and B becomes a mere debtor to A; but if the purpose is not carried out because it becomes impossible, a resulting trust in A's favour arises. Millet (1985) convincingly argues that a purpose trust analysis ought to be avoided. Of course, the true intentions of the parties must be discerned from all the surrounding circumstances, and it is not in every case where A transfers money to B and a purpose for the money is stated will a *Quistclose*-type trust arise; there may be no trust at all, the transfer merely being a loan from A to B with a contractual condition on B's application of the money; or, A may really intend to transfer property to B on trust for C, so that the 'purpose' amounts to no more than the specification of C's equitable interest in the property – if this had been the interpretation in *Quistclose* the property would have been held upon trust for the shareholders regardless of the insolvency of the company; however, according to Millet A never relinquishes the beneficial ownership of the trust property until B makes the intended payment, for B holds it upon bare trust for him. The 'purpose' is accomplished when B exercises his power as legal owner of the property and carries out A's revocable instruction to spend the money as A instructs. When B does this, under A's contract with B, B becomes A's debtor for the equivalent sum. A's instruction to B is an order which B must follow under A's contract with B; this sort of contractual order is called a 'mandate.' A's mandate to B does not bind A in any way as a matter of property law, since A is the beneficial owner of the trust property; A may, however, contract with B not to revoke his instruction; if A then revokes, B will commit a breach of trust if he goes ahead and spends the trust money to carry out the original instruction; B may, however, sue A for breach of contract for any damages A's revocation causes him. If B cannot carry out A's instruction because supervening events make that impossible, then A merely retains his beneficial ownership. *Nota bene*: on this interpretation, the impossibility of carrying out A's instruction does not give rise to a ART as it would under a purpose trust which fails. There is no resulting trust at all; A has tried to apply his money with his mandate, but has failed, so he is in the same position as he started in when the arrangement was set up, as the beneficiary under a bare trust.

Powers for purposes

9.17   The beneficiary principle applies to trusts, not to powers of appointment, even if those powers are held by a trustee who must consider exercising those powers from time to time and make such a survey of the possible options so as to make a reasonable decision with respect to their exercise. Since, however, there is no obligation to exercise powers, there is no similar problem of finding a true beneficiary to enforce their exercise, and the courts have expressed their willingness to uphold powers to devote trust property to purposes. In *Re Douglas* (1887) the court was willing to uphold a power to appoint money to 'such charities, societies, and institutions' as the power-holder should select, even if on the proper construction this allowed the appointment to non-charitable societies or institutions. Although this case concerned a power to appoint property to institutions, not to purposes *per se*, such institutions would themselves apply the property to particular purposes, so the case is cited as evidence of judicial willingness to uphold powers for purposes. In *Re Shaw* (1957), George Bernard Shaw had in his will devoted funds for the purpose of devising a 40-letter alphabet for the English language. Harman J accepted that a power to devote funds to the purpose would have been valid, but having decided that the provision imposed a trust to carry out the purpose, he relied on *IRC v Broadway Cottages Trust* (1955) to hold that a valid power is not to be spelled out of an invalid trust (**7.7**).

9.18   In the case of powers of appointment, there will always be someone who will take in default of appointment. That person will have standing to ensure that the power-holder does not exercise the power improperly. He cannot, however, insist that the power-holder exercise the power; he would be unlikely to insist even if he could, for every such exercise will diminish the amount of property he will receive in default. Thus while a settlor can empower someone to spend the trust property on a purpose, there will be no one who is interested in ensuring that the power is exercised. Therefore a settlor creating a power cannot ensure that the trust property will be applied to the purpose he desires, though, obviously, if he gives the power to someone who is loyal to him and shares his devotion to the purpose, he may be confident that the property will be applied to it despite the absence of any legal means of enforcement.

9.19   A power to appoint property to purposes must be expressed with sufficient precision for the power-holder and the court to know with certainty what will count as appointing property to the purpose, in case any person who would take in default of appointment were to challenge a particular expenditure by the power-holder. As we have seen,

Roxburgh J in *Re Astor* would have held the trust to fail for uncertainty if not for lack of beneficiaries, and so even a settlor who wishes to create a mere power to appoint property to purposes must take care to express those purposes with care. Save for *Re Astor* and *Re Shaw*, no recent cases give any clear guidance as to the nature and extent of certainty in this area. Since the capricious creation or exercise of a power is also invalid (**7.55**), one presumes that a power to appoint property to purposes will founder if capricious.

Anomalous valid purpose trusts

9.20 The most significant exception to the 'no purpose trusts' rule is charitable trusts. Charitable trusts are trusts for purposes 'beneficial to the public' as defined by the law of charities (chapter 13). The other exceptions are all testamentary trusts. These are trusts for the maintenance of particular animals owned by the testator (a horse, *Pettingall v Pettingall* (1842); horses and hounds, *Re Dean* (1889)) and for the construction and maintenance of graves and funeral monuments (*Mussett v Bingle* (1876); *Re Hooper* (1932)). In *Re Endacott* (1959) a testator left his entire residuary estate, which amounted to more than £20,000, 'to the North Tawton Devon Parish Council for the purpose of providing some useful memorial to myself'. The gift was not allowed as an exceptional testamentary trust to construct a monument: Lord Evershed MR said, 'It would go far beyond any fair analogy to those decisions'. There also appears to be a similarly-grounded exception for the saying of private masses for the repose of the testator's relatives' souls (*Bourne v Keane* (1919)). These trusts are sometimes called 'trusts of imperfect obligation', for there are no beneficiaries of these trusts, and thus no obligations to any beneficiaries who may enforce them to carry out the purpose against the 'trustee'. However, this does not mean that the legal holder of the money to be devoted to the purpose may spend the money as he likes. If a testamentary gift is upheld as a purpose trust of this kind, the court will make a '*Pettingall*' order (named after the order made in that case). The trustee must undertake to the court to carry out the purpose, and the 'interested' parties, ie those persons who would take if the trust were to fail and who will take any funds surplus to the requirements of carrying out the purpose, are given leave to apply to the court if the trustee applies the property outside of the intended purpose. Thus the 'enforcement' of these 'trusts' is essentially identical to the enforcement of powers of appointment.

9.21 Two final points on these exceptional trusts, one serious, one trivial. The serious point concerns a case which is regularly cited in the textbooks as a *possible* case of a valid anomalous purpose trust. In *Re Thompson* (1934) a testator left money to a friend in trust for the purpose of promoting fox-hunting. Clauson J decided that he could make a *Pettingall* order because there was a residuary legatee who as an interested party could enforce the trust by applying to the court. But on this basis any purpose trust of whatever kind could be enforced; the *Pettingall* order is devised to deal with a trust of imperfect obligation only if it is found to fall within the class of exceptions to the general no purpose trust rule in the first place. It is getting things absolutely the wrong way round to find that a purpose trust is valid whenever one can devise a *Pettingall* order.

9.22 The trivial point is simply that leaving property for their maintenance is as much as you can do for your pets after you die. The idea that a millionaire may leave his fortune to his favourite cat is a cartoon fiction having no basis in law, just in case you were wondering. Your animals are your property in law, and you can't leave property to property; in legal terms, leaving property to your cat, Fred, is no different from leaving property to your toaster. The most you can do is leave a reasonable sum to keep Fred in the condition to which he has become accustomed.

Valid trusts for persons 'limited by a purpose': *Sanderson* trusts

9.23 Certain trusts which can be thought of as 'purpose trusts' have always been allowed by equity. This is a category of trusts under which the beneficiary is only allowed to take a certain amount which is determined by the costs of carrying out a purpose. Here's an example: '£100,000 to be paid by my trustees to my daughter Barbara in amounts equivalent to those she has expended on her education, the remaining funds to go to my son Peter'. The gift to Barbara is a gift to pay the costs of her education, and on that basis it appears that the settlor (usually in these cases, a testator) has created a trust for the purpose of educating Barbara. Nevertheless, one should not regard this sort of gift as an anomalous valid purpose trust. Consider this gift: '£100,000 on trust to pay Julia £1,000 on each occasion that Chelsea FC wins a match during the regular football season of 2000-2001, all funds remaining to be paid to Timothy'. This trust is perfectly valid, if unusual: the settlor has simply chosen an unusual way of carving up the beneficial interests between the two beneficiaries; it would be odd if such a gift were valid but a gift which limits the amount that a beneficiary receives on the basis of what it costs to educate him were not. That is why it is better to frame such a gift as a 'trust in which the subject matter is apportioned in reference to the costs of carrying out a well-defined purpose' rather than as a purpose trust. The purpose in these trusts is not to be regarded as the replacement of the human *object of the trust* with a purpose; the purpose is part of a device or formula which defines the *subject matter* of the trust for a particular object, an object, ie a beneficiary, who is fully human. True, if the beneficiary does not incur any costs of the required kind, then that beneficiary will take nothing; in that way these gifts may certainly provide an incentive for the beneficiary to achieve the purpose, although not always: consider a trust to pay the rehabilitation expenses of members of a mountaineering society who injure themselves by falling off mountains.

9.24 The leading case concerning such trusts is *Re Sanderson's Trust* (1857). Here a testator left property upon trust to 'pay and apply the whole or any part of the [income] for and towards [the] maintenance, attendance, and comfort', of his imbecile brother for the remainder of his life. At the death of this brother there remained unexpended income, and the question was whether those funds should be held on trust for the residuary legatees under the testator's estate, or whether the money should go into the imbecile brother's estate. In other words, the question was whether the gift was limited to such portion of the income as was required to pay for the brother's maintenance, or whether it was an absolute gift of the whole.

9.25 Page-Wood VC distinguished the two possible interpretations of testamentary gifts of this kind as follows:

> In reference to gifts of this description, there are two classes of cases between which the general distinction is sufficiently clear, although the precise line of demarcation is occasionally somewhat difficult to ascertain. If a gross sum be given, or if the whole income of the property is given,

and a special purpose assigned for that gift, this Court always regards the gift as absolute, and the purpose merely as the motive of the gift, and therefore holds that the gift takes effect as to the whole sum or the whole income, as the case may be ... [If] an entire fund is given for the maintenance of children or the like, they take the whole fund absolutely, and the maintenance is treated in effect as simply the motive in making the gift; while, on the other hand, if a portion only of the fund is given for maintenance, then they are entitled to draw out so much only as may be necessary for the purpose specified.

Thus there developed a body of case law directed to determining whether the testator intended that the whole of the trust property should go to the beneficiary, the purpose of maintenance, or education, or whatever, merely indicating the motive of the gift, or whether he was creating a fund out of which money might be distributed only on the basis of meeting the costs or expenses of the purpose. In this case Page-Wood VC decided that the brother was only entitled to such part of the fund as was necessary for his maintenance, attendance, and comfort. Nevertheless, it is clear that the brother, and others who benefit under like trusts when the costs or expenses that the trusts cover are met, are just as much human beneficiaries as persons who are recipients of absolute gifts. In particular, they are not to be regarded as beneficiaries of discretionary trusts, in which the trustees, at their discretion, may or may not spend the money on the particular purpose, ie to pay the particular expenses the testator indicated. The beneficiaries are fully entitled to demand the requisite payments to meet the costs or expenses specified by the trust.

9.26 Settlors, then, may devote property to certain purposes *in the sense* that they may leave property on trust to spend any amount of the property, up to all of it, on certain well-defined expenses of named beneficiaries, and these beneficiaries can enforce these trusts, by demanding whatever amounts fall within the expenses or costs defined by the purpose from the trustees. Any property left when the purpose is accomplished will result either to the settlor or, in the case of a will, to the testator's residuary legatees, unless a specific gift over of the remainder is made.

9.27 The courts in the nineteenth century were well versed in enforcing trusts of this kind, in particular trusts to pay for the maintenance, education, and advancement of children. A trust for maintenance is one which will provide for a persons daily costs of living, a house over his head and food, clothing, etc; a trust for education is straightforward; a trust for advancement is a trust to pay sums of money to 'advance' someone in the world, usually an infant who is approaching adulthood, by paying the costs of getting him started in his career; a typical example of a payment for advancement in the nineteenth century would be the purchase of a 'living' for a cleric, ie an appointment to an office in the Church of England, or the purchase of a commission in the army. Because the nature of these costs and expenses were so familiar it is possible, and makes sense, to treat such trusts as trusts to pay certain well-defined expenses. It is not clear that other purposes could so easily be treated in this way; indeed, it might even be regarded as a test of the validity of *Sanderson*-type trusts that the 'purpose' can be clearly localised to a particular beneficiary as the payment of a certain share of a fund, that share determined by well-defined expenses which he may incur – in other words, only well-defined costs or expenses may be *certain* enough. The certainty here is the certainty of subject matter; if the 'purpose' doesn't provide an easily understood definition of the kind of expenses which over the course of the trust will clearly determine the share the beneficiary is to receive, then the testator has not defined with sufficient precision the subject matter of the trust in that beneficiary's favour.

9.28 In cases of this kind it may be difficult to determine whether a testator intended a gift of the whole fund with an attached motive or direction, or a gift of such part of the property as is required to meet the beneficiary's costs of achieving a purpose such as his education. A somewhat unusual case was *Re Skinner's Trusts* (1860). Here the Reverend Skinner left £1,000 in his will for the publication of his own work, 'intitled 'An Analysis of Language, and Symbols of the Worship of the Sun' in two volumes' the profits and copyright of which were to be used to provide his grandson funds for his education. The executors of the will set aside £1,000, and sought advice from an expert and the publisher, both of whom advised against its publication. The question was whether the grandson was entitled to the whole fund, the publication of the manuscript being only a suggested means by which he should benefit, or whether the trust was primarily for the publication of the manuscript, the benefits of which were to go to the grandson; in other words, was the grandson intended to be the absolute beneficiary of £1,000, or only the beneficiary of such profits or valuable copyright that the publication of the book would generate. On the latter view, it was argued that the trust had failed because the book was unpublishable. Page-Wood VC, while regarding the case on the borderline, decided for the grandson.

9.29   In *Re Bowes* (1905) £5,000 was left upon trust for the purpose of planting trees on an estate. The evidence of foresters indicated that only a fraction of the land would benefit from the planting at a cost of only £800. North J decided that the paramount intention of the gift was to benefit the persons entitled to the estate, and so this intention should prevail over the specific means of planting trees where that means, if carried out, would be actually disadvantageous to the beneficiaries. Thus the owners of the estate were entitled to the £5,000 absolutely.

9.30   The problem of inferring the settlor's intention has been particularly acute in 'appeal' cases, where an appeal has been made to raise funds to provide for individuals who have suffered some misfortune. It is obviously a vexed task to determine whether an amorphous group of often anonymous contributors had one intention or the other, and perhaps these cases should be regarded as in a class of their own. In *Re The Trusts of the Abbott Fund* (1900), one Dr Abbott of Cambridge placed money on trust for the support of his family, including two daughters who were deaf and dumb, but the trustee turned out to be a rogue and the trust money disappeared. Several persons in turn sought subscriptions on behalf of the two daughters, which were held by trustees who made quarterly payments to the two women. On the death of the survivor of the two some £366 remained. The only evidence of the intention of the subscribers was the circular making the appeal for funds, which stated that the fund was to enable the women to reside in Cambridge and to provide for their 'very moderate wants,' and, if the trustees so decided, to purchase annuities for them. Stirling J decided:

> I cannot believe that [the fund] was ever intended to become the absolute property of the ladies so that they should be in the position to demand a transfer of it to themselves, or so that if they became bankrupt the trustee in bankruptcy should be able to claim it. ... I think that the trustee or trustees were intended to have a wide discretion as to whether any, and if any what, part of the fund should be applied for the benefit of the ladies and how the application should be made. That view would not deprive them of any right in the fund, because if the trustees had not done their duty – if they either failed to exercise their discretion or exercised it improperly – the ladies might successfully have applied to the Court to have the fund administered according to the terms of the circular. In the

result, therefore, there must be a declaration that there is a resulting trust of the moneys remaining unapplied for the benefit of the subscribers to the Abbott fund.

9.31 In *Re Andrew's Trust* (1905) money was raised by subscription for the children of the Bishop of Jerusalem. Again, the evidence as to the objects of the trust were slim, which was found in a letter by the now deceased canon who had initiated the appeal, who described the money as having been collected:

> ... for and towards the education of Bishop Barclay's children, ... [and] that it was by no means intended for the exclusive use of any one of them in particular, nor for equal division, but as deemed as necessary to defray the expenses of all, and that solely in the matter of education.

The children's education having been provided for under their father's will, the trustees sought a declaration enabling them to distribute the fund to the children. Kekewich J decided as follows:

> Here the only specified object was the education of the children. But I deem myself entitled to construe 'education' in the broadest possible sense, and not to consider the purpose exhausted because the children have attained such ages that education in the vulgar sense is no longer necessary. Even if it be construed in the narrower sense it is, in Wood VC's language, merely the motive of the gift, and the intention must be taken to provide for the children in the manner (they all then being infants) most useful.

9.32 After reviewing these two decisions in *Re Osoba* (1978), Megarry VC said:

> [I]f a trust is constituted for the assistance of certain persons by certain stated means there is a sharp distinction between cases where the beneficiaries have died and cases where they are still living. If they are dead, the court is willing to hold that there is a resulting trust for the donors; for the major purpose of the trust, that of providing help and benefit for the beneficiaries, comes to an end when the beneficiaries are all dead and so are beyond earthly help, whether by the stated means or otherwise. But if the beneficiaries are still living, the major purpose of providing help and benefit for the beneficiaries can still be carried out even after the stated means have all been accomplished, and so the court will be ready to treat the standard means as being merely indicative and not restrictive.

While there is obvious sense in this, Megarry VC appears to take a dangerously *ex post* view of the interpretation of testamentary gifts. Surely any interpretive strategy should be primarily devoted to figuring out the testator's intention from the outset, when the trustees who are to administer the trust receive the funds. It is then that they must be certain whether the trust is a gift of the whole with a mere motive or a *Re Sanderson* trust only of a part. Second, do Megarry VC's words about the means in a gift of the whole, that they 'are intended to be in the forefront', mean that even where the gift is of the whole, the trustees must *first* apply the money according to the motive, to defray the expenses of maintenance or education or whatever, until such time as they are no longer incurred, as when the education of the beneficiary is complete? In other words, does the gift become an absolute one only upon the 'purposes' either being accomplished or no longer capable of fulfilment? (Cf *Re Bowes*.) If so, what happens if before the 'purpose' comes to an end, ie before the trustees distribute the property as an absolute gift, the beneficiaries all die? Whether the gift is a gift of the whole or only a part surely cannot turn simply on the time of the beneficiaries' death, for that would engender a lottery whereby the remaining surplus of a large gift for the education of Albert would go to into his estate if he died the day after graduation (the purpose being complete, the gift of the whole would now 'take'), but would go on resulting trust if he died the day before. Megarry VC's guidance on the construction of such gifts should, then, be followed with some care.

9.33   *Re Osoba* (1978, Ch D, 1979, CA) concerned a testamentary trust of residue for the maintenance of the testator's widow and his mother, and for 'the training of my daughter Abiola up to university grade'. There was no gift over which would take effect on the completion of the purposes. The testator's mother had predeceased him, and by the time the case came before the court the testator's widow was dead, and Abiola had finished her university education; the question was whether the surplus funds held on trust went to the residuary beneficiaries on resulting trust, all of the trust purposes now being fulfilled. Megarry VC said he would lean toward construing a gift of residue as an absolute gift, since otherwise any surplus would go on resulting trust to those who would take on intestacy, not an intention one would normally ascribe to a testator. Megarry VC construed the instructions as to how the money should be spent as a mere indication of motive, and decided that the wife and Abiola together became entitled to the whole fund absolutely on the testator's death.

9.34 There are two reasons for having gone into these cases in some detail. The first is simply to make clear that such trusts, which are in a sense a variation on purpose trusts, exist in the law but do not violate the beneficiary principle so long as they are interpreted as 'trusts in which the subject matter is apportioned in reference to the costs of carrying out a well-defined purpose'. Second, however, if the subject matter of a trust can be apportioned in this way, then it is clear that well-defined purposes may be taken into account in determining how a trustee should distribute the trust property, since such purposes indicate clearly how the subject matter may be expended. Thus these trusts raise the question: even in cases where the beneficiaries' interests are not limited by the purpose, should the trustees nevertheless take the settlor's purpose into account? Should they spend the money on the stated purpose first? Should, for example, the trustees have refused to give Abiola the whole trust fund until she was either educated up to University grade, or it became clear that carrying out the purpose was impossible (say Abiola was so thick that no University would admit her)? One might suggest that the courts should at least require the trustees to comply with the settlor's directions, not so as to ultimately limit the extent of the beneficial gift, but to give effect in so far as possible to the means by the settlor chose to give it. Thus, it might be right to say that until the beneficiaries use their *Saunders v Vautier* rights to vary or collapse the trust, individual beneficiaries should be able to insist that the trustees comply with the settlor's declared means of distribution in so far as it is certain. This view does not detract from the beneficiary principle, because the whole gift would still be to the beneficiaries. It would only properly limit the trustee's discretion through the enforcement of the settlor's intentions by the people who are appropriately entitled to do so, ie the beneficiaries.

Gifts to unincorporated associations

9.35 The purpose trust rule applies with just the same force to gifts to unincorporated associations as it does to gifts to individuals. The problems are slightly trickier here, however, because though a settlor may give property to an unincorporated association, he may not be giving the property on trust to carry out a particular purpose he chooses or any of the general purposes of the association; rather, he may just be giving the property to the association absolutely, *in the hope* that they will spend it as he wishes. Gifts of the latter kind are perfectly valid, while those of the former are, of course, invalid, as purpose trusts.

9.36   The leading case on the application of the beneficiary principle to gifts to unincorporated associations (UIs) is the PC decision in *Leahy v A-G for New South Wales* (1959). The gift in question was of a large estate called 'Elmslea':

> ... upon trust for such order of nuns of the Catholic Church or the Christian Brothers as my executors and trustees shall select ...

This wide power of selection allowed the trustees to select orders of nuns which were not charitable under the law. This trust was saved by the application of a New South Wales statute which restricted the power of selection to charitable objects. A majority in the High Court of Australia accepted that the gift would also be valid as a gift to a UI, given to the members 'for the benefit of the community'. Viscount Simonds, giving the decision of the PC, said:

> [A]n unincorporated society ... though it is not a separate entity in law, is yet for many purposes regarded as a continuing entity and, however inaccurately, as something other than an aggregate of its members. In law a gift to such a society simpliciter is nothing else than a gift to its members at the date of the gift as joint tenants or tenants in common. It is for this reason that the prudent conveyancer provides that a receipt by the treasurer or other proper officer of the recipient society for a legacy to the society shall be held a sufficient discharge to executors. If it were not so, the executors could only get a valid discharge by obtaining a receipt from every member ... [But] what is meant when it is said that a gift is made to the individuals comprising the community and the words are added 'it is given to the benefit of the community?' If it is a gift to individuals, each of them is entitled to his distributive share (unless he has previously bound himself by the rules of the society that it shall be devoted to some other purpose). It is difficult to see what is added by the words 'for the benefit of the community'. If they are intended to import a trust, who are the beneficiaries? If the present members are beneficiaries, the words add nothing and are meaningless. If some other persons or purposes are intended, the conclusion cannot be avoided that the gift is void. For it is uncertain and no doubt tends to a perpetuity ... it is to be noted that it is because the gift can be upheld as a gift to the individual members that it is valid, even though it is given for the general purposes of the association. If the words 'for the general purposes of

218

the association' were held to import a trust, the question would have to be asked, what is the trust and who are the beneficiaries? A gift can be made to persons (including a corporation) but it cannot be made to a purpose or to an object ... It is therefore by disregarding the words 'for the purposes of the association' ...and treating the gift as an absolute gift to individuals that it can be sustained.

The testator's words could only be construed as intending a trust for the purposes of the orders that might be selected, not a gift to their individual members, so, but for the statute the gift would have failed.

The contract-holding theory

9.37   In *Neville Estates Ltd v Madden* (1961), Cross J interpreted *Leahy* to hold that there are three possible constructions of a gift to a UI. The first is as a gift to the individual members as co-owners, whereby each may take their own share. Secondly the gift may be to the individual members:

> ... but subject to their respective contractual rights and liabilities towards one another as members of the association. In such a case a member cannot sever his share. It would accrue to the other members on his death or resignation, even though such members include persons who become members after the gift took effect ... Thirdly, the terms or circumstances of the gift or the rules of the association may show that the property in question is not to be at the disposal of the members for the time being, but is to be held in trust for or applied for the purposes of the association as a quasi-corporate entity. In this case the gift will fail unless the association is a charitable body.

In *Re Recher's Will Trusts* (1972), Brightman J expanded on the nature of the second kind of gift:

> In the absence of words which purport to impose a trust, the legacy is a gift to the members beneficially, not as joint tenants or as tenants in common so as to entitle each member to an immediate distributive share, but as an accretion to the funds which are the subject-matter of the contract which the members have made *inter se*.

This analysis of the way in which unincorporated associations receive gifts and hold property is generally termed the 'contract-holding theory', although it operates through a trust of the association members' money.

219

The treasurer-trustees of the association hold the association's funds on trust for the members of the association, to deal with the funds according to the rules of the association created by the contract of the members *inter se*. A gift which is an 'accretion to the funds' is therefore a gift to the treasurer-trustee of the UI to hold such property on the same trusts as he does the other funds of the UI. Thus the given funds become subject to the rules of the UI which determine the way the treasure-trustee deals with the members' funds. (See *Re Bucks Constabulary Widows' and Orphans' Fund Friendly Society (No 2)* (1979), per Walton J.)

9.38   The contract-holding theory explains how unincorporated associations may receive gifts which they can devote to their purposes, without such gifts being purpose trusts. That does not mean that a gift to an unincorporated association, properly construed, may not be on trust to carry out a purpose, and therefore invalid. *Re Lipinski's Will Trusts* (1976) concerned a gift to an unincorporated association which could well have been construed as a purpose trust. A testator left half of his residuary estate to 'the Hull Judeans (Maccabi) Association in memory of my late wife to be used solely in the work of constructing the new buildings for the Association and/or improvements to the said buildings.' Interpreting the provision, Oliver J felt that little turned on the fact that the gift was expressed as a memorial to the testators' wife – while that expressed a tribute the testator wished to pay, it did not, by itself, indicate a desire to create a perpetual endowment. Neither did the fact that money was to be available solely for construction or improvements indicate a perpetual purpose, for such money could be spend right away – 'improvements' is different in this respect from 'maintenance', which may well indicate a perpetual purpose trust. Framing the legacy in terms of a sole purpose only ruled out construing the gift as one to the members absolutely in equal shares.

9.39   Oliver J considered that the members of the association for the time being were an ascertainable class of beneficiaries, and given the existence of such a class, could see no reason why the trust should fail:

> If a valid gift may be made to an unincorporated body as a simple accretion to the funds which are subject-matter of the contract which the members have made inter se ... I do not really see why such a gift, which specifies a purpose which is within the powers of the unincorporated body and of

220

which the members of that body are the beneficiaries, should fail. Why are not the beneficiaries able to enforce the trust or, indeed, in the exercise of their contractual rights, to terminate the trust for their own benefit? Where the donee body is itself the beneficiary of the prescribed purpose, there seems to me to be the strongest argument in common sense for saying that the gift should be an absolute one within the second category, the more so where, if the purpose is carried out, the members can by appropriate action vest the resulting property in themselves, for here the trustees and the beneficiaries are the same person.

Oliver J argued that this interpretation of the law was at least consistent with *Leahy* as in that case there was no such ascertainable class. Second, there was authority in *Re Turkington* (1937):

> [T]here the gift was to a masonic lodge 'as a fund to build a suitable temple in Stratford'. The members of the lodge being both the trustees and the beneficiaries of the temple, Luxmoore J construed the gift as an absolute one to the members of the lodge for the time being.

Finally, Goff J's decision in *Re Denley* to uphold a purpose trust where there was such a class was 'directly in point'. Oliver J considered that although the gift was solely for a particular purpose, *Re Bowes*, amongst other cases, was authority for the proposition that where the entire amount of the gift was to go to the beneficiary, the purpose could be overridden as a mere motive or superadded direction. His conclusion, as we have seen (**9.14**), was that the gift was valid as one to the members, though expressed pretty plainly as a purpose.

Inward versus outward looking purposes

9.40　It appears that one criterion for Oliver J's holding was that the 'donee body is itself the beneficiary of the prescribed purpose', in other words that the purpose was 'inward-looking', as a benefit to the members themselves, rather than 'outward-looking', as one which might or necessarily benefit members of the community outside the association. Such a requirement is very doubtful. On the facts of this case, the objects of the association's constitution were clearly to benefit Anglo-Jewish youth generally, so such a requirement would have made the trust fail in the present case. In *Re Bucks Constabulary Widows' and Ophans' Fund (No 2)* (1979) Walton J said that the analysis of the way in which a UI holds its funds is no different:

... whether the purpose for which the members of the association associate are a social club, a sporting club, to establish a widows' and orphans' fund, to obtain a separate Parliament for Cornwall, or to further the advance of alchemy. It matters not. All the assets of the association are held in trust for its members – of course subject to the contractual claims of anybody having a valid contract with the association – save and except to the extent to which valid trusts have otherwise been declared of its property.

As long as the 'purpose' framing the gift is one which the members themselves pursue by spending their own money under the rules of their association, the gift is to their 'inward-looking' benefit, and the court can construe such a gift as an accretion to the association's funds. (See also *Re Recher's Will Trusts* per Brightman J.)

9.41   While requiring a gift framed as a purpose trust to be 'inward-looking' before finding it valid is, therefore, unnecessary in the case of a UI, it may well be necessary if the class of beneficiaries are not members of such an association. Recall that in *Re Denley* the purpose trust was only valid because it was considered to be directly or indirectly for the benefit of the class of ascertainable beneficiaries. If outward-looking purposes could be valid so long as the settlor named a class of beneficiaries, then *Re Astor* is essentially overthrown. For example, by naming a class of beneficiaries consisting of all the employees of national and regional newspapers in the UK, which class is ascertainable on the is or is not test, Viscount Astor could have provided a class which would indirectly benefit from the outward-looking purposes he intended, members of which class would have standing to enforce it but who for all intents and purposes could never get together under the principle in *Saunders v Vautier* to vary or end the trust. Thus, it must be the case that gifts expressed as trusts for outward-looking purposes may be valid if made to unincorporated associations just for the reason that the membership, as the class of ascertainable beneficiaries is, by definition almost, capable of getting together and deciding whether to carry out the purpose or not. This prevents the possibility that a *Re Astor* abstract and impersonal trust will ever actually gain an independent life.

9.42   *Re Lipinski* raises once again the status of the settlor's purpose – as Oliver J makes quite clear, the members of the unincorporated association are free to ignore it completely if they so wish. A prospective Mr Lipinski who wishes above all to see his purpose carried out may be well advised to frame his gift as a *Sanderson*-type trust, eg 'to the Hull Judean (Maccabi) Association in such amounts as equal its expenditure on new buildings' with a clear gift over of any remaining funds, or a gift on condition. A settlor should bear in mind that the certainty requirements for conditions subsequent, eg 'but if they fail to construct new buildings within five years of my death, then to the Red Cross', are strict, and if uncertain the gift will be treated as absolute (**3.43**), so care must be taken to frame the condition in a way which can be clearly applied.

The dissolution of unincorporated associations

9.43   The 'contract-holding' theory of the way in which unincorporated associations hold their property is now generally accepted. It must however, be distinguished from a different 'contractual' theory of UIs, which is of doubtful validity. Under this theory the property of UI's can only be explained as the holding of property on a true purpose trust, which would violate the beneficiary principle. In order to consider the merits of this theory, we must briefly return to the subject of automatic resulting trusts, or ARTs.

9.44   In *Re Gillingham Bus Disaster Fund* (1957) funds were raised on appeal to defray the cost of funerals for those who had been killed when a bus ran into a column of marching cadets, and to care for those who were disabled; any surplus funds were to be devoted to 'other worthy causes'. The gift was a *Sanderson*-type trust for the cadets, but the gift over 'to worthy causes' was void for being a non-charitable purpose trust (**13.34**). The Treasury Solicitor claimed the surplus as *bona vacantia*, ie goods without an owner. Harman J approached the question as follows:

> The general principle must be that where money is held upon trust and the trusts declared do not exhaust the fund it will revert to the donor or settlor under what is called a resulting trust. The reasoning behind this is that the settlor or donor did not part with his money absolutely out and out but only sub modo to the intent that his wishes as declared by the declaration of trust should be carried into effect. When, therefore, this has been done any surplus still belongs to him. This doctrine does not, in my judgment, rest on any evidence of the state of mind of the settlor, for in the vast majority of cases no doubt he does not expect to see his money back: he has created a trust which so far as he can see will

absorb the whole of it. The resulting trust arises where that expectation is for some unforeseen reason cheated of fruition, and is an inference of law based on after-knowledge of the event.

Since here the subscribers' expectations were 'cheated of fruition', an ART of the surplus arose in their favour in the proportions to which they had contributed. However, the resulting trust doctrine in appeal cases of this kind seems somewhat pointless for those who anonymously gave small amounts in collection boxes, for it means that the trustees must pay the money into court, where it will be held, essentially in perpetuity, on the off-chance that one of the anonymous subscribers of small amounts to the fund cares enough to get his proportionate share back to come forward and prove that he had made a donation is, hence the suggestion to treat the property as *bona vacantia*. Nevertheless, preferring to rely upon principle over matters of convenience, Harman J held firm on the resulting trust:

> In my judgment the Crown has failed to show that this case should not follow the ordinary rule merely because there was a number of donors who, I assume, are unascertainable. I see no reason myself to suppose that the small giver who is anonymous has any wider intention than the large giver who can be named. They all give for the one object. If they can be found by inquiry the resulting trust can be executed in their favour. If they cannot I do not see how the money could then ... change its destination and become bona vacantia.

9.45   Under the contract-holding theory, it is clear that the members of a UI own the society's property under the terms of their association, and therefore, upon dissolution of the society, the property is clearly not *bona vacantia*, but nor is there need for any resulting trust. The members have owned it all along, and therefore it is theirs to be distributed amongst themselves upon dissolution. Before this theory was articulated, however, there was a line of cases in which upon the dissolution of a UI the only alternative destinations of surplus funds were thought to be an ART and *bona vacantia*. In *Re Printers and Transferrers Amalgamated Trades Protection Society* (1899) contributions from the society's members funded benefits for the contibutors, in particular strike and lock-out benefits, and in *Re Hobourn Aero Components Ltd's Air Raid Distress Fund* (1946) employees contributed funds to pay benefits to members on war service or those injured in air raids. In both cases, on the dissolution of the associations the court held that there was a resulting trust of the remaining funds in

224

favour of the members in proportion to their contributions. By contrast in *Cunnack v Edwards* (1896), CA, where members contributed to provide widow's benefits, upon dissolution the court reasoned that the members had received all they had contracted for, ie the relevant widow's pensions, and so the surplus was *bona vacantia*.

9.46 *Re West Sussex Constabulary's Widow, Children and Benevolent (1930) Fund Trusts* (1968) falls into this line of cases. In 1968 the West Sussex Constabulary was amalgamated with other police forces, and therefore its benevolent fund, which paid allowances to the widowed mothers, widows, and children of deceased constables who were members, was to be wound up. The forces were amalgamated from 1 January 1968, and the remaining members of the fund held a meeting in June 1968 at which it was decided that the remaining funds, some £35,000, should be used to purchase annuities for those widows, etc, who were receiving benefits, the balance to be distributed to the members. Goff J reasoned that the amalgamation of the forces meant that there were no longer any members of the fund by June 1968, since the only persons who could be members were constables of the West Sussex constabulary, which had ceased to exist. Thus the June 1968 decision was invalid and the funds remained undisposed of. Goff J accepted that the members might have devoted the funds in this way had they met before the amalgamation, but they had simply acted too late. However, if it were true that the contract *inter se* between the members required that they be constables of the West Sussex force, then the amalgamation of the forces would have put their contract at an end. But that would only mean that the contractual rules of the association, such as whether a majority vote could bind all members, would no longer be operative. The death of this contract would do nothing to alter the *ownership rights* of the members to the fund, only their *contractual rights and duties* to deal with it in certain ways. Thus if the members were owners of the fund before 1 January 1968 (though bound by contract to deal with them under the rules), they remained owners afterward.

9.47 The former members then argued that they were the beneficial owners of the fund, as with any other UI, but Goff J rejected this argument; the fund simply did not look like a members' club, but was a pensions or dependant relatives fund; thus rather than being for the benefit of the members for the time being, only third parties could benefit.

9.48 The members then argued that there was a resulting trust in their favour. In rejecting this argument, Goff J advance the 'contractual' basis of the decision in *Cunnack*:

> In my judgment the doctrine of resulting trust is clearly inapplicable to the contributions of [the former and surviving members]. Those persons who remained members until their deaths are in any event excluded because they have had all they contracted for, either because their widows and dependants have received or are in receipt of the prescribed funds, or because they did not have a widow or dependants ... they and the surviving members alike are also in my judgment unable to claim under a resulting trust because they put up their money on a contractual basis and not one of trust ...

The only persons who had a claim, therefore, were those surviving members who had dependants who had not received any benefits yet – they might be able to claim against the fund on the basis of total failure of consideration or frustration of the contract. This application of 'contractual' reasoning must be wrong, since it requires that the funds were held on a perpetual pure purpose trust, ie a trust to enter into contracts to provide annuities and so on for members of a constabulary – in short, a trust to carry out a (non-profit) business; the funds are held not for any beneficiaries, but for the purpose of entering into and discharging contractual obligations.

9.49 In *Re Bucks Constabulary Fund*, a case with very similar facts, Walton J found himself 'wholly unable to square [Goff J's decision in *West Sussex*] with the relevant principles of law applicable', and applied the modern contract-holding analysis. The member/constables of the *Bucks* fund were entitled to it in equal shares on dissolution of the association.

9.50 However, though on the modern contracting holding theory there should have been no 'surplus' funds to dispose of in *Re West Sussex*, Goff J's treatment of undisposed of funds is regarded as correct if applied to cases where an ART properly arises, as in a case like *Gillingham Bus Disaster Fund*. The surplus is to be notionally divided in proportion to its sources, ie (1) Money raised by raffles or entertainments, whereby individuals contract with the association or trustees, the profits of which go into the fund; (2) small anonymous donations, such as those received in collecting boxes; and (3) identifiable donations, such as amounts contributed by cheque and legacies. An

ART arises only for the last category. No one in the first category who contributes to the fund incidentally as a function of buying a raffle ticket or attending an entertainment has given money upon trust; he receives his full benefit from the contract; Goff J reasoned that the purchaser may or may not be interested in aiding the cause, so therefore no trust intention can be imputed to him, and secondly, his contribution is indirect, via any profit, if any, accrues from his purchase. This does not seem particularly justifiable. If the trustees engage in commercially viable entertainments or raffles which make profits, which they then donate to the trust, of course the purchasers are out of the picture. But if, as is common, the purchasers 'purchase' entertainment or buy raffle tickets fully realising there is a large gift element, surely the intention to be presumed of such a purchaser is that the profits certain to be made are to be applied to, and only to, the purposes of the appeal. That they doubtless don't expect any money some day to return to them on failure or completion of the purpose of the appeal would put them in the same boat as any other contributor. Similarly, Goff J reasoned that the contributors of small anonymous donations must be assumed to have intended to part with their money absolutely in all circumstances. Again, distinguishing between large, identifiable contributors and small contributors or raffle ticket purchasers on the basis of their likely intentions is difficult to sustain. The better basis for the result is simply that the ART solution, though theoretically correct, Is so patently pointless in the case of the small contributors and purchasers, none of who will ever try to prove a valid claim to the money, that the *bona vacantia* solution is simply imposed as the most practical result in the circumstances. As Harman J points out in *Gillingham*, surely the only thing that distinguishes these classes of contributors is the possibility that they might actually be able to claim their money – there is no reason to believe that they were more or less likely to entertain any 'secondary' intentions governing the proper direction of their money if the primary trust failed. Unlike Harman J, however, for practical reasons that fact should not prevent the *West Sussex* result. As it stands then, neither *Gillingham Bus Disaster Fund* nor *West Sussex* disclose any factual settlor's intention which can displace the operation of an ART, and it is difficult to imagine one that realistically is likely to arise. What will displace it, apparently, is the inconvenience of the ART's effect in practice. It was therefore probably incorrect of Lord Browne-Wilkinson to have cited *West Sussex* as a case where settlors' actual intentions displaced an ART (**4.14**); that the ART there was supplanted by the *bona vacantia* solution is much better explained as a matter of convenience, not because the settlors' intentions so dictated.

9.51   The recent decision of Scott J in *Davis v Richards and Wallington Industries* (1990) makes matters less clear. There Scott J held *obiter* that in the case of a pension trust which had a surplus, ie more funds than necessary on actuarial principles to pay the various existing and future pensions, the proportion of the surplus deriving from the employer's contributions would be held on resulting trust for the employer. As regards the proportion deriving from the employees' contributions, however, such funds were to be treated as *bona vacantia*, one reason being the difficulties in working out the respective shares of the employees to the money held on resulting trust: different members who have historically contributed the same amount would be entitled under the scheme to different benefits through the formula for determining pensions (the difference in factors such as length of service and salary on retirement can bring about this result) and those who take a refund of contributions instead of a pension generally receive less value. This seems a quite unjustifiable application of the inconvenience test, since the shares of individuals to the surplus could be divided either on a past contributions basis or on a defined benefit basis as things stood when the surplus was to be distributed. That such a choice must be made is surely not so grave a problem that the money must be declared *bona vacantia*. As to the members claiming a refund, if they are in the scheme (ie have not taken their refund) when the actuary declares the surplus, they should take on whatever basis the others do; if they have already exited, they may justifiably be excluded.

Less than unincorporated associations – the case of political parties

9.52   In *Re Grant's Will Trusts* (1979), the testator left his entire real and personal estate to the Chertsey and Walton Constituency Labour Party. Vinelott J held that the gift was one to create a perpetual trust to further the purposes of the local Labour party, and therefore the gift failed. He held that the local Labour party was not an unincorporated association, because its rules were capable of being

228

altered by an outside body, the National Labour party, which could in fact direct the local party to transfer its assets to it. Furthermore, the local members could not:

> … alter the rules so as to make the property bequeathed by the testator applicable for some purpose other than that provided by the rules; nor could they direct that property to be divided amongst themselves beneficially.

It is not clear whether Vinelott J's reasoning on this point is sound. While there is no other case which discusses the issue directly, Cross J in *Neville Estates* proceeded on the assumption that the Catford Synagogue was an unincorporated association though affiliated with the United Synagogue which limited the power of the Catford members to alter their rules; moreover the United Synagogue could require the Catford Synagogue to transfer its real property to the United Synagogue.

9.53 In *Conservative and Unionist Central Office* the CA decided that the national Conservative Party was not an unincorporated association either. The party was an historical political movement, in which the various membership constituencies, the parliamentary party and the constitutency associations, had political but not contractual links. In particular, there were no rules by which the constituencies could control the leader of the party's or the central office's expenditure of the central office funds, and there was no historical point at which any contract between the members *inter se* could be said to have occurred.

9.54 If national political parties, and their local constituency parties, are not unincorporated associations, then how do they hold their property? In *Conservative Central Office* Brightman LJ suggested the 'mandate' theory to explain how *living* subscribers to the party donate their funds. Such funds are given upon an order from the donor, the principal, to the party treasurer, his agent; such an order is a mandate; if the treasurer fails to apply the money as the order specifies (here for party purposes) he may be sued to so apply it, and he may be restrained from misapplying it. The mandate becomes irrevocable once the treasurer mixes it with other party funds. Brightman LJ, however, acknowledged that this analysis would not explain testamentary gifts to political parties because:

... no agency could be set up at the moment of death between a testator and his chosen agent. A discussion of this problem is outside the scope of this appeal and, although I think that the answer is not difficult to find, I do not wish to prejudge it.

It is, unfortunately, quite difficult to find a way of making a testamentary gift which fits coherently with the mandate theory of *inter vivos* gifts. A better analysis may be that both *inter vivos* and testamentary gifts to political parties are conditional gifts at law or in equity **(4.17)**.

The rule against perpetuities

9.55   There are two principle cases in which the rule against perpetuities **(3.17** et seq) becomes relevant in the discussion of the beneficiary principle: the cases of the few, anomalous, true purpose trusts, and in the context of gifts for unincorporated associations. A true purpose trust, such as a trust for the upkeep of a grave, can last forever. Therefore, if the testator does not specifically limit his gift to a perpetuity period, the gift will be void for perpetuity. It may be the case that a testator is not entitled to choose the statutory perpetuity period of 80 years provided by the Perpetuities and Accumulations Act 1964. This turns on technical considerations regarding the interpretation of s 15(4) of the Act and the question whether the rule against perpetuities applies in a distinct way to pure purpose trusts (see Matthews (1996)), and no case has decided the point. A testator may, however, employ a lives-in-being-plus-21-years clause to indicate a perpetuity period. For this purpose a 'royal lives' clause is appropriate, for example, '£10,000 to my trustees on trust to maintain my grave, such trust not to extend beyond the expiry of 21 years following the death of the last surviving descendent of Queen Elizabeth II alive at my death'. Since there are no lives in being which are inherently relevant to the duration of a purpose trust, the testator must choose people whose lives shall count. The purpose of picking the descendants of a king or queen is simply that, being famous, it will be easy for the trustees to determine when the last surviving life in being dies. If the testator does not use a royal lives clause, and wishes to set an exact time period, then, assuming he is not entitled to use the statutory period of eighty years or less, he may only choose a period within the definable portion of the common law rule, ie the portion not determined by the duration of any lives in being, thus periods of 21 years or less. If the testator specifies that his gift is to continue 'for as long as the law allows' or

230

uses some similar phrase, courts have allowed the gift to last for 21 years (*Pirbright v Salwey* (1896); *Re Hooper* (1932)).

9.56 In the case of unincorporated associations, the problems are different. As we have seen, there are no valid pure purpose trusts for the purposes of an unincorporated association. For such gifts to be valid, they must be, or they must be interpreted to be, gifts to the members of the association themselves. But in some circumstances, the gift might properly be interpreted to be for the present and future members of the association, thus a gift to a fluctuating class, which may gain members as long as the association lasts. If the trust were not limited, the shares of any number of future individuals might vest for as long as the association lasts, hence indefinitely. Therefore a settlor who wishes to give a gift in these terms should ensure that it comes to an end within a suitable perpetuity period, either a stated period of eighty years or less, or a period determined by the relevant lives in being for the gift plus 21 years (here the relevant lives in being would be the members of the association at the time the trust takes effect), or a period determined by a royal lives clause. Even if the testator indicates no perpetuity period at all, the gift might possibly be saved by s 4(4) of the 1964 Act, which automatically closes the class of beneficiaries at the end of the period determined by taking the members at the time of the gift as the relevant lives in being, plus 21 years (see Hayton (1996a), 180-181).

Further Reading

Gravells (1977); Millet (1985); Rickett (1980); Green (1980).

Must read cases: *Re Astor's Settlement Trusts* (1952); *Re Denley* (1968); *Re Grant's Will Trusts* (1979); *Re Lipinski's Will Trusts* (1977); *Re Sanderson's Trust* (1857); *Re Osoba* (1977); *Leahy v A-G (NSW)* (1959); *Re Bucks Constabulary Widows' and Ophans' Fund* (1979); *Conservative and Unionist Central Office v Burrell* (1982).

Self-test questions

1.   Explain the rationale of the beneficiary principle; is this rationale less persuasive following the decision in *McPhail v Doulton* (1970)?

2. How may unincorporated associations hold property?

3. Smith dies, leaving £100,000 to the Aylesbury Morris Dancing Society 'for the purpose of building a Morris Dancing Centre as a memorial to myself'. Shortly after Smith's death the club decides to wind up, as most members wish to join another Morris dancing club. The treasurers report that the Society's current funds are £8,150, which amounts to a share of £163 for each of the fifty members, a figure which does not include the bequest of Smith, of which they have just been advised. Discuss.

4. Simon is a member of his local branch of the Socialist Workers Party, and is also a member of a Marxist reading group of about thirty people who raise money to buy publications by various means and who have a treasurer who holds the group's funds in a local bank. Simon has found out that he has six months to live. On his death he wants to ensure that his considerable fortune is devoted to the furtherance of Marxist causes. Advise him.

CHAPTER TEN

The Trust Up and Running

SUMMARY

The duty of investment

The Trustee Investments Act 1961

The standard of prudence in making trust investments

'Social' or 'ethical' investing

The delegation of trustee functions

The power of maintenance

The power of advancement

Variation of trusts

Appointment, retirement and removal of trustees

Custodian and judicial trustees

10.1   Trustees, as legal owners of the trust property, have all the rights and powers to deal with the trust property as would any other legal owner, though they must, of course, exercise these rights and powers solely in the interest of the beneficiaries. Because they are trustees, however, they have further particular powers and duties arising from their office, the most important of which are the duty of investment and the powers of maintenance and advancement.

The duty of investment

10.2   The duty of investment has two main aspects: (1) a duty to invest the trust property so as to be 'even-handed' between the different classes of beneficiaries; and (2) a duty to invest so that the fund is preserved from risk yet a reasonable return on capital is made.

Even-handedness between the beneficiaries

10.3 In many trusts the benefit of the property is divided between income and capital beneficiaries (**3.7**). In legal terms, income is whatever property actually arises as a separate payment as a result of holding the capital property. Thus on shares the dividends are the income, on land the rent is income, and so on. The income beneficiary is entitled to whatever income arises. On the other hand, if holding the property yields no new property rights, rental payments or dividends or so forth, there is no income, even if the shares or the land double in value, making a huge economic return on the investment. Some investments produce no income: eg currency, gold, antiques. Conversely, some investments will be 'all' income, what are called a 'wasting assets'; an example is a 20-year lease: the rent is income, though in economic turns it represents the return on the initial capital investment in the lease; in legal terms the capital just slowly reduces to zero as the lease runs its course. Therefore it is obvious that the trustee may favour the income beneficiary at the expense of the capital beneficiary, or *vice versa*, by making particular kinds of investments. The law therefore imposes a duty of even-handedness, which requires the trustee to balance their interests fairly in making his investment decisions.

10.4 The two chief characteristics of any investment are risk and return, and they correlate directly. That is, the higher a risk an investment presents, the greater the percentage return on capital any investor will demand. You will (at the time of writing) win a greater sum betting on Scotland to win the World Cup than on Italy (alas). Historically, the law has favoured the safety, or non-riskiness of trusts investments over high return. In particular, following the burst of the 'South Sea Bubble' in 1720, an orgy of speculation in shares of the South Sea Company which ended, as one might expect, in tears, equity regarded investment in company shares as a risk quite beyond the pale. Therefore, until this century trustees were restricted to investment in 'consols', fixed-interest government securities. Over time the range and type of 'trustee' investments has been expanded, and the current law which authorises trust investments is found in the Trustee Investment Act 1961.

10.5 Of course, the trust instrument itself may, and invariably does, empower the trustee to invest as the settlor allows, and in general, such investment clauses are very wide. Originally, again out of concern for the safety of the trust property, investment clauses were interpreted

234

restrictively, but now are given their plain meaning(Re *Harari's Settlement Trusts* (1949)). If there is no express investment clause, the statutory regime governs the trustee's investments, and because it is generally considered both a nuisance and a real fetter on the trustee's ability to secure a good return, Goodhart (1996) believes:

> ... that any professional person who drafts a trust instrument which leaves the powers of investment to be governed by the Trustee Investments Act would be guilty of professional negligence.

For this reason, the 1961 Act has limited significance in practice. Furthermore, as we shall see, even for those unfortunate enough to be governed by it rather than by an express clause, in recent years the restrictions have abated somewhat and look to do so even more. Accordingly it will be given fairly short shrift here. It is much more important that you grasp the general duties of even-handedness and prudence which apply to all trustees in their investment decisions.

The Trustee Investments Act 1961

10.6 The 1961 Act is one embodiment of an approach to regulating trustee investments which is generally called the 'legal list' approach. The legal list approach contrasts with the 'prudent man' approach. Under the former, the state in its wisdom chooses a number of particular kinds of investments which may be made by trustees; these investments are supposed to be safe but yield a reasonable return. A trustee may not make an investment which is not on the list; if he does he will be in breach of trust. Under the prudent man approach, the trustees are not legally prohibited from making any particular kind of investment. They will be found in breach of trust, however, if they do not invest as a prudent man would.

10.7 The 1961 Act expanded the legal list of investments from the much narrower list that obtained up to that time under the Trustee Act 1925. It allowed for the first time investment in some equities, ie shares of companies, which met certain criteria which were intended to establish their safety as investments.

10.8 The Act divides investments into three kinds: narrow-range investments, wider range investments, and special range investments (ss

1(1), 1(3), 2(1), 2(2),3(1)). Narrow range investments are the more traditional interest-generating trustee investments, and these are sub-divided into Part I investments which are the safest, eg national savings certificates, and the somewhat riskier debt instruments of Part II, whose capital value may fluctuate, eg company debentures and treasury stock. Wider range or Part III investments include equities, eg certain company shares. Special range investments are simply all those investments specifically authorised by the trust instrument. Originally trustees governed by the Act rather than by an express investment power in the trust instrument could invest up to 50% of the trust in Part III, ie equity, investments, but this proportion was extended to 75% by statutory instrument in 1996 (s 13 (1), SI 1996/845). Before investing in Part II or III investments, the trustee is required to obtain investment advice in writing (s 6 (2)-(5)), and this applies to investments of this kind whether the power to do so arises by virtue of the Act or by an express power in a trust instrument (see also *Re Whiteley* (1886); *Learoyd v Whiteley* (1887); *Cowan v Scargill* (1984)).

10.9   Where the trustee seeks to invest in Part III investments, he is required to divide the trust fund into separate funds, wider range investments to be made only with moneys from the fund segregated for that purpose. However, there is no requirement to periodically re-balance these separate funds so that the original proportions are maintained, and furthermore, since payments out of the trust can be made wholly out of one of the separate funds, nothing in the Act prevents the total share in wider-range investments from greatly exceeding the original allowable proportions over time. A draft order under the Deregulation and Contracting Out Act 1994 which would have further relaxed the restrictions on wider-range investments fell with the dissolution of the last Parliament. The measure was uncontroversial, and may be introduced again, but more substantial reforms, such as the repeal or substantial amendment of the Act, cannot be ruled out. Therefore, the basis of judging trustees generally must, to the extent that a trustee is not governed by a legal list, as most currently are not and in the near future none might be, be those principles which elaborate the duty of prudence.

10.10   One of the main sources of dissatisfaction with the Act is its out-of-date approach to the economics of investment. Today investment strategy is informed by 'modern portfolio theory', by which the risks of particular investments are balanced against the risks of others. Different

Investments are chosen which have offsetting risks; thus, for example, if natural gas sales rise at the expense of oil sales, investing in both offsets the risks of one against the other – if gas does well and gas shares rise, then oil shares will fall, and vice versa. Thus the overall risk of investing in both is less than the individual risk of either. The watchword, then, is 'diversification'; by diversifying the investment portfolio investments which singly pose substantial risks together provide a portfolio with a much more reasonable risk. Thus the modern prudent investor is to be judged not by the individual investment vehicles he chooses, in particular whether they are nominated on a legal list, but on the overall portfolio. Section 6(1)(a) of the 1961 reflects this by requiring the trustee to have regard:

> ... to the need for diversification of investments of the trust ...

and in *Nestle v National Westminster Bank plc* (1988) Hoffmann J said:

> Modern trustees acting within their investment powers are entitled to be judged by the standards of current portfolio theory, which emphasises the risk of the entire portfolio rather than the risk attaching to each investment taken in isolation.

The standard of prudence in making trust investments

10.11   A standard of prudence is a general standard applying both to trustees who invest from a legal list and to those who are given wider powers under an express clause. Such a standard cannot be spelled out in terms of black and white rules: like many other standards in the law, it is a standard which depends on a reasonable appreciation of the purposes the standard is to serve and the circumstances in which it applies.

10.12   In the leading case of *Speight v Gaunt* (1883), the trustee paid some £15,000 to a broker on the strength of a written 'bought note' which asserted that the broker had bought securities in that amount. The broker had never purchased the securities, and his fraud was not discovered before his subsequent bankruptcy, so all the money was lost. The trustee was not liable. The payment of funds to a broker in this way was in accord with the standard business practice of purchasing securities. Jessel MR said:

[A] trustee is not bound because he is a trustee to conduct in other than the ordinary and usual way in which similar business is conducted by mankind in transactions of their own. It could never be reasonable to make a trustee adopt further and better precautions than an ordinary prudent man of business would adopt, or to conduct the business in any other way.

The judgment was affirmed in similar terms by the HL.

10.13 In *Re Whiteley* (1886) a trustee was found liable for imprudently invested £3,000 upon a mortgage of a brickworks. The land itself was not so valuable as to provide sufficient security for the mortgage – only if the brickworks operation continued as a going concern, which, in the event it did not, was the loan likely to be repaid. In the CA Lindley LJ framed the standard thus:

The duty of a trustee is not to take such care only as a prudent man would take if he had only himself to consider; the duty rather is to take such care as an ordinary prudent man would take if he were minded to make an investment for the benefit of other people for whom he felt morally bound to provide.

In the HL (*Learoyd v Whiteley* (1887)) Lord Watson said:

As a general rule the law requires of a trustee no higher degree of diligence in the execution of his office than a man of ordinary prudence would exercise in the management of his own private affairs. Yet he is not allowed the same discretion in investing the moneys of the trust as if he were a person sui juris dealing with his own estate. Businessmen of ordinary prudence may, and frequently do, select investments which are more or less of a speculative character; but it is the duty of a trustee to confine himself to the class of investments which are permitted by the trust, and likewise to avoid all investments of that class which are attended with hazard.

10.14 A trustee is not required to 'beat the market' or save the trust investments from declining in value due to general economic conditions. In *Re Chapman* (1896) Lindley LJ said:

[A] trustee is not a surety, nor is he an insurer; he is only liable for some wrong done by himself, and loss of trust money is not per se proof of such wrong ... There is no rule of law which compels the court to hold that an honest trustee is liable to make good loss sustained by retaining an authorised security in a falling market, if he did so honestly and prudently, in the belief that it was the best course of action in the interest of all parties. Trustees acting honestly, with ordinary prudence or and within the limits of their trust, are not liable for mere errors of judgement.

(See also *Nestle v National Westminster Bank* (1979).)

10.15   Special considerations apply when the trust is a controlling shareholder in a company. In *Re Lucking's Will Trusts* (1967) a majority of shares in a family business was held on trust for the family members. One trustee, one of the family members, installed his friend as manager of the company, who proved most unsuitable, drawing large amounts of the company funds for his own use. The trustee failed to detect the manager's withdrawals until it was too late to recover them, and was held liable. Cross J said:

> Now what steps, if any, does a reasonably prudent man who finds himself a majority shareholder in a private company take with regard to the management of the company's affairs? He does not, I think, content himself with such information as to the management of the company's affairs as he is entitled to as shareholder, but ensures that he is represented on the board ... Alternatively, he may find someone who will act as his nominee on the board ... trustees holding a controlling interest ought to ensure so far as they can that they have such information as to the progress of the company's affairs as directors would have. If they sit back and allow the company to be run by the minority shareholders and receive no more information that shareholders are entitled to, they do so at their risk if things go wrong.

In *Bartlett v Barclays Bank Trust Co Ltd* (1979) almost all the assets of the trust consisted in private shares of a company which managed real property. The company embarked on a programme of hazardous and, as it turned out, disastrous property development, of which the trust company took little notice, implicitly trusting in the 'professional calibre' of the company board. The trust company was liable for the losses. Brightman J said:

> I do not understand Cross J [in *Lucking*] to have been saying that in every case where trustees have a controlling interest in a company it is their duty to ensure that one of their number is a director or that they will have a nominee on the board ... He was merely outlining convenient methods by which a prudent man of business (as also a trustee) with a

239

controlling interest in a private company, can place himself in a position to make an informed decision whether any action is appropriate to be taken for the protection of the asset. Other methods may be equally satisfactory and convenient, depending on the circumstances of the individual case. Alternatives which spring to mind are the receipt of the copies of the agenda and minutes of board meetings if regularly held, the receipt of monthly management accounts in the case of a trading concern, or quarterly reports.

A higher standard for paid trustees?

10.16 It is occasionally said that a higher standard of diligence will be expected of a paid trustee. In *Bartlett v Barclays Bank Trust Co Ltd* (1979) Brightman J opined that:

> ... a higher duty of care is plainly due from someone like a trust corporation which carries on a specialised business of trust management. A trust corporation holds itself out in its advertising literature as being above ordinary mortals. With a specialist staff of trained trust officers and managers, with ready access to financial information and professional advice, dealing with and solving trust problems day after day, the trust corporation holds itself out, and rightly, as capable of providing an expertise which it would be unrealistic to expect and unjust to demand from the ordinary prudent man or woman who accepts, probably unpaid and sometimes reluctantly from a sense of family duty, the burdens of trusteeship.

In *Re Waterman's Will Trusts* (1952) Harman J expressed almost identical views.

10.17 It is, however, questionable whether such a difference in standards is first, desirable, and second, is actually the law. First, it is said that the professional trustee has a more exacting duty, but nowhere is any real substance given to this 'higher' standard. Furthermore, all trustees have a duty to seek advice in areas where they are personally incapable of administering a trust, and they can charge the cost of this advice to the trust. Where the paid trustee is an investment expert his investment expertise is just being paid for in another way, through the paid trustee's general charge on the trust. The difference between these two situations does not suggest that there should be a difference of standards.

240

10.18   As to whether such a difference in standards actually exists, there is one obiter statement the other way (by Romer J in *Jobson v Palmer* (1892)), but more significantly such a distinction has never been applied as part of the *ratio decidendi* of a case, that is, a decision to hold a trustee liable or relieve him of liability has never turned on a difference of standards. In *Bartlett* the trustee bank was held liable on the ordinary prudent man basis – no recourse to a higher standard was necessary. And if ever there was a case where a higher standard of diligence might have been applied to a paid trustee it was the recently decided *Nestle v National Westminster Bank plc* (1994), but no difference in standards was referred to or applied. Only Leggatt LJ came anywhere close when he referred to the following passage from the Law Commission Report No 23 (1982), para 2.15:

> Professional trustees, such as banks, are under a special duty to display expertise in every aspect of their administration of the trust.

He followed this observation by the statement:

> The essence of the bank's duty was to take such steps as a prudent businessman would have taken to maintain and increase the value of the trust fund. Unless it failed to do so, it was not in breach of trust.

And he concluded the case with the line:

> But by the undemanding standard of prudence the bank is not shown to have committed any breach of the trust resulting in loss.

It should also be borne in mind that paid trustees will invariably insist on exemption clauses before undertaking the trust (**12.27** et seq), and such clauses provide that they will be liable only for their 'willful default', not mere negligence, so any higher standard for paid trustees will likely be of zero practical importance.

10.19   In *Nestle* a testamentary trust was created in 1922. When the holders of the life interests had all died, in 1986, the value of the capital was some £270,000 and the plaintiff remainderman claimed that the fund would have been worth well over £1m if it had been properly invested. The trustee had failed to understand the investment clause of the trust instrument, largely because it had failed to seek legal advice as to its meaning, and in consequence it believed that its investment options were much narrower than was the case and failed to review the investments properly. Although it was clear that the real value of the fund fell dramatically, the CA was not convinced that the investment decisions the trustees actually made would have been in breach of trust even had they understood their investment powers and regularly reviewed the investments. In particular, the trustees actions between 1922 and 1960 could not be judged by the standards of investment expertise of the post-1960 era, when modern portfolio theory favouring equity investment began to be generally applied. The CA accepted Hoffmann J's finding of fact that there was no provable loss to the fund given the advice of experts before the court on the standards of investment practice applicable over the history of the trust. It should not be assumed, however, that if a trust fund administered from the 1960s or later loses significant real value that will not indicate, at least *prima facie*, a failure to invest properly unless there are countervailing factors. Though that did happen to the trust in *Nestle*, there were such factors.

10.20   Roughly, from the 1960s onwards the trustee adopted a policy of investing large proportions of the funds in investments which were tax exempt for foreign residents, as both the living life tenants lived abroad. This resulted in low capital growth, but also savings in estate duty. The court did not find that the trustee breached his duty of even-handedness between the life tenants and the remainderman in adopting such a policy, because the saving in estate duty accrued to the remainderman as well. Staughton LJ said this on even-handedness generally:

> At times it will not be easy to decide what is an equitable balance. A life tenant may be anxious to receive the highest possible income, whilst the remainderman will wish the real value of the trust fund to be preserved. If the life tenant is living in penury and the remainderman already has ample wealth, common sense suggests that a trustee should be able to take that into account, not necessarily by seeking the highest possible income at the expense of capital but by inclining in that direction. However, before adopting that course a trustee should, I think, require some verification of the facts.

10.21   There are two especially significant points to be taken from *Nestle*: first, one cannot read the case without being impressed that the result very much turned on the defendant bank's winning the battle of the experts as to the investment expertise to be expected of a trustee, and this would seem to be an ineliminable element of adopting a prudent man approach. Secondly, while the bank was clearly 'in breach' to the extent that they woefully misunderstood the scope of the investment clause, they were not 'in breach' in so far as the investment decisions which they did make were held not to cause loss, because they *could have been justified* as valid investment decisions *had they known* their actual investment powers. In *Cowan v Scargill* (1984) Megarry VC stated this general principle as follows:

> If trustees make a decision on wholly wrong grounds, and yet it subsequently appears, from matters which they did not express or refer to, that there are in fact good and sufficient reasons for supporting their decision, then I do not think that they would incur any liability for having decided the matter on erroneous grounds; for the decision itself was right.

'Social' or 'ethical' investing

10.22   Trustees must invest in order to preserve and if possible, enhance the value of the trust property. This obligation is so strict that in *Buttle v Saunders* (1950) trustees were held to have a duty to 'gazump', that is accept a higher offer for the purchase of land they were selling even though this involved the dishonourable conduct of reneging upon their acceptance 'subject to contract' of a previous offer. Before the advent of 'social investing', the main effect of this concentration on the financial interests of the beneficiaries was simply to rule out benefits in kind as proper trust income (unless of course the trust instrument provided otherwise). For example, in *Re Power* (1947), trustees were barred from buying a house for the beneficiaries to live in. Jenkins J said that such a purchase:

> ... it is not necessarily an investment, for it is a purchase for some other purpose than the receipt of income.

10.23   *Cowan v Scargill* (1984) concerned a dispute between the trustees of the National Coal Board pension fund for miners. The trustees appointed by the National Coal Board wished to approve an investment plan which included investment in overseas securities and in the oil and gas industries. The trustees appointed by the National Union of Mineworkers refused to consent to a plan including overseas investment and investment in industries in direct competition with the coal industry. Megarry VC held that the NUM trustees' refusal to approve the scheme would be in breach of trust:

> When the purpose of the trust is to provide financial benefits for the beneficiaries, as is usually the case, the best interests of the beneficiaries are normally their best financial interests.

The fact that the NUM strategy might benefit present miners by perhaps assisting the health of the coal industry, which was by no means certain, would be of no benefit at all to retired miners who depended upon the financial performance of the investment to fund their current pensions, so the NUM strategy might also be regarded as not even-handed:

> In considering what investments to make trustees must put to one side their own personal interests and views. Trustees may have strongly held social or political views. They may be firmly opposed to any investment in South Africa or other countries, or they may object to any form of investment in companies concerned with alcohol, tobacco, armaments or many other things. In the conduct of their own affairs, of course, they are free to abstain from making any such investments. Yet under a trust, if investments of this type would be more beneficial to the beneficiaries than other investments, the trustees must not refrain from making the investments by reasons of the views that they hold.

However, Megarry VC also said:

> [I]f the only actual beneficiaries or potential beneficiaries of a trust are all adults with very strict views on moral and social matters, condemning all forms of alcohol, tobacco and popular entertainment, as well as armaments, I can well understand that it might not be for the 'benefit' of such beneficiaries to know that they are obtaining rather larger financial returns under the trust by reason of investments in those activities …

To the extent this last passage is taken to suggest that a trustee might make 'ethical' investment decisions in such circumstances, Megarry VC's words should be disregarded. If all the actual and potential beneficiaries are adults, then a trustee intending such a policy should present it to them in advance and get their consent, in which case the investment will not be in breach of trust. Otherwise it is a breach of trust, since trustees should not have the power to determine by their own lights what constitutes an 'ethical' or 'moral' benefit to their beneficiaries as a whole.

10.24   In *Evans v London Co-operative Society* (1976) trustees had regularly loaned the whole of a pension fund to the employer at below market interest rates. Although such loans were authorised by the trust instrument the trustees were liable for breach for not adequately exercising their discretion in properly negotiating an interest rate. However, Brightman J said that the trustees could

> ... give the parent financial concern accommodation on preferential terms if the trustees consider that the security of the employment of their members may otherwise be imperilled.

10.25   In the Scottish case *Martin v City of Edinburgh District Council* (1988) the local authority's policy to disinvest in companies with South African interests was found to be a breach of trust, because the decision was taken without considering the best financial interests of the beneficiaries.

10.26   Charities raise particular issues. In *Harries v Church Comrs for England* (1992) the Bishop of Oxford sought a declaration that the Church Commissioners should use their assets with the objective in mind of promoting the Christian faith, and were not entitled to act in a manner inconsistent with that object; he thus proposed an active investment policy of seeking out investments to forward Christian objects. The court disagreed. As with any other trust, the normal duty of charitable trustees is to seek the maximum return while investing prudently. While the Commissioners' policy of excluding certain investments, armaments, gambling, tobacco, newspapers, and companies with interests in South Africa was considered acceptable, a more restrictive policy of requiring them generally to invest on the basis of non-commercial considerations would create too great a risk to the trust. It thus seems that charity trustees may rightly choose not to invest in activities which directly contradict the purposes of the trust, so a charity for cancer research may rightly not invest in the tobacco industry, for it is assumed that such restrictions will leave the charity with an adequate range of investments to diversify a portfolio. Secondly charities may refuse to invest in otherwise sound investments if by so investing they would alienate those who give to the charity, thus reducing its overall financial position. But charities may not adopt a policy of accepting lower returns by treating their investments as a means of carrying out their charitable purpose. As Nobles (1992) points out, however, charities generally *give* their money away in pursuit of their purposes. Why should one mode of 'giving', ie investing in activities which may earn below-market returns, be disallowed, if it serves the charity's purpose? They are not, after all, trying to preserve and enhance the value of a sum of money for private beneficiaries.

10.27 Recently, Lord Nichols (1995) speaking extra-judicially has suggested that:

> The range of sound investments available to trustees is so extensive that very frequently there is scope for trustees to give effect to moral considerations ... without thereby prejudicing beneficiaries' financial interests. In practice, the inclusion or exclusion of particular investments or types of investment will often be possible without incurring the risk of a lower rate of return or reducing the desirable spread of investments. When this is so, there is no reason in principle why trustees should not have regard to moral and ethical considerations, vague and uncertain though these are. The trustees would not be departing from the purpose of the trust or hindering its fulfilment.

This suggestion should be firmly resisted. In the first place, regardless of the actual financial returns to the beneficiaries, trustees should never be entitled to take into account their own moral and ethical considerations in exercising any of their trust powers. Trustees are instruments of the trust. If they were ever to act on their own views in this way, they would be in breach of the rule that they are never to put themselves in conflict with the purpose of the trust; such considerations conflict with their duty because the trustee's ethical views are extraneous to the consideration of serving the beneficiaries' interests. Lord Nichols does not say that the trustees must implement the *beneficiaries'* moral or ethical views, but presumably, may act on their own. There is no warrant whatsoever to give trustees who are placed in a position of power and who are generally paid the right to engage their ethical preferences when investing so long as the beneficiaries cannot prove (see *Nestle*, **10.21**) that they have caused the trust loss by doing so. Who trusts the 'ethical' perspective of a large bank/trust company anyway?

10.28 Secondly, it is wrong to think that the range of investments is so great that a few ethical investment choices here and there will not affect the financial performance of the trust. As Langbein and Posner (1980) make clear, a decrease in the range of investments is not determined by the *number* of individual securities one does not invest in, but the percentage value of the investment market those securities represent:

> In 1979, Corporate Data Exchange, Inc identified ninety-nine companies that a socially responsible investor should avoid. The aggregate market value of the stocks of these companies was $342 billion. Yet the only criteria for exclusion were whether the company was predominantly non-unionised, had a poor record in occupational health and safety, failed to meet equal employment opportunity guidelines, or was a major investor or lender in South Africa. Although this is an arbitrarily limited set of criteria, it results in excluding such a large fraction (weighting numbers by market value) of listed equities as to create a degree of sampling error and sampling bias inconsistent with adequate diversification of the portfolio.

In other words, if a trustee refuses to invest in 'just two things', but those two happen to be cars and alcohol, he is unlikely to adequately diversify the trust portfolio because the car and drinks industries represent a major fraction of the overall economy. It is irrelevant that there are, in terms of numbers, thousands of other companies or securities to invest in. The resulting inadequate diversification will entail a riskier investment of the trust funds.

The delegation of trustee functions

10.29 Before 1926, unless specifically authorised by the trust instrument to do so, trustees could not delegate their administrative functions unless doing so was reasonably necessary for their administration of the trust to the standard of a prudent man of business (*Speight v Gaunt* (1883); *Learoyd v Whiteley* (1887)). Outside specific provision in the trust instrument, trustee's powers to delegate are now governed by the Trustee Act 1925, ss 23 and 25.

10.30 Section 23(1) is very broad, and essentially enables trustees to employ and pay an agent to perform any task in the administration of the trust. Section 30 (1) of the Trustee Act 1925 governs the liability of trustees for losses caused to the trust through the fault of their appointed agents appointed under s 23(1). The provisions state that a trustee shall be liable only for his own acts and defaults, unless the acts or defaults of others happen 'through his own wilful default'. Until *Re Vickery* (1931) it was assumed that in this context 'wilful default' indicated a want of reasonable care. Thus in line with *Speight v Gaunt* it was thought that a trustee who fell below the prudent man of business standard in his selection or supervision of agents committed a breach of trust and was liable for any resulting losses. This standard was applied by Cross J in *Re Lucking* (**10.15**) where the appointment of the agent to run a business was made by the company, not by the trustee under under s 23. In *Re Vickery* (1931) however, Maugham J decided that 'wilful default' comprised only conscious or reckless breach of duty. The result would appear to be that a trustee cannot be liable for the defaults of his agent unless he consciously or recklessly appointed an unfit agent or consciously knew of the agent's defaults and did nothing to stop them, or recklessly failed to detect them. While the decision has been cogently criticised (see Jones (1959)) it has not been overruled (see also *Steel v Wellcome Custodian Trustees* (1987)). Recently in *Armitage v Nurse* (1997) Millett LJ in the CA said:

> [T]he expression 'wilful default' is used in the cases in two senses. A trustee is said to be accountable on the footing of wilful default when he is accountable not only for money which he has in fact received but also for money which he could with reasonable diligence have received. It is sufficient that the trustee has been guilty of a want of ordinary prudence ... In the context of a trustee exclusion clause, however, such as s 30 of the Trustee Act 1925, it means deliberate breach of trust ... The decision [in *Re Vickery*] has been criticised, but it is in line with earlier authority.

It is difficult to know how authoritative this statement is, because Millett LJ does not discuss the earlier authorities which he cites, and therefore does not in terms dispel the standard criticism of *Re Vickery* that the authorities, on proper examination, did not support the decision.

10.31 The situation is different with respect to the trustees' discretions. In general a trustee may not delegate any of his discretions, whether dispositive, eg a discretion which beneficiaries will take under a discretionary trust, or administrative, eg the discretion as to the choice of investments. Even where the trustee seeks advice, for example in making investments, the actual decision as to the investment policy to be followed remains the trustee's. An example of a case where the prohibition on the delegation of discretion arose with respect to a power of advancement is discussed below (**10.42**). However, s 23(2) enables the trustee to appoint an agent where trust property is situated abroad, not only to administer the property, but to exercise any discretions or powers in respect of that property. Section 25 empowers a trustee to delegate to someone any or *all* of his duties, powers or discretions by power of attorney for a period not exceeding twelve months. If *Re Vickery* correctly states the standard of liability for appointments make under s 23(1), the standard of liability is stricter for the delegation of discretions under these sub-sections. Under s 23(2) a trustee is not to be held liable for losses caused by the appointment of the agent simply because he made the appointment; the *Speight v Gaunt* standards of prudence remain applicable to the selection and monitoring of the agent. Under s 25(5) the trustee is strictly liable for the acts and defaults of the agent given a power of attorney, ie they are to be regarded as his own acts and defaults.

The power of maintenance

10.32   The power of maintenance enables a trustee to spend income, but not capital, for the benefit of infant beneficiaries, ie those under 18. A settlor may specifically confer upon or deny the trustee this power, directing instead that the income should be spent on someone else or accumulated. In any other case, where property is held on trust for an infant, the Trustee Act 1925, s 31 confers on the trustee a power to apply, in their sole discretion income for the infant's maintenance. The section applies whether the infant's interest is vested, eg '10,000 shares of XYZplc on trust for my son Benjamin absolutely' or contingent, 'Blackacre to Bertram if he obtains the age of 25'. Once the beneficiary of a vested interest turns 18 then of course he is entitled to any income arising on the property, but under s 31(1)(ii) trustees must pay the income to a beneficiary even of a contingent interest upon his turning 18.

10.33   During his infancy, the trustees may pay such portions of the income for his maintenance as 'may, in all the circumstances, be reasonable', and must accumulate the rest. Unless, therefore, s.31 is excluded, even a beneficiary of an absolute interest will receive only such income as is required, in the trustee's discretion, for his maintenance. The trustees must have regard to the 'the age of the infant and his requirements and generally to the circumstances of his case, and in particular to what other income, if any, is available for the same purposes' (s 31(1)). In *Wilson v Turner* (1883) the trustees paid the income to the infant beneficiaries' father automatically without enquiring as to the beneficiaries' actual needs, and the father was required to repay the money.

10.34 Under s 31(2), income which is accumulated instead of being spent on maintenance in one year may be spent for the beneficiary's maintenance in later years. Thus income accumulated in the beneficiaries 10th and 11th years may be spent in his 17th when his expenses are greater. Also under s 31(2), where a beneficiary has a vested interest or an interest which vests upon his turning 18, when he turns 18 any income that instead of being spent for his maintenance was accumulated will then be held on trust for him absolutely – he can demand the immediate payment of it. This rule does not apply, however, where the vested interest is a conditional interest in land or an interest in personalty that may in any way be defeated, eg by the exercise of a power of appointment (see *Re Sharp's Settlement Trusts* (1972)). In that case, and in any case where the beneficiary's interest in the property does not vest until later, eg where his interest is contingent upon his turning 25, these pre-18 accumulations are held on the same trust as is the capital. Thus they will likewise be susceptible to the same contingency as is his interest in the capital. Therefore if his interest in the capital vests only when he reaches 25, then his interest in the pre-18 accumulations only vests when he reaches 25. In view of this, the trustees should consider making a final payment of past accumulated income shortly before the beneficiary's 18th birthday; after that, he will have no recourse to this money until his capital interest vests.

10.35 The income available for maintenance payments is only that income which arises on the property to which the minor beneficiary is, or will be, entitled. This is straightforward in the case of a beneficiary with a present vested interest. All of the income (ie dividends) on the shares in XYZ plc will be available to make maintenance payments to Benjamin in the example above. In the case of contingent or future interests, however, only income from property held on trust which 'carries the intermediate income' is available. This is best explained by example. If a testator gives Barbara a contingent pecuniary legacy, say £20,000 conditional upon her attaining the age of 25, it will be paid in due course out of the testator's residuary estate when she turns 25;

Barbara will not receive any accrued income or interest since no property was set aside for her on a special account. The gift, therefore, carries no intermediate income for maintenance payments if Barbara is a minor. The same will occur with a *future* pecuniary legacy, eg of £20,000 to Barbara on the death of her father. By contrast, in the case of any *inter vivos* trust, there is no 'residuary estate'; each gift has specific property allocated to it and therefore a contingent gift will be of specific property, and so until it vests it will carry the income that accrues on it and when the gift vests the beneficiary is entitled to that income. During the beneficiary's minority such income will therefore be available for maintenance payments. In all cases, however, any contrary indication in the terms of the trust will upset these rules, for example, a direction that the income should go to a different beneficiary.

10.36   By the operation of s 175 of the Law of Property Act 1925 and a number of cases which we shall not discuss, the following rules apply to different kinds of testamentary gift to determine whether they carry the intermediate income, assuming that there is no contrary intention. All testamentary gifts, whether of personalty or realty, and whether contingent or future, whether of specific property or residuary property, carry the intermediate income unless the gift is:

(1) a residuary bequest (ie a gift of residuary personalty) whether vested or contingent which is postponed to a future date (see *Re McGeorge* (1963));

(2) a contingent or future pecuniary legacy; but such a gift *will* carry the intermediate income where:

   (i) it appears that the testator intended to maintain the beneficiary; or

   (ii) the legacy has been set aside as a separate fund from the outset; or

   (iii) the legacy is contingent upon the beneficiary's attaining the age of majority, and the testator was his parent or stood *in loco parentis* to him, and there are no other funds available for the minor's maintenance.

The power of advancement

10.37 The power of advancement is the power to expend *capital* of the trust fund to benefit a beneficiary who has only a future or contingent interest in it. Thus if Betty is entitled to the trust property for life, and Barney in remainder, Barney has a vested future interest. If he is advanced capital before Betty dies, then he receives the benefit of the capital early. If Beatrix is given trust property conditional upon her attaining the age of 30, and she is advanced property at the age of 22, not only does she receive the benefit early, but if she dies at 28, she receives property she would not have received at all but for the advancement – there is no 'clawback' of advanced property if it turns out that at the end of the day the beneficiary doesn't meet the conditions entitling him to the contingent interest. An advancement is traditionally a significant sum intended to establish a beneficiary in life (**9.27**), although 'benefit' is now interpreted much more broadly (**10.40**).

10.38 A power to apply the capital of the trust to any object may be expressly given, but s 32 of the Trustee Act 1925 empowers trustees to advance capital to beneficiaries of future or contingent interests in the capital unless expressly excluded by the trust terms. Section 32 empowers trustees to advance a beneficiary up to one half by value of the capital interest he ultimately expects, his 'presumptive share', which must be taken into account when his final share is paid out. Subsequent advancements may be made over time so long as the beneficiary has not been paid out sums amounting to half of his presumptive share, but the method of accounting for past money advances used in practice can be 'monstrously unjust' (Law Reform Committee (1982), paras 4.43-4.47; Hayton (1987), 453; see Oakley (1994), 505 et seq for an example of the calculations). If, based on the calculation of the fund at the present time, a beneficiary is advanced an amount which, taking account of past advancements, gives him his full presumptive share in his capital interest, he may no longer be advanced any funds (*Re Abergavenny* (1981)), regardless of how much the value of the capital increases in future years.

10.39 In certain cases the trustees will need the prior consent of one beneficiary to advance money to another. Consider a trust of shares 'to A for life and then to B'. B has a future interest in the shares and is a candidate for advancement. But clearly, any advancement to B will reduce the capital in the trust, ie the number of shares, so A's income which comes from the dividends on the shares will decline. Section 32(1)(c) provides that the trustees may only make an advancement to B if A is *sui juris* and consents to the advancement in writing.

10.40 What counts as 'advancement' under s 32 is very wide indeed: In *Pilkington v IRC* (1962) Viscount Radcliffe said, 'It means any use of the money which will improve the material situation of the beneficiary', and in that case the HL would, but for the rules against perpetuity, have approved a proposed advancement which would have re-settled a five-year-old's expected interest when she attained 21 upon a new trust which would delay the vesting of her interest in the capital until she reached the age of thirty, in order to avoid the effects of death duty. In *Re Clore* (1966) the court approved an advancement to a rich beneficiary allowing him to make a charitable donation he felt morally obliged to make; it was a material, though not decisive, consideration that by the advancement of capital the beneficiary could make the donation with much less severe tax consequences than if he did so out of his income.

10.41 Trustees have an obligation to see that the money advanced actually goes to benefit the beneficiary. In *Re Pauling's Settlement Trusts* (1963) it was held that trustees could not advance money:

> ... without any responsibility ... even to inquire as to its application.

There large sums were advanced which the trustees were aware were being spent by the infants' father on the family's living expenses; the advancements were in breach of trust and the trustees were required to repay the money thus frittered away.

10.42 In *Pilkington* the HL decided that an advancement on re-settlement was permissable under s 32. This raises the possibility that funds advanced may be settled on discretionary trusts. Academic opinion is divided (see, eg Oakley (1994), pp 512-513; Hayton (1996), 677) as to whether an advancement under s 32 can be validly made which creates a trust under which the advanced beneficiary is, or may become (as under a protective trust), a discretionary beneficiary. The trustees under the new trust will have a discretion to benefit the beneficiary, and the general rule is that a trustee cannot delegate his discretion (**10.31**); by making an advancement on these terms it appears that that is just what he is doing. On the other hand, as pointed out by Oakley, all agree that the re-settlement itself might contain a power of advancement, and this confers a clear discretion on the new trustee. More to the point however, it would seem such a settlement should be judged by whether or not it confers a real 'benefit' on the beneficiary. Given his circumstances, it might appear that a protective trust in his favour might do that. This should be the over-riding consideration, and given that the benefit in *Clore* was acceptable, it seems possible that so might being a beneficiary under a discretionary trust. The delegation point, although raised in *Pilkington*, was not considered in any detail. Any express power of advancement can, of course, be framed to permit its exercise to re-settle part of the beneficiary's presumptive share on discretionary trust.

10.43 *Pilkington* also decided that for purposes of the rule against perpetuities, a power of advancement is to be treated as a special power of appointment, and therefore an advancement on re-settlement is subject to the time limitations of the original trust of the property (**3.22**). Where the re-settlement contains provisions void for perpetuity these will be void, of course, but the main trust for the beneficiary in whose favour the advancement is made will not fail *Re Hastings-Bass* (1975), unless the failure of the void provisions significantly alters the benefit the advancement was intended to achieve (*Re Abraham's Will Trusts* (1969)).

Variation of trusts

10.44 In general, a settlor may set whatever terms on a trust he desires. Because trusts generally last for some years, it is not uncommon for terms which seemed reasonable at the outset to cause problems or inconvenience later, eg terms which limit the trustee's power of investment, or modes of distribution of the assets which give rise to unforeseen tax liability. Furthermore, the beneficiaries may, even from the outset, be unhappy with the distribution of their particular beneficial interests. If the beneficiaries are all ascertained and *sui juris*, they may at any time combine to exercise their *Saunders v Vautier* rights to collapse the trust or vary its terms. Where this is not the case the assistance of the court must be sought.

10.45 The court has always had an inherent jurisdiction to vary trusts, though the scope of this jurisdiction is limited to variations which permit the trustees greater administrative or management powers, and then only in cases of 'emergency' (*Re New* (1910)); the court will not rearrange the beneficial interests (*Chapman v Chapman* (1954)). The only true exception to this rule is that the court will empower the trustees to apply income to maintain a settlor's minor children even where he directed the income to be accumulated. A court has also always been able to sanction a 'compromise' between beneficiaries' rights where they are the subject of doubt or dispute, but this is better seen as the court's settling what the beneficial interests are, not its remoulding of the beneficial interests.

10.46 Section 57 of the Trustee Act 1925 extends the court's jurisdiction to enhance the trustee's administrative powers to cases of expediency, ie to more than emergency situations. It clearly contemplates increasing the power of trustees to deal in particular ways with the trust property, not a wholesale re-writing of the trust, nor the remoulding of the beneficial interests (*Chapman v Chapman* (1954)).

10.47 An application to extend the trustee's investment powers provides a nice example of a variation under s 57. In *Trustees of the British Museum v A-G* (1984) Megarry VC refused to follow the (1961) decision In *Re Kolb's Will Trusts* which held that an extension of trust powers was to be approved only in special circumstances. He held that there should be a general power to widen investment powers based on a number of factors including: (1) the standing of trustees and their administrative plan for obtaining advice and controlling investments; (2) the size of the fund; and (3) the object of the fund (here capital growth was needed for the museum to be able to have an endowment for additions to the museum collection). In *Steel v Wellcome Custodian Trustees Ltd* (1987) Hoffmann J approved an extension of investment powers on similar principles.

10.48 The Variation of Trusts Act 1958 allows the variation of beneficial interests under trusts in cases where the beneficiaries are not in the position to do so by exercising their *Saunders v Vautier* rights. Essentially the Act allows the court to approve a variation on behalf of under-age beneficiaries and potential beneficiaries as yet unascertained. The variation is, therefore, effected by the unanimous exercise of the beneficiaries exercising their *Saunders v Vautier* rights – those who are *sui juris* and ascertained consent for themselves, and the court consents on behalf of those who are not; the Act does not give the court a general discretionary power to vary trusts at the application of an interested party (*Re Holt's Settlement* (1969); *Re Holmden's Settlement* (1968); *Goulding v James* (1997)). For this reason, recourse to the 1958 Act should be made only when the beneficial interests are to be varied. The mere extension of trustee powers, like the power of investment, should be sought under s 57 of the 1925 Act; in such a case the trustee is the proper applicant, not the beneficiaries, and since no need for the consent of all beneficiaries is required the s 57 application will be less costly (*Anker-Petersen v Anker-Petersen* (1991)).

10.49 The court will not consent on behalf of beneficiaries of full age even if their interests are contingent and extremely unlikely to vest in interest, even if obtaining their consent will be very inconvenient, as in *Knocker v Youle* (1986) where there were several dozen contingent *sui juris* beneficiaries, a goodly number in Australia, who were almost certain never to take under the trust. Should Parliament amend the Act to allow the court to consent on behalf of such beneficiaries? Is a court dealing with a *McPhail*-type trust able to do this in substance already, given its power to 'implement a scheme of distribution' proposed by a representative group of beneficiaries in order to enforce such a trust?

10.50 By s 1(1) of the Act the court may only approve an arrangement on behalf of a beneficiary if it would be to his 'benefit', unless (s 1(1)(d)) the beneficiary is an object of discretionary 'trust over' following the determination of the life interest under a protective trust in which case no 'benefit' need be shown. 'Benefit' has been construed broadly to include not only financial but moral and social benefits (*Re Holt's Settlement*). In *Re Weston's Settlements* (1968) Lord Denning MR refused to allow the export of a trust to Jersey where the settlor and the beneficiaries had recently moved to minimise tax liability. Considering social and educational benefits he said:

> I do not believe it is for the benefit of children to be uprooted from England and transported to another country simply to avoid tax.

10.51 The court will not require an absolute certainty of benefit – where subsequent events might make the variation disadvantageous to the beneficiaries on whose behalf the court consents, the scheme will still be approved if the more likely result is an advantage to them;

the court should undertake on the beneficiaries' behalf the same sort of risks which an adult would be prepared to take (*Re Cohen's Will Trusts* (1959); *Re Holt's Settlement*). However, where the effect of a variation might lead to a possible beneficiary under the old trust, even an as yet unborn individual, being excluded from the new trust entirely, the variation will not be approved because if such a person is born the variation would be wholly disadvantageous to him (*Re Cohen's Settlement Trusts* (1965)).

10.52 In *Re Steed's Will Trusts* (1960) the CA gave the testator's intentions significant weight where a life tenant under a protective trust applied for a variation to give her an absolute interest. The essence of the settlor's concern in creating the protective trust for his former housekeeper was that if absolutely entitled to the property she would be 'sponged upon by one of her brothers'. The CA refused to consent to the variation on behalf of the possible objects of the discretionary trust over, ie those who would take if the primary trust was forfeited. This decision seems quite out of line with the obvious import of the act, which if anything, should favour the variation of protective trusts to give the determinable life-interest holder an absolute interest: s 1 specifically provides that the court may approve a variation on behalf of the beneficiaries of the discretionary trust arising on the forfeiture of a protective trust even if the variation is of no benefit to them. In *Re Remnant's Settlement Trusts* (1970) an arrangement which overthrew the settlor's clear intentions was approved in the interest of family harmony and marital choice (a condition defeated a trust gift for objects marrying a Roman Catholic). Recently, in *Goulding v James* (1997), the CA made clear that the settlor's intentions are only relevant in so far as they contribute to assessing whether the proposed variation is of benefit to the class on whose behalf the court consents. The *sui juris* beneficiaries, like any other beneficiaries exercising their *Saunders v Vautier* rights, may propose an arrangement which directly contradicts the settlor's wishes *for them*. Although *Re Steed* was not in terms disapproved, it was largely confined to its particular facts.

10.53 The 1958 Act empowers the court to consent to 'any arrangement ... varying or revoking *all or any* of the trusts' (my italics). Given the breadth of this language, and furthermore the courts' interpretation that variations of trusts are to be understood as the exercise of *Saunders v Vautier* rights, it would seem that the court should happily countenance the complete revocation of the old trust and re-settlement of the property under a new one. Yet in *Re T's Settlement Trusts* (1963) Wilberforce J refused to approve a 'complete new resettlement' on the grounds that the Act was restricted to variations. However, in *Re Ball's Settlement Trusts* (1968) Megarry J said:

> But it does not follow that merely because an arrangement can correctly be described as effecting a revocation and resettlement, it cannot also be correctly described as effecting a variation of the trusts.

The most oft-quoted passage from the case is this, in which Megarry J quotes Martin J of the Supreme Court of Victoria in *Re Dyer* (1935):

> If an arrangement changes the whole substratum of the trust, then it may well be that it cannot be regarded merely as varying that trust. But if an arrangement, while leaving the substratum, effectuates the purpose of the original trust by other means, it may still be possible to regard that arrangement as merely varying the original trusts, even though the means employed are wholly different and even though the form is completely changed.

With respect, this is just so much verbiage. The original trust has no 'purpose' besides distributing the beneficial interests in the way it does. Any change in that changes its 'purpose', even if it does so for good reasons, eg to avoid tax. If something like the settlor's wishes is what 'purpose' means, it is clear that the statement is just wrong, since variations may freely defeat those (**10.52**). What *should* be quoted from Megarry J's decision is the following, which comes a couple of lines later:

> The jurisdiction of the Act is a beneficial one and, and in my judgment, the court should construe it widely and not be astute to confine its beneficent operation. I must remember that in essence the court is merely contributing on behalf of infants and unborn and unascertained persons the binding assents to the arrangement which they, unlike an adult beneficiary, cannot give. So far as is proper, the power of the court to give that assent should be assimilated to the wide powers which the ascertained adults have.

Precisely.

258

Appointment, retirement and removal of trustees

10.54 Over the course of any trust, old trustees may retire and occasionally trustees must be removed, and in both cases, depending upon how many trustees remain, new trustees may need to be appointed. Trustees may be individual persons or trust corporations, companies which specialise in acting as a trustee.

10.55 Any number of persons may be co-trustees of a trust where the corpus is made up entirely of personalty. There are restrictions upon any trust which contains interests in land: The Trustee Act 1924, s 34 sets a maximum of four (there are exceptions for charitable and other public purpose trusts); the Act also effectively sets a minimum of two trustees – while a sole trustee, ie a lone human trustee (not a trust corporation) of land is not prohibited, s 14(2) provides that a sole trustee cannot give a valid receipt for the purchase money to a purchaser of the land, and so no purchaser will knowingly deal with a sole trustee of land.

10.56 Trustees invariably hold property as joint tenants, so if one dies the survivor(s) alone continue as trustees (**1.15**). Only if a sole trustee dies does the legal title to the trust property pass to his personal representative, who in that case becomes a trustee. In the case of a trust created by will where all the intended trustees have predeceased the testator, the testator's personal representatives will be trustees until new trustees can be appointed, who may, of course, be themselves.

10.57 A trust will not fail for want of a trustee, but neither will anyone unwilling be forced to serve as a trustee. Thus if a testator by his will transfers property to Tom on trust for Beatrix, Tom may refuse to accept the role of trustee; the court, however, will ensure that someone undertakes the trust. If there is no one else willing, as a last resort the court may appoint the Public Trustee. The office of the Public Trustee was created by the Public Trustee Act 1906, largely to ensure the administration of trusts where no other person was willing to do so. While the Public Trustee may refuse to undertake a trust, he may not do so only because of its small value (Public Trustee Act 1906, s 2(3)). The Public Trustee is entitled to charge for his administration of the trust. Alternatively, the court may appoint a trust corporation, authorising it to charge for its services (s 42 of the Trustee Act 1925).

10.58 In the first instance, trustees are appointed by the settlor when the trust is created (by the testator by his will in the case of a testamentary trust), and he can choose whomever he wants. Once the trust is constituted, the trust terms themselves become operative, and these may give some individual(s), typically the settlor and the trustees for the time being, the power to appoint new trustees. However, such provisions are typically supplementary to the powers to appoint provided by s 36 of the Trustee Act 1925, which are generally regarded as adequate.

10.59 The basic purpose of s.36 is to ensure that there will be someone who can appoint trustees so that a court appointment is not required. It provides that where a trustee:

- has died (which includes the case of a trustee named in a will who has predeceased the testator (s 36(8)); or

- has remained outside the UK for over a year; or

- wishes to retire from the trust; or

- refuses to act, ie disclaims the role of trustee at the outset; or

- is unfit to act, eg bankrupt; or

- is incapable of acting, ie has a personal incapacity such as mental or physical infirmity; or

- is an infant; or

- has been removed by the exercise of a power in the trust instrument (s 36(2),

then a new appointment may be made, first, by anyone nominated to do so in the trust instrument, and failing that, by the trustees for the time being, and failing that because they have all died, by the personal representatives of the last surviving trustee. By s 36(8), refusing or retiring trustees are considered trustees for the time being so as to enable them to appoint their successors. It has been held (*Re Coates to Parsons* (1886)) that where some trustees intend to undertake the trust or continue as

260

trustees, but some refuse or Intend to retire, respectively, the appointment of new trustees by the continuing trustees without the concurrence of a refusing or retiring trustee will make the appointment invalid if it is shown that the latter was competent and willing to act. It is therefore advisable that all trustees for the time being participate in any appointment. Section 36(6) permits the appointment of additional trustees up to a maximum of four trustees in total. An appointment must be made in writing, though a last surviving trustee may not appoint a successor by will (*Re Parker* (1894)). An appointment is usually made by deed in order to vest the property in, ie transfer the legal title to, the new trustees at the same time (**10.62**). Nevertheless, s 37(7) provides that a new trustee becomes fully liable as a trustee as soon as he is appointed, even if the vesting of the property occurs sometime later. Even if a purported appointment is void, a new trustee who deals with the property as a trustee will be liable as one (**12.31**).

10.60   Section 19 of the Trusts of Land and Appointment of Trustees Act 1996 gives beneficiaries what amounts to a power to both remove and appoint trustees, although the power can be excluded by the settlor. If all are *sui juris*, the beneficiaries may unanimously direct any trustee to retire from the trust, or direct the trustees to use their power to appoint new trustees in favour any person they choose.

10.61   Although the court has the power to appoint trustees under its inherent jurisdiction over trusts s 41 provides that the court may appoint trustees where it is found 'inexpedient, difficult, or impracticable to do so without the assistance of the court', and in particular to replace a trustee who is mentally incompetent, bankrupt, or where a corporate trustee is in liquidation or has been dissolved. Clearly, then, this power is regarded as a long-stop provision where no one empowered by the instrument or s 36 may practicably appoint. The court has also appointed where, for example, all the trustees nominated by will predeceased the testator (*Re Smirthwaite* (1871)), where an elderly testator was physically and mentally incapable of carrying on (*Re Lemann* (1883)), and where a trustee had permanently left the UK (*Re Bignold* (1872)). In appointing trustees the court will be guided by criteria stated by the CA in *Re Tempest* (1866): (1) the wishes of the settlor, (2) the interests of all the beneficiaries, and (3) the efficient execution of the trust. Following the enactment of s 19 of the 1996 Act, recourse to the court should be rare.

10.62 Except in the case of custodian trustees (**10.64**), the trust property must be vested in the new body of trustees when a new trustee is appointed. Section 40 of the Trustee Act 1925 allows a deed of appointment of new trustees to serve also as a vesting instrument, which vests the legal title in the new body of trustees. In the case of registered land, the Registrar must give effect to such an instrument by revising the registered title accordingly. Some property cannot be vested in this way, the most important example of which is company shares. The shares must be transferred into the names of the new trustees in the normal way so that the new trustees are registered as owners in the company's books.

10.63 A person may disclaim the role of trustee from the outset, may retire from the trust, or may be removed. Although one should disclaim by deed, a disclaimer may be expressed in or implied from words or conduct. Once a person has accepted a trust, which in general is found whenever he exercises any function of a trustee in respect of the trust, he cannot disclaim – he may then only retire from the trust. Under s 36 of the Trustee Act 1925 a trustee may retire from the trust on the appointment of a replacement; under s 39, a trustee may retire by deed if there remains at least two individuals or a trust company as trustee(s), and he obtains the consent of the other trustees and anyone else entitled to appoint new trustees. The beneficiaries may now direct a trustee to retire (**10.60**), which is tantamount to removing him, and the court under s 41 may remove one trustee to replace him with another (**10.61**). The court may also remove a trustee in exercise of its inherent jurisdiction without necessarily appointing a replacement, though the grounds for doing so are not well defined. Clearly, any trustee in breach of trust or otherwise in dereliction of his fiduciary duties is a suitable candidate for removal; in *Letterstedt v Broers* (1884) the PC refused to lay down any rule governing the exercise of the power, except to say that the general interest of the beneficiaries should guide any decision.

Custodian and judicial trustees

10.64 Two particular kinds of trustee should be mentioned. 'Custodian trustees' hold the trust property as legal owners, but the management of the trust, ie all the trust decisions, are taken by different persons, called 'managing trustees', which the custodian trustee executes in so far as a disposition of the legal title to the property is required. It is as if the custodian trustee were a bare trustee, but one who complies with the orders, not of the bare beneficiary, but of the managing trustees. The main advantage of a custodian trustee is that once the property is vested in him, the managing trustees may retire or be removed and new managing trustees appointed, without having to revest the property each time. Only trust corporations, the Public Trustee and other specified public bodies or officers may be custodian trustees, i.e never private individuals.

10.65   A 'judicial trustee' is appointed by the court (Judicial Trustees Act 1896) in cases where some continuing court supervision is required because the administration of the trust has broken down; the court may give such directions as to the administration of the trust as it thinks fit.

Further Reading

Goodhart (1996); Law Reform Committee (1982); Langbein (1994); Langbein and Posner (1980); Nichols (1995).

Must read cases: *Speight v Gaunt* (1883); *Learoyd v Whitely* (1887); *Nestle v National Westminster Bank plc* (1994); *Bartlett v Barclays Bank Trust Co Ltd* (1979); *Cowan v Scargill* (1984); *Re Holt's Settlement* (1969); *Pilkington v IRC* (1962); *Re Pauling's Settlement Trusts* (1963); *Goulding v James* (1997); *Re Ball's Settlement Trusts* (1986).

Self-test questions

1.   The trustees of the substantial funds of the London Ecumenical Christian Church are given by the trust instrument a power to invest in any investments they see fit, subject only 'to their legal duty of prudent investment'. For 15 years they have left half the funds in a building society account, earning a low rate of interest. The remainder has been invested in shares of two companies. The share price of one of the companies has recently dropped by 30% in line with a general collapse in the stock market. The trust has a holding of 55% in the second company. The company has recently gone into receivership following the failure of a

speculative venture. The trustees had not known about the venture, and generally took no interest in the company's activities.

(a) Advise the trustees whether they have committed a breach of their duty of prudent investment; and

(b) Consider to what extent, if at all, the trustees are subject to a duty to ensure that trust funds are not invested in 'unchristian business activities'.

2.   What limitations are there on trustees' powers to delegate his functions as trustee? In what circumstances will he be liable for the defaults of his appointed agents?

3.   Bill, 14, and Bob, 23 are beneficiaries of a testamentary trust under they are each entitled to a sum of £25,000 contingent upon their attaining the age of 25, and to a half share of a large share portfolio contingent on their attaining the age of 30. To what extent may the trustees use their statutory powers of maintenance and advancement in Bill and Bob's favour?

4.   What differences are there between the rules which govern the variation of trusts (i) to modify the administrative powers of the trustees and (ii) to alter the beneficial interests?

5.   What powers have (i) the trustees, (ii) the beneficiaries, and (iii) the court, to appoint and remove trustees?

CHAPTER ELEVEN

The Fiduciary Nature of Trustee Obligations

SUMMARY

Authorised profits

Unauthorised profits and the liability to account for them

The 'no conflict' rule

The 'self-dealing' rule

The 'fair dealing rule'

The proprietary and personal nature of the liability to account

11.1   To begin with, review the description of fiduciary obligations at **2.2-2.3**. It is essential to realise, as Millet LJ makes clear in his recent review of the nature and scope of fiduciary duties in *Bristol & West Building Society v Mothew* (1996), that just because A stands as a fiduciary to B, that does not mean that every duty he owes B is a fiduciary duty:

> The expression 'fiduciary duty' is properly confined to those duties which are peculiar to fiduciaries and the breach of which attracts legal consequences differing from those consequent upon the breach of other duties. Unless the expression is so limited it is lacking in practical utility. In this sense it is obvious that not every breach of duty by a fiduciary is a breach of fiduciary duty ... It is ... inappropriate to apply the expression to the obligation of a trustee or other fiduciary to use proper skill and care in the discharge of his duties ... A fiduciary is someone who has undertaken to act for or on behalf of another in a particular matter in circumstances which give rise to a relationship of trust and confidence. The distinguishing obligation of a fiduciary is the obligation of loyalty. The principal is entitled to the single-minded loyalty of his beneficiary. This core liability has several facets. A fiduciary must act in good faith; he must

not make a profit out of his trust; he must not place himself in a position where his duty and his interest may conflict; he may not act for his own benefit or the benefit of a third person without the informed consent of his principal ... [Where] the fiduciary deals with his principal... he must prove affirmatively that the transaction is fair and that in the course of the negotiations he made full disclosure of all facts material to the transaction. Even inadvertent failure to disclose will entitle the principal to rescind the transaction ... The nature of the obligation determines the nature of the breach. The various obligations of a fiduciary merely reflect different aspects of his core duties of loyalty and fidelity. Breach of fiduciary obligation, therefore, connotes disloyalty or infidelity. Mere incompetence is not enough. A servant who does his incompetent best for his master is not unfaithful and is not guilty of a breach of fiduciary duty.

As Millet LJ points out, the duty of loyalty has been elaborated in the form of a number of more particular duties, concerning profits from the trust, conflicts of interest, and transactions with the trust property. We shall examine each in turn.

Authorised profits

11.2 Most trusts are today undertaken by professional trustees, so it is clear that there is no rule of equity which prevents a trustee from profiting from his position as trustee. The rule is that a trustee may not obtain any *unauthorised* profits. Most trusts contain express remuneration clauses in the trust instrument. If there is no such provision the trustee is not entitled to any remuneration whatsoever. All trustees are, however, entitled to the reimbursement of their out-of-pocket expenses incurred in carrying out the trust terms, such as the costs of employing solicitors or brokers, or to pay those expenses directly from the trust funds (s 30(2) of the Trustee Act 1925).

The rule in Cradock v Piper

11.3 The only true exception to the rule disallowing unauthorised profits is the rule in *Cradock v Piper* (1850). Just like any other trustee, unless authorised by the trust instrument a solicitor trustee cannot charge for any professional legal work done for the trust. Nor may he retain his own firm to do any such work, for he will indirectly benefit from the firm's revenue (*Christophers v White* (1847)), though he may employ a partner of his firm on the basis that he will receive no share of the profits (*Clack v Carlon* (1861)). Under the rule in *Cradock v Piper*, a solicitor trustee is allowed his usual charges for litigation work done for the body of trustees, which include himself, so long as his being one of the parties has not added to the expense of the litigation. This limited exception for litigious work is illogical and has not been extended to other cases. The rule is of limited practical importance since any competent solicitor undertaking a trust will insist that the instrument contain an appropriate provision allowing him to charge for his professional services.

The inherent jurisdiction to authorise remuneration

11.4   The court has inherent jurisdiction to authorise remuneration for trustees and other fiduciaries, and to increase the remuneration beyond that provided in the trust terms. The general principles were examined in the leading case, *Re Duke of Norfolk's Settlement Trusts* (1981). In this case a trust's charging clause provided a level of payment well below the current market standard; furthermore, due to changes in the nature of the trust holdings, the work required by the trustee had increased significantly. The CA decided that the inherent jurisdiction covered not only the power to allow remuneration for past services, and to allow remuneration for future services upon the appointment of a trustee, but to increase the level of remuneration beyond that fixed in the trust instrument. Two arguments stood in the way of the court's increasing the trustee's remuneration: first, if one regards the remuneration provision as a contract between the settlor and the trustee, then the trustee should, on contractual principles, live with the bargain he has made. Second, it was argued that by increasing the level of remuneration the court would in effect vary the beneficial interests under the trust because less would then go to the beneficiaries, and the court had no inherent jurisdiction to vary beneficial interests (**10.45**). The CA rejected both arguments. Fox LJ said this of the contractual analysis:

> It might have some appearance of reality in relation to a trustee who, at the request of the settlor, agrees to act before the settlement is executed and approves the terms of the settlement. But very frequently executors and trustees of wills know nothing of the terms of the will until the testator is dead … It is difficult to see with whom, in such cases, the trustees are

to be taken as contracting. The appointment of a trustee by the court also gives rise to problems as to the identity of the contracting party. The position, it seems to me, is this. Trust property is held by the trustee upon the trusts and subject to the powers conferred by the trust instrument and the law. One of those powers is the power given to the trustee to charge remuneration ... [I]t seems to me to be quite unreal to regard them as contractual. So far as they derive from any order of the court they simply arise from the court's jurisdiction and so far as they derive from the trust instrument itself they derive from the settlor's power to direct how his property should be dealt with.

Brightman LJ said:

> [The contractual conception] also seems to me, in the context of the present debate, to give little weight to the fact that a trustee, whether paid or unpaid, is under no obligation, contractual or otherwise, to provide future services to the trust. He can at any time express his desire to be discharged from the trust and in that case a new trustee will in due course be appointed ... The practical effect therefore of increasing the remuneration of the trustee (if the contractual conception is correct) will merely be to amend for the future, in favour of a trustee, the terms of a contract which the trustee has a unilateral right to determine.

In so far as these reasons are intended to justify the court's power to increase a trustee's remuneration, they are inadequate. Although Fox LJ emphasises that a trustee may have no say in determining the particulars of a remuneration clause, still, trust obligations are always voluntarily undertaken (no one is forced to become a trustee of any particular trust), and when a trustee does undertake a trust with an express remuneration clause, he must be assumed to accept the clause as adequate. In this respect his agreement to take on the trust is very like his agreeing to enter into a contract. The voluntariness of the trustee's undertaking is made clear by Brightman LJ's observation that a trustee has an escape route, retirement, if he later feels underpaid. Therefore the court should be slow to upset the 'bargain' represented by the remuneration clause, because, especially in the case of a professional trustee, his voluntary acceptance of the trusts is very close to contractual. The court should not exercise its inherent jurisdiction simply to allow him to escape from a bad bargain, ie an agreement to undertake a trust which later turns out not to be as profitable as expected. If he wishes to retire, so be it, and if a new trustee will only

268

undertake the trust on better remuneration terms, it may be better to consider increasing the remuneration for him, not for the original trustee. Such an approach would prevent a trustee from being in the position, by reason of his incumbency, to hold the trust to ransom.

11.5 With regard to the second argument, the CA held, quite rightly, that in authorising a trustee's remuneration of a trustee the court was exercising its jurisdiction to ensure the adequate administration of the trust. In doing so the court did not concern itself with the beneficial interests as such, and so cannot be regarded as varying them.

11.6 When considering increasing the remuneration of an incumbent trustee, Fox LJ said this:

> [T]he court has to balance two influences which are to some extent in conflict. The first is that the office of trustee is, as such, gratuitous; the court will accordingly be careful to protect the interests of the beneficiaries against claims by the trustees. The second is that it is of great importance to the beneficiaries that the trust should be well administered. If therefore the court concludes, having regard to the nature of the trust, the experience and skill of a particular trustee and to the amounts which he seeks to charge when compared with what other trustees might require to be paid for their services and to all the other circumstances of the case, that it would be in the interests of the beneficiaries to increase the remuneration, then the court may properly do so.

In his opinion Brightman LJ referred to the court's 'power to increase *or otherwise vary* the future remuneration of a trustee who has already accepted office' (my italics). It would be interesting to see in what circumstances the court will exercise its inherent jurisdiction to *reduce* the remuneration provided by the trust instrument, and whether a trustee opposing such an application would fare any better with the contractual argument, insisting that a bargain is a bargain.

11.7 Finally, although it has been said that the jurisdiction 'should only be exercised sparingly, and in exceptional cases' (*Re Worthington* (1954) per Upjohn J), Fox LJ in his reasons said that he and Brightman LJ were both of the impression that orders authorising increases in remuneration had been made in chambers since the 1950s, which might suggest that the exercise was not, in practice, all that exceptional.

11.8   These principles were applied recently in *Foster v Spencer* (1995) in which trustees of a cricket club were awarded remuneration for having tackled various problems 'vigorously and unremittingly' over the course of twenty years to enable the club to sell its ground. The court disagreed with the proposition that it could only allow remuneration, whether for past or future service, in order to engage or retain the services of the particular trustees for the future, ie to obtain the future services of trustees who would not act unless remunerated.

> Where, as in this case, there were no funds out of which to pay remuneration at the time of their appointment, nor was a true appreciation of the extent of the task possible, a prospective application would be impracticable, if not impossible. The refusal of remuneration ... would result in the beneficiaries being unjustly enriched at the expense of the trustees. The right of a trustee to remuneration for his past services cannot depend upon the circumstance that at the time he seeks it, his services are further required so that he is in a position to demand remuneration for the past as a condition of continuing in office.

Here one trustee was awarded a retrospective annual fee, and another a percentage of the sale price of the ground which took into account his successful effort in obtaining planning permission for the development of the site.

11.9   The court may even award unauthorised remuneration to trustees or fiduciaries in breach of their fiduciary duties. In *Boardman v Phipps* (1966), fiduciaries who acted in breach of the no conflict rule, though they did so honestly and in so doing created a large profit for the trust, received remuneration on a 'liberal scale', and in *O'Sullivan v Management Agency Ltd* (1985) remuneration including a profit element was allowed for management and production companies which had procured a contract from an artist through undue influence, but whose efforts were clearly in part responsible for the artist's financial success. In *Guinness plc v Saunders* (1990) a director who had negotiated on behalf of a company in a takeover bid sought an allowance from the court for his efforts. The HL questioned whether the court should ever authorise exceptional remuneration to a director, since the company articles specifically provided for the payment of directors – the exercise of the inherent jurisdiction:

> ... may be said to involve interference by the court in the administration of a company's affairs when the company is not being wound up. (per Lord Goff)

The court would definitely not do so in this case where the director had plainly put himself in a position of conflict of interest by agreeing to provide his negotiation services for a fee the size of which depended on the price his company would pay in the takeover.

Unauthorised profits and the liability to account for them

11.10   The rule regarding unauthorised profits is boldly framed in the oft-quoted statement of Lord Herschell in *Bray v Ford* (1896):

> It is an inflexible rule of the court of equity that a person in a fiduciary position … is not, unless otherwise expressly provided, entitled to make a profit; he is not allowed to put himself in a position where his interest and duty conflict. It does not appear to me that this rule is, as has been said, founded on the principles of morality. I regard it rather as based on the consideration that, human nature being what it is, there is danger, in such circumstances, of the person holding the fiduciary position being swayed by interest rather than by duty, and thus prejudicing those whom he was bound to protect.

It is clear from this statement that the prohibition on unauthorised profits arises to avoid conflicts of interest. If a trustee were entitled to profit from the trust as he saw fit, his own interests would be in conflict with his fiduciary duty to act solely in the interests of the beneficiaries.

11.11   Perhaps the extreme example of the no profit/no conflict rule is *Keech v Sandford* (1726). A trustee held a lease for a minor beneficiary, which he sought to renew. The lessor refused to renew the lease in favour of the minor. The trustee took the new lease for his own benefit. King LC required the trustee to hold the lease on trust for the beneficiary, even though his interest when he acquired it could not, strictly speaking, be in conflict with his duty to the beneficiary, since the lessor absolutely refused to renew to a minor. Lord King accepted that the consequence of the rule's application was that:

> … the trustee is the only person of all mankind who might not have the lease; but it is very proper that the rule should be strictly pursued, and not in the least relaxed; for it is very obvious what would be the consequences of letting trustees have the lease, on refusal to renew to the cestui que trust.

11.12   In *Protheroe v Protheroe* (1968) the CA, without a review of the relevant authorities, held that the rule in *Keech* applied to a trustee's purchase of the reversion upon a lease so that it was automatically to be held on trust for the beneficiary. While on the authorities this would be a clear extension of the rule, Hayton ((1996), 342) argues that the decision is right on a strict application of the no conflict rule (see *Boardman v Phipps*, below **11.21**), because the trustee would, as landlord, have interests in conflict with his role as fiduciary holder of the lease, or 'trust-lessee', for the beneficiary.

11.13   Normally, it is said that a fiduciary is 'liable to account' for any unauthorised profits which he receives as a result of his fiduciary position. What does 'liable to account' mean? A trustee has a primary obligation to 'account' for his stewardship of the trust, that is, his exercise of his fiduciary powers over the beneficiary's property. He must, on the insistence of the beneficiary, reveal and explain all of his dealings in his capacity as trustee. In the case of a trust, this will primarily involve the production of the trust accounts, showing his dealings with the trust property. If the trustee received an unauthorised profit, he will be made 'liable to account' for the profit, that is he will be required to bring the profit into account as an accrual to the trust. Similarly, a non-trustee fiduciary who makes an unauthorised profit out of his position is liable to account, ie liable to pay the profit to his principal. In this way the right to demand the 'taking of an account' is the beneficiary's remedy against the fiduciary who takes an unauthorised profit.

11.14   The difficult question which the trustee's liability to account raises is whether the beneficiary's right that the trustee bring the profit into account is merely a personal right against the trustee to pay the value of the unauthorised profit into the trust, or whether he has a proprietary right to the profit in the actual form of the property the trustee received, ie whether the trustee holds the unauthorised profit on trust for the beneficiary from the moment he receives it, as in *Keech* with respect to the lease which the trustee obtained. Clearly, if the trustee is insolvent, only the trust will ensure that he receives the value of the property; furthermore, if the property rises in value, a right to the property itself will be superior to a merely personal claim against the trustee that be must pay the value of the property at the time he received it into the trust. Bear in mind this distinction between a personal and a proprietary 'liability to account' as we consider the different situations in which this liability arises. We will consider the issue in detail at **11.39** et seq.

Incidental profits

11.15 A typical example of an incidental unauthorised profit is a commission a trustee receives by directing the trust business to a particular company. In *Williams v Barton* (1927) a trustee had a contract with a brokerage firm under which he received a commission on work for clients which he had introduced to them; he was accountable to the trust for the commission he earned by directing trust business to the firm. In *Swain v Law Society* (1981), CA; (1982), HL, a solicitor claimed that the Law Society was acting as a fiduciary vis-à-vis solicitors when it procured liability insurance for the profession, and so it held its share of a broker's commission on trust for the members of the Society. The argument succeeded in the CA, but it was decided in the HL that the Law Society was acting under a statutory duty to secure insurance cover and not as a fiduciary for the members; there was, however, no doubt that had the Society been acting as a fiduciary the commission would have been an incidental profit for which it would have been accountable to the members.

11.16 Another example is directors' fees. Trustees must safeguard the trust investments and it will be appropriate and sometimes necessary for a trustee to be appointed to the board of directors of a company in which the trust has a large shareholding (**10.15**). The general rule is that their directors' fees are incidental profits of their position for which they must account to the trust (*Re Macadam* (1945)), unless of course their retention of the fees is authorised. The decision in *Re Dover Coalfield Extension Ltd* (1907) is problematic. In that case two directors of the Dover company were appointed to the board of the Kent company, in which Dover held shares. In order for the appointments to be effective, the directors were required to hold a certain minimum number of shares in Kent. Sufficient shares were transferred from Dover into their names as trustees for Dover; though the beneficial interest remained with Dover, their legal title to the shares was sufficient to qualify them as directors. The CA held that the directors were not liable to account for their directors' fees. The basis of the decision is unclear, although the judgments seem to rest on two grounds; first, since they became directors of Kent at Dover's request, this amounted to an authorisation

273

from Dover to retain their fees; secondly, because the appointment to Kent was obtained before they acquired Dover's shares in Kent, and the fact that 'they did the work' as directors, the contract between the directors and Kent was a bona fide agreement for their services, ie so that they were not on the board simply as trustee-monitors of Dover's interests. In *Re Gee* (1948) Harman J, after reviewing the authorities explained the law as follows:

> [A] trustee who either uses a power vested in him as such to obtain a benefit (as in *Re Macadam*) or who (as in *Williams v Barton*) procures his co-trustees to give him, or those associated with him, remunerative employment must account for the benefit obtained. Further, it appears to me that a trustee who has the power, by the use of trust votes, to control his own appointment to a remunerative position, and refrains from using them with the result that he is elected to a position of profit, would also be accountable. On the other hand, it appears not to be the law that every man who becomes a trustee holding as such shares in a limited company is made ipso facto accountable for remuneration received from that company independently of any use by him of the trust holding, whether by voting or refraining from so doing. For instance, A who holds the majority of shares in a limited company becomes the trustee of the estate of B, a holder of a minority interest; this cannot, I think, disentitle A to use his own shares to procure his appointment as an officer of the company, nor compel him to disgorge the remuneration he so receives, for he cannot be disentitled to the use of his own voting powers, nor could the use of the trust votes in a contrary sense prevent the majority prevailing.

In *Re Gee* the trustee-director was not liable to account for his remuneration as a director because the company resolutions to appoint and pay him were unanimously voted by the shareholders, and since there was only a minority of shares held on trust, the resolutions did turn on the voting of the trust shares – even if the trust shares had been voted against the resolutions, that would not have changed the result.

Secret profits

11.17 One important subset of incidental profits are what are sometimes called 'secret' profits; while the term might be regarded simply as a synonym for unauthorised commission or profits, including, for example, the commission in *Williams v Barton*, it is useful to restrict the term to bribes and hidden commissions which the trustee knowingly obtains in breach of his fiduciary position. In *Reading v A-G* (1951) a

274

sergeant in the British Army stationed in Egypt assisted smugglers by riding in their lorries wearing his uniform so that they would not be stopped at check points. The British authorities seized £20,000 of the money he was paid for these services. In an action to recover the money Reading argued that while he had obtained it wrongfully, the Crown had no right to retain it; the HL held that as a non-commissioned officer he stood in a fiduciary relationship to the Crown and therefore he was liable to account for any profits he obtained by the misuse of his position. This is, to be sure, a somewhat odd extension of the notion of fiduciary, since it is not clear that Reading could really be regarded as having the power legally or practically to affect the Crown's interests (**2.2**).

11.18 In *A-G for Hong Kong v Reid* (1994), Reid, the acting Director of Public Prosecutions, accepted bribes to obstruct the prosecution of criminals. Reid was liable to account for the bribe money to the Crown in right of Hong Kong. Lord Templeman said:

> Where bribes are accepted by a trustee, servant, agent, or other fiduciary, loss and damage are caused to the beneficiaries, master, or principal whose interests have been betrayed. The amount of loss or damage resulting from the acceptance of a bribe may or may not be quantifiable. In the present case the amount of harm caused to the administration of justice in Hong Kong by Mr Reid in return for bribes cannot be quantified.

It seems, then, that the money is accountable to the principal whether or not the principal has himself suffered loss, and this affirms the decision in *Reading* – although the British authorities undoubtedly suffered embarrassment, clearly it was the Egyptian authorities who directly suffered a loss from Reading's acts.

11.19 In *Islamic Republic of Iran Shipping Lines v Denby* (1986) a solicitor accepted a 'commission' of $200,000 from the opposite side for securing the settlement of a legal action brought by his client. Legatt J said, 'What he received was, quite simply, a bribe', and was liable to pay the sum to his client.

The 'no conflict' rule

11.20 In certain cases what counts as a conflict between a fiduciary's interest and his duty to his principal is more complicated than in the fairly straightforward case of incidental profits, and here, what might be specifically called the 'no conflict' rule comes into its own. Under the 'no conflict' rule, a fiduciary is liable to account for any profit he obtains in circumstance where his interests *may* conflict with his duty to his principal. The rule is exceptionally stringent, in that it is framed – '*may* conflict' – in terms of the possibility of conflict, not in terms of there being an actual conflict of interest.

11.21   The leading case is *Boardman v Phipps* (1966). The defendants were Boardman, the solicitor to the Phipps family trust, and Tom Phipps, one of the beneficiaries. The trust held a significant holding in a private company which was ailing. Boardman and Phipps decided that with new and effective management the company could generate significant profits for the shareholders. With the informed consent of the two active trustees (a third trustee was the settlor's widow who was senile), Boardman and Phipps, as proxy holders of the trust shares, tried to get Phipps elected to the board, and failed. They also failed to negotiate a splitting up of the business between the Phipps holding and the other major block of shareholders. The two active trustees made it clear that they would not buy any more shares of the company for the trust. Finally, Boardman and Phipps purchased sufficient shares with their own money to enable them, with the support of the trustees, to take control of the company. As a result, they were able to sell off certain of the company assets, paying out large dividends while at the same time maintaining a high share price. Tom's brother, John Phipps, another beneficiary under the family trust, then sued Boardman and Tom Phipps, calling upon them to account for the profits they had earned on the shares they had purchased, as profits acquired in breach of their fiduciary duties to the trust, because acquired in conflict of interest with the trust. The HL, by a 3:2 margin, found Boardman and Phipps liable to account for the profits they earned. Clearly Boardman stood in a fiduciary position as solicitor to the trust; unfortunately, the case was argued and decided on the basis that Tom Phipps should be treated equally with Boardman whatever the outcome though Phipps, as a beneficiary under the trust, did not obviously stand in the same fiduciary capacity. Lord Guest's finding that Boardman was liable was straightforward:

> In the present case the knowledge and information obtained by Mr. Boardman was obtained in the course of the fiduciary position in which he had placed himself. The only defence available to a person in such a

fiduciary position is that he made the profits with the knowledge and assent of the trustees. It is not suggested that the trustees had such knowledge or gave such consent.

Thus because the information was acquired in the course of his dealings with the trust, and he was a fiduciary to the trust, any profits made from using that information would be profits arising from his fiduciary office; unless authorised, they must be accounted for. Simple. Two points should be noted. First, this simple equation of liability with Boardman's having profited from information acquired in his conduct of the trust would not have led to the liability of Tom Phipps, for as a beneficiary under the trust he could well argue that he obtained any information in that capacity, not as a fiduciary to the trust. Second, Lord Guest speaks of the consent of the *trustees*. (There was no informed consent by *all* the trustees, since the third, senile, trustee, was not informed at all.) This poses something of a puzzle. Normally, the consent of the beneficiaries is required to authorise any act which would otherwise be a breach of trust. Where a trustee employs a fiduciary agent, the agent owes his duties to the trustee, and the trustee may then authorise what would otherwise be a breach of that agent's fiduciary duty. But, if he does so for insufficient reasons, then he would be liable to the beneficiaries for a breach of trust, ie for failing himself to carry out his duties properly. However in this case Boardman was liable to the beneficiaries directly, so it can only be the case that because of his close relationship with the trustees and the beneficiaries he owed a fiduciary duty directly to them.

11.22 Lord Hodson took a similar line. Pointing out that in *Keech* the beneficiary could not have acquired the disputed assets himself, it was irrelevant that the trustees had decided not to purchase further shares in the company. Any profit obtained by a fiduciary made possible by his fiduciary position was to be accounted for unless consented to, although Lord Hodson made it clear that the consent required was that of the complaining beneficiary.

11.23 Unlike Lords Guest and Hodson, Lord Cohen did not wholly rely upon the *Keech* rule, as if any use of information acquired in the course of dealing with the trust to generate a profit for the fiduciary automatically entailed that the profit was to be accounted for. He stated:

[I]n my opinion, Mr. Boardman would not have been able to give unprejudiced advice if he had been consulted by the trustees [about acquiring further shares for the trust] and was at the same time negotiating for the purchase of the shares on behalf of himself and Mr. Tom Phipps. In other words, there was, in my opinion, at the crucial date ... a possibility of a conflict between his interest and his duty.

11.24   Lord Upjohn dissented and said:

The phrase 'possibly may conflict' requires consideration. In my view it means that the reasonable man looking at the relevant facts and circumstances of the particular case would think that there was a real sensible possibility of conflict; not that you could imagine some situation arising which might, in some conceivable possibility in events not contemplated as real sensible possibilities by any reasonable person, result in a conflict ... it has been assumed that it has necessarily followed that any profit made by [a fiduciary] renders him accountable to the trustees. This is not so.

In Lord Upjohn's opinion the 'no conflict' rule was not to be applied automatically, for that would only lead to the harsh and inequitable consequences of the majority decision. In order for a fiduciary to be accountable, he reasoned, the fiduciary must have made a profit (1) earned within 'the scope and ambit of his duty', and (2) in circumstances where he had placed himself in a position where there was a 'real sensible possibility of conflict' between his duty and his interest.

11.25   The majority decision in *Boardman* can certainly be criticised for what appears to be an unjustifiably harsh result. Although Boardman and Tom Phipps were allowed remuneration for their efforts on a liberal scale, they were stripped of all their profits from investing their own money in an endeavour which hugely profited the trust beneficiaries on the basis of what was quite clearly an unrealistic possibility of conflict.

11.26   At this point it is worth reconsidering the court's inherent jurisdiction to authorise or increase the remuneration of a trustee (**11.4** et seq). A trustee seeking remuneration, or an increase in remuneration, is clearly not in a situation where his interest and duty *may* conflict; they definitely are in *actual* conflict. The court, therefore, must be astute to assess the trustee's claims that he 'requires' such and such a level of remuneration. In the case of an increase of remuneration, taking a strict *Keech* approach would mean that the only person who could not benefit from the trustee's advice to the court that the remuneration of the trust was Insufficient would be that trustee himself, because of the 'very obvious consequences' which would ensue if a trustee were able to argue for an increase in remuneration which would be to his own benefit; thus a court would only accept a trustee's argument that the proper administration of the trust required an increase on the basis that a new trustee who would take advantage of the increased remuneration would be appointed. To state this is not to argue that the court should adopt such a rule, but only to question whether the court's strict and automatic application of the 'no conflict' rule is justifiable when *Re Norfolk's Settlement Trusts* shows that the court thinks itself fit to determine an appropriate division of benefits between the beneficiary and the trustee in a clear situation of actual conflict of interest.

The 'no conflict' rule and company directors

11.27 The leading case applying the 'no conflict' rule to company directors is *Regal (Hastings) Ltd v Gulliver* (1942). The defendants were directors of a company, Regal, which owned and operated a cinema. Two other local cinemas were available for lease, and the directors decided to create a subsidiary company which would acquire leases to these cinemas, and that Regal would then sell its holding in all three cinemas as a going concern. The landlord of the two cinemas was not prepared to grant the leases to the subsidiary unless either a personal guarantee was given by the directors, or the subsidiary had paid-up capital of £5,000. The directors were reluctant to provide personal guarantees, so the second route was chosen. However, the directors decided that Regal could not put up more than £2,000 of the required £5,000. Four directors then each subscribed for shares worth £500, as did the solicitor to Regal at the request of the director; one director acquired £500 worth of shares for third parties. With £5,000 paid-up capital the subsidiary acquired the leases. As it turned out, Regal did not sell its interest in the three-cinema business; rather, the shareholders of Regal and the subsidiary sold their shares to a purchaser. The directors who had put up part of the capital for the subsidiary company received a handsome profit for their investment. The purchaser installed a new board of directors, and Regal, now under their control, launched this action against the former directors, calling for them to account for the profits they had made on their sale of the subsidiary shares. Regal succeeded in the HL. In the lower courts the directors successfully defended the claim, by arguing the decision they made for Regal to invest no more than £2,000 in the subsidiary was *bona fide* – indeed it might have been a breach of trust to have risked more of Regal's money; therefore, the directors putting up their own money *secured* a benefit for Regal which it could not otherwise have obtained, and so there was no basis for holding them liable to account for the profits they had personally made. The HL unanimously rejected this interpretation of the case, applying the rule in *Keech* in its full rigour. Lord Russel said:

> The rule of equity which insists on those, who by use of a fiduciary position make a profit, being liable to account for that profit, in no way depends on fraud, or absence of *bona fides*; or upon such questions or considerations as whether the profit would or should otherwise have gone to the plaintiff, or whether the profiteer was under a duty to obtain the source of the profit for the plaintiff, or whether he took a risk or acted as he did for the benefit of the plaintiff, or whether the plaintiff has in fact been damaged or benefited by his action. The liability arises from the mere fact of a profit having, in the stated circumstances, been made. The profiteer, however honest or well intentioned, cannot escape the risk of being called to account.

None of the non-director subscribers of shares in the subsidiary, including the solicitor, were accountable, for none were fiduciaries subject to the rule. The solicitor took up his shares at the request of the company (a request made, of course, through its directors), and Lord Russel said:

> I know of no principle or authority which would justify a decision that a solicitor must account for profit resulting from a transaction which he has entered into on his own behalf, not merely with the consent, but at the request of his client.

11.28 Note that the effect of the decision was to give the new purchasers of the company and subsidiary shares a windfall, for they were, by this action by Regal, able to secure the return of part of their purchase price to Regal's coffers – had the company itself just sold the cinema business, the purchasers would not have been able to make such a claim, for the 'injured company' which suffered by the directors' breach would not have been in their hands. Recognising this, Lord Porter said:

> This, it seems, may be an unexpected windfall, but whether it be so or not, the principle that a person occupying a fiduciary relationship shall not make a profit by reason thereof is of such vital importance that the

possible consequence in the present case is in fact as it is in law an immaterial consideration.

11.29 Note also that the directors' liability might easily have been avoided. Their decision to take up shares in the subsidiary could have been approved by the vote of a general meeting of the company, ie a general shareholders' meeting, and being in control of the company, they doubtless would have controlled the voting to ensure the result they desired. Such approval in the case of a company is equivalent to the informed consent of the beneficiaries under a trust. As pointed out by Lowry (1997), the fact that company directors are typically able to control the voting at a general meeting makes the court's ringing endorsement of the application of the rule in *Keech* somewhat hollow, for any well-advised company directors who control by proxy a sufficient number of the companies shares may, by ensuring the approval of a general meeting, engage in profit-taking of this kind as they please.

11.30 The *Regal Hastings* principle was applied in *Industrial Development Consultants Ltd v Cooley* (1971). Cooley was the former chief architect of the West Midlands Gas Board. He joined IDC as their managing director, principally in order to procure work in the gas industry. He was approached by representatives of the Eastern Gas Board with respect to some large contracts for work to be done in the near future. The evidence indicated that the Eastern Gas Board would not have entered into contracts with IDC, as they disagreed in principle with 'the set-up' of IDC; the Board was willing, however, to enter into contracts with Cooley personally. Cooley secured his release from his position at IDC by lying to them that he was seriously ill, and secured the lucrative contracts for himself. Roskill J found that Cooley had clearly placed himself in actual conflict with IDC; it was his fiduciary duty to inform IDC of the Eastern Gas Board's plans and not to keep secret his dealings with the Board to his own advantage; the court declared that he held the profits of the contracts on trust for IDC. Roskill J realised that his decision secured for IDC a profit which it would never would have obtained if Cooley had complied with his fiduciary duty, but he accepted that:

> ... [i]t is an over-riding principle of equity that a man must not be allowed to put himself in a position in which his fiduciary duty and his interests conflict.

281

11.31   The strictness of *Regal Hastings* has not been followed in North American jurisdictions. For example, in *Peso Silver Mines v Cropper* (1966) the Canadian Supreme Court found that directors were not liable to account for their profits from the exploitation of mining claims after the company's board decided in good faith not to pursue the claims because of its straightened finances. (See also *Canadian Aero Services v O'Malley* (1973).) In the US the courts have developed a 'corporate opportunity doctrine', the purpose of which is to determine which opportunities for profit 'belong' to a company, from which directors may not personally profit (*Guth v Loft Inc.* (1939); *Broz v Cellular Information Systems Inc* (1996)). There are signs that the inflexibility of the *Regal Hastings* approach may no longer be so acceptable to English judges either. The PC, in an appeal from Australia, *Queensland Mines Ltd v Hudson* (1978), decided that Hudson, a former managing director of a company who had resigned from the board to take up mining licences personally which the company had decided, due to its financial difficulties, not to pursue itself, was not liable to account to the company for the profits he earned. The court reasoned that although the opportunity came Hudson's way in his role as a fiduciary to the company, the company board knew of his interest and had given their fully informed consent. This decision directly contradicts both *Regal Hastings* and the received wisdom generally, since it is not the directors but the shareholders in a general meeting who are capable of giving such consent. The PC also decided that the good faith rejection of the opportunity placed the opportunity 'outside' the scope of Hudson's fiduciary duty. But as Sullivan (1979) points out:

> This [ground for the decision] enables the directors when exercising their managerial prerogative to reject corporate opportunities to thereby remove those opportunities from the restrictions imposed by their fiduciary duties … The orthodoxy is that the director's legal powers of management are subject to the equitable obligations imposed by their fiduciary role; *Queensland* stands this on its head in allowing a managerial decision to delineate the scope of a fiduciary duty.

This aspect of the decision is particularly significant, since if it represents the law, a board's rejection of an opportunity may now be challenged only on the basis that it was not in good faith, raising all the difficulties of proof which such a charge may entail.

11.32   Two more recent first instance English cases are also of relevance. It is, as you might imagine, a rule that a trustee may not operate a business in competition with the trust (*Re Thompson* (1930)), and this applies to other fiduciaries vis-à-vis their principals as well. However, in *Island Export v Immuna* (1985) Hutchison J decided that, while a director's fiduciary obligations did not cease utterly upon the termination of his post, the mere fact that he entered into competition with his former company following his departure did not make him liable, so long as he did not capture a 'maturing business opportunity' of the company. (The phrase comes from the Canadian case *Canadian Aero Services v O'Malley* (1973).) Hutchinson J said:

> In this context counsel for the defendants rightly stresses the fundamental principles relating to contracts in restraint of trade. It would, it seems to me, be surprising to find that directors alone, because of the fiduciary nature of their relationship with the company, were restrained from exploiting after they ceased to be such any opportunity of which they had acquired knowledge while directors. Directors, no less than other employees, acquire a general fund of knowledge and expertise in the course of their work, and it is plainly in the public interest that they should be free to exploit it in a new position.

Similarly, in *Balston Ltd v Headline Filters Ltd* (1988), Falconer J stated:

> [A]n intention by a director of a company to set up business in competition with the company after his directorship has ceased is not to be regarded as a conflicting interest within the context of the principle, having regard to the rules of public policy as to restraint of trade, nor is the taking of any preliminary steps to investigate or forward that intention so long as there is no actual competitive activity, such as, for instance, competitive tendering or actual trading, while he remains a director.

11.33 As the US case law reveals (see in particular *Broz v Cellular Systems Inc* (1996)), and Lowry and Edmonds point out (1997, 1998), the common law rules are likely to have little influence in the vast majority of cases simply because the directors, if agreeing that all or some or one of them may exploit a corporate opportunity, will be able to secure the ratification of their decision at a general meeting. In many cases even a single director, because of his influence over the board and control of general meetings, may secure the ratification of exploits undertaken entirely for his own benefit. This leaves the common law to deal with the infrequent *Cooley* situation where the fiduciary will undoubtedly be liable under any regime of accountability because of his subterfuge and bad faith. The problem of ensuring the safety of shareholders from the illegitimate capture of corporate opportunities by directors is only likely to be achieved by changes in company law.

The self-dealing rule

11.34 The self-dealing rule prohibits a trustee from purchasing the trust property unless specifically authorised to do so, and explicit authorisations are strictly construed (*Wright v Morgan* (1926)). The rationale, as explained by Lord Eldon in *Ex p Lacey* (1802), is that because the trustee acts both as vendor for the beneficiaries and purchaser, he places himself in an obvious conflict of interest and it is impossible to determine whether he has served the beneficiaries interests properly in securing the best price for them. In consequence, if a trustee sells trust property to himself, the sale may be set aside, i.e is voidable, at the insistence of any beneficiary, regardless of how fair the transaction is. The principle in all its rigour was affirmed and applied in *Re Thompson's Settlement* (1985) to a trustee-landlord's consent to the assignment of a lease; the principle essentially applies to all trust property transactions.

11.35 *Holder v Holder* (1968) is an exceptional case where the purchaser from a testator's estate, though not proving the will, admitted at trial that by having performed certain minor acts in the administration of the estate he had become an executor, and therefore a trustee. Innocent of his trustee status, he purchased the property at fair value at a public auction. The CA refused to set aside the sale. Harman LJ argued that the purpose of the rule was to prevent any sale by a person acting as both vendor and purchaser, but here the property was prepared for sale by the two proving executors of the will with no input from the purchaser:

> I feel the force of the judge's reasoning that if the [purchaser] remained an executor he is within the rule, but in a case where the reasons behind the rule do not exist I do not feel bound to apply it.

Danckwerts and Sacks LJJ both went further and questioned whether the rule should ever be applied automatically, doubting that it was beyond the court to determine whether the trustee had taken unfair advantage of his position. Vinelott J in *Re Thompson's Settlement Trusts* clearly preferred the traditional approach. Note that the problems of determining a trustee's good faith in the face of an actual conflict are just the same here as they were in *Regal Hastings*, where the court refused to mitigate the severity of the rule on evidence that the director's decision that Regal could invest no more than £2,000 in the subsidiary was *bona fide*.

The fair dealing rule

11.36 The fair dealing rule applies to purchases not of the trust property itself, but of a beneficiary's interest in the trust property, or a purchase of an agent of his principal's property. The rule is less harsh, for the simple reason that the danger here is less: since there are two real parties to the transaction with their own interests at stake, not a trustee selling to himself, the bargain is much more likely to be a real one. Therefore if a trustee purchases the beneficial interest of a beneficiary the transaction may not be set aside automatically at the beneficiary's insistence, but only if the trustee cannot show (and the onus is on him to do so) that he has taken no advantage of his position, has fully disclosed all relevant information to the beneficiary, that the beneficiary did not rely solely on his advice, and that the price was fair. (See, eg the characterisation of Meggary J in *Tito v Waddell (No 2)* (1977), cited in *Re Thompson's Settlement Trusts*.)

11.37 If a trustee attempts to circumvent the application of either the self-dealing or the fair-dealing rules by collusively selling to a third party, the sale is liable to be set aside as if the trustee were a party himself. In *Re Postlethwaite* (1888) the court did not set aside a sale to a third party just because the trustee entertained a hope of purchasing the property himself from him. Sales to family members or spouses will be viewed suspiciously, and a trustee will not be entitled to avoid the application of the rule by retiring from the trust in order to purchase trust property (*Re Boles and the British Land Company's Contract* (1902)).

11.38 Where a sale is liable to be set aside, the transaction is voidable, not void at the outset, so an innocent third party purchaser of the property from the fiduciary before a beneficiary acts will take a good title; in these circumstances the trustee will be liable to account to the trust for any profits made on the resale, or if it is shown that the resale was at an undervalue, the difference between the sale price and the true value. Where the transaction is avoided while the property is still in the hands of the fiduciary, the beneficiaries may together require the return of the property in return for the purchase price received, or may require a re-sale of the property on the open market – if the property fetches more on the open market than the price paid by the fiduciary the difference is theirs, of course (see *Holder v Holder* (1967)).

The proprietary and personal nature of the liability to account

11.39   Where a trustee is liable to account for an unauthorised profit, one might understand this as a claim that the trustee has failed to bring trust property into the account. That is, his liability to account is simply a recognition of the fact that the property is trust property in his hands which he has not properly accounted for, ie dealt with. It would follow from this analysis that the particular profit, as trust property, is held on trust for the beneficiary. It is important to realise that on this view, the property should be regarded as being held under an *express* trust, the express trust under which all of the other trust property is held. Such a profit would stand on the same footing as would the proceeds of the sale of any of the trust property, or the income from trust property, which a trustee might wilfully or inadvertently have paid into his own bank account. Such property, just like capital proceeds or income, is captured by and is within the terms of the express trust. On this view, then, there is no question of the court's *imposing* a constructive trust on the particular profits or the income earned on it, and of course the profit can be trace into the proceeds of substitutions. The trustee will, of course, also be personally liable to the trust for the value of the property if it has disappeared or cannot be traced, for that will be how he will satisfy the account if he cannot do so with the actual property itself or its traceable proceeds.

11.40   One can discern such an understanding of the liability to account from some of the cases. For example, in In *Williams v Barton*, Russel J decided that the perfectly honest trustee held the commission as a 'constructive trustee' and 'was liable to account' as if this meant much the same thing. In *Boardman*, when the HL affirmed the order of Wilberforce J at first instance, they affirmed that the shares were held on trust, though apart from Lord Guest all of their Lordships spoke only of the defendant's liability to account. Similarly, in *IDC v Cooley*, the court declared that Cooley was a trustee of the profits he earned from his contracts, and liable to account for those profits plus interest. On the other hand, whenever judges ever refer to the trust over these profits, they always speak of a *constructive* trust. Does that indicate that the trust does not follow from the liability to account, since if that were so bringing a profit into account would bring it under the express trust? Perhaps, but the use of 'constructive' in these circumstances may be little more than a judicial tic – it may be that the court has a tendency, when it must decide the entitlement in equity to a piece of property which the legal owner dispute belongs in equity to another, and it finds against him, to say that he holds it on 'constructive' trust. For example, if the trustee appropriates property which clearly belongs to the trust, any profits or income on the property are clearly trust property, ie property under the express trust. Yet, it is typically said that such profits are held on 'constructive' trust (eg Martin (1997), 607).

11.41   However, the 'liability to account' may properly be understood as a merely personal liability of the trustee or other fiduciary to pay the value of the profit, plus interest from the time it was received, to the beneficiary or principal. On this view the law obviously goes beyond the liability to account when a fiduciary is found to hold the profit on trust as soon as he receives it, and in this case the trust is a 'constructive' one. It is imposed by operation of law on the property; the property is not captured at the outset by the express trust.

11.42   In *Lister & Co v Stubbs* (1890) the CA clearly regarded the fiduciary's liability to account for a bribe to be personal, not proprietary. Stubbs was a purchaser for Lister & Co, who received large secret commissions from one of Lister's suppliers, Varley & Co, for ordering goods from them. Lister had invested part of the commission money in land, and Lister sought an interlocutory injunction restraining Stubbs from dealing with the land, arguing that the land, as an investment purchased with the commission money, belonged in equity to it. The CA refused. Here is the famous passage from Lindley LJ's judgment:

> Then comes the question, as between Lister & Co and Stubbs, whether Stubbs can keep the money he has received without accounting for it? Obviously not. I apprehend that he is liable to account for it the moment he gets it. It is an obligation to pay and account to Messrs. Lister & Co, with or without interest, as the case may be. I say nothing at all about

that. But the relation between them is that of debtor and creditor; it is not that of trustee and *cestui que trust*. We are asked to hold that it is – which would involve conseqences which, I confess, startle me. One consequence, of course, would be that, if Stubbs were to become bankrupt, this property acquired by him with the money paid to him by Messrs Varley would be withdrawn from the mass of creditors and be handed over bodily to Lister & Co. Can that be right? Another consequence would be that, if the Appellants are right, Lister & Co could compel Stubbs to account to them, not only for the money with interest, but for all the profits which he might have made by embarking in trade with it. Can that be right? It appears to me that these consequences show that there is some flaw in the argument. If by logical reasoning from the premises conclusions are arrived at which are opposed to good sense, it is necessary to go back and look again at the premises and see if they are sound. I am satisfied that they are not sound – the unsoundness consisting in confusing ownership with obligation.

Thus Stubbs's liability to account was treated as a purely personal obligation to pay over the commission, or bribe – he was in the position of debtor to his principal for that amount, not trustee of the bribe money for him. Thus his obligation to pay over the bribe, though a fiduciary obligation, was nevertheless still only an obligation – he did not become a trustee of, or in other words, Lister did not get equitable ownership of, the bribe money the moment it was received. While Lindley LJ was absolutely right to insist upon the distinction between ownership and obligation, he did not himself explain why, in this circumstance, had Stubbs only the obligation to pay over the value of the bribe, and not the obligation to hold the bribe money on trust as soon as he received it. For those reasons one must consider Cotton LJ's judgment. He appeared to decide that, if Lister had proceeded to set aside the contract with Varley, then any moneys paid by Lister to Varley and which were then paid by Varley to Stubbs as a bribe might be regarded as Lister's in equity. He also distinguished cases where the fiduciary or trustee had in his possession funds actually withdrawn from the trust. Thus the CA appeared to decide that the false fiduciary would only hold property in his possession on trust for his principal where the funds were previously funds of the trust; or rather, funds which prior to his defalcation *were already* trust property, and so remained trust property though wrongly dealt with by the trustee. Presumably the court would also have agreed that dividends payable on shares owned by the trust and paid to the trustee would be trust property the moment they were received, so that if a trustee put them into his own pocket rather than into the trust's bank account he would hold them on trust the moment he received them. Although not property of the trust prior to their receipt by the trustee, such income is payable by virtue of the ownership of the capital, and the beneficiaries are the beneficial owners of that.

11.43 Recently, however, the PC in *A-G for Hong Kong v Reid* (1993) decided that the recipient of a bribe held it on trust for his principal. There were two bases for the decision. On one hand, Lord Templeman quoted with approval the words of Sir Peter Millet, speaking extra-judicially:

> [The fiduciary] must not place himself in a position where his interest may conflict with his duty. If he has done so, equity insists on treating him as having acted in accordance with his duty; he will not be allowed to say that he preferred his own interest to that of his principal. He must not obtain a profit for himself out of his fiduciary position. If he has done so, equity insists on treating him as having obtained it for his principal; he will not be allowed to say that he obtains it for himself. He must not accept a bribe. If he has done so, equity insists on treating it as a legitimate payment intended for the benefit of the principal; he will not be allowed to say it was a bribe.

This analysis, of course, leads to a finding that the bribe is held as trust property from the outset, under an express trust, just as much as any other trust 'income', like the dividends on shares, would be. On this reckoning, the liability to account is a proprietary liability *per se*, as considered in **11.39** above, and *Lister* must be wrong because it is conceptually in error – there is just no such thing as a liability to account which means that the fiduciary has only a personal obligation to pay over the value of the property in question. But on the other hand, Lord Templeman also stated that the fiduciary was subject primarily only to an equitable obligation to pay the money over to the principal, ie was a 'debtor in equity', not a trustee of the bribe money at all. But:

> Equity considers as done that which ought to have been done. As soon as the bribe was received, whether in cash or in kind, the false fiduciary held the bribe on constructive trust for the person injured.

The application of this maxim in these circumstances is very questionable (see Crilley (1994)). Principally, however, as Swadling (1997) points out, the maxim does not work in the case of a debt:

> [T]hat debt can be satisfied by the payment of money belonging to the fiduciary taken from any source. It is not only discharged by the handing over of the very money received. And since there is no duty to pay over the bribe *in specie*, the application of the maxim 'equity considers as done that which ought to have been done' cannot give rise to any proprietary rights over those moneys, for the payment over of the bribe itself is not that 'which ought to have been done'.

The judgment is certainly subject to criticism for depending upon two apparently incompatible grounds for the decision, but furthermore, the PC was not, as was the court in *Lister*, willing to distinguish between situations where unauthorised profits are held on trust by the fiduciary from the outset, and those in which they are not. Rather, the PC appear to suggest that in line with the general application of the 'no conflict' rule, any and all such profits will be held on trust from the outset. The constructive trust in *Boardman*, for example (assuming one *was* actually imposed), was cited with apparent approval, and Lord Templeman cited *Sugden v Crossland* (1856) with approval for:

> ... dispos[ing] succintly of the argument ... that there is a distinction between a profit which a trustee takes out of a trust and a profit such as a bribe which a trustee receives from a third party. If in law a trustee who in breach of trust invests trust moneys in his own name holds the investment as trust property, it is difficult to see why a trustee who in breach of trust receives and invests a bribe in his own name does not hold those investments also as trust property.

In short, the decision pretty much abolishes the merely personal liability to account for an unauthorised profit – it is essentially proprietary in all cases. While the PC's decisions are technically only of persuasive authority in England and Wales, no one doubts that *Reid* will be followed here, although given the broad terms of its expression and the difficulties of its reasoning, its ambit has yet to be precisely settled.

11.44 Although the CA in *Lister* did not provide a complete set of principles for differentiating between a trustee's personal and proprietary liability to account, it is submitted that it is essential to do so, and that *Reid* must be faulted on this score. *Pace* Lord Templeman, it is one thing for equity to require a fiduciary to hold on trust a profit acquired by taking the trust property itself, or the income arising on it, but quite another thing to do the same for any property acquired in breach of any of his fiduciary duties. The consequence are particularly important in the context of insolvency (**2.32** et seq). If B has the obligation to pay A money, and B goes bankrupt, then A is an unsecured creditor; if B has breached his fiduciary obligations to A and has earned a profit in so doing, but not because his breach was one where he appropriated any of A's property (in equity), while B should owe A those profits as a result of his liability as a fiduciary, there seems to be no reason for A *to acquire* a proprietary interest in those profits, for that simply allows A to gain a priority over B's other creditors when B, *ex hypothesi*, has not appropriated or interfered with A's property. Where a trust is automatically imposed on B's unauthorised profit however innocently it was acquired, as in *Boardman*, A gains an unjustified advantage merely because the obligation that was breached was a fiduciary one; it is difficult to say that John Phipp's right to Boardman's profits is any more compelling than C's common law right to be paid by B for the property C has has provided him under a contract, for C has thereby increased the value of B's estate, or D's common law right to be compensated for B's running him down with B's car, for D has suffered an actual (monetary) loss at B's hands. C and D have no proprietary claim, of course.

11.45 Is a trust over property in the breaching fiduciary's hands which is not originally property of the trust, or its traceable proceeds, or income of that property, ever justified? A trust over some bribes may be justified. If the bribe in *Lister* can be regarded as a payment which was really part of the consideration in the contract between Lister and Varley, then the money, this 'rebate' on the purchase price of Varley's supplies, should have gone back to Lister in the first place. On this view, the trust over the bribe prevents an unjustified distinction between a case of embezzlement and fraudulent conversion: one should not allow the trustee to avoid holding the property on trust from the outset simply because he embezzled it (ie prevented property that should have gone into the trust from getting there by treating it as his own) rather than fraudulently converted it (ie appropriated the existing trust property to his own benefit); both are equally examples of theft. The argument is that this 'rebate' is akin to the income on property, like dividends on shares. the agent intercepts this payment to his principal, treating it as his own (ie embezzling it) rather than paying it over to his principal. In *Mahesan v Malaysia Government Officers' Co-operative Housing Society Ltd* (1977) an agent of the housing society took a one-quarter share of an overvalue of $488,000 on a price of $944,000 paid for a piece of land

291

the agent purchased for the society from the briber. The bribe of $122,000 clearly represented the agent's 'cut' of the overvalue. The housing society sued the agent for its loss on the purchase, $443,000, which was the amount of the overvalue minus certain costs. Having elected for that remedy, the society was unable also to claim the value of the bribe, since the value of the bribe clearly formed part of the total overvalue.

11.46 But there are bribes and bribes. Certainly the A-G for Hong Kong could hardly claim that it should have received the profits from Reid's suborning of the judicial process. In that sort of case, the principal, by having a claim against the fiduciary, is really stripping him of the profits of his wrong, not demanding property which was his from the outset, or was a payment made to him intercepted by his fiduciary. Similarly, in *Boardman*, Boardman did not appropriate any property of the beneficiaries, unless the use of the information was itself an acquisition of trust property. While Lords Hodson and Guest treated the information as trust 'property', the majority did not, and there is little to recommend that view (see Lord Upjohn's dissent on the point). In such a case it would be right to strip Boardman of his profits (assuming the case was rightly decided), but the profits should not be regarded as trust property from the outset.

11.47 One of the concerns which seems to motivate the imposition of the trust is that if the trustee invests his ill-gotten gains, perhaps earning substantial profits, and he is only personally liable to account, he will only be liable for the value of his initial receipt plus interest. Thus he will not be stripped of all the profits of his wrong. But there is no reason why the account should be rendered in this way. A personal liability to account might also include a liability to pay over the value of all profits obtained by investment of the money. Such an accounting of profits is a remedy available for patent infringement, though the remedy is personal, not proprietary, ie no constructive trust is declared over the profits (Cornish (1996), pp 63-64).

Further Reading

Swadling (1997); Crilley (1994); Birks (1994, Vol II, Part IV) Lowry (1997); Lowry and Edmonds (1998); Millett (1998).

Must read cases: *Re Duke of Norfolk's Settlement Trusts* (1981); *Keech v Sandford* (1776); *Re Gee* (1948); *Boardman v Phipps* (1966); *Regal (Hastings) Ltd. v Gulliver* (1942); *Lister & Co v Stubbs* (1890); *Holder v Holder* (1968); *A-G for Hong Kong v Reid* (1993).

Self-test questions

1. Discuss the scope and rationale for the conflict of interest rule as it governs a fiduciary's personal profits, and the remedies available to a principal or beneficiary where the fiduciary is liable under the rule.

2. Andrew is a farmer, who farms his own land and also manages and farms the land of Frank. Andrew recently purchased a load of seed cheaply, and now realises it is more than he can use on his own farm. He plants a ton of the seed on Frank's land, and charges Frank the going price, making a profit of £600. An agent of Superseeds Ltd rings up Andrew at his manager's office on Frank's farm and asks whether Frank will grow a new genetically-modified tomato Superseeds has developed. Frank has a policy against growing genetically-modified crops, and Andrew offers to grow the tomato on his own farm. The crop does spectacularly well, earning Andrew a profit of £20,000. Finally, Andrew offers to purchase half of Frank's acreage. He provides Frank with the accounts of his management of Frank's farm; they are in such disarray that it is impossible to determine how profitable the operation is, but Frank sells anyway. Discuss Andrew's liability to Frank.

3. What does 'liability to account' mean?

Remedies for Breach of Trust

Different sorts of breaches of trust

12.1   Breaches of trust fall into three broad categories. First, there are breaches of fiduciary duty by which a trustee gains an unauthorised profit, considered in chapter 11. Second, there are breaches by the trustee of his duty to act with care and skill in the administration of the trust which causes the trust loss, eg the claim made in *Nestle* (**10.20**). Finally, there are misapplications of trust property, for example where the trustee in breach of trust pays money to a third party, or where the trustee invests in an unauthorised investment, as in *Bartlett* (**10.15**).

12.2   The liability to account (**11.13**) is again the starting point for understanding the beneficiary's remedies for the breaches of trust considered here. The best explanation of this liability is given by Millet LJ, speaking extrajudicially (1998):

> The primary obligation of a trustee is to account for his stewardship [of the trust]. The primary remedy of the beneficiary... is to have the account taken, to surcharge and falsify the account, and to require the trustee to restore to the trust estate any deficiency which may appear when the account is taken. The liability is strict ... If the beneficiary is dissatisfied with the way in which the trustee has carried out his trust – if, for example, he considers that the trustee has negligently failed to obtain all that he should have done for the benefit of the trust estate, then he may surcharge the account. He does this by requiring the account to be taken on the footing of wilful default. In this context 'wilful default' ... means merely lack of ordinary prudence or diligence. The trustee is made to account, not only for what he has in fact received, but also for what he might with due diligence have received ... Where the beneficiary complains that the trustee has misapplied trust money, he falsifies the account, that is to say, he asks for the disbursement to be disallowed. If, for example, the trustee lays out trust money in an unauthorised investment which falls in value, the beneficiary will falsify the account by asking the court to disallow both the disbursement and the corresponding asset on the other side of the account. The unauthorised investment will then be treated as having been bought with the trustee's own money and on his own behalf. He will be required to account to the trust estate for the full amount of the disbursement – *not* for the amount of the loss. That is what is meant by saying that the trustee is liable to restore the trust property; and why common law rules of damage and remoteness are out of place.

Thus there are the two remedial functions taking an account may serve. When an account is 'surcharged' or taken on the footing of wilful default, a trustee is made liable for his negligence. When the beneficiary 'falsifies' the account the trustee must restore the value of misapplied trust property. In both of these cases, the trustee *compensates* the trust with money out of his own pocket for the loss he has caused it. Where trust

296

property is misapplied, the beneficiary has other remedies in addition to, but consistent with, this primary remedy of having an account taken (**12.39** et seq).

12.3   The beneficiary need not falsify the account if a *profitable* unauthorised investment is made, as Millet LJ further explains:

> If the unauthorised investment has appreciated in value, then the beneficiary will be content with it. He is not obliged to falsify the account which the trustee renders; he can always accept it. (It goes without saying that the trustee cannot simply 'borrow' the trust money to make a profitable investment for his own account and then rely on the fact that the investment was unauthorised to avoid bringing the transaction into account.) Where the beneficiary accepts the unauthorised investment, he is often said to affirm or adopt the transaction. That is not wholly accurate. The beneficiary has a right to elect, but it is really a right to decide whether to complain or not.

12.4   The PC in *Tang Man Sit v Capacious Investments* (1995) reviewed the law governing a plaintiff's election of alternative remedies, and Lord Nicholls stated:

> The basic principle governing when a plaintiff must make his choice is simple and clear. He is required to choose when, but not before, judgment is given in his favour and the judge is asked to make orders against the defendant. ... In the ordinary course, by the time the trial is concluded the plaintiff will know which remedy is more advantageous to him ... Occasionally, this may not be so ... A plaintiff may not know how much money the defendant has made from the wrongful use of his property. It may be unreasonable to require the plaintiff to make his choice without further information. To meet this difficulty, the court may make discovery and other orders designed to give the plaintiff the information he needs, and which in fairness he ought to have, before deciding upon his remedy.

12.5   The requirement of election is clearly to prevent the beneficiary from having it both ways – he cannot both 'adopt' the trustee's act which turns out to be profitable, and also claim damages for a loss on the footing that he wishes to disallow the transaction. In *Mahesan* (**11.45**) the court treated the housing society's claims to the bribe and to compensation for the loss it suffered as alternatives between which it must elect, and this is justified on the basis that its total loss included the bribe, since the bribe was clearly part of the inflated purchase price it paid. Where

297

a fiduciary makes a profit in breach of his fiduciary obligations he will be liable to account for the profit regardless of whether his principle gains or loses by the profitable transaction (*Boardman*, **11.21**). There might well be cases where there is both an unauthorised profit and a loss to the trust, but the profit is not, as in *Mahesan*, properly treated as value taken from the trust and thus representing a part of the loss. Consider *Reid* (**11.43**). If the Crown in Hong Kong was forced to undertake an expensive review of its procedures and launch a public relations exercise to restore citizens' faith in the office of the DPP, it should be able to claim against Reid for the costs incurred as consequential losses of his breach of fiduciary duty in addition to its claim for the bribe money – the very receipt of the bribe money did not represent those losses; if liable for those losses at all, he would be liable even if he had obstructed prosecutions for his own satisfaction, receiving no bribes at all. Thus where the bribe or unauthorised profit is not clearly a part or a share of some money transferred from the trust, the bribe is an independent profit not related to the loss, and the beneficiary or principal should not be required to elect between claims for the profit and claims for the loss. In principle at least, it should be possible to have concurrent claims for both in the right circumstances (see Birks (1996a)).

Compensation for loss caused by the trustee's negligence

12.6 Where a trustee causes loss to the trust by his negligence or lack of diligence, eg by his failing to meet a standard of prudence in his investments, he must personally compensate the trust. The claim is known as one for 'equitable compensation', though in this circumstance it is essentially identical to a claim for money 'damages' at common law for the tort of negligence. The general principles of equitable compensation were reviewed by the HL recently in *Target Holdings v Redferns* (1995). A solicitor of the firm Redferns acted both for Target holdings, a mortgage lender, and Crowngate, a prospective purchaser of land. Unbeknownst to Target, Crowngate was the final purchaser in a fraudulent land transfer scheme calculated to make the land appear much more valuable than it actually was: land purchased for £775,000 by one intermediary company was to be sold to another intermediary for £1.25m, which would then be sold to Crowngate for £2m. The solicitor was apparently fully aware of this series of transactions. Target agreed to lend Crowngate £1.5m for the final purchase in return for a mortgage over the land. As was usual in such transactions, Target transferred the loan money to Redferns in advance of the purchase, on instruction to pay the money to Crowngate for the purchase in return for an execution of a charge over the land in Target's favour. In breach of this instruction, the solicitor transferred the money to the two intermediary companies in furtherance of the series of purchases. However, the final sale to Crowngate was eventually completed and the charge in Target's favour secured. Crowngate became insolvent, and as mortgagee Target sold the land; it fetched only £500,000. Target sued Redferns for breach of trust for paying away the loan money in breach of its instructions. In the CA, Target successfully won summary judgment against Redferns for the entire £1.5m paid away less the £500,000 realised on the sale, even though, despite the breach, Target was in the same position it would have been in had the money been paid according to its instructions, since Target did receive a charge on the correct land for their loan advance of £1.5m. The reasoning advanced by the CA was that, having paid away the £1.5m in breach of trust, there was then an immediate loss to the trust of that amount, which Redferns became immediately liable, and remained liable, to make good.

12.7   The HL reversed the decision of the CA. Lord Browne-Wilkinson, with whose opinion all their Lordships agreed, stated that both at common law and in equity the principles of compensation for loss are fundamentally the same – a plaintiff may only recover for a loss caused by defendant's wrongful act, and the compensation is calculated to put the plaintiff in the position he would have been in had he not sustained that wrongfully caused loss. However, the rules governing *causation of loss and remoteness of damage*, ie the rules governing whether a particular loss which is causally connected to the defendant's act is compensatable, differ between the common law claim for damages and a claim for equitable compensation.

> Even if the immediate cause of the loss is the dishonesty or failure of a third party, the trustee is liable to make good that loss to the trust estate if, but for the breach, such loss would not have occurred ... Thus the common law rules of remoteness of damage and causation do not apply. However there does have to be some causal connection between the breach of trust and the loss to the trust estate for which compensation is recoverable, viz the fact that the loss would not have occurred but for the breach ... Equitable compensation for breach of trust is designed to achieve exactly what the word compensation suggests: to make good a

loss in fact suffered by the beneficiaries and which, using hindsight and common sense, can be seen to have been caused by the breach.

On these principles, Target obtained exactly what it would have obtained had there been no breach of trust, and so was entitled to no compensation. Target was, of course, entitled to pursue its claim that the solicitor had fraudulently procured the transaction by failing to inform Target of deceitful series of sales; if that claim were successful Target would, in lieu of rescinding the transaction, be able to claim the full value of the money paid away, because, but for *that* breach, ie the fraud, it would never have entered into the transaction at all. In other words, if Target could prove this, it would be entitled to falsify the account. The HL restored the original order of the first instance judge which gave Redferns leave to defend against this claim only on the payment of £1m into court.

12.8 With regard to the proposition that the rules of causation for equitable compensation should differ from those for common law claims for damages, in *Bristol & West Building Society v Mothew* (1996), Millett LJ said:

> Equitable compensation for breach of the duty of skill and care resembles common law damages in that it is awarded by way of compensation to the plaintiff for his loss. There is no reason in principle why the common law rules of causation, remoteness of damage and measure of damages should not be applied by analogy in such a case. *It should not be confused with equitable compensation for breach of fiduciary duty which may be awarded in lieu of rescission [ie instead of a contract being set aside for self dealing] or specific restitution [ie instead of an order to return specific property taken from the trust, where for example, the property is no longer in existence.]* (my italics)

In the case of equitable compensation where trust money is misapplied in breach of trust, there is no question of calculating the loss according to the common law principles of causation and remoteness for the loss is the loss of the trust property misapplied. If the trustee cannot restore the actual trust property, the equitable compensation that he must pay is simply the value of that property plus interest. Similarly, in cases where it is impossible or inequitable to rescind a self-dealing transaction (eg *Holder*, **11.35**), the compensation is again simply the value of the property minus the price the trustee paid plus interest. Indeed, according to Millett LJ speaking extra-judicially, *Target Holdings* should not have been regarded as a case of equitable compensation at all, so the rules of causation for loss need not have been considered:

> The solicitor held the plaintiff's money in trust for the plaintiff but with its authority to lay it out in exchange for an executed mortgage and the documents of title. He paid it away without obtaining these documents. This was an unauthorised application of trust money which entitled the plaintiff to falsify the account. The disbursement must be disallowed and the solicitor treated as accountable as if the money were still in his client account and available to be laid out in the manner directed. It was later so laid out. The plaintiff cannot object to the acquisition of the mortgage or the disbursement by which it was obtained; it was an authorised application of what must be treated as trust money. To put the point another way; the trustee's obligation to restore the trust property is not an obligation to restore it in the very form in which it he disbursed it, but an obligation to restore it in any form authorised by the trust.

On Millett LJ's view, then, there was no loss not because the rules of causation indicated there was none, but because the misapplication was fully corrected when the trust was properly restored according to its terms.

12.9 *Mothew* concerned a claim by a building society against a solicitor who had acted both for it and the borrower. The solicitor failed to include facts pertinent to assessing the creditworthiness of the borrower in filling out a standard form report to the society prior to the release of the mortgage loan; the facts indicated that he negligently failed to complete the report form accurately. Though he had been aware of the facts, he had forgotten or overlooked them when making the report. The CA held that while the solicitor's paying out the money for the purchase was certainly a payment of *trust* money (it was clearly held by him on trust), his action in paying it was not a breach of trust or fiduciary duty for there was no breach of loyalty or good faith (recall 11.1); the mortgagee was left to its claim against the solicitor for breach of their contract or for the tort of negligence.

12.10 The principles underlying equitable compensation for breach of fiduciary duty were recently considered again by the CA in *Swindle v Harrison* (1997). Mrs Harrison, at the instigation of her son, mortgaged her house to provide capital to purchase the Aylesford Hotel, in order that together they could operate a family restaurant business. She contracted to buy the hotel and paid a £44,000 deposit, which would have been forfeited if she did not pay the remainder of the sale price and complete the purchase. Unfortunately, by the date of completion, she and her son were unable to obtain sufficient money to complete the purchase. Her solicitor, the engagingly named Mr Swindle, arranged for his firm to provide a bridging loan so that she could complete. In breach of fiduciary duty, Mr Swindle failed to inform her of certain pertinent facts, in particular his firm's profit on the loan. It was clear that but for the bridging loan, Mrs Harrison would not have been able to purchase the restaurant, and she would have lost her £44,000 deposit. The restaurant business turned out to be a disaster, resulting in the loss of the entire sum she had raised on the equity in her home. Because the solicitor failed to disclose material facts to her in breach of his fiduciary duty, she was clearly entitled to rescind the bridging loan agreement; it was therefore argued that the solicitors' firm was liable for any losses which would not have resulted 'but for the loan', ie all the losses resulting from the restaurant business.

12.11　The CA found against Mrs Harrison. Both Evans and Hobhouse LJJ distinguished between what they called 'restitutionary' and 'compensatory' remedies for loss. It is important to note that this use of the term 'restitution' is special and misleading. It refers to the restitution of the trust property in the sense that a fiduciary must *restore* the trust property or its value. This *restoration* is not 'restitutionary' in the normal legal sense of the word, which refers to stripping the defendant of an unjust enrichment (**2.30**). In this context, it is irrelevant whether the defendant fiduciary has gained or not from his breach. His obligation is to restore the value of the trust. It is compensation for loss, pure and simple. Restorative compensation restores the trust to the position it would be in had the transaction never taken place, as where in taking an account an unauthorised investment is 'falsified' by the plaintiff, or where a sale invalid for self-dealing is set aside. The other measure for compensation takes the perspective that the plaintiff should be put into the position he would have been in now if the wrong had not occurred. On this measure, all the consequences of the wrong are taken into account, whatever the particular wrong is, whether a misappropriation of trust property or a negligent act by the trustee: if it was a trivial wrong which caused the plaintiff only a trivial loss that will be the extent of the compensation due. Under this regime of compensation, the effect of the wrong over the course of time is assessed.

12.12 Evans LJ opined that the restorative measure of compensation is only awarded when a plaintiff is induced to enter a transaction by conduct which amounted to equitable 'fraud', which essentially included any breach of fiduciary duty. Evans LJ agreed with Millett LJ in *Mothew*, however, that not every duty of a fiduciary is a fiduciary duty. Evans LJ discerned no 'breach of fiduciary duty which might be regarded as the equitable equivalent of fraud', and therefore Mrs Harrison was entitled only to the non-restorative measure of compensation, compensation for consequential loss. Since the facts indicated that Mrs Harrison would have proceeded with the transaction even if she had been informed of all the pertinent facts, the losses she suffered trying to run the hotel as a business were not losses caused by this breach of fiduciary duty, and therefore her claim failed. The problem with Evans LJ's analysis is that he assumed that Mr Swindle's failure to fully inform Mrs Harrison would allow her to set the loan transaction aside, and this *is* a breach of fiduciary duty which, if setting the transaction aside were inconvenient or impossible, would lead to an award of compensation in lieu of rescission which *would* be aimed at *restoring* the plaintiff to the position he would have been in had the transaction never taken place. Evans LJ appears to decide that a breach of fiduciary duty normally regarded as a species of 'equitable fraud' – here the solicitor's breach of the no conflict/self-dealing rule by failing to disclose material facts about the transaction – a breach sufficient for setting the sale aside, was not 'equitable fraud' for the purposes of equitable monetary compensation.

12.13 Hobhouse LJ's reasoning is to be preferred. He made essentially the same distinction between restorative compensation and compensation for consequential losses, using the terms 'restitution' and 'common law damages'. Hobhouse LJ's use of the term 'common law damages', while accurate in the sense that the normal measure of damages at common law is not restorative, may be faulted for implying that equitable compensation is never awarded on the consequential loss basis. It is, as Millet LJ makes clear (**12.8**): it is the routine measure applied in cases of compensation where the beneficiary 'surcharges' the account, claiming compensation for losses caused by the trustee's lack of due diligence. Nevertheless, Hobhouse LJ rightly held that the restorative measure of damages only applies to, and thus is limited to, the very transaction which takes place in breach of fiduciary duty. In this case it applied only to the loan transaction, and she was not claiming any loss arising specifically from that transaction (indeed, by the time of trial, the loan contract had already been rescinded by agreement). Hobhouse LJ agreed with Evans LJ that on the facts, it was clear that on normal principles of compensation for consequential losses, Mr Swindle's breach of fiduciary obligation did not cause the losses incurred in the restaurant business. In contrast to Evans LJ, however, Hobhouse LJ held that Mrs Harrison's complaint failed not because in this circumstance the breach of fiduciary duty attracts only the normal 'common law' measure of damages, but because the breach of fiduciary duty did not relate to her loss at all. That breach was fully remedied by rescission and restoration of the position vis-à-vis that transaction. Hobhouse LJ did not, as a consequence, have to hold that in some circumstances breach of fiduciary duty attracts only the 'common law' measure of damages. It always attracts the restorative measure. But the restoration is rightly restricted to the transaction complained of.

12.14 Mummery LJ's shorter discussion of the point seems somewhat in between the views of Evans LJ and Hobhouse LJ. He opined that in determining equitable compensation, the court must apply 'common sense' causation, following Lord Browne-Wilkinson in *Target Holdings*. The principles of causation, however, are only to be applied once the scope of the relevant duty is ascertained, and in explaining this scope he relied on the recent decision in the HL, *South Australia Asset Management Corpn v York Montague Ltd* (1996). The case concerned claims by mortgage lenders for losses flowing from their reliance on negligent over-valuations of property in advancing mortgage loans. Lord Hoffman drew a distinction between reliance on information intended to enable a person to undertake a course of action he had decided upon, and reliance on information or advice as to what course of action to take. In this case, since the breach of fiduciary duty only related to the disclosure of certain information concerning the bridging loan, it was not relevant to Mrs Harrison's decision to purchase the hotel, since had she known all the facts she would have proceeded anyway. Thus Mrs Harrison's losses did not flow from the breach of fiduciary duty. Like Hobhouse LJ, then, Mummery LJ finds that the breach of fiduciary duty was not related to Mrs Harrison's loss because the duty did not relate to the hotel/restaurant business, but only to the loan transaction. Like Evans LJ, however, Mummery LJ does not rely upon deciding this point on the nature and scope of equitable remedies for breach of fiduciary duty, but rather on the basis of the normal 'common law' principles of causation to determine the measure of damages.

12.15   It is submitted that Hobhouse LJ's reasoning is to be preferred, since it makes clear that the remedy for breach of fiduciary duty is distinct, and not to be assimilated with the position of damages at common law, as both he and Millet LJ have pointed out. Where compensation is provided in place of rescission or specific restoration of property to the trust, this compensation only arises because the primary restorative remedy, rescission or specific restoration, cannot be carried out. It is compensation in lieu of a transfer of property, the value of which is known. One does not need to go into principles of causation to determine the value of the compensation. In other words, restorative compensation never compensates for what might be called 'consequential losses'; restorative compensation just gets the beneficiary or principal his property back. If because of the breach of trust, there *are* consequential losses, for example, because of a misapplication of trust property a beneficiary was not paid his normal income allowance and therefore in desperation sold some family antiques at undervalue to pay the rent, these losses are certainly compensable but must be found to be caused by the breach on normal principles of causation. Only Hobhouse LJ's decision grounds the distinction between restorative compensation and compensation for consequential losses in equity's allowing the plaintiff to set aside, or reverse, transactions invalid for breach of fiduciary duty or misapplications of trust property, without any inquiry into consequential losses.

12.16   In cases where an unauthorised investment causes loss, the beneficiary may 'falsify' the account and the trustee must restore to the trust the full value of the moneys disbursed on that investment, and pay an amount representing what would have been earned if the money were invested appropriately. In general, in assessing the amount of this compensation, the trustee may not offset gains made by other investments on the basis that 'overall, the trust fund is in good shape'. However, in *Bartlett* (**10.15**), the court held that the disastrous investment in one property development project was part of a larger investment policy favouring land development. In taking the account, then, this decision required the beneficiary to 'falsify' both the winning and losing projects as one invalid investment, with a resulting reduction in the amount of compensation.

12.17   Where an investment loss is caused by the trustee's lack of due diligence, the problem is to determine how much more the trust property would have increased in value. In *Nestle* (**10.20**), the plaintiff beneficiary failed to prove that the trust company's negligent misunderstanding of the trust instrument caused any loss; had she done so, however, Dillon LJ said *obiter* that the trustee would have to pay 'fair' compensation, ie an amount sufficient to restore the trust fund to a value it would have achieved if a proper investment policy had been followed, 'not just the minimum that might have just have got by without challenge'.

Liability of trustees *inter se*

12.18   The general equitable rule is that individual trustees are only liable for their own breaches of trust, not for the breaches committed by their co-trustees. However, equity does not recognise a 'sleeping' or 'passive' trustee, ie a trustee who does not fully participate in the administration of a trust. As Cotton LJ stated in *Bahin v Hughes* (1886):

> [I]t would be laying down a wrong rule that where one trustee acts honestly, though erroneously, the other trustee is to be held entitled to an indemnity who by doing nothing neglects his duty more than the acting trustee.

On this basis a trustee would be liable for breaches of their co-trustees to the extent that they were negligent or fell below the standard of prudence in monitoring their co-trustees' behaviour. Section 30(1) of the Trustee Act 1925 now governs the liability of trustees in this respect, as it does their liability for agents appointed under s 23(1) – see **10.30**. It thus appears that trustees will not be liable for the acts of their co-trustees unless they consciously or recklessly failed to monitor their behaviour.

12.19   Where two or more trustees are each liable for a breach of trust, they are 'jointly and severally' liable, which means that the suing beneficiary may claim the whole loss against the trustees together, or against any one trustee separately. Between themselves trustees may rely upon the Civil Liability (Contribution) Act 1978, which gives the court a discretion to apportion the share of liability each defendant trustee will bear, according to their relative individual responsibilities for the loss. In certain cases a trustee, though himself liable for breach of trust, may demand that his co-trustee indemnify him for any compensation he must pay – the effect of this, where that co-trustee is solvent, is to make him alone pay the compensation. Two such circumstances were stated in *Bahin v Hughes*:

> [W]here one trustee has got the money into his own hands, and made use of it, he will be liable to his co-trustee to give him an indemnity.

Second, a trustee may claim an indemnity against his co-trustee where that trustee is a solicitor who has exercised a controlling influence over the conduct of a trust; a solicitor trustee is not bound to indemnify his co-trustees, however, simply because he is a solicitor (*Head v Gould* (1898)). Third, where a breaching co-trustee is also a beneficiary under the trust, special considerations apply because of this dual status (**12.23**).

Beneficiaries' consent to a breach of trust

12.20   An adult beneficiary who freely consents to, or participates in, a breach of trust, may not sue the trustee to make good any loss caused by the breach. In *Re Pauling's Settlement Trusts* (1963) the trustee of a family settlement succumbed to the pressure of one beneficiary, the father, to make 'advancements' to his children, which in reality were not advancements at all: the money was not intended to benefit the individual children, but to defray the family's extravagant living expenses, including the cost of purchasing family homes. The children, though of full age, were not taken to have consented because, though they were aware of the true purposes of the advancements, the court held that their approval was procured by the undue influence of their father. The fact that several children received benefits to themselves from the advancements did not bar them from claiming against the trustee for breach of trust, though they did have to offset these benefits against their claim for compensation.

12.21   To truly consent a beneficiary must be fully aware of the facts, though not necessarily of his legal rights. Wilberforce J described the court's general approach in *Re Pauling's Settlement Trusts*:

> [T]he court has to consider all the circumstances … with a view to seeing whether it is fair and equitable that, having given his concurrence, he should afterwards turn round and sue the trustees … it is not necessary that he should know that what he is concurring in is a breach of trust, provided

that he fully understands what he is concurring in, and that it is not necessary that he should himself have directly benefited by the breach of trust.

These principles were adopted in *Holder* (**11.35**), where the plaintiff, suing to set aside the purchase of trust property by his brother who had technically acquired the status of an executor, was held to have acquiesced in the sale though unaware at the time of the legal position. He had subsequently received part of the purchase price as a beneficiary under the will, and throughout had full knowledge of all the facts concerning the sale. Besides considering these facts which go to determining actual consent, in *Holder* the 'fair and equitable' requirement for allowing the beneficiary now to 'turn round and sue' was applied. Although it was clear that the plaintiff did not know his legal rights to block or set aside the sale until afterward, the court felt that his conduct throughout, which appeared to be motivated largely by animosity towards his brother, and the fact that in failing to discover the brother's technical breach, he and his brother stood on an equal footing as both were legally advised, made it inequitable for him now to have the sale set aside.

12.22   The court has an inherent power to 'impound' the beneficial interest of a beneficiary who has requested, instigated, or consented to a breach of trust. By 'impoundment' is meant that the beneficiary's interest will be applied, to the full extent of the interest, to compensating the trust for the loss incurred by the breach. The result of this is that a beneficiary whose interest is impounded is not only prevented from suing the trustee for the breach, but is made to indemnify the trustee for the latter's participation in it. It seems from *Chillingworth v Chambers* (1896) that where the beneficiary merely consents to a breach initiated by the trustee, ie in circumstances where the beneficiary has not instigated or requested the breach, his interest may only be impounded if he had consented in order to benefit from the breach himself. Section 62 of the Trustee Act 1925 now supplements the inherent jurisdiction, allowing the court to impound a beneficiary's interest if he consented to a breach irrespective of any benefit to himself, so long as his consent is made in writing.

12.23   Where the beneficiary is also a trustee, two rules come into operation. Normally a trustee may claim contribution from his co-trustees for a share of the compensation to be paid (**12.20**). In the case of a beneficiary-trustee, the rule in *Chillingworth v Chambers* applies:

where a beneficiary-trustee and his co-trustee are liable for a breach of trust from which the beneficiary-trustee alone has benefited, then the beneficiary-trustee's beneficial interest is impounded to its full extent, and only if his interest is insufficient to cover the loss will he be able to claim contribution from his co-trustee. Under the rule in *Re Dacre* (1916), whether his interest is impounded or not, the trustee-beneficiary is not entitled to receive any part of his beneficial interest until his breach *qua* trustee is remedied, nor is any assignee of his equitable interest.

Trustee Act 1925, s 61

12.24 Section 61 of the Trustee Act 1925 relieves trustees of liability for breach of trust in certain circumstances. It reads:

> If it appears to the court that a trustee, whether appointed by the court or otherwise, is or may be personally liable for any breach of trust... but has acted honestly and reasonably, and ought fairly to be excused for the breach of trust and for omitting to obtain the directions of the court in the matter in which he committed such breach, then the court may relieve him either wholly or partly from personal liability for the same.

The court's exercise of the power is not governed by hard and fast rules. In *Re Pauling's Settlement Trusts* Upjohn LJ said:

> Section 61 is purely discretionary, and its application necessarily depends on the particular facts of each case.

12.25 Relief under s 61 was sought in two cases we have already considered. In *Re Pauling's Settlement Trusts* the sole trustee was a bank. Wilmer LJ opined that:

> Where a banker undertakes to act as a paid trustee of a settlement created by a customer, and so deliberately places itself in a position where its duty as trustee conflicts with its interest as a banker, we think that the court should be very slow to relieve a trustee under [s 61].

Relief was refused with respect to an advancement which benefited the bank because it was used to reduce the mother's overdraft with it. This suggests that any breach carried out by a trustee acting in clear conflict of interest, though not in terms dishonest, cannot be reasonable. With respect to another transaction the court held that the bank's relying upon the consent of the children, though over 21, when clearly it was obtained by their father's undue influence, was unreasonable, and so relief under s 61 was unavailable. The court did afford the bank relief in respect of one advancement where the bank trustee's solicitors and the solicitor who separately advised the sons were largely at fault.

12.26 The trustees also sought relief under s 61 in *Bartlett* (**10.15**). Brightman J tersely dismissed the plea, though covering each of the three criteria of the section:

> There is no doubt that the bank acted honestly. I do not think it acted reasonably. Nor do I think it would be fair to excuse the bank at the expense of the beneficiaries.

Trustee exemption clauses

12.27 Should the law allow trustees to be exempted from liability for their negligence in carrying out the trust by the insertion of an exemption clause in the trust instrument? Matthews (1989) has suggested that such clauses should be capable of excluding a trustee's liability for negligence, but not gross negligence; the Ontario Law Reform Commission (1984) argues against the validity of exemption clauses generally in view of the court's power to relieve trustees of liability, as under s 61. Ham (1995) argues that, although the invalidity of such clauses might result in higher charges to cover the cost of insurance, this price is worth paying given the consequences of a serious default by trustees.

12.28 The CA in *Armitage v Nurse* (1997) has recently decided that such clauses are perfectly effective to exclude trustees' liability for gross negligence. The exemption clause in the instrument protecting the trustees from any loss or damage 'unless such loss or damage shall be caused by his own actual fraud'. Millet LJ pointed out that such a clause does not purport to exclude, and does not exclude, a trustee's liability for breach of fiduciary duty. Thus it would not prevent a beneficiary setting aside a sale of trust property to a trustee, for that would not involve relieving a trustee for liability *for a loss*; neither, on such a view, would such a clause prevent a trustee from being stripped of an unauthorised profit, nor presumably, from liability for misapplications of trust property where the trustee acted in conflict of interest for in both those cases the trustee would be in breach of his fiduciary duty of loyalty.

12.29 Millet LJ accepted:

> ... that there is an irreducible core of obligations owed by the trustees to the beneficiaries and enforceable by them which is fundamental to the concept of a trust. If the beneficiaries have no rights enforceable against the trustees there are no trusts. But I do not accept the further submission that these core obligations include the duties of skill and care, prudence and diligence. The duty of trustees to perform the trusts honestly and in good faith for the benefit of the beneficiaries is the minimum necessary to give substance to the trusts, but in my opinion it is sufficient ... [A] trustee who relied on the presence of a trustee exemption clause to justify what he proposed to do would thereby lose its protection: he would be acting recklessly in the proper sense of the term.

There was, in his opinion, no basis in authority for saying that an exemption clause which relieved a trustee of liability for his gross negligence was 'repugnant' ie conceptually inconsistent with their being a trust.

12.30 Millett LJ examined the pleadings in the case and found that none clearly alleged dishonesty, but at most, negligence, and therefore the trustees were not liable. The trust arose as a variation of a previous trust under which both the plaintiff daughter and her mother were beneficiaries. Under the new trust, the plaintiff was the sole beneficiary. However, the trust largely consisted of a holding of farmland, and the trustees appointed a company controlled by her mother and grandmother to farm it, which also farmed the mother's own land. In essence the claim was that the trustees had managed the trust property with the interests of the family in mind, not the plaintiff, though the plaintiff was the only object of the trust. Millett LJ did not find in the pleadings sufficient particular allegations to sustain this charge, but allowed the plaintiff to re-amend her pleadings, adding:

> I express no view on whether there is material which would justify counsel in advising such a course; and I would not wish to encourage it. They will no doubt bear in mind that at the material time the trustees of the settlement consisted of one professional man and two distant relatives; and that a charge of fraud against independent professional trustees is, in the absence of some financial or other incentive, inherently implausible.

This narrow focus on fraud, however, seems to undercut Millett LJ's previous point that such a clause would not relieve the trustee of any breach of fiduciary duty. Consider in particular the duty of even-handedness. In *Nestle* (**10.20**) the CA did not consider the trustee to have breached this duty by tailoring its investments to benefit the current life tenants, because the court's appreciation of the duty gave the trustee a very wide discretion, but one can imagine another court taking a somewhat narrower view. The trustee did not, apparently, give much thought to its duty of even-handedness, as the investments favouring the life tenant seemed to have been made simply in response to the hectoring of one of the life tenants. In any case, the duty of even-handedness must be regarded as one of the core trustee fiduciary obligations for only by being even-handed between the beneficiaries does a trustee meet his obligation of good faith and loyalty to *all* the beneficiaries. Indeed, the duty of even-handedness is just a specification of the duty of loyalty and good faith where there is more than one beneficiary. Therefore, an exemption clause cannot relieve a trustee from his liability to a beneficiary for failing to be even-handed towards him. If the plaintiff's claims were made out, *Armitage* is clearly *a fortiori* to *Nestle*, since the allegation was that the trustees were loyal to the interests of the plaintiff's mother, who was not a beneficiary at all. Consider also *Re Pauling's Settlement Trusts*. There the trustee bank acted solely at the instigation of one beneficiary of the settlement, the father. It was apparently the forcefulness of his personality which largely led it to ignore the children's interests and make the advancements it did. In neither *Nestle* or *Re Pauling's Settlement Trusts* did the professional trustees stand to gain significantly from the alleged breaches of trust; they did so in the absence of any 'financial incentive' and it is not clear what 'other incentive' they had beyond making their lives easier in the administration of the trust. So, although Millett J is right to suspect that any charge of actual fraud may be inherently implausible where the professional trustee gains no benefit by it, an allegation of a breach of the duty of even-handedness may be more plausible.

Trusteeship *de son tort*

12.31   Where an individual who is not a trustee 'intermeddles' with the trust affairs, though innocently, he may become liable as a trustee for any misapplication of trust property or other loss caused to the trust

(*Mara v Browne* (1896)); such a person is known as a trustee *de son tort*. Such a person is typically an agent of the trust who takes it upon himself to exercise trustee functions over the property beyond the scope of his agency. Trusteeship *de son tort* is not restricted to agents, though they are in most danger of acquiring this liability.

Accessory liability

12.32   A person who never actually receives or handles trust property may yet be 'liable to account as a constructive trustee' for assisting in a breach of trust; the traditional terminology for accessory liability is 'liability for knowing assistance'. In this context, the phrase 'constructive trustee' is misleading for the liability depends upon assisting the breach of trust, not because the accessory ever actually becomes a trustee of any trust property. Of course, in certain cases an individual may assist a breach of trust *and* receive trust property in the course of doing so, in which case he may be liable not only as an accessory, but also for receiving the trust property (**12.39** et seq). The reason he is said to be liable 'as a constructive trustee' is that he is liable to account personally for the loss to the same extent as the express trustee who commits the breach. Thus the beneficiary's claim against an accessory, if there is one, is additional to his claim against the trustee himself for the breach, which is particularly useful if the trustee has disappeared or is insolvent.

12.33   The principles governing accessory liability were recently reviewed by the PC in *Royal Brunei Airlines Sdn Bhd v Tan* (1995). Mr Tan was the principal shareholder and director of BLT, a company which was Royal Brunei Airlines' general travel agent in certain locations. Under the airline's agreement with BLT, the proceeds of ticket sales were to be held on trust for the airline. The proceeds, however, were never paid into a separate trust account, but into BLT's current account, and the money was used for BLT's general business purposes. The PC denied that an accessory could only be liable if the trustee was engaged in a dishonest or fraudulent design himself. That view derived from Lord Selborne LC's statement in *Barnes v Addy* (1874) that an accessory was not liable 'unless they assist with knowledge in a dishonest and fraudulent design on the part of the trustees'. The PC decided that the accessory's liability should turn on his own dishonest participation in the breach, whether the trustee committing the breach did so dishonestly or not.

12.34 What does 'dishonesty' mean? Lord Nichols said that though honesty has a strong subjective element, the standard of liability was objective:

> Honesty is not an optional scale, with higher or lower values according to the moral standards of each individual ... Unless there is a very good and compelling reason, an honest person does not participate in a transaction if he knows it involves a misapplication of trust assets to the detriment of beneficiaries. Nor does an honest person in such a case deliberately close his eyes and ears, or deliberately not ask questions, lest he learn something he would rather not know, and then proceed regardless.

In respect of cases where there is genuine doubt as to whether a transaction constitutes a breach of trust, Lord Nichols said:

> Acting in reckless disregard of others' rights or possible rights can be a tell-tale sign of dishonesty. An honest person would have regard to the circumstances known to him, including the nature and importance of the proposed transaction, the nature and importance of his role, the ordinary course of business, the degree of doubt, the practicability of the trustee or the third party proceeding otherwise and the seriousness of the adverse consequences to the beneficiaries. The circumstances will dictate which one or more of the possible courses should be taken by an honest person. He might, for instance, flatly decline to become involved. He might ask further questions. He might seek advice, or insist on further advice being obtained. He might advise the trustee of the risks but then proceed with his role in the transaction. He might do many things. Ultimately, in most cases, an honest person should have little difficulty in knowing whether a proposed transaction, or his participation in it, would offend the normally accepted standards of honest conduct. Likewise, when called upon to decide whether a person was acting honestly, a court will look at all the circumstances known to the third party at the time. The court will also have regard to personal attributes of the third party such as his experience and intelligence, and the reason why he acted as he did.

The PC found Mr Tan liable. He had assisted in the breach of trust by 'causing or permitting' BLT to undertake the transactions in breach of trust in full knowledge that the moneys were to be held on trust, and that amounted to dishonest conduct. BLT was also dishonest, since Mr Tan's state of mind as its director was to be imputed to the company.

314

Third parties and agents

12.35   Third parties or agents to the trust are, however, not to be liable as accessories for negligently, but not dishonestly, failing to discover a transaction to be a breach of trust due to their own negligence:

> [B]eneficiaries cannot reasonably expect that all the world dealing with their trustees should owe them a duty to take care lest the trustees are behaving dishonestly.

Recall, however, that in *Boardman* (**11.21**), although Boardman was not a trustee but merely an agent of the trust, he was regarded as a fiduciary to the trust so as to make him liable directly to the beneficiaries.

12.36   In *Agip (Africa) Ltd v Jackson* (1989); affd (1990), CA the test of 'dishonesty' was applied to a solicitor and an agent who managed companies set up entirely for the purpose of receiving moneys obtained by fraud and then passing them on to unknown others. The only purpose of the companies was to make it difficult to detect the fraud and to follow the money that had been fraudulently obtained. With respect to finding a third party dishonest, Millett LJ said:

> It is essentially a jury question. If a man does not draw the obvious inferences or make the obvious inquiries, the question is: why not? If it is because, however foolishly, he did not suspect wrongdoing or, having suspected it, had his suspicions allayed, however unreasonably, that is one thing. But if he did suspect wrongdoing yet failed to make inquiries because 'he did not want to know' ... or because he regarded it as 'none of his business' ... that is quite another. Such conduct is dishonest, and those who are guilty of it cannot complain if, for the purpose of civil liability, they are treated as if they had actual knowledge.

In *Agip*, there was evidence that the defendants might have believed that they were assisting in a scheme, not to defraud a company, but to avoid the currency exchange controls of Tunisia. Millett LJ said:

> [I]t is no answer for a man charged with having knowingly assisted in a fraudulent and dishonest scheme to say that he thought that it was 'only' a breach of exchange control or 'only' a case of tax evasion. It is not necessary that he should have been aware of the precise nature of the fraud or even the identity of its victim.

12.37   In the CA decision in *Lipkin Gorman v Karpnale Ltd* (1989 – the case went to the HL, but the decision on accessory liability did not form part of the appeal), a law firm sought to hold its banker liable because it allowed a partner of the firm, one Mr Cass, who was addicted to gambling, to withdraw money from the firm's client account for that purpose. The CA decided that given the contract between the banker and its client, the bank could not be liable unless it was in breach of its contract to its client to operate and monitor the account properly. In this case Cass's withdrawals were perfectly valid within the terms of their contract with their customers – Cass had full authority to draw on the client's account. And although the bank manager knew that Cass was a gambler, this was not a sufficient reason to suspect that he was looting the client account, and the CA held that it would impose an excessive burden on bankers to monitor all of their accounts to pick up suspicious withdrawals.

12.38   In *Finers v Miro* (1990) a firm of solicitors sought directions from the court concerning assets it held on trust for a client. The solicitors suspected that some portion of the assets represented the proceeds of a fraud the client allegedly committed by unlawfully transferring assets from a US company, now in liquidation. The CA directed the solicitors to inform the liquidator of the US company that they held assets which might be assets of the company. But for the strong suspicion of fraud, informing the liquidator would amount to a breach of their fiduciary duty of confidence to their client. The CA based its decision in part on the fact that the knowledge of the solicitors was now such that should they dispose of any of the property to the defendant they might well be liable as accessories to a breach of trust, following *Agip*.

Remedies for the misapplication of trust property

12.39   Where trust property is misapplied, someone obviously receives it. As we already know (2.22 et seq), the plaintiff beneficiary has the right to claim the property back from a subsequent recipient for he retains equitable title to the property, unless the recipient is a bona fide purchaser for value of a legal title to the property without notice. Besides merely 'following' the trust property into the hands of third party recipients, recall also that the beneficiary may trace the value of the property into the proceeds of exchanges. If the beneficiary can trace the value of the trust property, he may be able to make an equitable proprietary claim to those proceeds as well (**12.57** et seq). Finally, the beneficiary may have a *personal* claim against recipients of trust property or its traceable proceeds for its value.

12.40   The plaintiff will be able to rely only upon a personal claim against the recipient of trust property or its proceeds if the recipient has destroyed or dissipated the trust property or proceeds, as no proprietary claim can be made. Obviously this personal claim will only be significantly valuable if the recipient is solvent. By contrast, a proprietary claim is most valuable in the case of the recipient's insolvency, for if the beneficiary can establish a proprietary right to the property itself, it does not form part of the recipient's estate.

12.41   The preceding personal claim must be distinguished from personal liability for being an accessory to a breach of trust (**12.33** et seq), although the recipient of trust property might also be an accessory. Therefore, against a stranger to the trust (ie not a trustee), the beneficiary may have three claims in respect of the misapplication of trust property. One, a proprietary claim for the actual trust property or traceable proceeds that the stranger retains; two, a personal claim for his receipt of trust property or traceable proceeds; and three, a personal claim for his being an accessory to the breach. The last claim may well be a very extensive liability, making him liable for much more than the value of the trust property he received, since the scheme of misapplication may have resulted in trust property going to others besides himself. We shall consider the defendant's proprietary and personal liability for receipt of trust property in turn. First, however, it is necessary to consider in detail the rules of tracing. Remember throughout that the tracing of value through different transaction may serve two purposes: (1) to allow the beneficiary to establish a *proprietary* claim to property still in the defendant's hands; and/or (2) to allow the beneficiary to say that his property or his value was received by the defendant, in order to establish *personal* recipient liability.

Tracing

12.42   It is obviously easiest to trace value through direct substitutions of one item of property for another. If the trustee gives an antique chair which belongs to the trust to A who sells it for £500, then the beneficiary can claim that the £500 is the traceable proceeds of the chair. Almost all of the difficulty in tracing arises when the misapplied trust property is money, or once the value is traced into money, for what people tend to do with money is bank it. The reason why banking money causes problems is that bank accounts are typically *mixtures* of value, and tracing through mixtures of value raises a host of problems.

12.43 If A takes the £500 traceable proceeds and deposits in his bank account, which has a balance of £1,000, raising the balance to £1,500, what does this new balance of £1,500 amount to in law? One view is that a bank account is a series of individual debts which add up to the current balance. Here the bank owes A at least two debts, one for £500, and as many further debts as correspond to the deposits which made up the previous balance of £1,000. The alternative view is that A and the bank agree under their contract that the Bank will, in exchange for the title to the £500, replace A's right against the bank to be paid his current balance of £1,000, for a new right against the bank to be paid £1,500: in essence A exchanges the £500 plus one debt owed him by the Bank for a new, more valuable debt owed him by the Bank. Thus the old balance is fully replaced by a new balance, and a bank account balance at any one time is a simple whole or 'monolith', which is not made up of a series of debts. On either view it is clear that the bank is a purchaser of the £500 for value. The bank, either on the 'series of debts' or the 'monolithic debt' analysis, raises A's balance to £1,500, and thereby valuably enhances A's rights. Unless the bank has notice that the money is paid into the account in breach of trust, the bank is a purchaser for value of the £500 in cash, or of the rights represented in a cheque worth £500 if that is what A deposited. The beneficiary must trace the cash or cheque into the proceeds of this further exchange transaction with the bank, that is, into the new debt against the bank, either into the new debt of £500 on the 'series of debts' view, or into the new debt of £1,500 on the 'monolith' view. Of course a withdrawal is just the opposite of a deposit, and is just as much a purchase for value. The customer, in return for cash, or in the case of a cheque, in return for the payment of a third party to his order by the bank, gives value since under his contract with the bank the debt the bank owes him is extinguished in whole or in part to the value of the withdrawal.

The 'first in, first out' rule

12.44 The 'series of debts' view is the common law view of bank accounts for the purposes of regulating the relations between banker and customer. When a customer withdraws money from the bank account, he extinguishes one or more of the debts the bank owes him. So for example, assume A's account has had only two transactions so far, one deposit of £1,000 and one deposit of £500. If A withdraws £400, the bank in providing him with those funds has extinguished one of these debts by that amount. Either the £1,000 debt is reduced to £600, leaving debts of £600 and £500, or the £500 debt is reduced, leaving debts of £1,000 and £100. Which debt is it? At common law *Clayton's Case* (1816) decides that, where the intentions of the parties do not determine the issue, a 'first in, first out' rule applies. The first debt is paid off first, as if the debts stood in a queue waiting for extinction. So here the result of A's withdrawal is that the £1,000 debt is reduced to £600, and the £500 debt is untouched. If A had withdrawn £1,200, that would have first fully extinguished the £1,000 debt, and then reduced the £500 debt to £300.

12.45   *Clayton's Case* establishes the rule between A and the bank as to the disposition of their serial transactions on the 'series of debts' view – should it also regulate the relations between A and the beneficiary for the purposes of tracing withdrawals which follow the deposit of trust money? Here for example, the £1,000 debt would be created with A's money alone, and so the beneficiary could not trace into that; his value went into creating the £500 debt. Under the 'first in first out' rule of *Clayton's Case*, A's subsequent withdrawals up to the value of £1,000 would all be withdrawals of his value alone, and only withdrawals after that would represent value into which the beneficiary's value can be traced, for only they would be substitutions for the debt in which his value lies. The question arose in *Pennell v Deffell* (1953), and then again in *Re Hallett's Estate* (1880). Both were cases in which a trustee paid trust money into his own account. In *Pennell* the 'first in, first out' rule in *Clayton's Case* was applied by the CA in Chancery, to the detriment of the beneficiaries under the trust; *Clayton's Case* was considered to have settled what the correct approach to bank accounts was. The CA reconsidered this in *Re Hallett's*. There the trustee paid trust funds into his bank account first, and then added money of his own; he then made withdrawals of money which he dissipated. Under the 'first in, first out' rule, the trust money went into the dissipated withdrawals. The CA decided that the 'first in, first out' rule should not be applied; rather a presumption of honesty should be attributed to the trustee, so that he was taken to have withdrawn his own value from the account first. Thesiger LJ dissented:

> Equity has gone very far in aid of trust creditors when it holds that they may follow and obtain in priority to general creditors moneys paid to a banker, and, therefore, no longer existing in specie as moneys numbered and earmarked, but converted into debt, and it may be that the distinguished judges [in *Pennell v Deffell*] may have thought that equity had gone far enough, and that in the absence of express appropriation the general rule of appropriation of payments in and out of a bank account should apply to that debt when forming part of a larger debt made up as to the rest of moneys not trust moneys paid into the bank.

It is always worth remembering in respect of tracing that, the more favourable the rules are to trust beneficiaries, the less favourable they are not only to the trustee, but also to his creditors.

12.46 In *Re Oatway* (1903), the trustee purchased shares with money from a bank account in which trust money and other money (treated as his own by the court) had been combined. When the shares were purchased, there was enough value so that the value of the trust money was not needed for the purchase, so if the *Re Hallett's* presumption that the trustee spends his own money first applied, the shares would be his own. The remaining funds, however, were later all withdrawn and dissipated. Joyce J refused to apply the presumption:

> [W]hen any of the money drawn out has been invested, and the investment remains in the name or under the control of the trustee, the rest of the balance having been afterwards dissipated by him, he cannot maintain that the investment which remains represents his own money alone, and that what has been spent and can no longer be traced and recovered was the money of the trust ... the trustee must be debited with all the sums that have been withdrawn and applied to his own use so as to be no longer recoverable, and the trust money in like manner be debited with any sums taken out and duly invested in the names of the proper trustees. The order of priority in which the various withdrawals and investments have been respectively made is wholly immaterial.

The result of this decision is to give the beneficiary the right to control the book-keeping of the bank account to his advantage, claiming his value went into any profitable investment and denying it to went into any untraceable expenditure. However it is not clear whether there is a priority between *Re Hallett's* and *Re Oatway*, ie that the *Re Hallett's* presumption is to be applied first, so that where the remaining bank balance is sufficient to cover the beneficiary's value, the beneficiaries may only trace into that balance. Martin ((1997), 671) argues that *Re Tilley's Will Trusts* (**12.62**) suggests that this is the case, though there is no clear English authority. If it is not the case, a plaintiff beneficiary may 'cherry-pick' the profitable expenditures, treating them as trust investments, even though there remain ample funds in the account to restore the trust.

The 'lowest intermediate balance' rule

12.47   The extent of this right to control the book-keeping of the account extends, however, only to withdrawals. Subsequent *deposits* by the wrongdoing trustee to the bank account are not presumed to be repayments to replace any trust moneys that have been withdrawn and dissipated. If the trustee has the genuine intention to repay withdrawn trust funds, the repayment will of course count as such, but *not as the traceable proceeds of the beneficiary's original value*, for the replacement value did not come in any way from trust property, but as new property of the trust put in by the trustee, over which he declares a new express trust (*James Roscoe (Bolton) Ltd v Winder* (1913)). This decision leads to the 'lowest intermediate balance' rule of tracing into bank accounts. However the presumptions as to withdrawals are played, once a bank balance is reduced to say, £50, it is necessarily the case that the maximum traceable value that can possibly remain in the account is £50. If £500 of trust money were deposited, at least £450 must have been withdrawn, and so a beneficiary faced with such an intermediate balance can trace his value further only into the past withdrawals which reduced the balance to that figure.

Tracing amongst innocents

12.48   Different rules apply to tracing through bank accounts when the value that the trustee mixes in one bank account comes from different trusts, or when an innocent volunteer adds trust value to his own bank account. The rules which apply to tracing amongst these innocent parties *inter se* are different than the rules which apply between these innocents and a wrongdoing trustee. In a case where none of the wrongdoing trustee's money is involved, the general rule that apparently applies is the 'first in first out' rule of *Clayton's Case*. The application of the rule here has been criticised (see, eg Smith (1997), 193–194), and it is suggested that the innocents should be able to trace into all the withdrawals and into any value that remains in shares proportionate to the amounts of value that they contributed. Such a solution would be in line with the common law rule governing 'fluid' mixtures, ie mixtures of goods like oil where the separate identity of the mixed parts cannot be ascertained – the innocent owners of the mixed goods co-own the whole in proportion to the amounts they contributed. (See Birks (1992); *The Ypatianna* (1987)). However, the applicability of the rule in *Clayton's Case* to these situations has recently been affirmed by the CA in *Barlow Clowes International Ltd v Vaughan* (1992). The case concerned the proper means of allocating the remaining value in a pooled investment scheme amongst the contributing investors. All three judges, however, held that the authorities indicated that the rule was not to be applied blindly in all circumstances. In this case, because the investment scheme involved the pooling of investment funds, the contributors could be presumed to intend that their interests in the fund were proportionate to their contributions, so they were entitled to be traced as co-owners into the remaining funds in proportionate shares. Leggatt LJ's dissatisfaction with the rule in *Clayton's Case* was most apparent, saying it had 'nothing to do with tracing'. The mode of tracing between innocents Leggatt LJ preferred is called the 'rolling charge' or 'North American' solution (as it is applied in Canada and the US; see eg *Re Ontario Securities Commission and Greymac Credit Corpn* (1986)). The value contributed by innocents is traced into mixtures so that they become proportionate co-owners of the whole, but the 'lowest intermediate balance' rule is properly taken account of, as are the *Re Hallett's* and *Re Oatway* rules as between the trustee and the beneficiaries as co-owners of the trust value. Assume a rogue trustee, T, pays into his account £500 of beneficiary A's, and then £500 of beneficiary B's, which already contains £500 of his own, raising the balance to £1,500. Now assume T withdraws £750 and dissipates the money. By *Re Hallett's*, T will be presumed to spend his own £500 first and so only £250 of the trust money. As co-owners in proportionate shares, A and B will suffer the loss equally, each now tracing into a half share of £750. Now T add's £500 from beneficiary C. Under the principle of the lowest intermediate balance, it must be the case that A and B can only trace into the £750, which is all the trust money that remains when C's money is added, not into C's contribution. From now on, however, the mixing means that C's fate is linked with A's and B's as proportionate co-owners of the entirety of their traceable value: A and B each have a $(^1/_2 \times £750)/£1250 = {}^3/_{10}$ share, and C a $^4/_{10}$ share of the whole of £1,250 of trust value.

12.49 Under the same scenario, the rule in Clayton's case delivers the following result: The £250 trust money attributed to T's withdrawal of £750 will, under the 'first in first out' rule of *Clayton's Case*, be £250 from A's contribution alone, so if that is the end of the story, A will receive only £250, while B will receive his full £500 back. Assume now that T adds £500 of C's, who is also an innocent. T then withdraws £500. This withdrawal will wipe out A's remaining traceable value of £250, will reduce by £250 B's value, and leave C's value untouched. If the money the trustee withdraws is dissipated, and the story ends there, then the timing of the deposits will mean that though each contributed £500, A can trace into nothing, B into £250 in the account, and C his full value into £500 in the account.

12.50 Consider what might be called the 'opposing scenario': assume that T's first withdrawal of £750 is put in a desk drawer and kept safe. *Re Oatway* allows A and B to deny that T spent trust money first, so both will want to trace into the £750 cash still in the desk. If he draws on the trust money according to the 'first in first out' rule A's value will be drawn on first, and so A will be able to trace his full value into the cash in the desk, while B will be able to trace only into £250 in the account. Under the 'rolling charge' solution they would each trace a half share into the £750, and each recover £375. Notice that on either the 'first in first out' or the 'rolling charge' rule that C will recover nothing, since at the time the withdrawal is made, his value has not been added, so that there his no way that he can trace his value into the money in the desk.

12.51 Notice that both the 'rolling charge' mode and the 'first in first out' rule will require a careful examination of the transactions over the history of the account, which will be expensive, expenses which will, in an insolvency, reduce the total amount of funds available for distribution. This was the case in *Barlow Clowes*, and this was one consideration against applying the 'rolling charge' solution, though it is the most fair. Note that while the effect of the rule in *Clayton's case* is to prejudice early contributors, the effect of the proportionate co-ownership solution adopted in *Barlow Clowes* prejudices late contributors. Given that we are concerned with tracing the actual value of contributors, it must be the case that the lowest intermediate balance rule must apply. However the proportionate co-ownership solution ignores this rule, putting the contributor who paid in money long ago on the same footing as one who contributed last week, even though it is almost certain that on any realistic examination of the past account withdrawals, a significant proportion of the early contributor's value was withdrawn.

Tracing with respect to overdrawn accounts and backwards tracing

12.52   One 'backwards traces' when one traces value into property purchased by the recipient *before* he receives the value which is traced. If a rogue trustee buys an antique table worth £3,000 *on credit*, by taking a loan from a bank, or by using his overdraft facility, or with his credit card, and then later pays off the debt incurred with trust money, logically it is clear that the value of the trust money now resides in the antique table. As Smith (1997), 146) says:

> Suppose that D buys a car from C with some money. If we were tracing the value inherent in ownership of the money, we could trace it into ownership of the car. Now change the facts slightly, so that D buys the car on credit; he takes ownership of the car, but he is C's debtor in respect of the purchase price. A day later, D pays the debt with the money being traced. Can we trace from the money into the car as before? It is difficult to see why not. There is no substantial change in the transaction; the period of credit might be reduced to a minute or a second to better make this point. If that is right, then when money is used to pay a debt, it is traceable into what was acquired for the incurring of the debt.

Unfortunately, the law has not adopted this logical and compelling position, apparently as a result of some confusion about tracing into overdrawn bank accounts.

12.53   Normally, when money is paid into a bank account, there is no difficulty determining the substitution that has occurred. The bank takes title to the money, and gives value in exchange in the form of the increased bank balance. The increased bank balance is, of course, the traceable proceeds of the payment in of the money. Where £500 is paid into an account which is £500 in overdraft, resulting in a balance of zero, what are the traceable proceeds? In exchange for the title to the money, the bank gives value in the form of the reduction of the debt it is owed by the customer to zero. No debt now exists between the bank and the customer, and therefore no rights between them which can be the traceable proceeds of the £500 payment. For this reason, it is generally but wrongly assumed that the payment of a debt is the end of the tracing exercise, since there just *are no proceeds*. While it is absolutely right to deny that anything of value *in the account* is traceable by the plaintiff, for there is no existing right between the bank and customer, this does not mean that the tracing exercise must end when the rights between the bank and its customer 'run out'; if you stop there you have merely given up the tracing exercise prematurely; the tracing exercise has not come to a natural conclusion by itself. The overdraft was incurred by withdrawing funds, and the payment of the overdraft is therefore traceable into those funds, and into whatever those funds were spent upon. Of course, tracing into the proceeds of an overdraft may be evidentially difficult, and therefore may often be impossible in practice, but that is no reason to deny this form of backwards tracing in principle, especially in clear cases where it is apparent what was purchased on credit was subsequently paid off by trust funds. Consider the case of a trustee who uses trust money to pay off his credit card bill; all the card transactions are clearly recorded in his monthly statements and receipts, and it would seem preposterous for the court to refuse to trace into the television, antique table, and suit of clothes so manifestly acquired with the beneficiary's value.

12.54   The outlook for a general recognition of backward tracing in English law is not promising. It is clear that the Courts have implicitly allowed backward tracing: in *Agip* the Court allowed the plaintiff to treat a payment by Lloyds bank In London to the defendant as the transfer of his value even though the payment from the plaintiff to Lloyds correspondent bank in New York was made *later*. Thus Lloyds had made the payment to the defendant before, and in expectation of, receiving a corresponding amount from the plaintiff via a New York bank. (See also the tracing through credit facilities in *El Ajou v Dollar Land Holdings plc* (1993)). Furthermore, backward tracing necessarily underlies the ability of equity to trace through bank cheque clearing systems generally, since the settlement between banks is not simultaneous with the crediting and debiting of accounts. Nevertheless, the CA's recent consideration of backward tracing in *Bishopsgate Investment Management Ltd v Homan* (1994) is disappointing. At first instance Vinelott J was willing to allow backward tracing in limited circumstances, ie:

> ... where an asset acquired by [the defendant] with moneys borrowed from an overdrawn or loan account and there was an inference that when the borrowing was incurred it was the intention that it should be repaid

by misappropriation of [the plaintiff's] money. Another possibility was that moneys misappropriated from [the plaintiff] were paid into an overdrawn account of [the defendant] in order to reduce the overdraft and so make finance available within the overdraft limits for [the defendant] to purchase some particular asset.

Dillon LJ accepted this as correct, but Leggatt LJ found the contention utterly wrong on the basis that it was simply impossible for a claim to be made in respect of an asset acquired before the misappropriation took place. There is no majority decision on this point in the case, for the third judge, Henry LJ, simply agreed with both judgments, so it is not clear what the status of backward tracing of any kind in English law now is. (See also *Boscawen v Bajwa* (1995); **12.64**.)

12.55   As Smith (1995) points out, however, the basis for Vinelott's version of backward tracing is deficient in any event. As to the first case he mentions, it seems to violate the general principle of tracing to require that the defendant *intends* to use the misappropriated trust property to purchase the asset. All that is generally required is that he acquire the asset with the plaintiff's value – his intention is entirely irrelevant. As to the second case, this is in violation of the rules of tracing, for if the payment of the overdraft is traced, it should be traced into the value for which the debt *was incurred*, not for any new purchases enabled by the reduction of the overdraft. While those purchases might not have been possible 'but for' the payment in of the plaintiff's value, the new overdraft facility allows the defendant to use the *bank's value* to make more purchases, not the plaintiff's. The plaintiff's value can only be traced via the overdraft into what was purchased so as to give rise to the overdraft debt.

12.56   It remains only to mention in order to dismiss the 'swollen assets' theory of tracing. In *Space Investments Ltd v Canadian Imperial Bank of Commerce Trust Co (Bahamas) Ltd* ((1986), PC) Lord Wilberforce opined *obiter* that beneficiaries could trace trust money misappropriated by a bank into all the assets of the bank, without having to show in which assets of the bank the misappropriated value lay. This is called the 'swollen assets' theory because the beneficiary's ability to trace into all the assets is justified on the basis that the trust money 'swelled' the banks total assets, and that is all the plaintiff beneficiary need show to assert a right to all the bank's assets. The theory is inappropriate to tracing, for tracing is conceptually tied to following value through actual substitutions into specific items of property held by the defendant. Tracing is not needed to claim that the defendant was enriched, overall, by the receipt of the plaintiff's value, but nor can it be used to treat all the defendant's assets as one indistinguishable mixture of property, like one big bank account, for that is patently false. A defendant's wealth is made up of a number of properties, and the point of tracing it to show whether the plaintiff's value has gone into any of them, and if so, which ones. The swollen assets theory was rejected by the PC in *Re Goldcorp Exchange Ltd* (1994), and by the CA in *Homan*.

Proprietary claims to traceable proceeds – charges and equitable ownership

12.57 Once the process or exercise of tracing of tracing succeeds in locating the plaintiff's value, he may then make a claim in respect of that value. (See *Boscawen v Bajwa* (1995) per Millett LJ.) Note however, that the wrongdoing trustee may at any stage do his duty and reinstate or restore the trust. If he does so, he must do so properly. As Millett LJ points out parenthetically above (12.3), the trustee has no right to 'borrow' trust money for his own purposes and then just replace what he has borrowed. Thus if he uses £1,000 of trust money to buy shares now worth £2,000, he will only restore the trust if he then declares that he holds the shares on trust. If the shares fall in value to £500, he may only restore the trust by replacing the full £1,000 plus interest. If he uses £1,000 of trust value plus £1,000 of his own to buy shares for £2,000 now worth £5,000, he is likewise liable to hold half of the shares on trust. If the shares fall in value to £1,500, he must hold the shares as if charged by the trust to the value of £1,000 plus interest; only the remaining value counts as his own.

12.58 Where there have been no substitutions of trust property requiring tracing to locate the value taken from the trust, that is, where the beneficiary is able simply to follow the trust property into the hands of a third party (not a bona fide purchaser for value), the beneficiary simply demands the return of the property, and the court will order the third party to deliver it up or assign the legal title back to the trust. Here the beneficiary merely 'vindicates' his continuing equitable title in the trust property.

12.59 Where trust property is traced into proceeds, the beneficiary may elect either to claim ownership in the proceeds, or a charge on the proceeds for the value that went into their acquisition (see, eg *Re Hallett's* per Jessel MR). Where property is purchased by a trustee with a mixture of money from several trusts or innocents, each is entitled to a proportionate equitable co-ownership share in the property. Where a trustee has purchased property with a mixture of his own and trust money, the beneficiary is clearly entitled to a charge over the property, but there is some question whether the beneficiary may claim a proportionate equitable co-ownership interest in the proceeds – according to *Re Hallett's* he is restricted to a charge. It is however, generally accepted that the beneficiary should be entitled to such a share, and this was accepted *obiter* in *Re Tilley's Will Trusts* (1967). Normally, the beneficiary's election will turn on whether the value of the proceeds has increased. If £10,000 of trust value went unmixed with any other value into the purchase of shares now worth £20,000, the beneficiary will simply claim equitable ownership of the shares. If the shares have fallen in value to £5,000, then the beneficiary will claim a charge on the shares for the £10,000 plus interest – whatever is not recovered by realising the charge, ie selling the shares, the beneficiary will have to sue the trustee for personally. Assume that the £10,000 was half trust value, and half of the trustee's own money; in that case where the shares rise in value to £20,000, the beneficiary will, if he can, claim that he is a 50% co-owner of the shares, and if not, must settle for a charge for the payment of £5,000 plus interest. If they fall in value to £7,000, he will claim a charge over the shares, ie over all the shares, for the £5,000 value that went into them plus interest.

12.60   In *Foskett v McKeown* (1997), a trustee used trust funds to pay some of the premiums on a life insurance policy in favour of his wife and children. The beneficiaries claimed that they were entitled to a proportionate share of the proceeds of the policy which were paid when the trustee committed suicide. The CA held by a majority of 2:1 that the beneficiaries were entitled only to a charge on the proceeds to secure their restitutionary claim for the value of their money that went to pay the premiums. Scott VC and Hobhouse LJ held that the payment of the insurance policy premiums did not, in itself, generate any proprietary interest in the policy, and therefore since trust value can only be traced into property, the beneficiaries were not entitled to a proportionate share of the proceeds. Morritt LJ, dissenting, would have allowed the beneficiaries to trace into the policy proceeds in proportion to their contributions to the premium payments.

12.61   The claim of equitable (co-)ownership or a charge are not the only theoretical options. Hayton (1996), 839, fn 85) argues that where the trustee buys an asset with both trust money and some of his own, but the facts indicate that *but for the use of the trust money he would not have been able to acquire the asset at all*, then if the asset rises in value the beneficiary should be able to claim ownership of the whole asset subject to a charge in favour of the trustee for the value he put in. For example, if the trustee, because of his credit record is unable to borrow money to buy a house, puts in £40,000 of trust money with £10,000 of his own to buy a house now worth £100,000, why should the beneficiaries be restricted to a co-ownership share of four-fifths, ie £80,000? Should they not be able to claim the whole subject to a charge in favour of the trustee for the return of his £10,000 plus interest? This seems the approach consistent with the strict approach in *Boardman*, where the entire value of Boarman's shareholding went to the trust, minus his initial outlay for the shares. In Boardman's case he was allowed an additional sum, liberally calculated, for his investment skill, though that would seem inappropriate where a trustee misapplies trust funds.

12.62 Re *Tilley's Will Trusts* (1967) is an anomalous decision, in which a plaintiff was *restricted* to a claim for a charge over assets purchased with trust money which had risen in value. The widow of a testator was trustee of his testamentary trust, and thoroughly confused the trust moneys with her own funds. She made several profitable property investments, but Ungoed-Thomas J decided that because the trustee (1) did not deliberately use the trust moneys, and (2) she had ample overdraft facilities to make the property purchase she did, and so she did not *rely* on any of the trust value to fund her purchases, the beneficiaries were entitled at most to a charge over the acquired property. This decision might be justifiable in the case of an innocent volunteer recipient of trust funds who innocently mixed trust money with his own, and therefore, given his ample funds, could argue that the beneficiary should not benefit from his investment expertise he had exploited for his own benefit, but it seems wrong in principle to allow the same argument to be made by an 'innocent' *trustee*, since trustees are strictly liable for their misappropriations of trust property, and should be susceptible to all the normal equitable claims regardless of their intentions or innocence.

The multiplication of claims

12.63 It is perfectly possible for a beneficiary to be able to trace the trust value into a multiplying track of substitutions. Consider the case where the trustee sells a trust asset, say an antique clock, to X, who is not a bona fide purchaser for value, for £2,000. The beneficiary can trace into the proceeds of that exchange, the £2,000, but at the same time retains equitable title in the clock. If X sells the clock to Y for £3,000, and Y is also not a bona fide purchaser, then the beneficiary's array of claims expand again, since he can trace into the £2,000, the £3,000, and still retains title in the clock. This process can go on indefinitely in principle. In principle, the beneficiary should be able to make claims for an equitable charge or equitable (co-)ownership against the trustee, X, or Y, for title to the original trust property or to the immediate or subsequent traceable proceeds, limited only by the principle of double (or multiple) recovery, ie as soon as the beneficiary has recovered property or money to account for all the trust value misapplied, he should be barred from bringing any further claims.

Subrogation claims reliant upon tracing

12.64 Subrogation is the acquisition of another person's rights against a third party upon the making of a payment: very roughly, by making a payment the plaintiff 'purchases' those rights. The classic example occurs in the insurance context – if I am insured against injuries caused by the negligent acts of a third party, my insurance company, upon paying me an insurance award compensating me for my loss, is entitled to sue the tortfeasor, ie the negligent injurer, in my name for damages. Thus acquiring my right to sue, the insurance company is said to be 'subrogated' to my claim against the tortfeasor. A different sort of subrogation is relevant here. In certain circumstances, if X pays off Y's debt to Z, X will be subrogated to Z's right as a creditor. In other words, by paying off Z, X will in effect 'purchase' Z's right to the payment of the debt against Y. Thus, if trust money or its traceable proceeds is used to pay off Y's debts, in certain cases the beneficiary may claim to be subrogated to the original debt claims. This is what occurred in *Boscawen v Bajwa* (1995). Bajwa intended to sell his mortgaged land for a price roughly equal to what he owed under the mortgage to the Halifax Building Society; on the sale Bajwa would be required to use the purchase money to pay off the mortgage, which would leave him with little if any proceeds for himself. The purchasers raised £140,000 on a mortgage loan from Abbey National, and the money was transferred to solicitors in advance of the completion of the sale. In breach of trust the money was advanced

330

before completion and was applied to pay off the mortgage loan to Halifax. The sale never occurred, and as a result Bajwa ended up with an unmortgaged property, while Abbey National had advanced funds and received no mortgage on the property in return. The CA held that Abbey National was entitled to be subrogated to Halifax's mortgage on the land, thus entitling them to priority over a charge on the land which had been subsequently granted by the court to judgment creditors of Bajwa. The court clearly distinguished between the process of tracing, which allowed Abbey National to show that its value was received by Bajwa, and the claim to be subrogated. Millett LJ said:

> If the plaintiff succeeds in tracing his property, whether in its original or in some changed form, into the hands of the defendant and overcomes any defences which are put forward on the defendant's behalf, he is entitled to a remedy. The remedy will be fashioned to the circumstances … If the plaintiff's money has been applied by the defendant, for example, not in the acquisition of a landed property but in its improvement, then the court may treat the land as charged with the payment to the plaintiff of a sum representing the amount by which the value of the defendant's land has been enhanced by the use of the plaintiff's money. And if the plaintiff's money has been used to discharge a mortgage on the defendant's land, then the court may achieve a similar result by treating the land as subject to a charge by way of subrogation in favour of the plaintiff … Tracing was the process by which the Abbey National sought to establish that its money was applied in the discharge of the Halifax's charge; subrogation was the remedy which it sought in order to deprive Mr Bajwa … of the unjust enrichment which he would otherwise obtain at the Abbey National's expense.

12.65   Note that subrogation, while achieving a similar result in the case of a secured loan, is the opposite of backwards tracing. In backwards tracing, one traces into items purchase with the borrowed funds. In contrast, a subrogation claim allows the plaintiff to stand in the shoes of the lender; in the case of an unsecured debt, for example a credit card debt the plaintiff will acquire by subrogation nothing more than a *personal* claim for money against the defendant, for that is all the credit card company had. In the case of a mortgage, however, subrogation provides a result similar to backwards tracing. A backwards tracing claim would allow the plaintiff to trace his value into the property purchased with the credit given, and in the case of a mortgage of land, that will be the land itself, of course. The plaintiff will then claim either a proportionate share of the value of the land or a charge on it for his traceable value which went into it. By subrogation, the plaintiff will necessarily acquire a proprietary right in the land too, since the loan was a secured one, and the charge forms part of the right to which he is subrogated. But the plaintiff cannot acquire by subrogation an ownership or co-ownership share.

12.66   Note also that in this passage Millet LJ considers that a beneficiary is entitled to a charge over land which has been improved with traceable value. In *Re Diplock* (1948) such a charge was denied beneficiaries under a will where the innocent recipient was a charity who was mistakenly paid by the executor, on the ground that a charge, being enforceable by sale, might require the charity to sell the property, and therefore the consequences of imposing a charge would do more than merely restore the plaintiff's value, but cause the charity a significant actual loss.

Personal claims for the receipt of trust property or its traceable proceeds

12.67   A recipient of trust property or its traceable proceeds may also be personally liable to repay money equal to the value he has received. That is, he will be liable to pay the value of the trust property he received irrespective of whether he *retains* any traceable value of the plaintiff beneficiary, in respect of which the beneficiary may make a proprietary claim of some kind. All the beneficiary has to show by the tracing exercise in such a case is that the defendant *received* value originating in the trust. Traditionally this personal liability was called liability for 'knowing receipt', and as this term suggests, such recipient was only personally liable if he had some degree of knowledge, eg actual or constructive knowledge, of the plaintiff's right to the property received. The law governing the standard of knowledge required to fix a recipient of trust property with personal liability for its value is extraordinarily confused, for two related reasons. The first is simply that this personal liability can be justified in three completely different ways, which indicate different standards of knowledge.

Personal recipient liability as 'knowing receipt'

12.68   The first, traditional, way is framed by saying that someone liable for knowing receipt is 'liable to account as a constructive trustee'. In other words, the reason the recipient is liable is that, by his conduct, he should be in the same position as a trustee who has acted in breach of trust and misapplied trust property – he will not only be subject to the beneficiary's proprietary claims to the trust property itself or its traceable proceeds, but like a true express trustee who has breached the trust he will be personally liable to restore the value of the trust with his own money. In short, recipient liability *qua* '*knowing* receipt' is a *fault*-based liability, a version of 'knowing assistance' or accessory liability – the only difference between the two is that, since the recipient received trust property and was actually enriched, the standard of knowledge will apply differently, since one may have different means of discovering that one is assisting a breach of trust if one is actually in receipt of trust property by the breach from a person who is not. Many of the older cases seem to treat knowing assistance and knowing receipt as very similar, and discuss the standard of knowledge required for liability for one as applicable to, or at least closely related to, the other. This makes perfect sense if the recipient is being made liable to account in respect of the breach which results in his receipt of trust property as if he were the defaulting trustee himself.

Personal recipient liability as equitable 'conversion'

12.69   The other two bases for a personal claim against the recipient of trust property are directly analogous to two common law claims. The first is liability for conversion which, since the Torts (Interference with Goods) Act 1977, may more properly be called 'interference with goods'. A defendant is strictly liable for his possession of the plaintiff's chattel, ie his interference with the plaintiff's proprietary rights, even if he no longer retains the chattel. If A's toaster is stolen by B who sells it to C, then C, even if he buys from B in complete good faith, ignorant of B's theft, is strictly liable for the value of the toaster to A, even if he has sold it on to D. C is left to recoup his loss by in turn bringing an action against B. C's knowledge as to A's title is irrelevant. Liability for conversion protects the legal owner's proprietary rights in chattels, but notice the difference between this action and the beneficiary's proprietary equitable right to claim his equitable title to trust property in the hands of a third party, or (co-)ownership of or a charge on its traceable proceeds – the liability for conversion, because framed in terms of the wrong of interference, covers past interferences as well as currently ongoing ones, so C who has sold the toaster is still liable. The beneficiary, on the other hand, can only 'vindicate' his title in trust property or

333

proceeds against a recipient who retains the property in his hands. If personal recipient liability in equity is applied in analogy with conversion, the recipient of trust property should be strictly personally liable, regardless of his knowledge, even though he no longer retains the trust property or its traceable proceeds, just as the common law convertor is. Note, however, that because of the bona fide purchaser rule, the equitable 'converter', if he purchases the trust property for value without notice of the breach of trust, will take the property free of any of the beneficiary's claims. However, because liability is otherwise strict, *all volunteers* will be liable, whether innocent or not.

Personal recipient liability as restitution

12.70 The third option is to say the reason the recipient is liable is simply that he has received value to which he is not entitled, so he must give it back. Otherwise he would be unjustly enriched. This claim then, is not *compensatory*, but *restitutionary*. The analogy here is with common law restitutionary actions, such as the action traditionally called the action 'for money had and received': Where A mistakenly pays B £50, then B is strictly liable to repay this unjust enrichment of £50 to A. As with the standard of knowledge applicable to conversion, B's knowledge about A's mistake is irrelevant, although in practice of course B will usually only realise his liability to repay A when he learns of A's mistake. Unlike the case of conversion, in the case of a common law restitutionary claim, however, B is entitled to claim the defence of change of position in certain circumstances.

The defence of change of position

12.71 This defence was firmly established as part of English law only recently, in the HL decision in *Lipkin Gorman v Karpnale Ltd* (1991). A solicitor of the firm of Lipkin Gorman, Cass, used his signing authority to withdraw funds from the firm's client account which he then lost gambling. The firm sued Karpnale Ltd, which owned the Playboy Club in Mayfair where Cass gambled away the money. The money was clearly trust money, and Cass clearly stood in a fiduciary position with respect to the use of the money, if not as a trustee himself, so there was no question that had the case been argued on equitable principles, the trust money might have been traced, if the transactional links could be shown, into the hands of the Club. The case, however was argued only on common law principles of restitution. The HL decided that despite the fact that Cass became the legal owner of the money he withdrew from the client account, the firm retained a sufficient legal interest in the money (about which more below, **12.86**) to claim that the Club received the firm's value at common law. Since the firm clearly did not intend the money to go to the Club, indeed the firm was ignorant of the tranfer of the money, the Club would be unjustly enriched unless it was a bona fide purchaser of it. Because, however, the Club acquired title to the money by wagering contracts, and since such contracts are void, the Club did not in the eyes of the law give valuable consideration for the money, and therefore was held liable to a restitutionary claim. Because, however, the Club had paid Cass some winnings, the Club was able to reduce its liability on the basis that it had innocently 'changed its position' in response to its receipt of the money. Lord Goff said:

> Where an innocent defendant's position is so changed that he will suffer an injustice if called upon to repay or to repay in full, the injustice of requiring him so to repay outweighs the injustice of denying the plaintiff restitution. If the plaintiff pays money to the defendant under a mistake of fact, and the defendant then, acting in good faith, pays the money or part of it to charity, it is unjust to require the defendant to make restitution to the extent that he has so changed his position ... I am most anxious that, in recognising this defence to actions of restitution, nothing should be said at this stage to inhibit the development of the defence on a case by case basis, in the usual way.

12.72 At this point there is little guidance in the case law, but the following points about the nature and scope of the defence may be made. First, the defence can be either 'enrichment-based' or 'injustice-based' or both. With respect to the former, the defence may be available to those who are, at the time of trial, no longer truly 'enriched' by the receipt of the plaintiff's value. The clearest example of this is the case of one who receives the property of another which is then immediately stolen through no fault of his. The more typical but problematic case is that of the individual, who on receipt of the plaintiff's value and believing it to be his, spends an equivalent sum on an expenditure which he would not, but for the receipt, have made. For example, innocently believing that he has correctly received royalties of £2,000 for a book, he takes an expensive vacation he would not otherwise have done. Here the claim is that he is not really enriched *to the extent of* £2,000, because at his proper level of wealth, he would not have thought the vacation worth that much. It is only as a richer person, for whom each pound means

335

less (what economists call the declining marginal utility of money) that he would have regarded the vacation as worth £2,000 *to him*. Both cases may also serve as examples of 'injustice-based' claims to the defence – the two are not unconnected. With respect to the theft, if the money was paid to the defendant by the plaintiff's mistake, it might be argued that he should bear some or all of the risk of its theft, so that it would be unjust to demand the repayment of all of the money. In the second situation, in order to repay the money the defendant might be forced to sell property or take out a loan, and again, if the payment was the plaintiff's mistake, he may be regarded as in part responsible for the frivolous expenditure, for he created the appearance of greater wealth upon which the defendant relied. (See also *Re Diplock*, **12.79.**) In respect of the defendant's reliance upon the receipt of the plaintiff's value, in *South Tyneside Metropolitan Borough Council v Svenska International* (1995), the court held that the defence was available only to one who relied upon an actual receipt of wealth, and not on facts giving one grounds to expect a receipt of wealth which actually materialised. Martin's ((1997), 681) response to this seems correct:

> Thus an employee who spent money on a holiday in reliance on the promise of a forthcoming bonus would have no defence ... whereas an employee who spent a bonus [he received] on a holiday would have. To deny pre-enrichment reliance...places an unwarranted restriction on the flexibility of the defence.

The defence is obviously available only to innocent recipients. A wrongdoer, or one who knows that he has received the value of someone else, is under a duty to make restitution immediately – any change of position he undergoes will be taken for his own benefit, so could hardly go to diminishing his enrichment (on the enrichment-based version of the defence), or will be taken in conscience violation of the plaintiff's right, so it would not be unjust for him to make full restitution (on the 'injustice-based version) (see Nolan (1995)).

Ministerial receipt

12.73 One example Lord Goff gave of the previous partial recognition of the change of position defence in English law was the defence of ministerial receipt: where the plaintiff seeks to hold an agent personally liable for receiving trust property or its traceable proceeds, the agent will not be liable if the property came to him in his capacity as agent to the trustee or fiduciary, and he has accounted to his principal for the money before receiving notice of the plaintiff's claim (see further Swadling (1995)). The defence was successfully employed in *Agip;* even though the defendant's agents were held to be liable as accessories to the breach of trust, they did not have actual notice of the plaintiff's claim or the fraud against him before they passed on the payment they received to their principal.

12.74 There are indications that the courts are now in the process of re-formulating liability for the receipt of trust property as liability for unjust enrichment leading to a claim for restitution. In *Royal Brunei Airlines*, for instance, Lord Nicholls sharply distinguished accessory liability and recipient liability:

> Different considerations apply to the two heads of liability. Recipient liability is restitution-based, accessory liability is not.

In *El Ajou v Dollar Land Holdings plc* (1992) Millett LJ said:

> [Knowing receipt] is the counterpart in equity of the common law action for money had and received. Both can be classified as receipt-based restitutionary claims.

In *Lipkin Gorman* Lord Goff said the following:

> [T]he recognition of the [change of position] defence should be doubly beneficial. It will enable a more generous approach to be taken to the recognition of the right to restitution, in the knowledge that the defence is, in appropriate cases, available; and, while recognising the different functions of property at law and in equity, there may also in due course develop a more consistent approach to tracing claims, in which common defences are recognised as available to such claims, whether advanced at law or in equity.

In respect of the final sentiment, Millet LJ in *Boscawen*, dealing with the claims of an owner in equity for recipient liability against a defendant into whose hands he has traced his value, made it clear that the change of position defence should apply. Moreover, he said:

> The introduction of the defence not only provides the court with a means of doing justice in future, but allows a re- examination of many decisions

337

which the absence of the defence may have led judges to distort basic principles in order to avoid justice to the defendant.

12.75 On the other hand, in *Westdeutsche Landesbank v Islington London Borough Council* (1996) Lord Browne-Wilkinson quite clearly affirmed, *obiter*, the traditional formulation:

> Even if the third party [recipient of trust property], X, is not aware that what he has received is trust property B [the beneficiary] is entitled to assert his title in that property. If X has the necessary degree of knowledge, X may himself become a constructive trustee for B on the basis of knowing receipt. But unless he has the requisite degree of knowledge he is not personally liable to account as trustee.

However, taken in its context, the statement may be taken to be directed only to the question whether the third party recipient should, without knowledge, be regarded as having a *trustee*'s duties and liabilities such as the liability to account (the answer being 'no'), leaving entirely open whether the third party recipient might have personal liabilities arising on a different basis, ie on the basis of his unjust enrichment or his interference with the beneficiary's proprietary rights.

The current standard of knowledge

12.76 Until there is a definitive statement by the HL on the nature of recipient liability, one must assume that recipient liability is still 'knowing receipt' to the extent that the defendant must have knowledge to some degree to be liable. In *Baden v Société Générale* (1982) Peter Gibson J distinguished five categories of knowledge:

> ... (i) actual knowledge; (ii) wilfully shutting one's eyes to the obvious; (iii) wilfully and recklessly failing to make such inquiries as an honest and reasonable man would make;(iv) knowledge of circumstances which would indicate the facts to an honest and reasonable man; (v) knowledge of circumstances which would put an honest and reasonable man on inquiry.

Knowledge in all of these categories is sufficient to fix the defendant with 'notice', the standard of cognisance which applies in determining whether a person has 'notice' of a breach of trust or the beneficiary's rights. Category (i), actual knowledge, equates with 'actual notice', but categories (ii) to (v) cover only what might be called 'constructive knowledge', and constructive notice is broader. Constructive notice essentially sets a standard of due diligance, attributing to a person all that he would have discovered by making the proper inquiries. Categories (i) to (iii) might be regarded as 'dishonest' knowledge, ie if a defendant acts in violation of the plaintiff's rights with one of these levels of knowledge he can justly be regarded as acting dishonestly. Knowledge to the level of categories (iv) and (v) does not necessarily import dishonesty, for the defendant may fail to draw the right inferences or inquire appropriately because he was foolish or otherwise unreasonable, but not actually dishonest (See *Agip* per Millett LJ, above **12.36**).

12.77 The authorities do not indicate a uniform standard of cognisance that will fix a recipient of trust property or its proceeds with personal liability. In *Re Montagu's Settlement Trusts* (1987) Megarry VC was unwilling to fix a volunteer recipient of chattels in breach of a family trust, who later sold them, with personal liability to repay their value. He held that even if the recipient had once known that the chattels were property of the trust, he would not be personally liable where he had honestly forgotten that they were. Megarry clearly distinguished between notice, which the defendant had, and knowledge, which he did not; only the latter was sufficient for acquiring personal liability for receipt of trust property. Megarry clearly regarded personal liability for receipt as liability to account 'as a constructive trustee', ie on the traditional formulation, not on the conversion or restitution view. In contrast, Millett LJ in *Agip* and *El Ajou v Dollar Land Holdings plc* (1992) appeared to hold that constructive notice is sufficient. Comparing his view with that of Vinelott J's in *Eagle Trust plc v SBC Securities Ltd* (1992) he said:

> Vinelott J based liability firmly on inferred knowledge and not on constructive notice. For my own part, I agree that even where the plaintiff's claim is a proprietary one, and the defendant raises the defence of bona fide purchaser for value without notice, there is no room for the doctrine of constructive notice in the strict conveyancing sense in a factual situation where it is not the custom and practice to make inquiry. But it does not follow that there is no room for an analogous doctrine in a situation in which any honest and reasonable man would have made inquiry ... I am content to assume, without deciding, that dishonesty or want of probity involving actual knowledge (whether proved or inferred) is not a precondition of liability; but that a recipient is not expected to be unduly suspicious and is not to be held liable unless he went ahead without further inquiry in circumstances in which an honest and reasonable man would

have realised that the money was probably trust money and was being misapplied ... Moreover, I do not see how it would be possible to develop any logical and coherent system of restitution if there were different requirements in respect of knowledge for the common law claim for money had and received, the personal claim for an account in equity against a knowing recipient and the equitable proprietary claim. In the present case, for example, it would be illogical and undesirable to require the plaintiff to assert a proprietary claim he does not need in order to avoid the burden of having to prove dishonesty or ask the court to infer it.

So while Millett LJ reaffirms that constructive notice is sufficient, and explicitly does so on the basis that the standard of knowledge for personal and proprietary recipient liability should be the same, he accepts that the 'notice' must be adapted to the particular circumstances of dealing; notice, as it applies to land transfers because of the standard practices of inquiry, should not apply to transactions for which there is no such practice. As regards the standard of knowledge for a *volunteer* recipient, though Millett LJ cited the view of Megarry VC in *Re Montagu's* he regarded this issue as controversial, implicitly doubting whether Megarry VC got it right. Nevertheless, in *Westdeutsche Landesbank*, Lord Browne-Wilkinson specifically cited *Re Montagu's* in support of the passage quoted above at **12.74**.

12.78 In summary, then, it is probably fair to say that as things stand at the moment, a recipient who has given value for trust property will fail to be a bona fide purchaser if he has notice of the breach of trust, but the standard of notice will vary according to the normal practice of inquiry which attends the specific kind of transaction in issue, i.e whether he purchases land, securities, chattels, and so on. Where he is fixed with notice, so that the beneficiary can claim equitable title to the trust property or make some other proprietary claim to the proceeds if the recipient still retains them, it is not clear if the recipient is thereby also immediately personally liable because of his notice. Millett LJ would say 'yes' while others such as Vinelott J would require at least 'constructive *knowledge*'; though a proponent of strict liability under the restitutionary approach, Hayton ((1996a), 869-870) regards the current standard as one of dishonest knowledge, since this appears on *Re Montagu's* to be the correct standard on the traditional view that the recipient is liable to account as if he were a trustee in breach. As regards volunteers, Lord Browne-Wilkinson's approval of *Re Montagu's* in *Westdeutsche Landesbank* may indicate that Megarry VC's view will prevail. If so, then Hayton's view as to recipient liability for non-volunteers, ie that dishonesty is required, is strengthened, since if the traditional formulation is maintained, then there is no logical basis for different standards for purchasers or volunteers, any more than there should be a different standard of dishonesty for accessories to a breach who profit from it and those who don't. That is irrelevant to the accessory's or recipient's *fault*, which on this formulation is the basis of his liability.

12.79 Clearly, this area of law needs sorting out by the HL. As we have seen, Millett LJ believes that personal liability for the receipt of trust property should be regarded as the equitable equivalent of the restitutionary personal claim at common law for money had and received. This would entail that any recipient of trust property not a bona fide purchaser would be strictly liable to a personal claim by the beneficiary for the value of trust property or traceable proceeds received, though subject to the change of position defence. Some support in authority for this position is provided by *Re Diplock* (1948, CA; affirmed by the HL sub nom *Ministry of Health v Simpson* (1950)). In that case the executors of a will distributed a large sum of money to various charities. It was discovered that the charitable gift was void for uncertainty, and so the money ought to have gone to the next of kin. The CA, exercising its *equity* jurisdiction, found the charities strictly liable to the personal claims of the next of kin for the value they received, subject, however, to the next of kin first exhausting their personal claim against the executors for misapplying the funds. However, while the similarities between the circumstance of a legatee whose personal representative had paid the money to the wrong person and the beneficiary whose trustee misapplies trust property to the wrong person are patent, it seems that the *Re Diplock* claim is quite an anomalous remedy, 'mired in its own rather complex history' (Harpum, 1994) involving equity's assumption of the ecclesiastical court's jurisdiction over wills. The case certainly reveals that equity is not constitutively averse to awarding a personal restitutionary liability, but it is probably not a basis upon which a general and comprehensive restitutionary remedial framework encompassing both common law and equity can be built.

Recipient liability in equity – restitution or conversion?

12.80 Unfortunately, treating personal liability for the receipt of trust property or its proceeds as restitutionary liability is too simple. The simplest case of 'knowing receipt' is the case of the third party who receives trust property. According to the standard view, the plaintiff beneficiary retains his equitable title to the trust property, and so he just 'vindicates' his equitable title if the third party retains it. If the third party no longer retains it, then any strict personal liability which equity imposes upon him is analogous to the common law liability for conversion. That is, when the beneficiary claims that the third party (not being a bona fide purchaser) is personally liable for receipt of trust property, he claims that the third party interfered with his beneficial title – no beneficial title passed to the third party, so in equity's eyes he cannot have been *enriched* by the receipt; in order to be enriched in the eyes of the law or equity one must acquire title to the property. If one does not, one merely interferes with another's title, and it is that *wrong*, not any enrichment, for which one owes compensation. One is liable to *compensate*, not to *make restitution* – one has received no enrichment to make restitution of.

12.81 If that is the situation with respect to recipients of the original trust property, what do we say about recipients of its traceable proceeds? Here it is simply much harder to say that the beneficiary has an equitable title in the proceeds simply because he was the beneficiary under a trust of the original property, at least in the case of proceeds in the hands of strangers to the trust. In the case of the trustee himself it may be possible to maintain this. The express trustee is not, strictly speaking, a trustee only of the actual existing property in the trust at any one time. He is trustee of the trust property *as a fund*. Thus when he receives dividends or rents on the trust property, or sells trust investments and receives the proceeds of sale, those receipts are automatically captured by the trust. He does not have to declare a new trust over the received property each time, for the trust obligation covers the trust fund, thus all the individual items in it from time to time. Indeed, it may follow from *Reid* and *Boardman* (**11.43** et seq) that the trust has sufficient scope to capture automatically any secret profits earned by the trustee. If this is so, then even where the trustee in breach of trust uses trust property for his own purposes, any proceeds he acquires may rightly be regarded as automatically captured by the trust as well.

12.82 Now consider the third party recipient. Whatever he receives from the original trustee, whether original trust property or any proceeds acquired by the trustee in breach, is, according to what was just said, trust property, for it comes from the trustee himself and all proceeds in his hands are captured by the express trust. Now assume the third party himself acquires proceeds from what he has received – this will be the case whenever he receives money or a cheque from the trustee which he then banks in his account, the proceeds being, of course, his larger bank balance. We cannot say that these proceeds automatically become trust property, for the third party is not a trustee (in particular if he is innocent of the breach), and so his dealings with trust property or proceeds are not automatically captured by the express trust so as to give automatically an equitable title in them to the beneficiary. Any further traceable proceeds, whether in the hands of the third party, or if they can be so traced, in the hands of a fourth or fifth or sixth party, will similarly not be proceeds which are automatically captured by the express trust. In these cases, the beneficiary, even though he has the right to a proprietary claim, either a claim to equitable (co-)ownership of the property or to a charge, is not simply 'vindicating' a continuing equitable title that has bounced from the original trust property to the traceable proceeds one substitution after another. He is tracing his value to be sure, but at this stage his claim must be restitutionary. Equity, given its traditional proprietary means of dealing with value, will impose a constructive trust giving equitable (co-)ownership or will impose a charge on the proceeds in the beneficiary's favour, to reverse the recipient's unjust enrichment at the beneficiary's expense.

12.83 If this is correct, we can see the difficulty of applying the restitutionary analysis in any simple fashion to the question of recipient liability. To the extent that the beneficiary is claiming that the third party has received trust property in which he has a continuing equitable title, then his claim against that third party is equivalent to a claim in equity for conversion. Liability for conversion is strict, and in particular, *there is no change of position defence*. It is simply not true, then, that a new restitutionary analysis, with its change of position defence, will properly apply to every defendant. Consider the defendant in *Re Montagu's*; he received actual trust chattels. On analogy with the common law claim for conversion, he would be strictly personally liable for their value. But the defendant sold the chattels, and on the preceding analysis it then became the case that he did acquire title in his own right to the proceeds, and therefore was enriched; he was enriched at the beneficiary's expense because the beneficiary could easily trace into those proceeds. So the beneficiary *also* had a restitutionary claim against the defendant. Therefore, in analogy with the common law, the defendant was liable both for conversion of the original trust property and for restitution for receipt of the proceeds of sale. In this circumstance, why would a

343

plaintiff pursue the analogy with the restitutionary claim, with its change of position defence, when in analogy with conversion the defendant is strictly liable with no such defence?

12.84 It is clear that the present claim in equity for 'knowing receipt' does not operate in close analogy to conversion and restitution, in so far as it makes no distinction between claims based on interference with continuing equitable title and claims based on the receipt of traceable proceeds. As long as the defendant has 'knowledge' to the relevant standard, he is personally liable both for the receipt of original trust property and proceeds alike. While the claim for 'knowing receipt' may need to be reformed, the preceding discussion indicates the significant conceptual difficulties of applying a restitutionary analysis to the range of cases the present equitable claim covers. If we are in favour of strict personal liability for receipt of trust property or its traceable proceeds, but are also in favour of the change of position defence in all such cases, and if equity reforms itself on those lines, then equity would adopt a change of position defence in respect of both claims for compensation for conversion and restitutionary claims for unjust enrichment. That might be a good thing. Some find the strict common law liability of convertors unjust. In the spirit of fusion, however, and more importantly for the bedrock principle of justice that like cases should be treated alike, it does not do to allow the innocent volunteer recipient of a stolen television to be made strictly liable for conversion, while giving the innocent volunteer recipient of a television misappropriated by a trustee a change of position defence. If we treat the equitable title of the beneficiary seriously, it is important to realise that the move to treat all recipient liability in equity as restitutionary leads to this significantly different treatment purely on the basis of whether the title was legal or equitable. As it currently stands, the action for 'knowing receipt' leads to an equally unjust difference in results: the common law recipient of stolen chattels is strictly liable, whereas the recipient of trust property or its traceable proceeds is only liable if he is shown to have the requisite degree of knowledge of the trust.

Tracing at common law and the quest for a fiduciary relationship

12.85 For various complicated historical reasons, until recently it has been assumed that a plaintiff will have a much more difficult time establishing a claim to the proceeds acquired by a defendant who wrongly exchanges the plaintiff's property, where the plaintiff has *legal* beneficial title to it, ie where he just owns the property at law rather than having equitable title under a trust. The supposed reason is that the common law rules of tracing were much less sophisticated than those of equity. In particular, the legal owner of property had a much harder time claiming any rights in traceable proceeds once his value had been added to a bank account, because, it was believed, the common law could not trace through mixtures of value. The idea that the common law was mentally deficient in this respect is clearly belied by fact that the common law developed principles to deal with the mixing of goods, as where a quantity of one individual's oil was mixed with that of another (**12.48**), or the rule in *Clayton's Case*, whereby a bank balance is treated as a series of individual debts. The resistance of the common law to a plaintiff's claim to proceeds is better explained not as an inability to trace, but a resistance to the making of legal proprietary claims to proceeds (See Smith (1997), 321-339). The common law authority for the 'exchange-product' theory, ie that a legal owner may claim legal title to the proceeds acquired in exchange for his property, is frail. The foundational cases in favour of the theory are *Taylor v Plumer* (1815) and *Banque Belge v Hambrouck* (1921), but it is now generally accepted that the former case was decided on *equitable*, not common law, principles, (See Smith (1995)), and the latter case is unsatisfactory, first, because two judges in the CA based their decision on *Taylor,* and the other on equitable principles, and secondly, because the case is better explained in terms of a power *in rem* (Khurshid and Matthews (1979)), i.e a power of the plaintiff to acquire title in the proceeds, not on the basis that he automatically acquires title to the proceeds on exchange.

12.86   In *Lipkin Gorman* Lord Goff said the following:

> It is well-established that a legal owner is entitled to trace his property into its product, provided that the latter is indeed identifiable as the product of his property. Thus in *Taylor v Plumer* ... , where Sir Thomas Plumer gave a draft to a stockbroker for the purpose of buying exchequer bills, and the stockbroker instead used the draft for buying American securities and doubloons for his own purposes, Sir Thomas was able to trace his property into the securities and doubloons in the hands of the stockbroker, and so defeat a claim made to them by the stockbroker's assignees in bankruptcy. Of course, 'tracing' or 'following' property into its product *involves a decision by the owner of the original property to assert*

his title to the product in place of his original property. This is sometimes referred to as a ratification. I myself would not so describe it; but it has, in my opinion, at least one feature in common with ratification, that it cannot be relied upon so as to render an innocent recipient a wrongdoer. (My italics)

There are two things to note about this description of common law claims to traceable products. It is not an endorsement of the 'exchange-product theory', since it depends upon the owner's assertion of his title to the proceeds. On the exchange-product theory the owner acquires title to the product automatically upon the exchange. Second, the legal interest in the proceeds cannot 'be relied upon to render an innocent recipient a wrongdoer'. This means that the Playboy Club, which received the money innocently, was not deprived of the change of position defence. It also means that a third party who innocently received the proceeds could not be liable for conversion of the proceeds, for that is a wrong. Thus the legal interest in the product the legal owner gets is a distinctly peculiar one (see also Birks (1991); Smith (1997), 325-339)). Unfortunately for our understanding of the law, the Club conceded (somewhat inexplicably) that if it was shown that the firm had a legal interest in the money in Cass's hands, his mixing of the firm's money with his own would not prevent the firm's tracing the money into that received by the Club, so the HL did not have to deal with the possibility that the identity of the firm's value might have been untraceable given the way in which Cass had mixed it with his own since, as mentioned, it is commonly held that with regard to mixtures of value in bank accounts, at least, the common law would not trace through mixtures of value.

12.87 Because of the supposedly superior tracing process recognised in equity, and because equitable remedial rights in the form of an equitable charge or an equitable co-ownership claim are available to the plaintiff who can establish an equitable claim to traceable proceeds, the law of England has been coloured by plaintiffs arguing that the original misapplication of their property involved a breach of fiduciary duty. Like trustees, fiduciaries such as agents or company directors who misapply their principals' property are liable to account for the misapplication, and principals may trace the value of the property transferred using equitable tracing rules and avail themselves of equitable claims to the proceeds. These proprietary claims are, of course, most valuable in the case where the defendant is insolvent. The high watermark of this development occurred in *Chase Manhattan Bank v Israel British Bank* (1979), where Goulding J held that where a plaintiff paid money under a mistake, not only did he have the normal common law resitutionary personal claim against the recipient, but that immediately upon receiving the money the recipient had a *fiduciary* obligation to return that very money; therefore the recipient held it on trust for the payor. Accordingly the payor could claim any traceable proceeds acquired with the money as his in equity, thus withdrawing the proceeds from the pool of assets on the recipient's insolvency. In *Westdeutsche Landesbank v Islington London Borough Council* (1996) the HL held this reasoning to be wrong. (As we have seen, the HL also rejected the Birks/Chambers theory of the resulting trust which would have justified the decision (**4.26**).) However, Lord Browne-Wilkinson did state, *obiter*, that the result in *Chase Manhattan* could be justified on the basis that when the recipient bank learned of the mistaken payment, its conscience was affected, at which point equity would impose a *constructive* trust over the money received. This justification seems quite wrong, and as a mere *obiter dictum* should not be followed; the constructive trust seems to be raised on nothing more than the recipient's awareness that he owes the plaintiff a certain sum, ie that he must repay an equivalent amount to that which he received. This is just a normal everyday recognition of a legal liability to pay a debt, no different in principle than a recognition of any other kind of debt, such as a debt to pay one's credit card bill. The mere realisation that one is indebted does not turn one into a trustee, or a fiduciary, or a wrongdoer in equity, and therefore there is no basis for the imposition of a constructive trust here. The better view is simply that *Chase Manhattan* was wrongly decided. Lord Browne-Wilkinson further opined that money that is stolen is traceable in equity, because the thief will immediately hold the money under a constructive trust.

Further Reading

Birks (1991, 1992, 1995, 1996a); Harpum (1994); Millett (1998); Smith (1994, 1997); Swadling (1994, 1997).

Must read cases: *Re Pauling's Settlement Trusts* (1963); *Armitage v Nurse* (1997); *Target Holdings v Redferns* (1995); *Swindle v Harrison* (1997); *Bristol & West Building Society v Mothew* (1996); *Royal Brunei Airlines v Tan* (1995); *Agip (Africa) Ltd v Jackson* (1989); *Lipkin Gorman v Karpnale Ltd* (1991); *Re Hallett's Estate* (1880); *Re Oatway* (1903); *Barlow Clowes International v Vaughan* (1992); *Boscawen v Bajwa* (1995); *Westdeutsche Landesbank v Islington London Borough Council* (1996); *Re Montagu's Settlement Trusts* (1987).

Self-test questions

1. What is 'equitable compensation', and how is it measured in respect of different kinds of breach of trust?

2. '[I]t must be acknowledged that the view is widely held that these clauses have gone too far, and that trustees who charge for their services and who, as professional men, would not dream of excluding liability for ordinary professional negligence, should not be able to rely on a trustee exemption clause excluding liability for gross negligence.' (Millet LJ in *Armitage v Nurse* (1997)) Discuss.

3. Tom is the trustee of the Higgins family trust. He misappropriates £30,000 which he pays into his bank account raising the balance to £40,000. He makes the following payments from his account. He buys shares for £5,000, which are now worth £10,000. He uses £20,000 to pay off the mortgage on his flat. He then adds £10,000 of his own to the account, raising the balance to £25,000. He gives £10,000 to his son, Ted, who is ignorant of the source of the money. Ted uses it to buy ten cases of vintage wine; he drinks up five of the cases, and lays down the rest. Tom dissipates the remaining funds in the account.

With the knowledge of Harry Higgins, one of the beneficiaries, Tom misappropriates another £10,000 which they together spend on a world cruise.

Finally, Tom steals a painting from the Higgins house, which he sells for £2,000. He uses the money to buy a car, which he retains.

Discuss the liability of Tom, Harry, and Ted.

4. Discuss whether the current law governing the situation in question 3 is justified, or is in need of reform.

CHAPTER THIRTEEN

Charitable Trusts

SUMMARY

The character of trust purposes

Trusts for the relief of poverty

Trusts for the advancement of education

Trusts for the advancement of religion

Trusts for other purposes beneficial to the community

The public benefit requirement

A charity must be for exclusively charitable purposes

Preservation from failure: cy près

Reform

13.1 Charity has no essential connection with the law of trusts, as Matthews (1996) explains:

> [Charity] derived from the ecclesiastical jurisdiction, not from that of the Chancery. Charity did not need to be performed through the medium of the trust. It was not so in English law at the outset, and even today it need not be. It could, for example, be carried out through a company. And many legal systems have well developed laws of charity without recourse to, indeed without any knowledge of, trusts. It is a historical accident that the Court of Chancery hijacked the charitable gift and squeezed it (with some difficulty) into the pre-existing framework of the trust.

While there are some particular features of charitable trusts which concern their nature as trusts *per se* (eg the cy près doctrine, 13.40 et seq), this topic largely comprises particular aspects of the law of charities. Be warned, therefore, that what you learn here will, for the most part, have only marginal relevance to what else you have learned in this book, which is why it is at the end. The topic is, however, invariably covered in trusts courses, most likely because it is easy, providing at least one exam question on which all should do well. It also makes a welcome change for those who hate studying trusts, or more likely, for those who hate teaching it.

13.2 Charitable trusts are (1) trusts for purposes which benefit the public, which (2) on the authority of statute and common law are 'charitable'. Not all publicly beneficial purposes are considered by the law to be charitable. What counts as a charitable purpose is the source of a never-ending supply of case law.

13.3 Charitable trusts are not subject to the beneficiary principle. Charitable trusts are valid purpose trusts which are enforced, not by beneficiaries, but by the Attorney-General, or more recently, by the Charities Commissioners (who also have other duties, such as registering charitable trusts, monitoring the accounts of charitable trusts, investigating the running of charities to check abuses, and advising charitable trustees). Charitable trusts can last forever, and on that score are not subject to the rule against perpetuities (**3.17**). (Charitable gifts which are determinable or made upon condition subsequent, are however, subject to the rule as it applies to gifts of that kind.)

Fiscal benefits

13.4 Charities are generally exempt from income tax, capital gains tax, corporation tax, inheritance tax, and stamp duty, although they do have to pay VAT on the goods and services they purchase. They are also able to claim a 80% rebate on council tax for the land they hold, and local councils may refund the remaining 20% on a discretionary basis. Relief from inheritance tax, capital gains tax, and income tax is also available for donors who give to charities. Finally, charities are not taxed on the profits they earn from trading so long as the profits are applied to charitable purposes and the trading carries out the purpose of the charity.

The conditions for charitable status

13.5 In order for a purpose trust to be charitable:

- the *character* of the purposes must be charitable;

- the purposes must, on balance, be beneficial rather than detrimental;

350

- the trust must benefit a section of the public, not a collection of private individuals;

- the purposes must be *exclusively* charitable, and in particular, the purposes must not be political; and

- the trust must not be profit-distributing.

The character of the trust purposes

13.6 Charitable purposes are those which may be found amongst those listed in the preamble to the Charitable Uses Act 1601, or purposes which are analogous to those in the preamble and are within its 'spirit and intendment'. The relevant section of the preamble is as follows:

> ... some [property given] for relief of aged, impotent and poor people, some for the maintenance of sick and maimed soldiers and mariners, schools of learning, free schools, and scholars in universities; some for repair of bridges, ports, havens, causeways, churches, sea banks and highways; some for education and preferment of orphans; some for or towards the relief, stock, or maintenance for houses of correction; some for marriages of poor maids; some for supporting, aid and help of young tradesmen, handicraftsmen and persons decayed; and others for relief or redemption of prisoners or captives, and for aid or ease of any poor inhabitants concerning payment of fifteens, setting out of soldiers and other taxes ...

It seems that in 1601 this list consisted almost totally of purposes which would directly work a public benefit by lowering the local rates, since the persons and projects named would otherwise have been financially supported by the parish; thus an individual who devoted his funds to such purposes provided a very tangible public benefit indeed. There is a school of thought which holds that even today tax relief afforded to charities can only be justified to the extent that these charities provide services which would otherwise require the allocation of state funds.

13.7 Basing himself on the guidance the preamble provided, in *Income Tax Special Purposes Comrs v Pemsel* (1891) Lord Macnaghten produced his famous four-fold characterisation of what is charitable:

Charity in its legal sense comprises four principle divisions: trusts for the relief of poverty; trusts for the advancement of education; trusts for the advancement of religion; and trusts for other purposes beneficial to the community, not falling under any of the preceding heads.

13.8 In *Scottish Burial Reform Society v Glasgow Corpn* (1968) the HL decided that the Scottish Burial Reform Society, a non-profit making company whose main object was the inexpensive, sanitary disposal of the dead, particularly by cremation, was a charity. Lord Reid stated:

> [The] benefit [must be] of a kind within the spirit and intendment of the [Charitable Uses Act 1601]. The preamble specifies a number of objects which were then recognised as charitable. But in more recent times a wide variety of other objects have come to be recognised as also being charitable. The courts appear to have proceeded first by seeking some analogy between an object mentioned in the preamble and the object with regard to which they had to reach a decision. Then they appear to have gone further, and to have been satisfied if they could find an analogy between an object already held to be charitable and the new object claimed to be charitable.

13.9 In *Incorporated Council of Law Reporting for England and Wales v A-G* ((1972), CA Sachs and Buckley LJJ held that the Council, which produces the Law Reports, was a valid charity under the education head, and if not charitable under that head, under the fourth head of purposes beneficial to the community. Russell LJ felt that the Council was a valid charity under the fourth head only, but he also argued that proceeding by analogy from the preamble with respect to the fourth head was unnecessary; he argued that the court should just make a determination of whether the charity carries out a purpose beneficial to the public. This 'first principles' approach has since been doubted by Dillon J at first instance in *Re South Place Ethical Society* (1980), and clearly differs from the HL affirmation of the analogy approach in the Scottish Burial Society case.

13.10 The history of this expansion by analogy is not a particularly honourable one. Worries about testators disinheriting their families through gifts to the Church and to charities led to the Mortmain and Charitable Uses Act, 1736 (now repealed) which made most gifts of land on trust to charities void. In order to bring about the failure of as many gifts as possible under the Act, the boundaries of what counted as charitable slowly expanded. In particular, the wide scope for what counts as religion can be explained in part by the fact that a wide definition ensured that gifts of land to all sects were equally struck down. In the famous case of *Thornton v Howe* (1862), a trust to publish the writings of Joanna Southcott, 'an ignorant and foolish woman' who nonetheless believed herself with child by the Holy Spirit and about to give birth to the new Messiah, was held charitable, therefore void under the Act.

13.11   The *Charity Commissioners Annual Report*, (1987, para 24ff) outlines the Charity Commissioners approach to analogy. Although bound to follow the route of precedent and analogy, they try to do so 'constructively and imaginatively'.

Trusts for the relief of poverty

13.12   Poverty does not mean destitution; trusts for poverty are for those who would otherwise have to 'go short' *(Re Coulthurst* (1951)), so trusts for 'ladies of limited means' *(Re Gardom* (1914)) and for 'decayed actors' *(Spiller v Maude* (1881)) were valid. The charity can be limited to particular classes so long as it doesn't name individuals, nor include those who might not be poor. So trusts for poor employees *(Dingle v Turner* (1972)), or an individual's poor relations *(Re Scarisbrick* (1951); *Re Segelman* (1995)) are good, but a trust benefiting the working classes was not because being a member of the working class did not necessarily imply poverty *(Re Sanders' Will Trusts* (1954)). In *Re Niyazi's Will Trusts* (1978) a trust for a working man's hostel in Famagusta, Cyprus, where there was a grave housing shortage, was upheld as charitable, though Megarry VC opined that the trust was 'desperately near the border-line'.

Trusts for the advancement of education

13.13   This head obviously includes conventional education and training: thus trusts for schools, colleges, universities and other institutions of learning are valid. But this head extends to cover research, artistic and aesthetic education *(Royal Choral Society v IRC* (1943)), museums *(British Museum Trustees v White* (1826)), sport facilities provided for the young at school *(Re Mariette* (1915)), student unions *(London Hospital Medical College v IRC* (1976)), and professional bodies so long as they advance education *(Royal College of Surgeons of England v National Provincial Bank*

Ltd (1952)). However, courts are careful to ensure that this head is not used to provide charitable status for political purposes masquerading as education or research.

13.14 Education of the young must be taken in a broader sense than mere classroom learning. In *IRC v McMullen* (1981) a trust for the provision of facilities to play association football or other sports in schools or universities was held valid. In *Baldry v Feintuck* (1972) the charitable status of student unions was affirmed as part of the educational enterprise, but the devotion of funds to political campaigns by student unions was not, and could be restrained by injunction. However, the fact that a student union provides facilities to political clubs does not invalidate its charitable status.

13.15 The education head also covers the dissemination of useful knowledge. It was upon this basis that the CA decided that the production of the Law Reports was charitable in *Incorporated Council of Law Reporting v A-G*. It also covers the promotion of culture; in *Re Delius* (1957) a charity to promote the music of Delius was good.

13.16 Carrying out useful research is charitable under the education head as well, but the limits of charitable research are not entirely clear: in *Re Shaw* (1957) George Bernard Shaw's testamentary gift to be devoted to research into a 40 letter alphabet for English and the translation of one of his works into the new alphabet was held to be not charitable; this was probably a narrow decision, based on the idea that the gift did not contemplate education or teaching. In *Re Hopkins* (1965) however, a gift to the Francis Bacon Society 'to be earmarked and applied towards finding the Bacon-Shakespeare manuscripts', ie to finding evidence that Francis Bacon wrote the works attributed to Shakespeare was valid under the education head, on the basis that such a discovery would be of immense importance. In *McGovern v A-G* (1981), Slade J summarised the principles:

> (1) A trust for research will ordinarily qualify as a charitable trust if, but only if (a) the subject matter of the proposed research is a useful subject of study; and (b) it is contemplated that knowledge acquired [thereby] will be disseminated to others; and (c) the trust is for the benefit of the public, or a sufficiently important section of the public. (2) In the absence of a contrary context, however, the court will [readily construe] a trust for research as importing subsequent dissemination of the results thereof.

354

(3) Furthermore, if a trust for research is to constitute a valid trust for the advancement of education, it is not necessary either (a) that a teacher/pupil relationship should be in contemplation or (b) that the persons to benefit from the knowledge to be acquired should be [students] in the conventional sense. (4) ... [the court] must pay due regard to any admissable extrinsic evidence which is available to explain the wording of the will in question or the circumstances in which it was made.

13.17   The production of mere propaganda is not the advancement of education. *Re Hopkinson* (1949) is one of several cases in which trusts for educating adults in the principles of particular political parties were held invalid, in which the oft-cited words of Vaisey J appear: 'political propaganda ... masquerading as education is not education within the statute of Elizabeth'. *Re Koeppler's Will Trusts* (1986) concerned a trust for carrying on the work of the 'Wilton Park' Institution, which ran conferences for representatives of member nations of major western organisations to exchange views on political, economic, and social issues; though political figures participated, the conferences did not further any particular political viewpoint, and the trust was charitable under the education head.

Trusts for the advancement of religion

13.18   In general the law of charities assumes that any religion is better than none, but as between religions, stands neutral (*Neville Estates Ltd v Madden* (1961) per Cross J). Religion, however, requires a spiritual belief or faith in some higher unseen power. Trusts promoting morality or particular ethical ways of life are not religious. In *Re South Place Ethical Society* (1980) Dillon J said: 'Religion is concerned with man's relations with God, and ethics are concerned with man's relations with man'. The trust in question, one for the study and dissemination of ethical principles and the cultivation of a rational religious sentiment was not charitable under the religion head, but was as a trust for the advancement of education, as well as under the fourth head as contributing to mental or moral improvement. In *R v Register General, ex p Segerdal* (1970), the 'Church' of Scientology, based upon the American L Ron Hubbard's theory of 'dianetics', was held to be a philosophy of existence, not a religion, so not a charity. In the Australian case, *Church of the New Faith v Comr for Payroll Tax* (1983), scientology was held charitable under the religion head: the court considered any 'belief in a supernatural Being,

355

Thing, or Principle' to be sufficient so long as that belief was combined with canons of conduct giving effect to that belief.

Trusts for other purposes beneficial to the community

13.19 For obvious reasons this is the most difficult category for which to define what counts as charitable, and the 'growth by analogy' approach is most evident here. In *William Trustees v IRC* (1947) there was a gift on trust to establish and maintain an institute, to be known as the 'London Welsh Association', the purposes of which included maintaining an institute for the benefit of Welsh people in London, and promoting their language and culture. The various activities of the institute included lectures, dances, games, and provision of facilities for clubs. These purposes and activities not being exclusively charitable, the trust failed. Lord Simonds quoted Viscount Cave LC in *A-G v National Provincial Bank* (1924):

> ... it is not enough to say that the trust in question is for public purposes beneficial to the community; you must also show it to be a charitable trust;

and with respect to the fact that the gift is given to a particular section of the community, Lord Simonds said:

> If the purposes are not charitable *per se*, the localisation of them will not make them charitable.

Thus for a purpose under the fourth head to be charitable, it must be one of those in the Preamble, or one which has already been decided to be analogous to one in the Preamble, or one which the courts are prepared to hold for the first time is analogous to one of those. Simply because the gift is beneficial to a particular community is entirely insufficient.

13.20 The preamble specifically mentions the 'relief of aged, impotent and poor people'. This passage is construed disjunctively, so trusts for the provision of housing for the aged are charitable (*Joseph Rowntree Memorial Trust Housing Association Ltd v A-G* (1983)), as are trusts for blind children (*Re Lewis*(1955)), the seriously ill or wounded (*Re Hillier* (1944)), the permanently disabled (*Re Fraser* (1883)), and trusts for hospitals, even if they charge fees to patients, so long as they are not profit-distributing

(*Re Resch's Will Trusts* (1969)). (The same reasoning applies to make independent schools which charge fees charitable.) Trust for the relief of victims of disasters are charitable (*Re North Devon and West Somerset Relief Fund Trusts* (1953)), but only in so far as they provide relief from poverty, or in the case of sickness or disability, the class is a public one. The Charity Commissioners advise a restriction to those in need under the poverty head, for if the victims are a specific and identifiable group, it may lack public benefit vis-à-vis the relief of sickness or disability.

13.21   Certain public services and facilities are charitable under the fourth head, such as the production of the Law Reports (*Incorporated Council of Law Reporting v A-G*, above) and the work of the National Trust (*Re Verrall* (1916).

13.22   Although apparently far from the concerns evident in the Preamble, trusts for animal welfare such as the Society for the Prevention of Cruelty to Animals (*Tatham v Drummond* (1864)) and the preservation of wildlife through animal sanctuaries (*Re Wedgwood* (1915) (Wild Fowl Trusts)) are charitable. However, in *Re Grove-Grady* (1929) the CA held that a gift for an animal sanctuary which specifically excluded humans so that the animals would not be molested, was not charitable, for such a gift produced no public benefit. In the New South Wales case of *A-G for New South Wales v Sawtell* (1978) the court reasoned that there has been a general change in public opinion, which now recognises the intrinsic value of the preservation of wildlife, and held such a gift charitable. *Re Grove-Grady* should not be regarded as casting doubt on the ability to create wildlife sanctuaries, but rather suggests that such purposes be expressed in terms of education or environmental protection rather than as a trust purely to benefit the wild animals themselves.

13.23   Trusts for sport or recreation have had a difficult time. In *Re Nottage* (1895) trusts for mere sport, here yacht racing, were held not to be charitable purposes. On the other hand, the provision of land for a recreation ground for public use by the community at large is charitable (*Re Hadden* (1932)). In a Canadian case, *Re Laidlaw Foundation* (1985), it was held that amateur sports institutions would generally be regarded as charitable; the court reasoned that in contrast to the time of *Nottage*, when most people got exercise from manual labour and it was generally the rich who engaged in recreational activities like yacht racing, in these sedentary times amateur sport should be looked upon as promoting health. This approach was not followed by the Charity Commissioners in the case of the Birchfield Harriers (CC Annual Report, 1989, paras 48-55). They decided that the the Birchfield Harriers, an amateur athletic club which trained prospective top athletes including many Olympians, and was therefore not available as a facility for the public generally, was not a charitable institution. The Commissioners felt that Re Nottage was still the law in England. Similarly, in IRC v Glasgow Police Athletic Association (1953), the HL accepted that trusts which promote the efficiency of the police or the armed forces are charitable, but held that a trust for the purpose of promoting athletic sports and general pastimes for the Glasgow police was not, being more in the nature of a private trust for the advantage of the members. In IRC v Baddeley (1955) a trust to be administered by Methodist leaders for the promotion of religious, social and physical well-being of persons resident in West Ham and Leyton, by the provision of facilities for religious services and instruction and for the social and physical training and recreation of persons, who for the time being were or were likely to become members of the Methodist Church who had insufficient means to otherwise enjoy these advantages, was held not charitable by the HL. These recreational purposes were not charitable because there was insufficient public benefit. The public benefit requirement was considered particularly important in the case of charities under the fourth head. Viscount Simonds said that one must observe the distinction

> ... between a form of relief accorded to the whole community yet by its very nature advantageous only to the few, and a form of relief accorded to a selected few out of a larger number equally willing and able to take advantage of it ... I should in the present case conclude that a trust cannot qualify as a charity within the fourth class ... if the beneficiaries are a class of persons not only confined to a particular area but selected within it by reference to a particular creed. The Master of the Rolls in his judgement cites a rhetorical question asked by [counsel] ...: 'Who has ever heard of a bridge to be crossed only by impecunious Methodists?' The reductio ad absurdum is sometimes a cogent form of argument, and this illustration serves to show the danger of conceding the quality of charity to a purpose which is not a public purpose.

The Recreational Charities Act 1958

13.24   Lord Reid dissented in *Baddeley*, and the law was felt to be in some confusion. In response the Recreational Charities Act 1958 was passed. Section 1 states:

358

1. (1) Subject to the provisions of this Act, it shall be and be deemed always to have been charitable to provide, or assist in the provision of, facilities for recreation or other leisure-time occupation, if the facilities are provided in the interests of social welfare:

Provided that nothing in this section shall be taken to derogate from the principle that a trust or institution to be charitable must be for the public benefit.

(2) The requirement in the foregoing section that the facilities are provided in the interests of social welfare shall not be treated as satisfied unless —

(a) the facilities are provided with the object of improving the conditions of life for the persons for whom the facilities are primarily intended; and

(b) either —

(i) those persons have need of such facilities as aforesaid by reason of youth, age, infirmity or disablement, poverty or social and economic circumstances; or

(ii) the facilities are to be available to the members or female members of the public at large.

The act does not define its own public benefit requirement, and so it is not clear that it does much more than restate the law, except in so far as s 1(2)(b) allows facilities restricted to a class on the basis of social and economic circumstances which do not, apparently, simply mean poverty; the other restrictions appear to define classes which have an independent status in the law of charities: gifts for the poor, aged and impotent are good anyway, and recreational facilities for youth are generally treated as charitable as advancing education. The Act does not seem to overturn *Williams v IRC, Baddeley,* or the *Glasgow Police* cases.

13.25 In *IRC v McMullen* (**13.14**) the HL decided that the gift for sports fell under the education head, and so didn't consider the recreational charities act, but in its 1979 decision in the case the CA did; the majority held that the gift was not 'provided in the interests of social welfare', because it did not merely provide facilities for those deprived; second, it was not intended to 'improve the conditions of life of those for whom

359

the facilities were primarily intended', for it was intended as a gift for pupils generally, but would only benefit those who played, irrespective of their conditions in life. Bridge LJ dissented from this 'deprived class' view, saying, 'Hyde Park improves the conditions in life for residents in Mayfair and Belgravia as much as for those in Pimlico or the Portobello Road'. His dissent won the day in the HL in *Guild v IRC* (1992) where a gift for a public sports centre was held to be charitable.

The public benefit requirement

13.26 There are two aspects to the public benefit requirement. The first is that the purpose must be *beneficial* to the public, not detrimental. The second is that the purpose must be of benefit to a section of the public. This aspect of the requirement varies from category to category. Trusts for the relief of poverty are regarded as benefiting the public *per se*; In the case of trusts for the advancement of religion it seems to have been reduced almost to the vanishing point, while for the fourth *Pemsel* category, it appears to be of the essence of charitable status.

A detrimental purpose cannot be charitable

13.27 Though a purpose is public in nature, it must be to the public benefit, not to its detriment, to be charitable. Occasionally the courts seem willing, or perhaps feel they are forced, to make decisions about the ultimate benefits of certain purposes. In *National Anti-Vivisection Society v IRC* (1948) the HL decided to weigh the conflicting moral and material utilities of, on one hand, the advancement of morals and education which would result from a suppression of vivisection, and on the other, the benefits to medical science and research vivisection afforded. It decided that on balance the suppression of vivisection was not beneficial to the public. It departed from the earlier case of *Re Foveaux* (1895), which held that the court stood neutral on the public benefit of abolishing vivisection. In *Re Hummeltenberg* (1923) a gift for the training of spiritual mediums was held to provide no public benefit, and in the course of his decision in *Re Pinion* (1965) Harman J gave the illustration of schools for prostitutes or pickpockets as purposes which would not be charitable on this score. In *McGovern v A-G* (**13.35**) the court considered the possible detriment that Amnesty International's activities might have in the conduct of foreign affairs by the government.

360

13.28 In the case of religion the court appears to allow charities which it regards as having no benefit whatsoever, as in the case of *Thornton v Howe* (**13.10**). With respect to detrimental religious purposes, the Church of Scientology was held to be not charitable (**13.18**), and this may in part have reflected the pronouncements of judges in other cases not concerning scientology's charitable status; in *Hubbard v Vosper* (1972) Lord Denning said that scientology was 'dangerous material', and it was described by Goff J as 'pernicious nonsense' in *Church of Scientology v Kaufman* (1973). In the government white paper, *Charities: A Framework for the Future* (1989, Ch 2) the government considered the anxieties of those frightened by religions or cults which insist on members breaking ties with their families, or whose practices were regarded as tantamount to brainwashing. The paper sensibly held that no one had yet devised a definition of 'public benefit' which was workable to distinguish particular religions as actually detrimental, and said it was, in general, the *conduct* of some groups which was not in the public interest, not their religious objects *per se*. Any conduct which was detrimental was more properly addressed by the general criminal and civil law, not by the law of charities.

The requirement that a section of the public must benefit

13.29 In the case of trusts for the advancement of religion, the requirement that a section of the public benefit is minimal, though not non-existent. In *Gilmour v Coats* (1949) the HL held that a gift to a contemplative order of nuns was not charitable, reasoning that intercessory prayer on behalf of members of the public was not a sufficient public benefit; there must be some engagement with the public. In *Neville Estates v Madden* (1962) a gift to the Catford synagogue was good, for the court:

> ... is entitled to assume that some benefit accrues to the public from the attendance at places of worship of persons who live in this world and mix with their fellow citizens.

In *Re Hetherington* (1990), a gift for the saying of masses for the repose of the donor's husband and relations was charitable on the basis that the masses were said in public.

13.30 The public benefit requirement is more crucial in the case of trusts for the advancement of education. While independent schools are charitable though the benefits directly accrue only to those who are able to pay fees, the case of scholarships restricted to particular classes has caused problems. Trusts for the education of residents of particular localities, or for the children of members of various professions are valid. In *Oppenheim v Tobacco Securities Trust* (1951) a trust for the education of children of employees or former employees of the British-American Tobacco Company, whose employees numbered over 110,000, was held to be not charitable by the HL, on the ground of insufficient public benefit, employing what has been called the 'personal nexus' test: if a class is defined by a personal nexus to someone, and in this case the children's connection with their parent's employer stands on the same footing as one's connection with a relation, then that class is not a section of the public. Lord MacDermott dissented, asking whether there should there be a difference between a trust for the children of coalminers before all the pits were nationalised, which would be charitable, and one for the same children afterward, which would fail since they would all be joined by the employment nexus to the National Coal Board. He rejected the test and said that the court must consider all the circumstances of the case, and would have held the gift charitable. In *Dingle v Turner* (1972) Lord MacDermott's criticism of the personal nexus test was accepted by the HL, though this was *obiter*, as the gift in that case was a gift to relieve poverty, in respect of which there are no similar tests on the extent of the class.

13.31 Indeed, in respect of trusts to relieve poverty, it appears that the public benefit test means no more than that the trusts cannot be for named individuals; a gift for one's poor relations is perfectly valid (*Re Scarisbrick* (1951)). *Dingle v Turner* (1972) concerned a trust to pay pensions to poor employees. Being restricted to the poor, the trust was valid, but in the course of his judgment Lord Cross rejected the personal nexus test in favour of determining a trust's validity on the basis of all the circumstances of the case. This view was unanimous, but three of the five Law Lords refused to follow him when he said that the fiscal benefits of charitable status were relevant to the determination of charitable status:

> [T]he courts – as I see it – cannot avoid having regard to the fiscal privileges accorded to charities … [T]hey enjoy immunity from the rules against perpetuity and uncertainty and although individual potential beneficiaries cannot sue to enforce them the public interest arising under

them is protected by the Attorney-General. If this was all there would be no reason for the courts not to look favourably on the claim of any 'purpose' trust to be considered a charity if it seemed calculated to confer some real benefit on those intended to benefit by it whoever they might be and if it would fail if not held to be a charity. But that is not all. Charities automatically enjoy fiscal privileges which with the increased burden of taxation have become more and more important and in deciding that such and such a trust is a charitable trust the court is endowing it with a substantial annual subsidy at the expense of the taxpayer ... It is, of course, unfortunate that the recognition of any trust as a valid charitable trust should automatically attract fiscal privileges, for the question whether a trust to further some purpose is so little likely to benefit the public that it ought to be declared invalid and the question whether it is likely to confer such great benefits on the public that it should enjoy fiscal immunity are really two quite different questions.

In particular, he said that certain schemes like the educational scheme in *Oppenheim*, perhaps, were akin to fringe benefits for employees which should not be subsidised by the taxpayer.

13.32   The 'fringe benefit' appeared to be central in two cases which concerned the preferential treatment of a private class in educational trusts. *Re Koettgen* (1954) concerned a trust for the promotion of commercial education for members of the public who could not afford it, which, however, contained a provision stating that a preference should be given to the families of employees of a named company of up to 75% of the total fund; it was held charitable, though it is clearly very close to the line, if not incompatible with *Oppenheim*. The more recent CA decision in *IRC v Educational Grants Association Ltd* (1967) may better reflect the current judicial thinking. Here there was a fund devoted to the advancement of education in general terms, which was therefore charitable; the fund was maintained by payments from the Metal Box Company; in one year, however, when the claim was made for tax relief, between 76% and 85% of the income was paid for the education of children of persons connected with the company; the tax relief was denied, because it was held that it was not spent for charitable purposes only – the non-charitable payments were *ultra vires*.

13.33   The public benefit requirement is very much of the essence in respect of trusts under the fourth head. In particular, trusts will fail if the benefit appears to be unnecessarily or artificially restricted, as in

Baddeley, or restricted to what amounts to a class of private individuals, as in *Glasgow Police*. Such a gift is not bad on this count because the benefits are restricted to residents of a particular community, nor for the reason that only those able to pay fees may take advantage, as in *Re Resch's Will Trusts*. Nor does the trust's being restricted to victims of a disaster create an invalid class (*Re North Devon and West Somerset Relief Fund*), though being the victim of a disaster does not alone make one an object of charity – only if, and to the extent that, one is thereby impoverished, or disabled, etc.

A charity must be for exclusively charitable purposes

13.34 Trusts have failed for being expressed to be for more than charitable purposes. A classic example is *Morice v Bishop of Durham* (1805), where a trust for 'charitable or benevolent' purposes failed, since not every benevolent purpose would count as a charity under the law. However, charitable trusts may engage in subsidiary purposes or activities which are not themselves charitable, such as fund-raising, which contribute to the fulfillment of their main purposes. It is, however, the issue of charities engaging in political activity which has raised some of the thorniest issues. In general, political purposes are not charitable. The orthodox rationale for this was explained by Lord Simonds in the *National Anti-Vivisection Society* case:

> [Quoting Tyssen on Charitable Bequests:] 'However desirable the change may really be, the law could not stultify itself by holding that it was for the public benefit that the law itself should be changed. Each court in deciding on the validity of a gift must decide on the principle that the law is right as it stands.' ... Lord Parker [in *Bowman v Secular Society* (1917)] uses slightly different language, but means the same thing, when he says that the court has no means of judging whether a proposed change in the law will or will not be for the public benefit. It is not for the court to judge and the court has no means of judging.

Furthermore, Lord Simonds pointed out that the Attorney-General must supervise and enforce charities, and in some cases, formulate a scheme for their execution, and he should not be put in the position of forwarding a purpose which he and his government might feel to be quite against the interests of the general welfare.

13.35 *McGovern v A-G* (1981) concerned a trust set up by Amnesty International for those of its purposes which it felt were charitable. The relevant purposes were to secure the release of prisoners of conscience, to procure the abolition of torture and other cruel, inhumane or degrading treatment of prisoners, to undertake research into the maintenance and observation of human rights and to disseminate the same. Slade J held that where the political purpose was one of a change in the laws of a foreign country, there was no danger of the court 'stultifying' itself by having both to regard a law which it was bound to apply as both right and needing to be changed, since the law was a foreign one. But such a trust would still fail the public benefit test for the court would in such a case have even less means of judging whether the proposed change in the law was of benefit to the local inhabitants. Furthermore, the court would have to take into account the substantial risk that such activity by an UK charity would prejudice the foreign relations of the UK with that country. Precisely the same dangers would apply to changing the administrative practice of a foreign government if the purpose could be achieved by that end. Therefore trusts whose central purposes involved a change in the law, government policy, or administrative practice either in the UK or abroad were political and thus not charitable.

13.36 On the requirement that trust purposes must be wholly and exclusive charitable, Slade J said:

> [Each] and every object or purpose designated must be of a charitable nature. Otherwise, there are no means of discriminating what part of the trust property is intended for charitable purposes and what part for non-charitable purposes and uncertainty in this respect invalidates the whole trust. Nevertheless, ... a distinction of critical importance has to be drawn between (a) the designated purposes of the trust, (b) the designated means of carrying out these purposes and (c) the consequences of carrying them out. Trust purposes of an otherwise charitable nature do not lose it merely because, as an incidental consequence of the trustees' activities, there may enure to private individuals benefits of a non-charitable nature. Thus, for example, in *Incorporated Council of Law Reporting* the Court of Appeal rejected contentions that the Council of Law Reporting was a non-charitable body merely because publication of the law reports supplied members of the legal profession with the tools of their trade. Similarly, trusts purposes of an otherwise charitable nature do not lose it merely because the trustees, by way of furtherance of their purpose,

have incidental powers to carry on activities which are not themselves charitable ... The distinction is ... one between (a) those non-charitable activities authorised by the trust instrument and which are merely subsidiary or incidental to a charitable purpose, and (b) those non-charitable activities so authorised which in themselves form part of the trust purpose. In the latter but not the former case, the reference to non-charitable activities will deprive the trust of its charitable status.

13.37 Slade J found that both securing the release of prisoners of conscience and securing the abolition of torture and other degrading or inhuman punishments were not charitable purposes. As to the former, the purpose:

> ... must be regarded as being the procurement of the reversal of the relevant decisions of governments and governmental authorities in those countries where such authorities have decided to detain prisoners of conscience, whether or not in accordance with local law. The procurement of the reversal of such decisions cannot, I think, be regarded as one possible method of giving effect to the purposes ... it is the principal purpose itself.

Making reference to the Amnesty International statutes, Slade J construed the latter purpose as including the abolition of capital and corporal punishment, and found as its main object:

> ... to procure the passing of the appropriate reforming legislation for the purpose of abolishing inhuman or degrading punishments by process of law, including capital and corporate punishment ...

Had research into human rights and dissemination of the result thereof been the only purpose, Slade J would have found the trust charitable, but given that the other purposes were not, it fell with the rest.

13.38 The Charity Commissioners produce guidelines form time to time on ancillary political activities by charities. The most recent is *Political Activities and Campaigning by Charities* (1995). In summary, it advises charitable trustees that they may engage in political activity if there is a reasonable expectation that the activity concerned will further the charitable purpose, to an extent justified by the resources spent on the activity, and if the views expressed are 'based on a well-founded and reasoned case and are expressed in a responsible way'. Charities may express views of this kind by making representations to national or local

366

government or individual politicians, but must not participate in party political demonstrations nor support any political party. In the government white paper, *Charities: A Framework for the Future* (1989, paras 2.37-2.46), the government suggested that the law in this area 'commands general agreement', and expressed no intention to reform it.

A charity must be non-profit-distributing

13.39 . Charitable trusts may engage in activities to raise funds, including charging fees for their services (*Re Resch's Will Trusts* (1969)), though they must not distribute profits. This goes for charitable companies as well as charitable trusts, obviously. As for earning profits, in *Oxfam v Birmingham District Council* (1976) the HL held that a charity shop was not entitled as a charity to relief from rates, because it was used for the purpose of fund-raising and was not directed to the charitable purposes themselves. The general rule, therefore, is that the profit-earning activities of charities are liable to the same rates and taxes, such as VAT, as are any other businesses, though various exceptions exist. For example, The Rating (Charity Shops) Act 1976 overturned the *Oxfam* ruling in respect of those shops which are used solely or mainly for the sale of donated goods, the proceeds of which are used solely for charitable purposes.

Preservation from failure: the cy près doctrine

13.40 Where a charitable purpose would fail because the means chosen by a testator for its implementation are either impractical or impossible to carry out, the cy près doctrine, and more recently, s 13 of the Charities Act 1960 can be applied so that it will not fail. 'Cy près' is law French, originally meaning something like 'as near as possible'. The cy près power of the courts allows the court to direct that the trust property be applied to a purpose as close as possible to the one intended by the settlor. Cy près can save charitable trusts from failure at the outset, or from subsequent failure when carrying out the purpose becomes impossible or impractical.

Preservation from failure at the outset

13.41 In order for the court to re-direct trust money intended for a charitable purpose which fails by applying the cy près doctrine, the court

367

must find that the donor manifested a 'general' or 'paramount' charitable intention, ie an intention to give the money to charitable purposes of which the particular gift was but a specification; if the intention was to give only to the specific charity or charitable purpose, and the charity is defunct or the purpose impossible to carry out, then the gift fails.

13.42 What is a general charitable intention? In *Re Lysaght* (1965) Buckley J said:

> A general charitable intention ... may be said to be a paramount intention on the part of a donor to effect some charitable purpose which the court can find a method of putting into operation, notwithstanding that it is impracticable to give effect to some direction by the donor which is not an essential part of his true intention – not, that is to say, part of his paramount intention. In contrast, a particular charitable intention exists where the donor means his charitable disposition to take effect if, but only if, it can be carried into effect in a particular specified way, for example, in connection with a particular school to be established at a particular place, *Re Wilson* (1913), or by establishing a home in a particular house: *Re Packe* (1918).

13.43 The courts have employed cy près effectively to strike out conditions on trusts for scholarships. In *Re Lysaght* (1965) an endowment of medical studentships at the Royal College of Surgeons was to be restricted to recipients not of the Jewish or Roman Catholic faith; the College would not accept the gift because the condition was 'so invidious and so alien to the spirit of the college's work as to make the gift inoperable in that form'. In *Re Woodhams* (1981), music scholarships were restricted to boys from two particular groups of orphans' homes. In both cases the condition was regarded as an inessential element of the testator's bequest, specifying particular means of carrying out his general charitable intention to fund the said scholarships, and the conditions were deleted. It is said (Hayton (1996), 566; Martin (1997), 432) that these cases are an exception to the rule that a trust will not fail for want of a trustee, since it was considered essential to the gift that the scholarships were at the named institutions. Despite the words of the judges in the cases, however, this betrays a misunderstanding. While the *participation* of the named institution was essential for the gifts, so that had they refused to allow their students to take up the scholarships the charitable purpose would indeed have failed, this has nothing to do with who held the funds on trust. The gifts would have failed even if the money was to

368

be paid by another trustee to students nominated by the institutions. A trust never fails for want of a trustee, but a charitable purpose may fail if carrying it out requires the participation of a particular individual or institution and that individual or institution refuses.

13.44 Many cases in which charitable gifts are saved from failure at the outset concern testamentary gifts to charitable institutions or bodies which operated when the testator made his will but have since been amalgamated with others or have gone defunct. Three cases must be distinguished. The first concerns gifts to particular named charities which no longer exist in their own right, but whose purposes are continued by other charities. In *Re Faraker* (1912) there was a testamentary gift to 'Mrs Bayley's Charity, Rotherhithe' which had, with other local charities been consolidated into a trust for the poor in Rotherhithe. The CA held that the gift should go to the consolidated charity because it continued the named charity. This is not an example of cy près, for the gift is regarded as being successfully made to the intended charity. This is so even in the circumstances where, as in *Faraker*, the continuing charity has substantially different overall purposes; the original charity was for poor widows, and the consolidated charity was for the poor generally, so that there was no guarantee that any of the gift actually went to poor widows.

13.45 Second, where the particular charitable institution named to be the recipient of the gift no longer exists, the gift will not fail if on a true construction of the testator's intentions he intended to create a charitable purpose trust and merely indicated this institution to serve as the trustee. Since a trust will not fail for want of a trustee, the court will find another trustee to carry out the charitable purpose. This construction is much more likely in the case of a gift to an unincorporated charitable body than an incorporated one, for the following reasons given by Buckley J in *Re Vernon's Will Trusts* (1960):

> Every bequest to an unincorporated charity by name without more must take effect as a gift for a charitable purpose. No individual or aggregate of individuals could claim to take such a bequest beneficially. If the gift is to be permitted to take effect at all, it must be as a bequest for a purpose, viz., that charitable purpose which the named charity exists to serve. A bequest which is in terms made for a charitable purpose will not fail for lack of a trustee ... A bequest to a named unincorporated charity, however, may on its true interpretation show that the testator's intention to make the gift at all was dependent upon the named charitable

organisation being available at the time when the gift takes effect to serve as the instrument for applying the subject matter of the gift to the charitable purpose for which it is by inference given. If so and the named charity ceases to exist in the lifetime of the testator, the gift fails: *In re Ovey* (1885). A bequest to a corporate body, on the other hand, takes effect simply as a gift to that body beneficially, unless there are circumstances which show that the recipient is to take the gift as a trustee. There is no need in such a case to infer a trust for any particular purpose ... the natural construction is that the bequest is made to the corporate body as part of its general funds, that is to say, beneficially and without the imposition of any trust. That the testator's motive in making the bequest may have undoubtedly been to assist the work of the incorporated body would be insufficient to create a trust.

This reasoning is inventive but unpersuasive. Surely most testators don't know whether the institutions to which they give are unincorporated or not, and second, most probably do not register a distinction between a gift to a charitable body as an accretion to its funds or a gift for the charitable purposes it carries out; how then, can such a distinction be used to discern the testator's intentions? Nevertheless, the distinction is accepted as good law; it was applied in *Re Finger's Will Trusts* (1971), so that a gift to a now defunct unincorporated association was valid as a purpose trust, whereas a gift to a defunct incorporated body failed, though the latter was saved by applying the money cy près. *Re Vernon* and *Re Finger* were both cited with apparent approval by the CA in *Re Koeppler's Will Trusts* (1985). Such a purpose trust is a trust for that specific purpose only; a particular charitable institution serving as trustee must not treat the gift as a general accretion to its funds, but must apply it only to the specific purpose (*Re Spence* (1978)). In contrast, testamentary gifts to an incorporated charity which took effect following a court order that it be wound up, but before its actual dissolution, were, on the same principles, held by Neuberger J not to be gifts on trust for a charitable purpose, but gifts in accretion to the corporation's funds; the gifts went into the general assets of the charitable corporation for distribution to its creditors (*Re ARMS (Multiple Sclerosis Research) Ltd* (1997)).

13.46 True cases of cy près only occur where the intended charitable gift actually fails, as in the gift to the incorporated body in *Re Finger's Will Trusts* above. In *Re Rymer* (1895) the testator gave money to a particular seminary, which at the time of the testator's death has ceased to exist, although its current students were transferred to another seminary. The gift could only be saved by application of the cy près doctrine, but since the court found that the gift was to the particular seminary only, there was no general charitable intention, so cy près could not be applied.

13.47 *Re Harwood* (1936) established something of a general rule that a gift to a particular charity that once existed but is now defunct, is interpreted, unless there are indications to the contrary, as a gift intended for that body alone, disclosing no general charitable intention, whereas in the case of a gift to a named charity which never existed it is much easier to find a general charitable intention. In *Re Spence* Megarry VC extended the principle to the case where the testator has selected a particular charitable purpose, here the purpose of benefiting the residents of a particular old folks home which at the testatrix's death ceased to exist. He explained the rule's rationale as follows:

> I do not think that the reasoning of the In re Harwood line of cases is directed to any feature of institutions as distinct from purposes. Instead, I think the essence of the distinction is in the difference between particularity and generality. If a particular institution or purpose is specified, then it is that institution or purpose, and no other, that is to be the object of the benefaction. It is difficult to envisage a testator as being suffused with a general glow of broad charity when he is labouring, and labouring successfully, to identify some particular specified institution or purpose as the object of his bounty. The specific displaces the general. It is otherwise where the testator has been unable to specify any particular charitable institution or practicable purpose, and so, although his intention of charity can be seen, he has failed to provide any way of giving effect to it. There, the absence of the specific leaves the general undisturbed. It follows that in my view in the case before me, where the testatrix has clearly specified a particular charitable purpose which before her death became impossible to carry out, [there is] that level of great difficulty in demonstrating the existence of a general charitable intention which was indicated by In re Harwood.

13.48 Section 14 of the Charities Act 1993 usefully provides that where collections are on public appeal for a charitable purpose, eg purchasing a work of art for the National Gallery so that it remains within the UK, which fails at the outset, eg not enough money is raised for the purpose, the money will be applicable cy près as if given for charitable purposes generally.

Preservation from subsequent failure

13.49 When a charitable trust has been effectively carried out for a time, but then its purposes become impossible or impractical to carry out, the court may modify the purposes, on the basis that they are giving effect to the settlor's intention to give property 'out and out' to charity. Up to the turn of the century, the cy près power to modify the terms of a trust was narrowly construed, and only if the original terms were actually impossible or impractical to carry out would the court intervene. So, as Martin (1997), 430) remarks, cumbersome, uneconomical, and inconvenient trusts for 'the distribution of loaves to the poor or of stockings for poor maidservants' continued well into this century. Courts have increasingly taken a more extensive view of the cy près power, and more importantly, s 13 of the Charities Act 1993 has expanded the scope for the doctrine, in particular providing that a cy près modification may occur where the original purposes have been adequately provided by other means, which encompasses statutory services in a welfare state. Section 13, though often used by the Charities Commissioners, has not been frequently litigated. In *Re JW Laing Trust* (1983), it was held that s 13 applied only to permit alterations in the purposes of a trust, not variations of settlor's directions which were merely administrative, though in this case, such a direction, that the capital and income be fully distributed within a short time period, was deleted under the court's inherent jurisdiction (**10.45**).

Reform

A statutory definition of charitable purposes

13.50 The current 'definition' of what is charitable, by reference to the preamble by way of the four *Pemsel* categories is cumbersome and lacks any clear justification. Should a new definition be legislated? Parliament could create a new list more in keeping with the times. Such a list would, of course, be subject to judicial interpretation, and this might lead to the recognition of further purposes by analogy as with present judicial practice. A statutory definition might be framed not as a list, but rather in terms of a general definition, like 'purposes beneficial to the community'.

13.51 The government white paper, *Charities: A Framework for the Future* (1989), indicates things are likely to stay as they are; in particular, the paper argues against a statutory definition of what should count as charitable, because such a statutory definition might (1) reduce flexibility and development, and (2) might lead to some long recognised charitable purposes becoming non-charitable. Furthermore, (3) any list would soon become encrusted with judicial decisions, becoming as complex as the old law. (4) Defining charity to be 'purposes beneficial to the community' would be likely to render any non-private, not profit-seeking trust charitable, and this would also be a vague and very subjective standard. Point (2) is of particular interest, and must be tackled by anyone who seeks reform of this kind. Would it be satisfactory simply to abolish the charitable status of a number of existing charities? Could such trusts carry on as private purpose trusts, and if so, enforced by whom? Would it be right to apply such money to other charitable purposes if it was clear the new definition allowed no similar trust which might be considered within the general charitable intentions of the donors to the old one? There is also a problem if one decides to 'grand-father' existing charities of the banned kind, but allow no new ones. This creates invidious distinctions between the old and new, and would be particularly invidious if one of the newly banned categories were religious purposes.

13.52 The charitable status of trusts for the advancement of religion poses a particular problem. Can it be said in these secular and pluralistic times that the money now devoted to religious organisations benefits the public, on balance? Should their charitable status be simply abolished, or, in contrast, would it be better to adopt a broader view of the spiritual? It may be worth recalling that in times past organised religious organisations like the Church of England had quasi-governmental and quasi-judicial roles in the community, and thus were a second institution with public power alongside, or in competition with, the modern state. In pluralistic societies this role is vestigial, and their public benefit seems largely to do with moral inculcation or education or relief of poverty. Should religious bodies only be considered charitable to the extent they continued to fulfil these purposes? Can the public recognition of charitable status (and whatever fiscal benefits flow from that) be justified in regard to all 'religious' activities. We may be living through a new age of faith, but as has been said before, the problem with the death of God is not that people believe in nothing, but that people will believe in anything, crystals, dolphins, heaven only knows what nonsense. Finally, can we admit the charitable status of religions while at the same time drawing a line around unacceptable conduct which is the direct result of religious belief? Can one support the belief without indirectly, and culpably, supporting the conduct to which it leads? Should charitable status turn on the conduct of adherents acting upon their beliefs? For example, should a Muslim charity be de-registered if its officers try to carry out the fatwah against Salman Rushdie?

Dissociating validity from fiscal privilege

13.53   Are the taxation exemptions that automatically follow from charitable status the real cause of worry about which purposes are charitable, as Lord Cross appeared to think in *Dingle*? Even if that is so, simply abolishing the automatic fiscal advantages of charitable status might not diminish the real problem of defining 'charity'; it might only displace it. Immediately following abolition there would be a strong argument that those purposes truly directed to the public benefit should receive fiscal recognition of some kind. The idea is sometimes mooted that the best way would be for the state to give money directly to those 'true' charities. If that were to be done on a fair and transparent basis, however, it would simply require a definition of 'charity' all over again, though under the rubric 'public benefit'. If the government of the day was able to subsidise whichever charities in whatever amounts it liked, then one is faced with the concern that the independence of charities to pursue public goals which might be politically unpopular would be discouraged, leading some charities at least to tailoring their purposes for political reasons; furthermore, smaller charities which could not muster the political support to lobby for a state subsidy would be unfairly disadvantaged.

Further Reading

Gravells (1977); Moffat (1994), ch 17; White Paper (1989); Charity Commissioners (1995); Economist (1995).

Must read cases: *McGovern v A-G* (1981); *Re Lysaght* (1965); *Incorporated Council of Law Reporting for England and Wales v A-G* (1972); *IRC v McMullen* (1981); *IRC v Baddeley* (1955); *Oppenheim v Tobacco Securities Trust* (1951); *Dingle v Turner* (1972); *Re Faraker* (1912); *Re Vernon's Will Trusts* (1960); *Re Finger's Will Trusts* (1971); *Re Spence* (1978).

Self-test questions

1. Are the following purposes charitable? If not, should they be?

- to set up an amateur sporting institute, for the better training of Great Britain's most promising young amateur athletes;

- to provide birth control to students in schools in London;

- to provide tennis rackets to the unemployed of Manchester;

- to provide a national health service in a poor third world country where the predominant religion prohibits blood transfusions;

- to further the activities of a religious sect which counsels its adherents to withdraw from the world and live in remote communes;

- to provide scholarships to assist students to learn ballroom dancing while at university, with the condition that the trustees may, in applying up to 75% of the income of the trust, give preference to children of employees of Y Ltd.;

- to provide funds to the Sisters of 2001, an association of Roman Catholic nuns whose sole activity is to persuade the Vatican to allow the ordination of women priests.

2. What is the public benefit requirement, and how does it operate with respect to the different categories of charity?

3. How does the law operate to save charitable trusts from initial failure? Describe and critically assess the law governing the court's finding of a 'general charitable intention'.

Select Bibliography

Baker, J (1990) *An Introduction to Legal History*, 3rd edn (London: Butterworths)

Bell, A (1989) *Modern Law of Personal Property* (London: Butterworths)

Birks, P (1992) 'Mixing and Tracing' 45(2) *Current Legal Problems* 69

Birks, P (1996a) 'Inconsistency between Compensation and Restitution' 112 *Law Quarterly Review* 375

Birks, P (1996b) 'Equity in the Modern Law: An Exercise in Taxonomy' 26 *University of Western Australia Law Review* 1

Birks, P (1991) 'The English recognition of unjust enrichment' [1991] *Lloyd's Maritime and Commercial Law Quarterly* 473

Birks, P (1992) 'Restitution and Resulting Trusts' in Goldstein, *Equity and Contemporary Legal Developments* (Oxford, Oxford University Press)

Birks, P, (ed) (1994) *The Frontiers of Liability, Volumes I and II* (Oxford: Oxford University Press)

Birks, P, (ed) (1995) *Laundering and Tracing* (Oxford: Clarendon Press)

Burn, E (1994) *Cheshire and Burn's Modern Law of Real Property*, 15th edn (London: Butterworths)

Chambers, R (1997) *Resulting Trusts* (Oxford: Clarendon Press)

Charity Commissioners (1995) 'Political Activities and Campaigning by Charities'

Crilley, D (1994) 'A Case of Proprietary Overkill' [1994] *Restitution Law Review* 57

Cornish, W (1996) *Intellectual Property* 3rd edn (London: Sweet & Maxwell)

Economist (1995) 'Not as deserving as they seem' (July 15, 1995) *The Economist* 22

Elliot, D (1960) 'The Power of Trustees to Enforce Covenants in Favour of Volunteers' 76 *Law Quarterly Review* 100

Emery, C (1982) 'The Most Hallowed Principle – Certainty of Beneficiaries of Trusts and Powers of Appointment' 98 *Law Quarterly Review* 551

Endicott, T (1997) 'Vagueness and Legal Theory' 3 *Legal Theory* 37

Gardner, S (1993) 'Rethinking Family Property' 109 *Law Quarterly Review* 263

Goodhart, W (1996) 'Trust Law for the Twenty-first Century' in Oakley AJ (ed) *Trends in Contemporary Trust Law* (Oxford: OUP, 1996), 257

Gravells, N (1977) 'Public Purpose Trusts' 40 *Modern Law Review* 397

Green, B (1980) 'The Dissolution of Unincorporated Non-Profit Associations' 43 *Modern Law Review* 626

Green, B (1984) 'Grey, Oughtred, and Vandervell – A Contextual Reappraisal' 47 *Modern Law Review* 385

Grubb, A (1982) 'Powers, Trusts and Classes of Objects' [1982] *Conveyancer* 432

Ham, R (1995) 'Trustee's liability' 9 *Trust Law International* 21

Hackney, J (1987) *Understanding Equity and Trusts* (London: Fontana)

Harpum, C (1994) 'The Basis of Equitable Liability' in Birks, P (ed) *The Frontiers of Liability, Volume I* (Oxford: Oxford University Press), 9

Hayton, D (1996a) *Hayton and Marshall: Commentary and Cases on the Law of Trusts and Equitable Remedies* 10th edn (London: Sweet & Maxwell)

Hayton, D (1996b) 'The Irreducible Core Content of Trusteeship' in Oakley, A (ed) *Trends in Contemporary Trust Law* (Oxford: Oxford University Press), 47

Hayton, D (1994) 'Uncertainty of Subject-Matter of Trusts' 110 *Law Quarterly Review* 335

Hayton, D (1987) *Underhill and Hayton: Law of Trusts and Trustees* 14th edn (London: Butterworths)

Hodge, D (1980) 'Secret Trusts: The Fraud Theory Revisited' [1980] *Conveyancer* 341

Hopkins, J (1971) 'Certain Uncertainties of Trusts and Powers' [1971] *Cambridge Law Journal* 68

Hornby, J (1962) 'Covenants in Favour of Volunteers' 78 *Law Quarterly Review* 228

Jones, G (1959) 'Delegation By Trustees: A Reappraisal' 22 *Modern Law Review* 381

Jones, G (1968) 'Unjust Enrichment and the Fiduciary's Duty of Loyalty' 84 *Law Quarterly Review* 472

Kodilinye, G (1982) 'A Fresh Look at the Rule in Strong v Bird' [1982] *Conveyancer* 14

Khurshid, S and Matthews, P 'Tracing Confusion' (1979) 95 *Law Quarterly Review* 78

Langbein, J and Posner, R (1980) 'Social Investing and the Law of Trusts' 79 *Michigan Law Review* 72

Langbein, J (1994) 'The new American trust-investment Act' 8 *Trust Law International* 123

Law Reform Committee (1982) *23rd Report: The Powers and Duties of Trustees*, Cmnd 8733

Lowry, J (1994) '*Regal (Hastings)* Fifty Years On: Breaking the Bonds of the *Ancien Regime*' 45 *Northern Ireland Legal Quarterly* 1

Lowry, J (1997) 'Directorial Self-Dealing; Constructing a Regime of Accountability' 48 *Northern Ireland Legal Quarterly* 211

Lowry, J and Edmonds, R (1998) 'The Corporate Opportunity Doctrine: The Shifting Boundaries of the Duty and its Remedies' 61 *Modern Law Review* 515

Macnair, M (1988) 'Equity and Volunteers' 8 *Legal Studies* 172

Martin, J (1997) *Hanbury and Martin's Modern Equity* 15th edn (London: Sweet & Maxwell)

Matthews, P (1989) 'The Efficacy of Trustee Exemption Clauses in English Law' [1989] *Conveyancer* 42

Matthews, P (1979) 'The True Basis of the Half-Secret Trust?' [1979] *Conveyancer* 360

Matthews, P (1996) 'The New Trust: Obligations without Rights?' in Oakley AJ (ed) *Trends in Contemporary Trust Law* (Oxford: Oxford University Press), 1

McKay, L 'Re Baden and the Third Class of Uncertainty' (1974) 38 *Conveyancer* 269

Millet, P (1998) 'Equity's Place in the Law of Commerce' 114 *Law Quarterly Review* 214

380

Millett (1985) 'The *Quistclose* Trust – Who Can Enforce it?' 101 *Law Quarterly Review* 269

Moffat, G (1994) *Trusts Law: Text and Materials* 2nd edn (London: Butterworths)

Nichols, Lord (1995) 'Trustees and their broader community: where duty, morality, and ethics converge' 9 *Trust Law International* 71

Nobles, R (1992) 'Charities and Ethical Investment' [1992] *Conveyancer* 115

Nolan, R (1995) 'Change of Position' in Birks, P (ed) *Laundering and Tracing* (Oxford: Clarendon Press), 135

Oakley, A (1994) *Parker and Mellows Modern Law of Trusts* 6th edn (London: Sweet & Maxwell)

Perrins, B (1985) 'Secret Trusts: The Key to the *Dehors*' [1985] *Conveyancer* 248

Rickett, C (1980) 'Unincorporated Associations and their Dissolution' 39 *Cambridge Law Journal* 88

Rose F (1996), 'Gratuitous Transfers and Illegal Purposes' 112 *Law Quarterly Review* 386

Sealy L (1962) 'Fiduciary Relationships' [1962] *Cambridge Law Journal* 69

Sheridan, L (1951) 'English and Irish Secret Trusts' 67 *Law Quarterly Review* 314

Simpson, A (1986) *A History of the Land Law*, 2nd edn (Oxford: Clarendon Press)

Smith, L (1997) *The Law of Tracing* (Oxford: Clarendon Press)

Smith, L (1995) 'Tracing in *Taylor v Plumer*: Equity in the Court of King's Bench' [1995] *Lloyd's Maritime and Commercial Law Quarterly* 240

Smith, L (1994) 'Tracing, 'swollen assets' and the lowest intermediate balance: *Bishopsgate Investment Management Ltd v Homan*' 8 *Trust Law International* 102

Sullivan, G (1979) 'Going it Alone – Queensland Mines v Hudson' 42 *Modern Law Review* 711

Swadling, W (1997) 'Property and Unjust Enrichment' in JW Harris (ed) *Property Problems: From Genes to Pension Funds* (London: Kluwer), 130

Swadling, W (1996) 'A new role for resulting trusts?' 16 *Legal Studies* 110

Swadling, W (1995) 'The Nature of Ministerial Receipt' in Birks, P (ed) *Laundering and Tracing* (Oxford: Clarendon Press), 243

Swadling, W (1994) 'Some Lessons from the Law of Torts' in Birks, P (ed) *The Frontiers of Liability, Volume I* (Oxford: Oxford University Press), 41

Treitel, G (1987) *The Law of Contract* 7th edn (London: Stevens & Sons)

Waters, D (1967) 'The Nature of the Trust Beneficiary's Interest' XLV *Canadian Bar Review* 219

Watkin, T (1981) 'Cloaking a Contravention' [1981] *Conveyancer* 335

White Paper (1989) 'Charities: A Framework for the Future' Cmnd 694

Worthington, S (1996) *Proprietary Interests in Commercial Transactions* (Oxford: Clarendon Press)

Youdan, T (1984) 'Formalities for Trusts of Land, and the Doctrine in *Rochefoucauld v Boustead*' 43 *Cambridge Law Journal* 306

Index

383